AF890227

SUSTAINABLE FINANCE AND CLIMATE CHANGE

ELGAR FINANCIAL LAW AND PRACTICE

Series Editor: Jeffrey Golden KC (Hon), *Arbitrator and Mediator, Joint Head of Chambers, 3 Hare Court; Founder and Chair Emeritus of the P.R.I.M.E. Finance Foundation*

The Elgar Financial Law and Practice series is a library of works by leading practitioners and scholars covering discrete areas of law in the field of banking and finance. Titles in the series are both analytical and descriptive in approach, highlighting and unpicking the legal issues that are most critical and relevant to practice. Designed to be detailed, focused reference works, the books in this series offer an authoritative statement on the law and practice in key topics within the field, from Financial Collateral to Private Equity, from Secured Transactions to Financial Crime, and from Financial Derivatives and Hedge Funds to Bank Resolution and Bank Capital.

For a full list of Edward Elgar published titles, including the titles in this series, visit our website at www.e-elgar.com

SUSTAINABLE FINANCE AND CLIMATE CHANGE

Law and Regulation

Edited by

RENÉ SMITS

Professor Emeritus, Law of the Economic and Monetary Union, University of Amsterdam, the Netherlands

ELGAR FINANCIAL LAW AND PRACTICE

Edward Elgar
PUBLISHING

Cheltenham, UK • Northampton, MA, USA

© The Editor and Contributors Severally 2024

All rights reserved. No part of this publication may be reproduced, stored in a retrieval system or transmitted in any form or by any means, electronic, mechanical or photocopying, recording, or otherwise without the prior permission of the publisher.

Published by
Edward Elgar Publishing Limited
The Lypiatts
15 Lansdown Road
Cheltenham
Glos GL50 2JA
UK

Edward Elgar Publishing, Inc.
William Pratt House
9 Dewey Court
Northampton
Massachusetts 01060
USA

A catalogue record for this book
is available from the British Library

Library of Congress Control Number: 2024930508

This book is available electronically in the **Elgar**online
Law subject collection
http://dx.doi.org/10.4337/9781800377288

ISBN 978 1 80037 727 1 (cased)
ISBN 978 1 80037 728 8 (eBook)

EE

CONTENTS

EXTENDED CONTENTS

CONTRIBUTORS

Georges Affaki is Professor of Law at the Université Paris-Panthéon-Assas (Paris-II), a judge at the Qatar International Court and admitted to practice before the Court of Appeal of Paris, France. He is a chartered arbitrator and a member of the ICSID Panels of Arbitrators and Mediators. He has served as a member of the ICC International Court of Arbitration for two terms. He is consistently listed by Chambers and Partners among France's Most in Demand Arbitrators.

Professor Affaki is Fellow of the Chartered Institute of Arbitrators and Fellow of the Australian Centre for International Commercial Arbitration (ACICA). He sits on the Board of Directors of the Saudi Center for Commercial Arbitration, and was appointed to the International Financial Legal Experts body of the Shanghai High People's Court. He chaired the revision of the P.R.I.M.E. Finance Arbitration Rules and co-chaired (with Claudia Salomon) the ICC Task Force on Financial Institutions and International Arbitration. He also chaired the French Arbitration Committee working group on Arbitration in Banking and Financial Matters. He acted as Rapporteur for the International Law Association Resolution on international jurisdiction over foreign bank branches, and chaired a Paris Europlace working group on dispute resolution in Islamic finance.

Professor Affaki is a governor of the UNIDROIT Foundation and a council member of the ICC Institute. He led or participated in several law reforms in transition economies. In 2019, he was nominated as Foreign Trade Counselor of France by a Decree of the Prime Minister and was awarded the European Prize for Interdisciplinary Research. He holds trustee positions in a number of non-profit organisations and is actively engaged in community projects.

Megan Bowman is Professor in Law and Founding Director of the Centre for Climate Law and Governance at King's College London. She leads the King's/United Nations Environment Programme research impact partnership on Legal Readiness for Climate Finance, consults to governments and NGOs on implementing the Paris Agreement and has been principal investigator on several research grants, including a prestigious Leverhulme Fellowship for work on climate-related financial and corporate regulation in Europe and the UK. Her first book, *Banking on Climate Change: How Finance Actors and Transnational Regulatory Regimes are Responding* (Kluwer 2015), was internationally acclaimed by practitioners and scholars. Megan is a qualified barrister and solicitor of the High Court of Australia and Supreme Court of Victoria with an LLM in Comparative Law (McGill) and a PhD in regulatory theory (Australian National University).

David Brinkman is Principal Legal Counsel in the DG Legal Services of the European Central Bank, in the Supervisory Law Division. Before his time at the ECB, David worked as an attorney-at-law in a large Dutch law firm. He has been an in house-counsel for a listed bank insurance conglomerate and has worked as a supervisor for the Dutch Central Bank, in the Market Access Department. David holds an LLM in law from the University of Amsterdam.

Heikki Cantell is General Counsel, Head of Legal Department and Secretary General of the Nordic Investment Bank (2007–). He has extensive experience in managing all legal aspects of the activities of international financial institutions, having previously served as General Counsel of the Council of Europe Development Bank (CEB) from 1995 to 2007. Prior to his career as General Counsel, he was Head of the Paris branch of Heikki Haapaniemi Law Firm, and was a legal counsel for the Finnish Cultural Foundation.

Mr Cantell has a number of professional engagements in addition to his role as General Counsel, including Conseiller du Commerce Extérieur for the Republic of France and board appointments on two Finnish holding companies. He has been nominated as an arbitrator by the International Chamber of Commerce in international commercial litigations.

Mr Cantell also lectures widely at universities and conferences and has published articles in legal and commercial publications in France and in Finland. He holds a LLM (Master of Law) degree from the University of Helsinki and a postgraduate degree in commercial law from the University of Paris II. He has also graduated from the Harvard Business School Advanced Management Program.

Ida Levine is Principal with Two Rivers Associates Limited consulting on public policy, strategy and governance. She is a non-executive director of the Impact Investing Institute and serves as its Lead Expert on Policy and Regulation. She also sits on the Financial Markets Law Committee and the Advisory Board of the UCLA (University of California, Los Angeles) Institute for Carbon Management. Ida was a founding Director of the Investor Forum and is the former Chair of the International Securities Regulation Committee of the International Law Association.

Previously Ida was a Board Director and Senior Vice-President and Senior Counsel of Capital Group and served as its Director of Public Affairs in Europe. Before Capital Group, Ida was European Counsel with JP Morgan Investment Management and a partner at the international law firm Jones Day (London and New York).

Jonathan Maphosa is Managing Partner and founder of Maphosa Attorneys, a law firm with expertise in corporate and commercial law, banking and financial services regulation (including sustainable finance and payments regulation), mining and environmental and tax law.

Jonathan regularly advises South African and regional banks and financial institutions on the structuring and implementation of cross-border financial transactions, bond issuances (including green bonds), the regulatory aspects of payment systems operations and the merger, disposal and acquisition of heavily regulated banking assets.

In 2016 Jonathan was appointed a member of the Expert Group for the review of the South African National Payment Systems Act. Since 2019 he has been a P.R.I.M.E Expert. Jonathan was recognised in November 2020 by the Global Banking Regulation Review as one of the '45 Under 45' regulatory experts in the world, being the only nominee from Africa. Jonathan is also a member of the Committee on International Monetary Law of the International Law Association (MOCOMILA), which is dedicated to the study of legal aspects of money, payments, currency and financial stability. Jonathan is a Fellow of the Mandela Washington Fellowship (Georgia State University, Andrew Young School of Policy Studies).

Prior positions held by Jonathan include Nedbank Group Chief Legal Counsel and General Counsel for BankservAfrica, the largest automated clearing house and payments system operator in Africa. He is the former Deputy General Counsel and Head: Monetary and Financial Law Division of the South African Reserve Bank and was lead legal counsel for the South African Reserve Bank in the negotiation of the BRICS multilateral Inter-Central Bank Agreement which governs the swap transactions and instruments ratified by all BRICS countries. He has served on the board of the Corporate Counsel Association of South Africa. Jonathan's articles have appeared in legal journals, magazines, websites and business media. Jonathan has published a book on green tax laws.

Tamlyn Mills is Partner at Norton Rose Fulbright in Melbourne, Australia. Tamlyn is an experienced dispute resolution practitioner with a broad practice encompassing commercial and corporate litigation, international arbitration and related court proceedings, including the enforcement of arbitral awards and foreign judgments in the Australian courts.

Taking a commercial and pragmatic approach to matters, Tamlyn provides clients with strategic pre-action advice, assists them to achieve the early and efficient settlement of disputes through alternative dispute resolution mechanisms and acts in proceedings before the State and federal courts and before arbitral tribunals. Throughout her career, Tamlyn's practice has focused on significant and complex disputes, often raising novel and untested points of law. She has represented clients at both first instance and appellant level, including up to the High Court, and has acted in proceedings in the Supreme Courts of Queensland, New South Wales, Victoria and Western Australia.

Habib Motani is an English solicitor and a leading international financial markets lawyer. He is a consultant to Clifford Chance LLP, having spent more than 30 years as a partner in the firm's banking and finance practice. He is a Visiting Professor at the School of Law at the University of Edinburgh. He has particular expertise in relation to derivatives, securities lending, repo, netting and collateral and clearing and settlement systems. He specialises in OTC and securitised derivatives, structured capital markets products including derivative linked retail and wholesale structured products, investment banking sales and trading advisory work, Islamic derivatives, securities lending and repos, netting and collateral and their regulatory capital treatment and in the infrastructure aspects of the financial markets, such as payment and settlement systems, clearing systems, prime brokerage and custody.

René Smits is Professor Emeritus of the Law of the Economic and Monetary Union (EMU), University of Amsterdam; a consultant on EMU law, EU banking regulation and sustainable finance; and a member of the European Central Bank's Administrative Board of Review. He has been general counsel of *De Nederlandsche Bank* (the Dutch central bank) and an assessor at the Belgian Competition Authority, and has been working in various legal capacities at the NMa, the Dutch Competition Authority, and its successor the ACM (Authority for Consumers & Markets). He is a member of the Committee on International Monetary Law of the International Law Association (MOCOMILA) and an Expert on the Panel of Recognized International Market Experts in Finance (P.R.I.M.E. Finance).

Jaap Winter is Professor, International Corporate Law at the University of Amsterdam, and Professor, Corporate Law, Governance and Behaviour at Amsterdam's other university (Vrije Universiteit), where he has been chair of the executive board. Professor Winter is also Distinguished Visiting Professor

Corporate Governance, INSEAD; Chair of the Supervisory Board of the Royal Schiphol Group (Amsterdam International Airport); Chair of the Supervisory Board of Erasmus University Rotterdam; and Partner, Phyleon Governance & Leadership. Previously, Professor Winter has been an attorney at the law firm De Brauw Blackstone Westbroek. He has published extensively on corporate law, notably on companies' objectives and role in society.

Elisa de Wit is Partner at Norton Rose Fulbright, based in Melbourne. Elisa is an environment and planning and climate change lawyer. She leads the Australian climate change and sustainability practice and the firm's global carbon markets practice. Elisa has practised in the areas of environmental, planning and climate change law for more than 30 years, including eight years of practice in the United Kingdom.

Elisa has a detailed understanding of the legislative and policy frameworks aimed at greenhouse gas reduction or mitigation and has provided extensive advice to a wide range of clients on the obligations and opportunities which flow from these frameworks. Elisa's climate change practice also includes advising on climate risk, climate disclosure and climate change-related litigation.

FOREWORD

Tackling the ongoing climate and environment crises is this generation's defining task. Undeniably, our planet is warming and its nature degrading. The effects are becoming ever more clear with each passing year. One million of the eight million species on the planet are at risk of being lost. Forests and oceans are being polluted and destroyed. These are not my words but those of the European Commission[1] when introducing the European Green Deal in 2019. Since then many steps have already been taken by governments, central banks and supervisors and other authorities. At the same time, the urgency of the twin crises has increased.

In the journey to climate and environmental sustainability, the financial industry has a key role to play. To give an example: to achieve the goals set by the European Green Deal, the Commission has pledged to mobilise at least €1 trillion in sustainable investments until 2030. The role of the financial industry is also expressly acknowledged in the Paris Agreement, the European Climate Law and the many legislative initiatives coming out of the European Green Deal. And this is not just a European view. The key role that finance has to play is endorsed by 127 central banks and supervisors from all over the world that are cooperating in the Network for Greening the Financial System.

Finance moves hand-in-hand with the evolving legislative and regulatory framework steering society and the economy towards climate and environmental neutrality. Yet, the global financial industry should not just wait and see what the legislator and regulator impose on it. Finance has the opportunity to be the Great Facilitator. In managing their climate-related and environmental risks – which besides the physical and transition risks includes litigation and liability risks banks can support their clients to transition to a sustainable business model in line with the Paris objectives. Insurers can improve the resilience of their customers to climate change and environmental degradation but should expect and contractually require that their clients in return do their utmost to mitigate the origins of the climate and environment crises. The

---

1 COM(2019) 640 final

entire financial industry will see that investment being redirected into sustainable projects will cause new business opportunities to emerge.

That being said, we should not ignore that there will be challenges for the industry to resolve. This is why I am very excited about the publication of this necessary book. It delves into the many aspects that need to be considered in understanding sustainable finance from a legal perspective. With this broader picture, we can discuss and challenge each other's role in the transition. I welcome the discussion being advanced by this book, with contributions from scholars in law and finance. In view of the increasing effects of the ongoing climate and environment crises it is, in fact, vitally important.

Frank Elderson, Member of the Executive Board and Vice-Chair of the Supervisory Board of the European Central Bank

1 August 2023

ABBREVIATIONS

ACCR	Australian Centre for Corporate Responsibility
ACPR	Autorité de Contrôle Prudentiel et de Resolution (France)
ADB	Asian Development Bank
ADEME	Agence de la Transition Ecologique
AIFM	Alternative Investment Fund Manager
AIFMD	Alternative Investment Fund Managers Directive
AMF	Autorité des Marchés Financiers (France)
anti-SLAPP	Massachusetts anti-Strategic Litigation Against Public Participation statute
APP	Asset Purchasing Programme (of the ECB)
APP	Atmospheric Pollution Prevent
ASA	Advertising Standards Authority (UK)
ASCB	Advertising Standards Complaints Board (**New Zealand**)
AUM	Assets under management
BASA	Banking Association South Africa
BCBS	Basel Committee on Banking Supervision
BCEAO	Banque Centrale des Etats de l'Afrique de l'Ouest
BEPGs	Euro Area specific broad economic policy guidelines
BITs	bilateral investment treaties
C&E risk	climate-related and environmental risk
CBAM	Carbon Border Adjustment Mechanism
CCS	Carbon capture and storage
CDP	Carbon Disclosure Project
CDSB	Climate Disclosure Standards Board
CJEU	Court of Justice of the European Union
COP	Conference of the Parties (the highest decision-making body within the UNFCCC)
CRA	Credit Rating Agency
CRISA	Code for Responsible Investing in South Africa
CSDD	Corporate Sustainability Due Diligence

CSI	Corporate Social Investments
CSPP	Corporate Sector Purchasing Programme (of the ECB)
CSRD	Corporate Sustainability Reporting Directive
CTB	Climate Transition Benchmark
DETEC	Swiss Federal Department of the Environment, Transport, Energy and Communications
DLAG	Disclosures and Labels Advisory Group (of the FCA)
E&S	Environmental and Social
EBA	European Banking Authority
EBRD	European Bank for Reconstruction and Development
ECB	European Central Bank
ECCB	Eastern Caribbean Central Bank
ECHR	European Convention on Human Rights
ECON	European Parliament's Committee on Economic and Monetary Affairs
ECT	Energy Charter Treaty
EEA	European Environment Agency
EFRAG	European Financial Reporting Advisory Group
EGD	European Green Deal
EIB	European Investment Bank
EIOPA	European Insurance and Occupational Pensions Authority
EMU	Economic and Monetary Union
EP	Equator Principles
EPA	Environmental Protection Agency (US)
EPBC Act	Environment Protection and Biodiversity Conservation Act 1999 (Australia)
EPFI	Equator Principles Financial Institutions
ERISA	US Employee Retirement Income Security Act of 1974
ESAs	European Supervisory Authorities (EBA, ESMA, EIOPA)
ESCB	European System of Central Banks
ESG	Environmental, Social and Governance
ESMA	European Securities and Markets Authority
ESRS	European Sustainability Reporting Standards
ETS Directive	Emissions Trading Scheme Directive
EU	European Union
EU EUTS	EU Emissions Trading Scheme
FCA	Financial Conduct Authority (UK)

FET	Fair and Equitable Treatment (FET)
FMP	Financial Market Participant
FPS	Full Protection and Security
FRF	Future Regulatory Framework Review (UK)
FSB	Financial Stability Board (EU)
FSOC	Financial Stability Oversight Council (US)
GBP	Green Bond Principles
GBS	EU Green Bond Standard
GCF	Green Climate Fund
GEF	Global Environment Facility
GFANZ	Glasgow Finance Alliance for Net Zero
GHG	Greenhouse Gas
GLP	Green Loan Principles
GRI	Global Reporting Initiative
HEG	High-level Expert Group on Sustainable Finance (EU)
HM	Her/His Majesty
IASB	International Accounting Standards Board
ICC	International Chamber of Commerce
ICJ	International Court of Justice
ICMA	International Capital Market Association
ICSID	International Centre for Settlement of Investment Disputes
IFC	International Finance Corporation
IFIs	International Financial Institutions
IFRS	International Financial Reporting Standards
IIRC	International Integrated Reporting Council
IMF	International Monetary Fund
IOSCO	International Organization of Securities Commissions
IPBES	Intergovernmental Science-Policy Platform on Biodiversity and Ecosystem Services
IPCC	Intergovernmental Panel on Climate Change
IPP	Independent Power Producers
IPSF	International Platform on Sustainable Finance
IRP	Integrated Resource Plan
ISSB	International Sustainability Standards Board
JSE	Johannesburg Stock Exchange
LMA	Loan Market Association

MEP	Member of the European Parliament
mHREDD	mandatory human rights and environmental due diligence
MiFiD 2	Directive and Markets in Financial Instruments Directive
MOCOMILA	The Committee on International Monetary Law of the International Law Association
MRC	Environmental Advertisement Code (*Milieu Reclame Code*) (The Netherlands)
NAFTA	North American Free Trade Agreement
NBB	National Bank of Belgium
NCA	National Competent Authority (EU)
NCB	National Central Bank
NDCs	Nationally Determined Contributions
NERSA	National Energy Regulator of South Africa
NFRD	Non-Financial Reporting Directive
NGFS	Network of Central Banks and Supervisors for Greening the Financial System
NGOs	Non Governmental Organisations
NRC	Dutch Advertisement Code (Nederlandse Reclame Code)
OECD	Organisation for Economic Co-operation and Development
OJ	Official Journal of the European Union
PCA	Permanent Court of Arbitration
PEPP	Pandemic Emergency Purchasing Programme (of the ECB)
POP	Persistent Organic Pollutants
PSC	Production Sharing Contracts
PSPP	Public Sector Purchasing Programme (of the ECB)
RDS	Royal Dutch Shell
REIPPPP	Renewable Energy Independent Power Producer Procurement Programme
RTS	regulatory technical standards
SARB	South African Reserve Bank
SASB	Sustainability Accounting Standards Board
SCC	Stockholm Chamber of Commerce
SDGs	Sustainable Development Goals
SEC	Securities and Exchange Commission (US)
SEE	Social, Economic and Environmental
SFDR	Sustainable Finance Disclosure Regulation
SRB	Single Resolution Board

SSM	Single Supervisory Mechanism (EU)
TCFD	Task Force on Climate-related Financial Disclosures
TEC	European Community Treaty
TEU	Treaty on European Union
TFEU	Treaty on the Functioning of the EU
UNCITRAL Transparency Rules	UNCITRAL Rules on Transparency in Treaty-Based Investor-State Arbitration
UNCLOS	UN Convention on the Law of the Sea
UNEP	United Nations Environment Programme
UNFCCC	UN Framework Convention on Climate Change
US	United States (of America)
USMCA	United Mexican States and Canada
VCPOL	Vienna Convention for the Protection of the Ozone Layer
VRF	Value Reporting Foundation
WBA	World Benchmarking Alliance
WEF	World Economic Forum

TABLE OF CASES

INTERNATIONAL CASES

European Union

European Court of Human Rights (ECtHR)

International Centre for Settlement of Investment Disputes (ICSID)

Permanent Court of Arbitration (PCA)

SCC Arbitration Institute

UNCITRAL

NATIONAL CASES

Australia

Belgium

Brazil

Canada

France

Germany

Lliuya v RWE AG, Case No 2 O 285/15, Higher Regional Court of Hamm (Fifth Civil Senate), Judgment 30 November 2017 **11.057, 11.060–11.063**

Metz et al v Wintershall Dea AG, Regional Court of Kassel, Statement of Claim, filed 4 October 2021 **11.090–11.092**

Neubauer v Germany, Case No 1 BvR 2656/18, 1 BvR 78/20, 1 BvR 96/20, 1 BvR 288/20, Federal Constitutional Court, Judgment 24 March 2021 **11.034–11.037, 11.091**

Neubauer v Germany, Constitutional Complaint regarding Federal Climate Protection Act, filed 6 February 2020 **11.034–11.037**

Guyana

Thomas v EPA, Application for Judicial Review, made on behalf of the applicant Troy Thomas, 21 May 2020 **11.203, 11.205**

The Netherlands

HBG: HR 21 February 2003, NJ 2003, 182; ECLI:NL:HR:2003:AF1486 **4.18**

ABN AMRO: HR 13 July 2007, NJ 2007, 34; ECLI:NL:HR:2007:BA7972 **4.18**

Cancun: HR 4 April 2014, NJ 2014, 286; ECLI:NL:HR:2014:797 **4.17**

Urgenda Foundation v State of the Netherlands, Case No C/09/456689/ HA ZA 13-1396, District Court of The Hague, 24 June 2015, ECLI:NL:RBDHA:2015:7196 **11.008–11.012, 11.210**

State of the Netherlands v Urgenda Foundation, Case No 200.178.245/01, The Hague Court of Appeal, Judgment of 9 October 2018, ECLI:NL:GHDHA:2018:2610 **11.008–11.012**

State of the Netherlands v Urgenda Foundation, Case No 19/00135, Supreme Court, 20 December 2019, ECLI:NL:HR:2019:2007 **7.15, 10.55, 11.006, 11.007, 11.008–11.012, 11.210**

Milieudefensie v Royal Dutch Shell, Case No C/09/571932 / HA ZA 19-379, District Court of The Hague, Judgment of 26 May 2021 **11.059, 11.076–11.079, 11.211**

Complaint to the Dutch Advertising Committee regarding Shell advertisements, File 2021/00190, 26 August 2021 **11.146–11.149**

New Zealand

Smith v Fonterra Co-operative Group Limited [2020] NZHC 419 **11.080–11.083**

Smith v Fonterra Co-operative Group Limited [2021] NZCA 552 **11.080–11.083**

Norway

South Africa

Switzerland

United Kingdom

United States of America

TABLE OF LEGISLATION

EUROPEAN UNION LAW

Treaties

Regulations

Directives

Acts of EU Institutions and Bodies

European Banking Authority

European Central Bank

European Commission

INTERNATIONAL TREATIES, CONVENTIONS AND OTHER INSTRUMENTS

NATIONAL LEGISLATION

Australia

Barbados

Brazil

Canada

Fiji

France

Germany

Guyana

United States of America

1

INTRODUCTION TO SUSTAINABLE FINANCE AND CLIMATE CHANGE: LAW AND REGULATION

René Smits

This book brings together contributions on law and regulation addressing sustainable finance and climate change. The team of authors develops the theme from various angles, together setting forth a picture of where we stand in these ever developing fields of law. The authors cover finance and investment law, corporate law, environmental law and central bank law, as well as litigation and arbitration. These key topics represent a selection of the manifold and ever evolving issues in this field. A word of gratitude is due here for the patience of the contributors, as the book's creation took much longer than anticipated, the idea having been conceived just before the COVID-19 pandemic broke out. **1.1**

In his chapter, with a title in line with the book's emphasis ('An Overview of the Legal and Regulatory Issues'), Heikki Cantell, general counsel of the Nordic Investment Bank, provides a general introduction to the book's themes. He sets the stage for the chapters that follow by indicating the severity of climate change and biodiversity loss, and presenting the main actors and actions taken at government (including central banking) and corporate levels thus far. Cantell mentions public climate funds and how the financial sector has responded to the need for environmental, social and governance (ESG) integration. He sees sustainable finance as 'regulated by a complex interplay of ever-emerging public law and private norms, including binding rules at the regional and domestic levels and a plethora of "soft" law voluntary, market-driven elements'.[1] Cantell argues that 'climate change requires a fundamental shift in how our financial systems work'.[2] **1.2**

1 See p. 13.
2 See p. 17.

1.3 Megan Bowman, Reader in Law and director of the Centre for Climate Law & Governance at King's College London, follows up with reflections on the role of law and regulation in providing sustainable finance. In her chapter, 'Sustainable Finance and Implementing the Paris Agreement: The Key Role of Jurisdictional Legal and Regulatory Architecture', she notes that implementing Paris Agreement objectives requires mobilising finance at the necessary scale. Taking as a starting point a typology of financial mechanisms (direct mobilisation of funds by a variety of means, including stopping fossil fuel subsidies) and facilitative modalities (an enabling environment, including disclosures, taxonomies and prudential regulation), Bowman defines 'climate finance'. She sets out the arguments for national and regional jurisdictional regulatory architecture that shows legal readiness for climate finance: to enable, attract and leverage that finance in-country, regionally and globally. As sustainable finance is facilitated by disclosure frameworks, Bowman argues that corporate disclosure is a means, not an end, to addressing climate risk, just as climate risk itself is not synonymous with the climate crisis but merely one indicator of it. As disclosure alone cannot guarantee the systems-level change required to mainstream green finance, regulating climate finance will greatly benefit from what Bowman terms a pluralistic and complementary instrument approach comprising financial mechanisms and facilitative modalities that can expediate 'legal readiness' for climate finance, through 'regulator ecosystems for sustainable finance'.[3]

1.4 Jaap Winter, an eminent expert of corporate governance and company law and a professor at the University of Amsterdam, makes a passionate plea for a different approach to the corporation's objectives. In 'The Role of the Board, Societal Responsibility and Climate Change', Winter argues that a fundamental reset is required: a duty of societal responsibility should be imposed on the board of the corporation. Alluding to changes taking place already in law, including in the 2022 edition of the Dutch Code of Corporate Governance, he pleads for a specific duty for the board to commit the corporation to being a responsible corporate citizen in society. This call fits well in the context of the companies having to adjust to climate change and to adapt to ESG reporting requirements.

1.5 The need for investors to adapt, and the rules to which they are made subject, is the topic of the next chapter, by Ida Levine: 'The Role of the Investor'. As principal consultant at Two Rivers Associates Limited and a non-executive

---

3 See p. 31.

director of the Impact Investing Institute, and with her roles in international securities regulation, Levine is well placed to set out the expectations that ever evolving standards require of investors. She introduces policy drivers in the EU, the UK, the US and internationally; identifies market themes and discusses how a common language of definitions and standards is in the process of forming. Setting out sustainable finance regulation, Levine takes the reader on a deep dive into the EU taxonomy legal acts and discusses the UK's post-Brexit regulation and US regulatory action (legislative, executive and agency). She discusses whether 'fiduciary duty' nowadays entails more than working solely for the financial interests of beneficiaries or has evolved to include considerations of stewardship. Levine presents accounting standards on ESG emerging, writing that 'global consensus on sustainable finance standards and regulation is becoming more of a possibility'[4] while intimating that we may be 'at a tipping point, with much of the ambitious regulatory programme of the EU and UK coming into effect – and a global framework for sustainability disclosure starting to emerge'.[5]

Turning to the European Union context, three authors present climate **1.6**
change-related changes and implications: Habib Motani, English solicitor and consultant to Clifford Chance LLP and visiting professor at the School of Law at the University of Edinburgh, sets out the European Green Deal ('The European Green Deal'); David Brinkman, principal legal counsel in the Supervision Division of the European Central Bank's Legal Services, presents the EU's climate regulation ('Climate Law'), and René Smits, professor emeritus of the Law of the Economic and Monetary Union (EMU), University of Amsterdam, delves into the mandate of the European Central Bank in relation to climate change and biodiversity loss ('The ECB's Mandate in the Face of Climate Change and Biodiversity Loss'). This triptych of chapters gives an overview of how the EU envisages to address climate change, interprets the European Central Bank (ECB)'s mandate and provides legal background to the EU's goal of becoming climate-neutral by 2050. Motani describes the current position of the EU's Green Deal and sketches obstacles in the road ahead. Brinkman sketches the history of the Climate Law against the backdrop of the Paris Agreement, and interprets the binding nature of the provisions of both legal acts. He draws a wider canvas on EU regulation for the net-zero goal and discusses enforcement of the Climate Law's requirements in respect of EU institutions, including the ECB. The development of

4 See p. 93.
5 See p. 99.

the latter's mandate is the topic of the following chapter. Smits outlines how the ECB's primary and secondary mandates have been interpreted over time. He concludes that the mandate of the EU's central bank not only *permits* but *requires* the ECB to take full account of climate change and biodiversity loss, giving additional arguments derived from other provisions of primary EU law. The author discusses the requirement to take climate and biodiversity into account in the ECB's monetary policy and other basic tasks as well as in its specific task of prudential supervision of banks. He summarises the steps the ECB has already taken in respect of climate change and biodiversity loss and also examines the application of the EU Climate Law to the European Union's central bank.

1.7 Pivoting to Africa, Jonathan Maphosa, an attorney in South Africa with a deep financial sector background, provides an overview of South African initiatives, standards and progress on sustainable finance in his chapter ('A South African Perspective'). Maphosa identifies types of climate-related risks and presents best practices in the financial sector, including South Africa's Code of Corporate Governance and Green Finance Taxonomy. He discusses adherence to the Equator Principles; green loans and bonds (with three case studies on Morocco, Nigeria and South Africa); and sustainable banking in South Africa (again with case studies, of two major banks). Finally, Maphosa outlines recommendations to the South African banks on how to transition towards sustainable finance.

1.8 Focusing on dispute settlement in the context of sustainable finance, two contributions provide insights and overviews on arbitration and litigation, respectively. Georges Affaki, avocat in Paris, professor of law at Université Paris-Panthéon-Assas (Paris-II) and arbitrator, clearly sees arbitration playing a key role in the resolution of climate change disputes. In his chapter ('Arbitration in Climate Change Finance') Affaki expresses his expectation that we will see a great increase in green technology and investment disputes, sketches a number of such disputes and discusses how climate-related issues may be settled under international investment agreements, with investors claiming or respondent states defending climate-related disputes. Affaki recalls how outside expertise may be invoked in arbitration and discusses transparency and the involvement of third-party *amici curiae*. He cites a specialist saying that arbitration may well become 'a tool of global climate governance'.[6]

6 See p. 290

At the same time, litigation is on the rise, as becomes clear in the book's final chapter, written by Elisa de Wit and Tamlyn Mills of Norton Rose Fulbright Australia ('Climate Change Litigation'). They provide an extensive overview of litigation which is identified on the basis of different legal bases for claims: actions based on (i) human rights and constitutional law, (ii) tort law, (iii) consumer law, (iv) corporate law and (v) administrative and environmental law. The case summaries and references in the chapter allow the reader to follow the, often still ongoing, proceedings and discover how these have been concluded where this is the case, thus providing a wealth of data for potential litigants (and defendants) in climate law litigation. **1.9**

2

AN OVERVIEW OF THE LEGAL AND REGULATORY ISSUES

Heikki Cantell[1]

A. THE NATURE OF CLIMATE CHANGE AS THE DEFINING ISSUE OF OUR TIME

2.01 The United Nations Secretary-General has called climate change 'the defining issue of our time'.[2] The climate-related risks to health, livelihoods, food security, water supply, human security and economic growth if climate change continues to increase are well known, as is the critical risk of a simultaneous loss of biodiversity.[3] There is strong scientific agreement that the foremost driver of climate change is human behaviour and activities; however, the subject of climate change itself remains in dispute. Political ideology, economic interests and rising scientific scepticism have led to a lack of alignment in the global response to climate change. This book is an important contribution to the field. It explores the relationships between climate change, sustainable financing and the evolving legal and regulatory landscape. With a clearer idea of

1 General Counsel and Secretary General, Nordic Investment Bank.
2 www.un.org/sg/en/content/sg/statement/2018-09-10/secretary-generals-remarks-climate-change-delivered#:~:text=Climate%20change%20is%20the%20defining,boom%20SOS%20across%20our%20world.
3 www.ipcc.ch/site/assets/uploads/sites/2/2018/07/SR15_SPM_version_stand_alone_LR.pdf, p.11.

how to harness the power of sustainable financing, investment can be directed towards solutions that facilitate the green transition and contribute to the wellbeing of future generations.

The nature of climate change itself does not lend itself well to simplicity of facts. As it operates on long timescales and involves complex interactions across our ecosystems, it can be difficult to grasp the magnitude of the changes occurring in the climate. Such difficulty in directly observing patterns of, for example, weather events can lead to doubts about its seriousness and consequences. Climate change is a variable, complicated issue, the multifaceted dimensions of which only serve to feed into debates on its existence. However, both anecdotal evidence and scientific consensus remain steadfast as to the existence of climate change, humans being the majority cause and the need for crucial, time-critical action to address its impacts. 2.02

Inherent in those impacts is biodiversity loss, to which climate change is a significant contributor. From habitat loss to species extinction, from disruptions in precious ecological cycles to consequential aggravations on trophic levels, the disruption which climate change has caused, and will continue to cause, in our elaborate ecosystems is all-encompassing. Biodiversity loss has also been highlighted by the European Central Bank as a major disturbing factor for the financial sector.[4] The two predicaments of climate change and biodiversity loss are devastatingly interconnected: mitigating climate change's effects would aid in preserving the existence of our planet as we know it, and protecting biodiversity would help to reinforce resilient ecosystems to aid in that climate change mitigation. 2.03

The societal and financial consequences of climate change and biodiversity loss cannot be underestimated. The effects stretch beyond our ecosystems, to touch societies and economies at every level and in all aspects of everyday life. 2.04

B. A GLOBAL REACTION TO A GLOBAL ISSUE: THE INTERNATIONAL COMMUNITY HAS RESPONDED

Before focusing on the specificities of the finance sector's response to climate change, it is prudent to first gain an understanding of the wider global responses that are progressing. On the international level, a multitude of international and regional initiatives, partnerships, entities and activities have 2.05

4 www.ecb.europa.eu/press/inter/date/2023/html/ecb.in230608~7247c0aaca.en.html.

been mobilized or established to respond to the effects and reduce the causes of climate change.[5] The UN Framework Convention on Climate Change (UNFCCC), signed in 1992 with almost universal membership, provides the main intergovernmental forum for regulating the global response to climate change.[6] The first-ever universal, legally binding global climate change agreement came about in 2015, when parties to the UNFCCC adopted the landmark Paris Agreement, aimed at limiting global warming to below 2 degrees Celsius above pre-industrial levels.[7] That year, all UN Member States also adopted the 2030 Agenda for Sustainable Development, which includes the 17 Sustainable Development Goals (SDGs).[8] One of those goals is 'climate action', and several other SDGs also relate to climate change.[9]

2.06 The EU Taxonomy Regulation,[10] which was adopted in 2020, is expected to have a significant impact. It contributes to the EU's goal of becoming climate-neutral by 2050 by channelling investments towards environmentally sustainable activities to assist with the green transition. Related to that is the EU's Sustainable Finance Disclosure Regulation,[11] which mandates financial institutions to disclose the sustainability characteristics of their products and aligns them with the EU Taxonomy. On a regional level, the European Commission's European Green Deal provides a 'roadmap' to boost resource efficiency to a cleaner economy, restore biodiversity and reduce pollution.[12]

2.07 International climate funds such as the Global Environment Facility[13] and the Green Climate Fund[14] work with developing nations by providing financial support with the aim of climate change mitigation. There are also other institutions and organizations that have mobilized collective action to address

5 www.unenvironment.org/explore-topics/climate-change/about-climate-change/climate-change-initiatives-and-partnerships.

6 The 2030 Agenda for Sustainable Development provides that the United Nations Framework Convention on Climate Change 'is the primary international, intergovernmental forum for negotiating the global response to climate change'.

7 https://unfccc.int/files/essential_background/convention/application/pdf/english_paris_agreement.pdf.

8 https://sustainabledevelopment.un.org/post2015/transformingourworld.

9 E.g. Goals 1, 7, 11, 12, 14 and 15 www.unenvironment.org/explore-topics/climate-change/about-climate-change/climate-change-initiatives-and-partnerships.

10 Regulation (EU) 2020/852 of the European Parliament and of the Council of 18 June 2020 on the establishment of a framework to facilitate sustainable investment, and amending Regulation (EU) 2019/2088, OJ L 198, 22.6.2020, p.13.

11 Regulation (EU) 2019/2088 of the European Parliament and of the Council of 27 November 2019 on sustainability-related disclosures in the financial services sector, OJ L 317, 9.12.2019, p.1.

12 https://ec.europa.eu/info/strategy/priorities-2019-2024/european-green-deal_en.

13 www.thegef.org/.

14 www.greenclimate.fund/.

climate change, such as the C40 Cities Climate Leadership Group[15] and the Science Based Target[16] initiative. Although the response of states and regions is perhaps more uneven, it is clear that the global community has recognized the issue of climate change and is acting to address it. The breadth of the issue of climate change necessitates the international community working together to implement initiatives that can help address the challenge of climate change.

C. SUSTAINABLE SOLIDARITY: THE FINANCE SECTOR HAS RESPONDED TOO

2.08 'Sustainable finance' is a term now widely used in the financial industry. Sustainable financing takes into account climate change and other environmentally based considerations when making investment decisions. The concept of sustainable finance is broad, in that it includes climate, green and social finance and other considerations relating to the longer-term economic sustainability of projects or entities receiving funding. The range of financial instruments it covers is extensive, and includes green bonds, impact investing, responsible lending and environmental, social and governance (ESG) integration. Sustainable finance may also take into account the role and stability of the financial and economic system more generally.[17] Sustainable finance has emerged as a powerful tool in redirecting capital towards climate solutions. However, it is not only focused on climate change; instead, sustainable finance includes a multitude of financial practices that consider ESG factors when making financial decisions. Such a change in investment attitudes allows, for example, risk management and sustainability to be at the forefront of decision-making.

2.09 As in so many other areas of life, here too it is of vital importance to involve the financial sector in order to achieve meaningful impact of scale. Even a decade ago, the attributes 'green' and 'climate' were more of a curiosity than a focus in the financial sector. International financial institutions (IFIs), each established by treaty to promote a given mandate, by their very nature of being mandate-driven have been at the forefront of including climate and environmental considerations among the criteria for their financing. Such financing

15 www.c40.org/.

16 https://sciencebasedtargets.org/.

17 See for example ICMA, 'Sustainable Finance: High-level Definitions', May 2020. Available at www.icmagroup.org/assets/documents/Regulatory/Green-Bonds/Sustainable-Finance-High-Level-Definitions-May-2020-110520v4.pdf.

has an impressive impact, with the recent Finance in Common[18] event in Paris in June 2023 noting that IFIs and their related national development institutions hold USD 23 trillion in assets and invest USD 2.5 trillion annually, corresponding to 15 per cent of the market.[19] These same organizations were also the first to introduce the concept of 'green' in their funding activity by creating the 'green bond' concept. At that time, with the exception of IFIs, the rest of the market tended to consider the 'green' label in a bond issue more as a marketing tool than as representing any financial interest. During the past few years, however, bond issues that target financing of environmental projects have been receiving a small advantage in pricing because of the good purpose they promote. This builds financial motivation, which in turn becomes a driving force in directing investments towards more environmentally friendly projects. This broad trend in the financial sector has been very much driven by international conventions such as the Paris Agreement, reflecting the political will but also the general opinion requiring increasingly strong consideration of environmental issues in investments. In addition, legislation and regulation have followed and enhanced the trends of accountability, transparency and social responsibility of borrowers. One of the key actors is the Task Force on Climate-related Financial Disclosures,[20] established in 2015 by the Financial Stability Board to develop recommendations for disclosing climate-related financial risks and opportunities. Alongside these developments, international standards for the taxonomy of 'green' have been created and are being developed in order to assess the credibility of the green label and thus prevent 'greenwashing'.

D. ESG IS AN INCREASING PART OF FINANCING – AND LONG HAS BEEN

2.10 Closely related to sustainability is the concept of ESG. Climate change is obviously a core aspect of the environmental component of ESG, as are issues such as biodiversity loss, deforestation and pollution. ESG is closely related to or even synonymous with 'responsible investing', which refers to investment strategies and practices that include ESG considerations in decision-making and 'active ownership'.[21] ESG has emerged as a core concept in defining sustainability in concrete terms. There is now a wide range of industry-led

18 https://financeincommon.org/.

19 www.idfc.org/news/idfc-contribution-to-the-summit-for-a-new-global-financial-pact/.

20 www.fsb-tcfd.org/.

21 PRI, 'What Is Responsible Investment?' www.unpri.org/introductory-guides-to-responsible-investment/what-is-responsible-investment/4780.article. Last accessed 3 July 2023.

or supported sustainability initiatives and other normative documents that link ESG with financing, such as the UN Environmental Programme Financial Initiative, Equator Principles, Global Impact Investing Network and Principles of Responsible Investment.

In a sense, looking beyond mere profit maximization or shareholder value creation is not necessarily new to modern banking. In the medieval period, Italian banks acted locally and regionally and were motivated by Christian moral and ethical principles and concerns.[22] For instance, some banks set caps on interest rates for ethical reasons; the environment, too, was part of the normative framework of life and the economy at the time.[23] In addition, Islamic finance,[24] not always well known in the mainstream financial sector, is a useful modern-day mode to address climate change risks and promote sustainable development. Its inherent principles,[25] based on Islamic law, promote ethical and socially responsible financing and environmental concerns.[26] We can see that the rapidly accelerating re-allocation of capital for environmental reasons is something of a return to the practice and spirit of early modern banking. **2.11**

E. CAN WE REGULATE A SCIENTIFIC PHENOMENON?

Ultimately, parliaments have the authority and public power to formulate policy responses and make binding rules addressing climate change. Central banks and supervisory agencies similarly have a critical role to play in policy and regulatory responses to integrate sustainability into finance. In terms of domestic governments' actions, market regulatory initiatives to connect sustainability to finance can be seen in some of the most highly populated and growing economies of the world, including China, India, Indonesia and Nigeria.[27] In addition, national and exchange-led actions connecting sustainability and finance at the domestic level have occurred in both the global north **2.12**

22 Weber, Olaf, Sustainable Banking – History and Current Developments (10 October 2012). Available at SSRN: https://ssrn.com/abstract=2159947 or http://dx.doi.org/10.2139/ssrn.2159947, pp.4–5.

23 Olaf, p.4.

24 Hussain, Mumtaz, Shahmoradi, Asghar, and Turk, Rima, An Overview of Islamic Finance, WP/15/120, at: www.imf.org/external/pubs/ft/wp/2015/wp15120.pdf.

25 Visser, Hans. *Islamic Finance: Principles and Practice*. 2nd (Edward Elgar Publishing, 2013).

26 See, also the Islamic Financial Services Board, at: www.ifsb.org/.

27 ICMA, 'Sustainable finance: Compendium of international policy initiatives & best market practice' (February 2020), pp.13–16. Available at www.icmagroup.org/assets/documents/Regulatory/Green-Bonds/ICMA -Sustainable -finance -Compendium -of -international -policy -initiatives -best -market -practice -February-2020-200220.pdf.

and south in a variety of economic contexts, including the United States, Brazil, South Africa, Norway, Mexico and the United Kingdom.[28]

2.13 On a regional or supranational government level, a prominent policy response integrating sustainability in finance is the EU Action Plan on Financing Sustainable Growth adopted by the European Commission in March 2018, as well as the related measures that implement several key actions in the Plan.[29] Notable actions in the Plan connecting finance with sustainability are the goal of establishing a clear taxonomy for sustainable activities,[30] establishing EU labels for green financial products, introducing measures to clarify asset managers' and institutional investors' duties regarding sustainability and bolstering the transparency of companies regarding their ESG policies.[31]

2.14 Governments and regulatory bodies are increasingly demanding that companies disclose their climate-related risks, opportunities and strategies. The recommendations of the Task Force on Climate-related Financial Disclosures have been embraced around the world to assist businesses in reporting on their climate-related financial information.

2.15 Transnational government networks of a different nature also play an indirect role in shaping sustainable finance law and regulation. The Coalition of Finance Ministers for Climate Action,[32] launched in 2019, aligns more than 80 countries to lead the response to climate change and ensure a 'just' transition towards a low-carbon economy. The Network for Greening the Financial System[33] is a global network of central banks and supervisory bodies, set up in 2017, which, along with addressing climate change, aims to promote sustainable financing. Another example is the Basel Committee on Banking Supervision,[34] which is the main standard-setter globally for the prudential regulation of banks and provides a forum for cooperation on banking supervisory matters.[35] It could be argued that the information-sharing, benchmarking and peer pressure generated by such coalitions is contributing to a gradual

28 Ibid.

29 European Commission, 'Renewed Sustainable Finance Strategy and Implementation of the Action Plan'. Available at https://ec.europa.eu/info/publications/sustainable-finance-renewed-strategy_en

30 See: https:// finance .ec .europa .eu/ sustainable -finance/ tools -and -standards/ eu -taxonomy -sustainable -activities_en.

31 Ibid.

32 www.financeministersforclimate.org/.

33 www.ngfs.net/en.

34 www.bis.org/bcbs/.

35 See: www.bis.org/topic/green_finance.htm.

harmonization of standards and practices on climate change-related financial risks and sustainable finance more generally.

Concurrent with these government responses, the financial industry itself is **2.16** increasingly factoring climate change and other environmental considerations into its practices when legislation faces challenges in keeping up with new market-driven requirements. Indeed, the winds are changing quickly in international finance. There is a growing momentum towards recognition within the industry that it must play its role alongside government and consider a broader range of stakeholders when engaging in financing activities. By way of example, the world's largest asset manager is a party – alongside the countries of France and Germany – to a novel public entity called the Climate Finance Partnership,[36] whose goal is to accelerate the flow of capital into climate-related investments in emerging markets.[37] Private banks, too, are playing a role in 'green financing' by directing financial flows towards climate change and other environmental and sustainable development priorities. Meanwhile, the G20's Sustainable Finance Study Group[38] aims to develop strategies and policies for scaling up sustainable finance globally.

Sustainable finance is, therefore, regulated by a complex interplay of **2.17** ever-emerging public law and private norms, including binding rules at the regional and domestic levels and a plethora of 'soft' law, voluntary, market-driven elements.[39] Key legislation regulates sustainable finance alongside normative considerations, such as measuring, reporting, standard-setting and issuing of labels by non-government entities. An example is the non-government organization the Sustainability Accounting Standards Board (SASB).[40] Its mission is to make and improve industry-specific disclosure standards across financially material environmental, social and governance topics to foster communication and decision-making between companies and investors.[41] SASB does not exercise formal public authority. Nevertheless, its standard-setting has a quasi-regulatory function. In the capital markets, another non-governmental entity that exercises a similar regulatory function regarding aspects of sustainable finance is the International Capital Market Association (ICMA).[42]

36 https://oneplanetsummit.fr/en/coalitions-82/climate-finance-partnership-cpf-198.

37 www.bloomberg.com/press-releases/2020-01-22/davos-2020-climate-finance-partnership-press-release.

38 https://g20sfwg.org/.

39 See e.g. Carlarne, Cinnamon P., *Climate Change Law and Policy: EU and US Perspectives* (Oxford University Press, 2010).

40 https://sasb.org/.

41 www.sasb.org/governance/

42 www.icmagroup.org/.

ICMA's members include public and private bodies, such as private and public issuers, banks and securities houses, credit rating agencies, asset managers and other investors, capital market infrastructure providers, central banks and law firms.[43] Through its different committees and working bodies, ICMA is a forum for information gathering and exchange and a source of normative documents and standards that affect the operation of the market. An example can be found in the fixed income market, where the framework created by ICMA's Green Bond Principles, Social Bond Principles and Sustainability Bond Guidelines clearly plays a role in directing and regulating the behaviour of market actors.[44]

2.18 Similarly, in the loan market, a move towards integrating climate change and sustainability is being pushed by the financial sector. In this regard, the role of the Loan Market Association (LMA) is worth noting. The LMA is the trade body for the syndicated loan market in Europe, the Middle East and Africa, with members including commercial and investment banks, institutional investors, law firms, service providers and rating agencies.[45] The LMA's work focuses on documentation, market practice and guidance, loan operations, education and dialogue with legislators and regulators.[46] The LMA, like ICMA, states publicly that it is committed to developing sustainable finance markets and consistent market standards regarding sustainable financing.[47] In 2019, the LMA issued its Sustainability Linked Loan Principles. This framework was designed to develop and strengthen the sustainability linked loan product by operating as guidelines to be applied by market participants.[48] Admittedly, the growth in green loans has not matched that of green, social and sustainability bonds in terms of its uptake and impact. Nevertheless, the LMA is playing a quasi-regulatory role in developing sustainable finance through issuing normative documents, such as guidelines, and setting standards in the market.

43 ICMA, www.icmagroup.org/membership/.

44 For more on these normative documents, see www.icmagroup.org/green-social-and-sustainability-bonds/.

45 LMA, www.lma.eu.com/about-us.

46 Ibid.

47 www .lma .eu .com/ application/ files/ 9515/ 9464/ 2541/ LMA _responds _to _European _Commission _Consultation_on_the_Renewed_Sustainable_Finance_Strategy_.pdf.

48 LMA, 'Sustainability Linked Loan Principles', p.2. Available at www .icmagroup .org/ assets/ documents/ Regulatory/Green-Bonds/LMASustainabilityLinkedLoanPrinciples-270919.pdf.

F. FROM PROFIT TO PURPOSE: THE ROLE OF FINANCIAL INSTITUTIONS

International organizations – including multilateral development banks and IFIs – continue to play a critical role in shaping standards domestically, regionally and internationally. This includes by functioning as platforms for ongoing dialogue, by contributing to the development of a common regulatory vocabulary and, obviously, through developing international legal and policy instruments.[49] In this sense, IFIs are part of a complex and decentralized global 'web' of public entities that, alongside the financial industry itself and other actors, contributes to developing the law and regulation of sustainable finance.[50] **2.19**

IFIs also continue to play an important role in generating normative practices and standards in the private sector. For example, the Nordic Investment Bank,[51] owned by the Nordic and Baltic countries, began to focus on financing environmental projects in the late 1980s. In recent years, the Bank's mission has been to finance projects that improve the productivity and benefit the environment of the Nordic and Baltic region. Borrowers are incentivized to improve the environmental aspect of their projects by better pricing if they achieve higher goals. By financing such projects, NIB also shares its expertise with public and private external stakeholders. More generally, it contributes to a broader normative discourse around sustainable finance and climate change. **2.20**

Such institutions play an important role in promoting and crystallizing norms and rules on sustainable finance transnationally. In the EU, sustainable finance is a work stream aimed at supporting the European Green Deal by channelling private investment to the transition to a climate-neutral economy, as a complement to public money.[52] The EU is also actively engaging the financial industry's input into developing sustainable financing with InvestEU,[53] a budgetary guarantee to assist in financing riskier projects and leveraging private investments, which has sustainable infrastructure among its main policy areas. **2.21**

---

49 www.oecd.org/gov/regulatory-policy/international-organisations-and-role-in-irc.htm.

50 For a discussion of how governments are increasingly cooperating via transnational networks to respond to issues of shared interest, see Slaughter, Anne Marie. *A New World Order: Government Networks and the Disaggregated State* (Princeton University Press, 2004). DOI: https://doi.org/10.1111/j.1477-7053.2004.00119.x.

51 www.nib.int/.

52 https:// ec .europa .eu/ info/ business -economy -euro/ banking -and -finance/ sustainable -finance/ what -sustainable-finance_en.

53 https://investeu.europa.eu/index_en.

2.22 The earlier mentioned green bonds issued by a number of IFIs provide an insight into the fragmented and decentralized nature of current sustainable finance law and regulation globally. 'Green bonds' are forms of debt financing the proceeds of which are dedicated to environmental projects and activities. These bonds play an important role in financing assets for the low-carbon transition.[54] Although there is currently no uniform green bond legal standard in the EU, progress is being made, with political agreement reached in March 2023 between the European Parliament and the Council on the Commission's proposal for a European Green Bond Regulation.[55] Also, frameworks for green bonds and climate bonds have been developed by market actors. This market-driven quasi-regulatory framework may crystallize into hard formal law given the European Green Deal Investment Plan's 2020 announcement that the European Commission will establish an EU Green Bond Standard (GBS).[56] This tool will be interconnected and mutually supportive with the EU Taxonomy. The alignment of the EU GBS with EU Taxonomy means that the EU will work towards preventing 'greenwashing' and promoting transparency in the green bond market. Nevertheless, green bonds remain largely unregulated and shaped mainly by private governance regimes that compete in the market and help generate an evolving regulatory framework for this aspect of sustainable finance law.[57] Central banks and government regulatory and supervisory bodies, both domestically and transnationally, also have the potential to use their public authority to mitigate climate change risks and re-orientate public policy in the direction of more sustainable practices in the financial industry. Indeed, it could be argued that they have the duty to do so.

2.23 As the contributions to this book show, the rapid move to sustainable forms of financing raises a range of questions. How can the impact of climate change risk be estimated over the long run? How can that risk be assessed in the framework of capital requirements? What kinds of climate change or ESG-related information should be disclosed, by whom, to whom? There are important

54 https://ec.europa.eu/info/business-economy-euro/banking-and-finance/sustainable-finance/eu-green-bond-standard_en.

55 Proposal for a Regulation of the European Parliament and of the Council on European green bonds, COM/2021/391 final; at: https:// eur -lex .europa .eu/ legal -content/ EN/ TXT/ ?uri = CELEX %3A52021PC0391.

56 https://ec.europa.eu/info/business-economy-euro/banking-and-finance/sustainable-finance/eu-green-bond-standard_en.

57 See also Stephen Kim Park, 'Investors as Regulators: Green Bonds and the Governance Challenges of the Sustainable Finance Revolution' 54 *Stan. J. Int'l L.* 1 (2018).

issues of governance, too, raised by sustainable finance, such as the legitimacy and accountability of market-driven private regulatory norms and frameworks.

G. CONCLUSION

Climate change is a global issue that requires a global response. Increasing the financing of investments that provide environmental, social and corporate governance benefits is a critical element of global efforts to mitigate the causes and effects of climate change. Indeed, incorporating ESG-related considerations in investments and ensuring sustainable patterns of production and consumption will become particularly critical in the aftermath of the COVID-19 pandemic and the currently ongoing war in Ukraine. The socio-economic consequences of both will continue to resonate throughout the world economy. To respond to the risks caused by climate, parliaments, and increasingly the private sector itself, are creating regulations and normative guidelines that regulate ESG considerations in the process of financing. The result is that the governance of sustainable finance is, like that of the response to climate change more generally, a multifaceted interplay between public and private rules, norms and institutions. Legislation, both domestically and internationally, is emerging – however slowly – that facilitates investments towards sustainable ends that mitigate the risks of climate change and subsequent biodiversity loss. **2.24**

Sustainable finance is having an increasing impact, and the growing enthusiasm of market participants is cause for optimism. In time, with improved working taxonomies used by the market and better harmonization and regulation, sustainable finance will play an increasingly prominent role in mitigating the causes and effects of climate change. Taking climate change and other ESG aspects into account is, simply put, part of good business, and leads to sustainable development. Sustainable finance is a vehicle to ensure that a healthy environment, human flourishing and economic prosperity go hand in hand. The multitude of frameworks and initiatives under construction will fuel the critical global response to mitigating climate change and biodiversity loss, and sustainable financing is a crucial part of the equation. The calibration of climate change mitigation and financing will be fundamental to move the green transition forward with the goal of ensuring a robust, environmentally friendly and sustainable future. **2.25**

The reality of climate change requires a fundamental shift in how our financial systems work. From green bonds to impact investing, from carbon pricing to the integration of environmental, social and governance factors, we have **2.26** witnessed the transformative power of aligning financial decisions with sustainability objectives. The transition to sustainable financing is not without hurdles. We have encountered barriers rooted in short-term thinking, lack of awareness and systemic inertia. However, the momentum for change is palpable. Governments, international organizations and regulatory bodies have laid the groundwork for sustainable finance through policy frameworks and regulatory standards. Financial institutions are increasingly recognizing the materiality of climate risks and the need to integrate sustainability into their strategies. Sustainable financing holds the potential to catalyse the transition towards a low-carbon, climate-resilient and inclusive future. It is not merely a financial imperative, but a moral one. By harnessing the power of finance and aligning it with environmental objectives, we can pave the way for a sustainable and thriving planet.

3

SUSTAINABLE FINANCE AND IMPLEMENTING THE PARIS AGREEMENT: THE KEY ROLE OF JURISDICTIONAL LEGAL AND REGULATORY ARCHITECTURE

Megan Bowman[1]

A. INTRODUCTION: RECALIBRATING OUR LENS FROM MEANS TO END

Much analysis regarding the role of law in sustainable finance has tended to focus on Environmental, Social and Governance (ESG) reporting and corporate disclosure frameworks.[2] This is not surprising given that the predominant **3.01**

---

1 The research underpinning this chapter occurred in several stages and was funded variously by a Leverhulme Fellowship RF-2020-441\8 (2020–2), British Academy/Leverhulme Small Research Grant SRG\171352 (2018-2019) and King's Together Seed Award (2017–18) for which I am very grateful.

2 As a good indicator of the disclosure zeitgeist, all practitioner contributions to the United Kingdom Environmental Law Association (UKELA)'s *E-Law* newsletter in April 2022 (Issue 129) focused on ESG disclosure. See also: E Webster (2020) 'Information Disclosure and the Transition to a Low-Carbon Economy: Climate-Related Risk in the UK and France', *Journal of Environmental Law* 32(2): 279–308; M Bowman and D Wiseman, 'Finance Actors and Climate-Related Disclosure Regulation: Logic, Limits and Emerging Accountability' in *Criminology and Climate: Insurance, Finance and the Regulation of Harmscapes*

regulatory modality in G20 countries for facilitating the transition to net zero and attaining the Paris objectives is climate-related reporting and disclosure by corporate actors and financial institutions.[3] The rise of disclosure frameworks and associated regulatory expectations is due largely to legal and policy initiatives arising from the 2017 recommendations of the Financial Stability Board's Task Force on Climate-related Financial Disclosures (TCFD).[4] Those recommendations encourage individual firms to voluntarily provide forward-looking information on risks and opportunities posed to their business by climate change for stakeholders (investors, lenders and insurers) using scenario analysis regarding governance, strategy, risk management and metrics and targets. The underlying logic of the TCFD Recommendations is that making greener financial choices and reducing climate-related business risks will require more and better information among market participants about the companies and products in which they invest and to which they provide finance.

3.02 Yet it is crucial to realise that reporting frameworks are a means, not an end, to addressing climate risk, and that climate risk itself is not synonymous with the climate crisis but merely one indicator of it.[5] More specifically, climate-related disclosure can best be described as a logical first step in the net-zero transition process to provide data to regulators and market participants to accurately price risk, identify firm- and market-level vulnerabilities and gauge net-zero progress. But, as evidenced by recent empirical research, disclosure alone cannot guarantee the systems-level change required to mainstream green finance.[6]

3.03 So, in this chapter, I wish to re-focus our sights on the end goal by starting with it. The clear message arising from recent international climate summits

---

(C Holley and C Shearing, eds, Routledge 2021), 153–78; M Bowman and E Webster, 'Courage in Private Financing to Implement the Paris Agreement: The UK Case Study' in *Courage, Contributions & Compliance: Advancing Climate Law and Governance Innovation* (M-C Cordonier Segger, C Voight and A Harrington (eds), Routledge 2023).

3 P D'Orazio and L Popoyan (2022) 'Realising Central Banks' Climate Ambitions through Financial Stability Mandates' *Intereconomics* 57(2): 103–11.

4 Task Force on Climate-Related Financial Disclosures, *Final Recommendations* (Basel: Financial Stability Board 2017).

5 FourTwentySeven, *Article 173, Lessons Learned from Climate Risk Disclosures in France* [Newsletter] (21 March 2018); M Bowman and D Wiseman, 'Finance Actors and Climate-Related Disclosure Regulation' (n2); B Caldecott, *Aligning Finance for the Net Zero Economy: Achieving Alignment in Finance* (EIT Climate-KIC 2020); M Baer, E Campiglio and J Deyris, 'It Takes Two to Dance: Institutional Dynamics and Climate-Related Financial Policies' (April 2021) Grantham Research Institute on Climate Change and the Environment *Working Paper No. 356 ISSN 2515-5717.*

6 M Bowman, *Regulatory Leadership for a Net Zero Transition: Central Banks and Financial Regulators: Levers and Limits* (King's College London, September 2022). Also S Waygood and T Tayler, 'Act Now: A Climate Emergency Roadmap for the International Financial Architecture' (Aviva Investors, 1 November 2022); and UNFCCC, *Climate Action Pathway: Finance: Vision and Summary 2021* (Marrakech Partnership and Global Climate Action United Nations Climate Change 2021).

in Glasgow and Sharm El-Sheik (also known as COP26 and COP27 respectively) is that we must turn the talk of finance promises into action if we are to implement the Paris Agreement and stay within the temperature guardrail of 1.5 degrees Celsius. In so doing, a key priority is to ensure that finance for green and resilient investment is flowing at scale to the countries and sectors that most need it. This will certainly implicate multilateral channels of finance such as the Green Climate Fund,[7] and avenues at international law such as market mechanisms under Article 6 of the Paris Agreement and state obligations of developed countries under Article 9 of the Paris Agreement.[8] Yet mobilising climate finance at the necessary scale will also require coherent jurisdictional (national and regional) regulatory architecture and implementation to enable, attract and leverage that finance in-country and globally.[9]

Importantly, a key argument of this chapter is that regulating climate finance will greatly benefit from a pluralistic and complementary instrument approach. The types, form and intent of such tools, and who can or should wield them, are the subject of recent research which also acknowledges that new tools will likely need to be created and deployed as the climate emergency escalates.[10] Nonetheless, jurisdictional legal and regulatory instruments can be most usefully categorised, designed and deployed by having regard to a two-fold typology of climate finance regulation comprising *financial mechanisms* and *facilitative modalities*.[11] **3.04**

Financial mechanisms directly mobilise or leverage finance, especially private capital, through pecuniary incentives (and disincentives) to steer market and financial action in a greener and sustainable direction. The main examples in this category to date include: blended financing to incentivise private sector engagement through concessional arrangements, guarantees and use of insur- **3.05**

7 M Bowman and S Minas, 'Resilience through Interlinkage: The Green Climate Fund and Climate Finance Governance' [2018] Climate Policy 342.

8 See eg MA Mehling, 'Advancing International Cooperation under the Paris Agreement: Issues and Options for Article 6' (MIT Center for Energy and Environmental Policy Research, November 2021); DA Wirth and L Benjamin, 'From Marrakesh to Glasgow: Looking Backward to Move Forward on Emissions Trading' [2021] Climate Law 245; A Zahar, *Climate Change Finance and International Law* (Routledge 2018); Hao Zhang, 'Implementing Provisions on Climate Finance under the Paris Agreement' [2019] Climate Law 21.

9 M Bowman (2022) 'Turning Promises into Action: Legal Readiness for Climate Finance and Implementing the Paris Agreement', *Carbon & Climate Law Review* 16(1): 41–55.

10 M Bowman, *Regulatory Leadership for a Net Zero Transition* (n6); L Clarke, 'Opinion: This is How Law Leads Non-State Actors to Decarbonise', *Race to Zero* (UNFCCC Climate Champions, 23 April 2023); P Bolton, M Despres, P Da Silva, F Samama and R Svartzman, *The Green Swan: Central Banking and Financial Stability in the Age of Climate Change* (Bank for International Settlements 2020); N Gunningham (2020) 'A Quiet Revolution: Central Banks, Financial Regulators, and Climate Finance', *Sustainability* 12(22): 1–22.

11 M Bowman (2023) 'Polaris and Pluralism: Presenting a Legal Analytical Framework for Climate Finance', *Carbon & Climate Law Review* 17(1): 3–26.

ance to reduce risks and increase returns; carbon pricing; green bonds; tax credits; feed-in tariffs; and green subsidies. Just as importantly, this category includes the elimination of fossil fuel subsidies that counteract regulatory efforts to incentivise investment that is low-carbon and climate resilient.

3.06 By contrast, *facilitative modalities* are non-pecuniary measures that facilitate an enabling environment for mobilising greener private capital by building up knowledge, know-how, capacity and accountability among market players and decision-makers in the medium to longer term. Key examples include: climate-related corporate disclosure; taxonomies that provide a common classification for investments and financial products as green or dirty; prudential regulation of supervised firms (usually banks and insurers); and knowledge sharing and capacity building among market participants and technicians through training and matchmaking. This category is particularly dynamic and ever-expanding, including emerging tools such as anti-greenwashing regulation and mandatory transition planning.

3.07 This typology makes explicit where and how disclosure fits within regulatory architecture. It also enables clear vision about the insufficiency of disclosure as a stand-alone instrument. In short, complementary combinations of facilitative modalities and financial mechanisms will be required for getting finance, especially private capital, to flow at scale to where it is needed and away from unsustabinable activity. As explored in this chapter, this presents a new challenge – and opportunity – for jurisdictional law and policy makers around the world in addressing the climate crisis.

B. POST-PARIS: THE NATURE OF FINANCE

3.08 While there is no internationally agreed definition of 'climate finance' as yet,[12] conceptions have evolved since Paris beyond state-financed lateral funding to include private capital. This is evidenced in the language and infrastructures associated with climate negotiations post-Paris. For example, the United Nations Framework Convention on Climate Change (UNFCCC) Secretariat has started to acknowledge that climate finance includes not only public capital (usually through bilateral or multilateral channels such as the Green Climate Fund which has a specific mandate to support the Paris Agreement)[13] but also

12 For a helpful account of the debate regarding the definition of 'climate finance' see C Di Leva, 'Financing Climate Mitigation and Adaptation' [2017] CCLR 4, 315–17.

13 Art 9(8) UNFCCC Paris Agreement (adopted on 12 December 2015, entered into force 4 November 2016) FCCC/CP/2015/L.9/Rev.1.

private investment and market finance to support mitigation and adaptation actions.[14] Moreover, the COP26 summit in Glasgow in 2021 was informally dubbed the 'Finance COP' for its inclusion of discussions about private sector finance (not just public finance) and the resulting Glasgow Climate Pact explicitly interweaves non-state actors and private finance into the delivery of Paris objectives.[15] Further, some argue that Article 2(1)(c) of the Paris Agreement, which stipulates the objective to make 'finance flows consistent with a pathway towards low greenhouse gas emissions and climate resilient development', is a clarion call for *all finance* to become sustainable in a radical move away from business as usual.[16] This expansive conceptualisation of climate finance is both new and necessary given that the multi-trillion-dollar investment needed for a global economic transition is well beyond government bursaries.[17]

Indeed, at COP26, an international consortium of private finance actors mobilised by Mark Carney (UN Special Envoy on Climate Action and Finance) promised to help deliver the multi-trillion-dollar funding required for a net-zero transition. This pledge was made under the banner of the Glasgow Finance Alliance for Net Zero (GFANZ) that collectively supervises US$130 trillion of assets under management. It is a world first; yet its faithfulness will be judged by the extent to which that market finance is mobilised to address climate change and also to support implementation of Nationally Determined Contributions (NDCs) especially in developing countries.[18] **3.09**

C. THE ROLE OF JURISDICTIONAL REGULATORY ARCHITECTURE AND THE CONCEPT OF 'LEGAL READINESS FOR CLIMATE FINANCE'

The imperative and also the challenge of turning financial promises into climate action highlights the critical role of jurisdictional law and regulation in implementing the Paris Agreement. Achieving a low-carbon and climate-resilient **3.10**

14 UNFCCC website, *Introduction to Climate Finance* at https:// unfccc .int/ topics/ climate -finance/ the -bigpicture/introduction-to-climate-finance accessed 22 February 2023, describing 'climate finance' as 'local, national or transnational financing – drawn from public, private and alternative sources of financing – that seeks to support mitigation and adaptation actions that will address climate change'.

15 UNFCCC Glasgow Climate Pact (signed 13 November 2021) Decision -/CP.26, paras 14, 28, 40, 54, 55

16 Eg LH Zamarioli and others, 'The Climate Consistency Goal and the Transformation of Global Finance' [2021] Nature Climate Change 578; M Bowman (2022) 'Turning Promises into Action' (n9). The scope of Article 2(1)(c) and its complementarity with Article 9 of the Paris Agreement is to be explored in the international climate negotiations: *Sharm el-Sheikh Implementation Plan*, 2022, Decision -/CMA.4 (par 68).

17 McKinsey recently estimated that US$275 trillion is required by 2050 to achieve a global net zero transition: 'The net-zero transition: What it would cost, what it could bring' (McKinsey & Company, January 2022), 8.

18 Bowman 'Turning Promises into Action' (n9).

global economy will not only rely on more efficacious multilateral funding and more plentiful microfinance transactions, but also requires a critical mass of legal and regulatory frameworks at national and regional levels that are fit for purpose.

3.11 There are three reasons for this. First, legal and regulatory reform will be required to set out rights and responsibilities of regulated firms, to create and govern markets and to steer economic actors and activities via regulatory incentives, penalties and norm-setting.[19] Second, within a very tight time-frame, climate change considerations will need to be fully incorporated into domestic legal and regulatory frameworks for effective NDC implementation. Third, while investments in emerging economies can deliver high returns combined with high impact, the risks (perceived and actual) tend to deter foreign private capital.[20] Law and regulation that is 'fit for purpose' helps to provide the certainty so desirable to market actors. It informs business case analyses for investment in climate mitigation and adaptation activities by modifying risks and returns as well as facilitating necessary data for greener decision-making. This, in turn, influences whether private actors will get on board and to what extent finance can flow at the necessary scale to where it is needed most.

3.12 Yet, attracting capital directly from the private sector, rather than through multilateral financial institutions, presents challenges. For example, investor attention can be scattered due to competing business cases for investment in different sectors, and some activities (especially in adaptation) do not generate a sufficient return on investment to satisfy business case imperatives. Moreover, there are information asymmetries and disparate terminologies used between government, business and civil society, with, for example, different stakeholders being motivated or deterred by the words 'sustainability', 'climate change' or 'energy security', and also different perceptions of key terms such as 'clean energy' and 'climate finance', such that metrics for measuring 'greenness' and determining flows and proceeds of capital are multifarious and contested. Further, in emerging economy markets specifically, the cost of borrowing (known as the 'cost of capital') is also significantly increased due to macroeconomic issues.[21]

---

19 T Morita and C Pak, 'Legal Readiness to Attract Climate Finance: Towards a Low-Carbon Asia and the Pacific' [2018] CCLR 6. Also, D Levi-Faur, 'Regulatory Capitalism' in Peter Drahos (ed), *Regulatory Theory: Foundations and Applications* (ANU Press 2017).

20 M Carney, 'Country Platforms Action Plan' (Bloomberg Professional, 3 November 2021).

21 V Songwe, N Stern and A Bhattacharya (2022) *Finance for Climate Action: Scaling up Investment for Climate and Development* (Independent High-Level Expert Group on Climate Finance, November), at 45–50.

Therefore, to engage private capital, a starting question for jurisdictional law and policy makers is how to overcome institutional and local barriers through interventions that can reduce risk and increase opportunities, leverage reputational considerations (a particular soft spot of financial institutions) and ensure policy integrity.[22] A related question is how best to interact with financiers and investors without being captured or railroaded by their business case imperatives. **3.13**

All this presents challenges for policy makers and regulators around the world regarding how best to turn promises into action. **3.14**

One emerging concept to help navigate this challenging terrain is that of 'legal readiness for climate finance'. The term was created in international policy circles and has been developed by practitioners such as the Legal Office of the Asian Development Bank (ADB) and research-impact partnerships such as that between King's College London and the United Nations Environment Programme (UNEP).[23] It can be defined as the degree to which a country has coherent regulatory architecture in place, together with requisite domestic technical expertise and institutional capacity, to systematically attract and mobilise finance at scale to address climate change and its impacts. Moreover, the concept is expanding beyond regulatory architecture created by government agencies and legislatures to also include interventions and accountability by courts and tribunals. This is because some climate litigation has 'the aim of producing policy or social change with respect to the issue' rather than directly addressing greenhouse gas pollution as per the parties.[24] Known as 'strategic climate litigation', these types of case are 'taking a long view beyond the immediate success or failure of individual cases' to leverage improved policy outcomes and regulatory environments more generally.[25] Looking forward, increasing attention will be given to how climate-related adjudicatory processes impact upon financial culture, finance flows and the regulatory architecture that steers and supports them both. **3.15**

---

22 M Bowman (2015) *Banking on Climate Change: How Finance Actors and Transnational Regulatory Regimes Are Responding* (Wolters Kluwer, International Banking and Finance Law Series (vol. 24): The Netherlands).

23 Morita and Pak, 'Legal Readiness to Attract Climate Finance' (n19); M Bowman and K Steenmans (contributing), 'Legal Readiness for Climate Finance: Private Sector Opportunities, Report and Findings of Roundtable held at King's College London, 25 January 2019' (UNEP, April 2019).

24 J Peel, H Osofsky and A Foerster, 'A "Next Generation" of Climate Change Litigation? An Australian Perspective' [2018] Oñati Socio-Legal Series 275, 280. See also: G Ganguly, J Setzer and V Heyvaert, 'If At First You Don't Succeed: Suing Corporations for Climate Change' [2018] Oxford Journal of Legal Studies 841, Section 2.

25 K Bouwer and J Setzer, *Climate Litigation as Climate Activism: What Works?* (The British Academy, 2020).

3.16 Previous publications on legal readiness have highlighted its relevance for developing countries,[26] including my own argument that optimal legal and regulatory design frameworks can both 'call in' external (multilateral) climate-related funding and 'put out' endogenous (domestic) investment opportunities to strengthen country ownership in financial processes for sustainable development.[27] Yet I want to emphasise here that legal readiness is applicable to all nations, whether developed or developing. The reason is that we need urgently to reach a point where all countries have internal regulatory consistency to ensure the necessary global critical mass for a 1.5 degrees Celsius world.[28] There is also a moral argument that developed countries are responsible for causing the climate crisis and therefore need to lead the charge on addressing it by role-modelling ambitious and effective actions, domestically and globally. To this end, legal readiness for climate finance can encourage private sector engagement by incentivising green and sustainable investments, penalising and prohibiting continued fossil fuel investment, reducing perceived and actual investment risks (financial, regulatory, sovereign and information asymmetry) and encouraging innovation. Fulfilling these aims is just as necessary in G7 countries as it is for those in the G77.

3.17 What does a path to legal readiness for climate finance look like? There is no cookie-cutter one-size-fits-all approach. The climate finance space is inherently dynamic and regulatory choices must be informed by local context and extant legal culture rather than blind jurisdictional replicability. What has worked in one country may not transfer readily to another; optimal frameworks will depend on cultural, economic, social and legal contexts.[29]

3.18 Nonetheless, broadly speaking, regulatory tools for climate finance fit within the categories of financial mechanisms or facilitative modalities, as described earlier, and can occur across multiple legal and regulatory domains and manifest in various legal forms, ranging from hard legislation to soft law, financial and market regulation, contractual arrangements and, ever increasingly, corporate climate litigation.[30] Non-exhaustive examples include: enacting

---

26 Morita and Pak, 'Legal Readiness to Attract Climate Finance' (n19); Bowman 'Turning Promises into Action' (n9).

27 Bowman 'Turning Promises into Action' (n9).

28 Intergovernmental Panel on Climate Change (IPCC) (*IPCC Sixth Assessment Report: Climate Change 2022: Impacts, Adaptation and Vulnerability* (IPCC 2022).

29 E Scotford and S Minas, 'Probing the Hidden Depths of Climate Law: Analysing National Climate Change Legislation' [2018] *Review of European, Comparative & International Environmental Law* 67.

30 Exemplified by *McVeigh*, being the first case on disclosure and due diligence brought by a beneficiary against their public pension fund: *McVeigh v Retail Employees Superannuation Pty Ltd* (2018) NSD1333/2018. For a thorough discussion of this category see the 'corporate climate litigation platform' launched in 2024 by the

a new umbrella Climate Change Act with relevant financial and investment provisions contained therein; amending constitutional law to enable private sector investment in the energy sector; enacting new investment legislation or amending taxation legislation to include tax credits for renewable energy investments; enhancing prudential regulation and supervisory tools such as capital requirements and senior management accountability; and ensuring company legislation and financial regulation include climate-related disclosure.

D. GOING BEYOND DISCLOSURE FOR LEGAL READINESS

Despite the suite of options outline above, TCFD-based disclosure is currently the predominant climate-related financial regulatory tool in G20 jurisdictions and, notably, the UK and Europe. Indeed, since 2017 when the TCFD Recommendations were first published, the disclosure regulation space has moved quickly in terms of scope, content and legal obligation. **3.19**

- Emphasis has shifted from historical entity-level greenhouse gas emissions and peripheral ESG/non-financial reporting to forward-looking climate-related risks and opportunities as financially material to business.
- We have entered an unprecedented phase of disclosing business plans for a net-zero transition, including supply chain considerations and double materiality evaluations of business impact on the planet.
- In a relatively short time, the preferred jurisdictional regulatory form has morphed from a voluntary market-led exercise to a mandatory legislative regime.

For example, the European Commission's (EC) 2018 Action Plan on Financing Sustainable Growth is part of its response to the Paris Agreement; it aims to reorient capital flows towards sustainable investment and leverage financial markets to address sustainability challenges, especially climate change, while fostering transparency and long-termism.[31] To fulfil that aim the Action Plan precipitated several legislative initiatives, including: the Sustainable Finance Disclosure Regulation (SFDR)[32] (in force March 2021), requiring financial market participants and advisers to publicly disclose (on **3.20**

British Institute of International and Comparative Law (BIICL). See also A Foerster, 'Climate Justice and Corporations' [2019] King's Law Journal 305.

31 European Commission, Communication from the Commission to the European Parliament, the European Council, the Council, the European Central Bank, the European Economic and Social Committee and the Committee of the Regions. Action plan: financing sustainable growth (8 March 2018) COM/2018/097 final.

32 Regulation (EU) 2019/2088 of the European Parliament and of the Council of 27 November 2019 on sustainability-related disclosures in the financial services sector, OJ L 317, 9.12.2019, p.1.

their websites and through periodic reporting) how they integrate sustainability risks into their advice and decisions about investment and insurance; and the Corporate Sustainability Reporting Directive (CSRD)[33] (in force January 2023), which replaced the Non-Financial Reporting Directive to require companies in scope to report on double materiality being sustainability risks (to business) as well as business impacts (on sustainability). Both the SFDR and the CSRD require companies to disclose alignment with the EU Green Taxonomy, which is a classificatory tool in force since July 2020 for assessing economic activities as sustainable.

3.21 Similarly, pursuant to the UK's 2020 Roadmap Towards Mandatory Climate-related Disclosures, the UK government, led by its Treasury department, is to introduce swathes of TCFD-aligned reporting across the whole UK economy by 2025:

- Since 1 January 2021, premium-listed companies have been required to disclose their climate risks in alignment with TCFD Recommendations via changes to the Financial Conduct Authority's FCA Listing Rules.[34] This is a comply-or-explain requirement whereby companies must include a statement in their annual report confirming disclosures have been made (or explain why they have not) and indicating where in the annual report or supplemental document they can be found.[35]
- Since October 2021, trustees of certain occupational pension schemes are required to, among other things, produce and publish a TCFD-aligned report annually, conduct scenario analysis every three years, obtain emissions data of the scheme's assets and use such data to assess the risks and opportunities of the scheme on an 'as far as they are able' basis[36] (in acknowledgement that Trustees will be navigating variable data availability).
- Since 1 January 2022, updated FCA Rules also require TCFD-aligned disclosures at entity and product level by asset managers and FCA-regulated asset owners (life insurers and pension providers) on an absolute mandatory basis (not comply-or-explain).[37]

---

33 Directive (EU) 2022/2464 of the European Parliament and of the Council of 14 December 2022 amending Regulation (EU) No 537/2014, Directive 2004/109/EC, Directive 2006/43/EC and Directive 2013/34/EU, as regards corporate sustainability reporting, OJ L 322, 16.12.2022, p.15.

34 *FCA Listing Rules* per FCA Policy Statement PS20/17 'Proposals to enhance climate-related disclosures by listed issuers and clarification of existing disclosure obligations' (December 2020).

35 FCA Handbook LR 8.8.6B-LR 9.8.6E.

36 *Occupational Pension Schemes (Climate Change Governance and Reporting) Regulations 2021 (2021/839)* in force 1 October 2021.

37 Per FCA Policy Statement (PS 21/24) 'Enhancing climate-related disclosures by asset managers, life insurers and FCA-regulated pension providers' (Dec 2021).

– Since April 2022, changes to the Companies Act 2006 (UK) require TCFD-aligned disclosures on a comply-or-explain basis by all large companies (including financial institutions)[38] in the form of a non-financial and sustainability statement within the strategic report.[39]

These UK and EU climate-related disclosure regulations have been introduced only in the past few years. Due to their nascency, financial regulators and supervisors are at an early stage of checking that disclosures comply with regulatory requirements rather than assessing the ambition of those disclosures as aligned to Paris Agreement goals.[40] In addition, regulators face capacity and funding challenges to monitor and enforce errant disclosures, especially given the wide scope of their everyday duties beyond climate issues. There is a very real concern that TCFD-aligned reporting will be tick-box in nature, rather than helping to embed risk identification, management and reduction throughout an organisation[41] – let alone to instigate the level of sectoral change required to address the climate crisis. **3.22**

Indeed, although these legal initiatives are to be applauded, such reporting cannot single-handedly deliver a net-zero transition or the systems change required to mainstream sustainable finance as portended by Article 2(1)(c). There are several main reasons for this. The disclosure space is notoriously plagued by logistical issues of disparate international reporting standards, variable data availability and quality, and lags in know-how and implementation by key players, namely companies, auditors and regulators.[42] Moreover, the TCFD Recommendations were not designed to achieve net zero or align markets to 1.5 degrees;[43] nor do they reference entwined social imperatives **3.23**

38 Defined as: within the financial year are not small or medium-sized, and are a traded, a banking, insurance or undertaking insurance market activity, is a company trading securities on the Alternative Investment Market, or, a high turnover company (more than £500 million) in the financial year: Companies Act 2006 (UK) s 414CA(A2)(1)(a)–(e) and (1A).

39 Companies Act 2006 (UK) 414CB(1); 414CA(A1)–(2); (2A); 'Explanatory Memorandum to the Companies (Strategic Report) (Climate-Related Financial Disclosure) Regulations 2022' (n 13) para 2.1.

40 Bowman, *Regulatory Leadership for a Net Zero Transition* (n6).

41 J Lipskyte and H Koster, 'Evaluation of Sustainability Reporting under EU Directive 2014/95' (2018) 29(8) *International Company and Commercial Law Review* 522, 522; CZ Wagner, 'Evolving Norms of Corporate Social Responsibility: Lessons Learned from the European Union Directive on Non-Financial Reporting' (2018) 19 *Transactions: The Tennessee Journal of Business Law* 619, 633–4.

42 Bowman, *Regulatory Leadership for a Net Zero Transition* (n6).

43 Caldecott, 'Aligning Finance for the Net Zero Economy' (n5); S Waygood (2021) 'Harnessing the International Finance Architecture to Deliver a Smooth and Just Transition, Sustainable Finance Proposals for the G7 and G20', *Aviva Investors* online (22 April).

such as a just transition.[44] Thus, TCFD-aligned disclosure regimes, without more, cannot attain the level of change required.

3.24 As such, it is crucial to realise that reporting frameworks are a means, not an end, to addressing climate risk, and that climate risk is merely one ingredient of a much larger planetary crisis. Specifically, mandatory climate-related disclosure can best be described as a logical first step in the transition process. It is a regulatory tool that, when implemented and utilised effectively, can provide data (via reporting) and assessments (via scenario analysis and stress testing) to regulators and market participants to assist in accurately pricing risk, identifying micro- and macro-prudential vulnerabilities and realigning investment portfolios. It also provides a building block for other regulatory activities such as risk-based and qualitative measures by financial regulators, monitoring and enforcement by supervisors and engagement and activism by other stakeholders (investors, shareholders, beneficiaries and civil society).

E. THE NEED FOR AN INTEGRATED REGULATORY APPROACH

3.25 Depending on country context and resource availability, law and policymakers could introduce mere *stand-alone* or piecemeal changes as a way of picking low-hanging fruit to begin the net-zero journey. They might choose to focus on a specific financial mechanism, such as launching a sovereign green bond, or legislating tax credits to incentivise renewable energy investments, or strengthening existing facilitative regulation such as specifying requirements for climate-related disclosure.

3.26 However, to achieve legal readiness for climate finance, a more comprehensive strategy will be required, what I term an *integrated regulatory approach.* This approach comprises a complementary mix of financial mechanisms and facilitative modalities across multiple legal domains that adjust or reform a country's legal and regulatory architecture to account for climate change and enable greater flows of climate finance.[45] An integrated regulatory approach is still tailored to country needs. For example, focus might be given to various financial mechanisms such as legislatively establishing an In-country Climate Fund for blended finance and green subsidies together with facilitative modalities such as green taxonomy creation and mandatory transition planning.

44 N Robins, 'Financing a Just Transition: How to Connect the Environmental and Social Dimensions of Structural Change' in *Making the Financial System Sustainable* (P Fisher ed, Cambridge University Press 2020), 237–57.

45 Bowman, 'Turning Promises into Action' (n9).

It could also provide a balanced package of reforms to overcome cognitive biases through rewards and trade-offs, such as removing fossil fuel subsidies in agriculture-dominant countries.[46] Or it may entail a Paris-aligned legal and policy overhaul that spans company and prudential regulation, constitutional reform, energy law, environment and planning law, employment law, and more. Indeed, given that initial NDC Synthesis evaluations showed that most countries are very far from the Paris Agreement temperature goal in Article 2.1(a), it is ideal to be ambitious.[47]

In short, to mainstream climate and sustainability into financial decision **3.27** making, disclosure must be nested within a matrix of complementary legal and regulatory measures for a low-carbon and climate-resilient economy. In this way, an integrated regulatory approach facilitates institutional coherence and seeks to create a consistent investment environment where all rules point in the same direction – to low-carbon and climate resilience – such that the private sector knows where and how to invest.

Research has further revealed that, in addition to the type and mix of law **3.28** and regulation, a critical ingredient of an integrated regulatory approach is enhanced inter-agency communication and collaboration, which I term 'regulator ecosystems for sustainable finance'.[48] Rather than remaining in siloes, collaboration is becoming essential between Treasuries, Ministers of Finance, central banks and financial regulators, parliamentarians, departments of energy, environment and business – even though climate finance may not be seen as their traditional field of expertise. Collaboration and coordination can be encouraged by policy or mandated by legislation. For example, under French law's Article 29 of the Energy and Climate Law[49] and former Article 173 of the Energy Transition Law, financial supervisors in France, the French ACPR and the AMF share technical task management such as scrutinising disclosures and enforcing supervisory remits. Specifically, the Autorité de Contrôle Prudentiel et de Resolution (ACPR) and Autorité des Marchés Financiers (AMF) jointly monitor and evaluate climate and coal-related net-zero commitments by financial institutions and convene two advisory Climate and Sustainable Finance Commissions, which comprise large banks

46 KL Milkman and others, 'Policy Bundling to Overcome Loss Aversion: A Method for Improving Legislative Outcomes' [2012] Organizational Behaviour and Human Decision Processes 158; M Bowman, 'Nudging Effective Climate Policy Design' [2011] International Journal of Global Energy Issues 242.

47 'NDC Synthesis Report' (UNFCCC, 2021).

48 Bowman, *Regulatory Leadership for a Net Zero Transition* (n6).

49 *LOI no 2019-1147 du 8 novembre 2019 relative à l'énergie et au climat*; JORF no 0261 of 9 November 2019; www.legifrance.gouv.fr/jorf/article_jo/JORFARTI000039355992.

and insurers, academics and institutional bodies. These Commissions have helped to inform recommendations regarding exclusion of coal lending by banks, portfolio alignment for green investment and carbon footprints of portfolios, and have begun to evaluate fossil fuels and non-conventional sources more broadly.[50]

F. DIRECTION OF TRAVEL: FROM TRANSITION FINANCE TO TRANSITIONING THE FINANCIAL SYSTEM

3.29 In summary, to be most effective, this chapter has argued for emerging climate finance law and regulation that:

- comprises a complementary blend of financial mechanisms and facilitative modalities, having regard to potential effectiveness, efficiency and equitable impacts;
- takes account of local context, including legal and regulatory capacity and resources[51] and pre-existing legal culture;[52] and
- is embedded within an institutional matrix that promotes sectoral reform and supports coherence within and between government ministries and agencies.

3.30 It is also clear from the preceding discussion that efficacy and sufficiency of a country's efforts along the legal readiness path will depend on not only political will and cooperation but also resourcing. Indeed, embedding an integrated regulatory approach within an institutional matrix requires precursory 'regulatory mapping' to assess legal and institutional strengths, barriers and gaps for a net-zero transition and the extent of alignment with Article 2(1)(c), as well as identifying and costing the reforms required for implementation, all of which can be expensive and requires technical expertise.

3.31 For developing countries, multilateral funding can and should be sought for such mapping. Some examples already exist. The ADB together with the International Finance Corporation (IFC) and Baker & McKenzie solicitors provided technical assistance to Fiji to critically assess the general investment

---

50 AMF (2021) 'The ACPR and AMF Publish Their Report on Climate-related Commitments of French Financial Institutions', *AMF News Release* (28 December); ACPR-AMF (2020) *Coal Policies of Paris Financial Centre Participants (Banks, Insurers, Asset Managers): First Joint ACPR/AMF Monitoring and Evaluation Report.*

51 Morita and Pak, 'Legal Readiness to Attract Climate Finance' (n19).

52 Scotford and Minas, 'Probing the hidden depths of climate law' (n29).

environment and create a legal roadmap for climate finance,[53] including a review of investment policy and related legislation, enacting the new International Arbitration Act 2017 and Personal Properties Securities Act 2017 to improve market processes and evaluating legal barriers to investment in the renewable energy and transportation sectors.[54] Similarly, the Inter-American Development Bank Group created 'NDC Invest' to provide technical and financial support for Latin American and Caribbean countries, including strengthening the capacity of governments and academia to help implement the Paris Agreement.[55] Moreover, transnational initiatives include the African Union's Green Recovery Action Plan[56] and the multi-member NDC Partnership[57] in recognition that regulatory innovation and technical capacity building of local policy makers and financiers is often a precursor to effective financial mechanisms such as green bonds and tax credits.

Indeed, there is a heightened need for multilateral funding and jurisdictional **3.32** agency collaboration to occur in a systematic way with the aim of helping countries to take an integrated regulatory approach and thus facilitate NDC implementation and SDG goals. To this end, comprehensive reform of the international financial architecture (including World Bank and International Monetary Fund (IMF) processes) has been demanded in the 2022 Bridgetown Agenda and acknowledged for the first time in formal documentation of the COP27 Outcome Decision, which notes that 'transformation of the financial system and its structures and processes' is required for a global and just low-carbon transition.[58] If this represents the direction of travel, then it is clear that such massive systems changes will require unprecedented institutional coordination to deliver the necessary investment, to correct market failures and to harness the scale and power of markets to allocate capital in the long-term global interest.[59] This will be an exciting space to watch.

53 'Fiji Legal Roadmap for Climate Finance and Investments' (COP23) https://cop23.com.fj/events/fiji-legal-roadmap%20-climate-finance-investments/ accessed 23 February 2023.

54 Morita and Pak, 'Legal Readiness to Attract Climate Finance' (n19).

55 M Jaramillo and V Saavedra, 'NDC Invest: Supporting Transformational Climate Policy and Finance' (Inter-American Development Bank, June 2021).

56 'African Union Launches a Continental Green Recovery Action Plan' (African Union, 15 July 2021).

57 'NDC Partnership, Fact Sheet' (NDC Partnership, December 2020).

58 Barbados Government, *The 2022 Bridgetown Initiative for the Reform of the Global Financial Architecture* (Barbados Government Information Service, 23 September 2022); Sharm el-Sheikh Implementation Plan, Decision 1/CMA.4 and 1/CP.27, Art XI.

59 Waygood and Tayler, 'Act Now' (n6).

4

THE ROLE OF THE BOARD, SOCIETAL RESPONSIBILITY AND CLIMATE CHANGE

Jaap Winter[1]

A. INTRODUCTION

4.01 A fundamental reset is required in corporate and financial regulation in order to deal with the enormous challenges societies and the world are facing. This text was initially written during the COVID lockdown to develop thoughts on how corporate law can and should be reimagined in order to address the problems that at least in part are caused by how corporations are understood to function. Many and extensive are the analyses of recent years on how capitalism is failing us. A core element of most analyses is the shareholder primacy doctrine that has taken hold of corporate law and corporate governance in the wake of Milton Friedman's watershed 1970 article in the New York Times Magazine. "In a free-enterprise, private-property system," Friedman wrote, "a corporate executive is an employee of the owners of the business. He has direct responsibility to his employers. That responsibility is to conduct the business in accordance with their desires, which generally will be to make as

1 For a more detailed treatment of this topic see Jaap Winter, 'Addressing the Crisis of the Modern Corporation: The Duty of Societal Responsibility', https://ssrn.com/abstract=3574681.

much money as possible while conforming to the basic rules of the society, both those embodied in law and those embodied in ethical custom [...] there is one and only one social responsibility of business, to use its resources and engage in activities designed to increase its profits so long as it stays within the rules of the game."[2] Friedman may not have intended to free the corporation of all moral responsibility and much can be argued against the idea that shareholders are the owners of a business. Nonetheless, his idea of the corporation has been understood, elaborated upon, and practiced during the past 50 years to generate a corporate reality that the corporation is largely responsibility-free beyond the responsibility to create value to shareholders. The costs to others, such as employees, customers, and wider society (environmental and climate costs, for example), of shareholder value creating actions are of no concern to the corporation itself. In the hands of the capital markets, investment banks, institutional investors, hedge funds, and heavily incentivized executives' corporations have become, if not immoral, at least amoral. What matters in corporate decision-making is the prospective financial outcome for shareholders, not much else. I oversimplify, I am aware; but I am afraid I am not oversimplifying too much.

The COVID-19 pandemic and the governmental lockdown measures to **4.02**
"flatten the curve" created a massive shock to societies, people, and corporations across the world. With the lockdowns, a unique global pause button had been pushed. At least temporarily, everything had to be done differently; priorities shifted, and new ways of collaboration could have been explored. If ever there was a time that society needed business to take responsibility beyond its own immediate financial success, that time was during the pandemic. We can no longer afford for corporations to be amoral. The challenge is to ignite a sense of societal responsibility within corporations. This can only come from the people who make the corporation an actor in society. In this chapter I argue that a duty of societal responsibility should be imposed on the board of the corporation. I will first put forward my analysis of the problem of the (lack of) responsibility of business in society. A critical factor is that the amoral corporate context is man-made. But, paradoxically, often we believe there is little we can do about it. Shareholder primacy has been applied as a dogma but fails as a theory. Proposals have been made to generate a change in this corporate reality. In all solutions that have been put forward so far to address aspects of the problem, the role of the board is crucial. But the proposals do not address

2 Milton Friedman, 'A Friedman Doctrine – The Social Responsibility of Business Is to Increase Its Profits', The New York Times, Sept. 13, 1970.

adequately what is needed for the board to commit the corporation to being a responsible corporate citizen in society. A specific duty for boards to do so could be introduced in corporate law. Such a duty will have to be elaborated in corporate law and corporate governance practices. I conclude with regulatory initiatives in the Netherlands and at EU level that seek to introduce such a duty of societal responsibility in corporate law.

B. THE HEART OF THE MATTER: THE MODERN CORPORATION HAS BECOME AMORAL

4.03 In a recent paper[3] I set out a number of factors that have contributed to a context of corporations that I have described as dehumanized; stripped of human inspiration, meaning, and judgment; disengaged from society, from what the people who make up society believe is important. My analysis is by no means complete. It is focused on the human aspects of the context of the modern corporation, both how this context is created by ourselves and how it affects us. This is essential. The core of the problem is not outside of us; it is in us. It is in how we design our corporate reality and how we conduct ourselves within it. By the combination of design and conduct we shape the context in which corporations exist and act in society. Solutions therefore are also not beyond us, but are within our reach; they are about us.

4.04 Let me summarize my argument as to how the corporation has become amoral. Five factors jointly and interactively cause concern regarding the state of the modern corporation: (i) the *dominant theory* of the firm; (ii) *the way capital markets and institutional investors have come to view corporations*; (iii) *efficiency-driven organizational practice*; (iv) *the effects of regulation*; and (v) *the remuneration of executives*.

(i) The shareholder primacy theory of the firm that originated from Friedman's work has come to dominate corporate thought and practice. In corporate thought, it was developed into the agency theory: managers are primarily seen as agents who should act in the interest of shareholders as their principals. As managers act rationally in their self-interest, they will not always further the interests of shareholders. Corporate law and corporate governance have the function to ensure that managers do act in the interests of shareholders. In corporate practice, executive remunera-

3 Winter, Jaap (2019), The Dehumanisation of the Large Corporation, published in Dutch in Ondernemingsrecht 2019/2, available in English at https://ssrn.com/abstract=3517492.

tion and takeover bids have been developed as mechanisms that discipline managers to do so. Executive remuneration aligns managers' interests with those of shareholders. Takeover bids may force managers out of their jobs if they underperform for shareholders. Other stakeholders who have interests in the corporation and its business, such as employees, customers, and the wider community, are no longer seen as relevant principals for whom managers should act as agents. Externalities such as the costs of environmental and climate damage or the social damage caused by restructuring are not factored into this shareholder value model. Put in a different way: in today's dominant corporate context only financial capital is rewarded, at the expense of human capital (well-being of employees), social capital (public goods, social infrastructure, community), and natural capital (resources, environment, and climate).[4]

(ii) Building on this theory of the firm, capital markets and their main players have over time come to view corporations as bundles of assets and liabilities. They represent separate units of financial value that can be realized at specific prices. Listed corporations do not *have* a balance sheet, they *are* a balance sheet, with assets and liabilities that can be realized in individual transactions. The financial value of those individual transactions, the price somebody apparently is willing to pay, is justification for breaking down the corporation as an integrated entity that is connected to society in myriad ways. Derivative financial instruments further remove investors from the reality of the corporation as an organization in which real people work and that is connected to society through a multiplicity of parties and relationships. In financial capitalism, investors are only interested in the financial value that emerges from these instruments. Institutional investors who excessively diversify their portfolios are no longer investing in individual corporations, but search for mathematically calculated absolute and relative returns. Intermediation of the entire investment process even further removes investors from the corporations they invest in. Financial capital is uncommitted to the corporations in which it invests.[5]

(iii) The world of modern management as taught in business schools and practiced in corporations is characterized by its endless search for efficiency improvement and cost savings as a means of maximizing shareholder value. Employees are a cost factor and staff reductions maximize shareholder value. Employees who stay are directed through key performance

4 Mayer, Colin (2018), Prosperity, Oxford University Press.

5 Ibid.

indicators, control systems, target-setting, and measuring and compliance e-tools to ensure they perform and behave according to plan—a plan that is overly based on illusions and scientific pretensions of certainty, while in reality corporations are constantly faced with uncertainty and unpredictability. The dominant organizational pattern is mechanistic, steering toward predetermined objectives and controlling employees through formalistic accountability procedures in bureaucratic processes. Employees' capacity for human judgment is vastly underutilized.

(iv) The managerial-control bureaucracy is augmented with more and more external regulation defining what corporations can, must, and may not do. After every new crisis, new rules give a false sense of control over a reality that was never under control before the crisis hit, with more and more external supervision through regulatory authorities. The paradoxical consequence has been to reduce the sense of responsibility that people have, from a responsibility for the consequences of their behavior toward others to a responsibility to comply with the rules. We actually feel less responsible and no longer train our moral muscle—a regulatory crowding-out effect. This has become what I call a "Perfect System Syndrome," taken from T.S. Eliot and colleagues' 1934 pageant play *The Rock*:

> They constantly try to escape,
>
> From the darkness outside and within,
>
> By dreaming of systems so perfect that no one will need to be good.

(v) Since the mid-1990s, executive remuneration has been developed on the back of the agency theory. Significant short- and long-term incentives seek to align the interests of executives with the interests of shareholders. They produce their own crowding-out effect: executives start to believe they are working hard for the extrinsic motivation of financial reward, rather than an intrinsic motivation to do well and act pro-socially. It is no longer in the personal interests of executives to consider any interests other than shareholders' interests as relevant for their decision-making.

4.05 These factors combined may have devastating results, as we see in the numerous cases of environmental degradation and neglect of employees, customers, and wider communities by corporations. A theme that is common throughout these factors is an excess of rationalization and system building, in an attempt to control reality, with a view to ensuring one particular outcome: value for shareholders. Such formal rationalization through bureaucracies, systems, and processes comes at the cost of human values, as Max Weber already explained some 100 years ago.[6] Weber, one of the founding fathers of sociology, points at one specific factor that is crucial. In a formally rational economy, "decisive are the need for competitive survival and the conditions of labor, money and commodity markets; hence matter-of-fact considerations that are simply *non-ethical* determine individual behavior and impose *impersonal* forces between the persons involved." Weber believed this formal rationality would come to overtake substantive rationality, in which choices are guided by some larger system of human values. As a result, we were to be left in the modern world with people who simply followed the rules without regard to larger human values.[7] Later, Erich Fromm would describe the process in different words. Fromm was a German psychoanalyst who moved to the United States in the 1930s. In 1956 he described modern American society from a psychoanalytic perspective in his book *The Sane Society*, in which he writes about alienation and conformity. Alienation for Fromm is related to idolatry, man building an idol that he then worships as if it is outside of him. The idol typically is a projection of one partial quality in man himself, which then stands over and above him. Man becomes a servant of a Golem,[8] which his own hands have built. "The very fact that we are governed by laws [of the market—JW] which we do not control, and do not even want to control, is one of the most outstanding manifestations of alienation. *We* are the producers of our economic and social arrangements, and at the same time we decline responsibility." Authority is no longer overt, but anonymous, invisible, alienated authority. "The mechanism through which anonymous authority operates is conformity. I ought to do what everybody does, hence, I must conform, not be different.. I must not ask whether I am right or wrong, but whether I am adjusted, whether I am not peculiar, not different."[9]

Weber's and Fromm's descriptions preceded the work of Friedman and the way **4.06**
in which shareholder primacy has come to dominate the corporate context. But it is striking to see how their insights precisely describe the transformation of the corporate context since the 1970s. In this corporate context the sole objective is to generate value for shareholders; other considerations are not relevant. As academics we theorize, research, and teach about aspects of the corporate context from this perspective. Within corporations we steer and organize to

6 Ritzer, Georg (2007), The Weberian Theory of Rationalization and the McDonaldization of Contemporary Society, www.corwin.com/sites/default/files/upm-binaries/16567_Chapter_.pdf.

7 Weber, Max (1921/1968), Economy and Society (3 vols), Bedminster Press 1186.

8 See www.myjewishlearning.com/article/golem/ for an explanation of the concept of a Golem in Jewish tradition.

9 Fromm, Erich (1956), The Sane Society, Routledge 2nd ed., p.153.

maximize efficiency towards this objective, through rational mechanisms that create impersonal forces between the persons involved. Through executive remuneration with substantial short- and long-term incentives, executives have a personal interest in maintaining the system. We have made the financial value-maximizing corporate context an idol, something to cherish and worship, that we benefit from the worship of. In the process we have started to conform to a corporate context created by ourselves as if this is beyond us, for which we bear no responsibility, and which cannot be contested. We have thus successfully alienated ourselves (in the sense of worshiping and not taking responsibility) from the corporate context we have created. The corporation has no responsibility beyond its objective to generate value for shareholders, and neither do we, who can only live with this matter-of-fact, anonymous and impersonal law of the market. And so the corporation and its inhabitants have become amoral. Moral responsibility, in the sense of having responsibility for the consequences of one's behavior toward others, has become an externality itself: it only is meaningful and relevant for and within the corporation to the extent to which the external world imposes it on the corporation and its inhabitants through laws or other moral codes, as Friedman's quote in the introduction shows. Our ability to conform to this perceived corporate reality-as-a-matter-of-fact is amazing, even frightening.

C. SHAREHOLDER PRIMACY IS A THEOREM THAT DOES NOT HOLD TRUE IN REAL LIFE

4.07 In the years since Friedman made his claim it has often been treated as a doctrine, triggering a religious reaction rather than a more balanced academic debate, as Zingales recently wrote.[10] Zingales proposes to restate Friedman as a theorem: under what conditions is it socially efficient for managers to focus only on maximizing shareholder value? Zingales describes three conditions: (1) companies should operate in a competitive environment, with firms being both price- and rules-takers; (2) there should not be externalities, or the government should be able to address perfectly these externalities through regulation and taxation; and (3) contracts are complete, in the sense that we can specify in a contract all relevant contingencies at no cost. If you read these conditions, they express that everybody else's interests are sufficiently addressed by either complete contracts or complete regulation (including on competition). If that is the case, the corporation can and should pursue only shareholders' interests.

10 Zingales, Luigi (2020), Friedman's Legacy: From Doctrine to Theorem, in: Zingales, Kasperkevic, Schechter (eds), Milton Friedman 50 Years Later, Stigler Center Chicago.

It is clear that in real life, in which corporations operate, none of these three conditions are in fact met. They have not been met over the past 50 years and I would hold that it is humanly impossible to design an economy and society with such institutions in which competition, regulation/taxation of externalities, and contracts are complete. Reality is too complex, uncertain, and unpredictable for us to achieve anything close to regulatory completeness, through private contract or public regulation. This does not mean that there is no role for government to constantly seek to improve the competitive environment and, for example, adapt existing competition principles in new ways for the digital world and big tech or invent fundamentally new competition principles to deal with the challenges they pose. Governments should also continuously seek to address externalities in terms of environmental, biodiversity, and climate damage through regulation and taxation. But as these attempts will never fully address all concerns, there remains an open space for corporations to act without clear and effective external rules of the game. The question is what corporations ought to do in that open space. **4.08**

The challenges currently faced by societies and the living world as a whole are pressing on a scale that we have not seen before. We can no longer afford to have corporations undertake their business without regard to these externalities. The corporate form with limited liability, which can attract capital that is rewarded when success is achieved, is a powerful tool that can bring about human qualities such as creativity, determination, and courage. The challenge is to ensure that through the corporate form these human qualities are applied to help solve the problems of the world, not to cause or aggravate them. Business actually is needed to solve problems of society that governments and individuals cannot solve. The shareholder primacy concept of the corporation is basically preventing this, telling directors to ignore externalities and simply pursue shareholder value maximization. This is where corporate law comes in. Something needs to change within the corporation and how it is understood and regulated to ensure that corporate conduct benefits society. **4.09**

D. THE BOARD AND THE DUTY OF SOCIETAL RESPONSIBILITY

Attempts are made in various ways to change the corporate context such that corporations become less focused on shareholder value maximization. A first way is to make corporations less vulnerable to shareholder pressure, by restricting shareholder rights. A second way is to emphasize that the corporation should have a purpose that explicitly addresses its role and objective in society. A third way is to involve stakeholders other than shareholders explicitly in **4.10** the corporate decision-making.[11] In each of these three approaches to address the problem of the responsibility of the corporation, the role of the board[12] is crucial. Without commitment of the board to direct the corporation to conduct itself in a way that benefits society and our planet, it is unlikely that the corporation will indeed do so.

4.11 This brings us to the core question that is not answered in these approaches: how do we ensure that the board is indeed committed to a broader responsibility of the corporation beyond merely serving the financial interests of shareholders? Mayer stresses the need for commitment but believes this commitment can only be generated when the corporation is owned by large, long-term oriented shareholders:

> [The] United Kingdom, in particular, with its dispersed ownership, is dominated by short-term shareholders rather than long-term shareowners, and is therefore a low commitment economy [...] Where corporations do not or are unable to offer the level of commitments that society demands of them, then it resorts to prescriptive regulation in place of permissive enabling legislation.[13]

4.12 But why should we stop there? Why should we accept that when a corporation only has dispersed, uncommitted shareholders, external, prescriptive regulation will have to bring about the level of responsibility that society expects of corporations? In such a view, societal responsibility of the corporation with dispersed owners indeed remains an externality: it only exists to the extent external regulation imposes it on the corporation and its board, as per the Friedman doctrine. We can do better, by turning to ourselves. The core of the problem of the amoral corporation is a human failure of succumbing to self-made formal rationalization and alienation. This human failure can only be overcome by addressing who we are as humans in the corporate context. We need to look at the board of the corporation, the people who make up the board, as the corporation's prime agent. It is people who act on behalf of the corporation, who allow for it to participate in economic activity.[14] Without people, the corporation cannot participate in society. This may change at some point in the future as computer systems with artificial intelligence start to take over more and more from human agency. It is an essential human challenge

11 See more extensively the source document in fn 1.

12 I refer to the board in this article as to include both the singular board in the one-tier model as well as both boards in a two-tier model.

13 Mayer, Colin (2018), Prosperity, Oxford University Press, pp.164–5.

14 Rönnegard, David and Velasquez, Manuel (2017), On (Not) Attributing Moral Responsibility to Organizations, in: Orts, Craig Smith (eds), The Moral Responsibility of Firms, Oxford University Press, pp.123–42.

to equip these systems with a sense of human morality, of other-regard.[15] If we cannot have human morality determine what corporations do when they depend on human agency, we will be much worse off when human agency is taken out of the equation.[16] The quality of taking moral responsibility, that is, responsibility for the consequences of one's acts, is a human quality.[17] It requires empathy, the ability to imagine what others would experience, and more broadly human emotions such as remorse and guilt. In order for societal responsibility to come from within the corporation, the responsibility of the people who are its agents needs to be activated. The board is legally responsible for the actions of the corporation.[18] It takes its core decisions and directs the people and the organization of the corporation. The board is the key body that should consider interests of different stakeholders and the uses of different forms of capital. In the board also rests the authority within the corporation to ensure that others who act on its behalf are guided by the principles and values determined by the board. In order to address the amoral character of the corporation, corporate law could formulate a duty of the board and the directors to ensure that the corporation acts responsibly with a view to the interests of society and the way the corporation uses financial, human, social, and natural capital. I would call this the duty of societal responsibility, a duty to ensure that the corporation acts as a responsible corporate citizen in society. I take these latter words from the King IV Corporate Governance Report of South-Africa (2016), principle 3: "the governing body should ensure that the organization is and is seen to be a responsible corporate citizen."[19] If this were to be not just an aspirational statement, but a firm duty of the board and directors, it would generate a commitment from within the corporation to drive the corporation toward fulfilling the needs of society. Such a duty can be seen as the counterpart of the limited liability with which society allows corporations and their shareholders and directors to operate. In exchange for unlimited upside opportunity and limited downside risk, society may expect of those who make use of the corporate form that when using this form they avoid harm to others and more positively contribute to fulfilling the needs of society.

15 Tegmark, Max (2017), Life 3.0. Being Human in the Age of Artificial Intelligence, Allen Lane.

16 See also Armour, John and Eidenmueller, Horst (2019), Self-Driving Corporations? https:// ssrn .com/ abstract=3442447.

17 Comte-Sponville, André (2009), Le Capitalisme est-il Moral? Albin Michel.

18 This does not mean that board members therefore face personal liability for everything the corporation is doing. Liability may follow from such responsibility, but typically follows only if certain threshold conditions have been met.

19 See for the full code https://cdn.ymaws.com/www.iodsa.co.za/resource/collection/684B68A7-B768-465C -8214-E3A007F15A5A/IoDSA_King_IV_Report_-_WebVersion.pdf.

E. ELABORATIONS OF THE DUTY OF SOCIETAL RESPONSIBILITY IN CORPORATE LAW AND CORPORATE GOVERNANCE

4.13 A duty of societal responsibility of the board of directors would complement the duty of loyalty and duty of care that are generally recognized as core director duties, in different ways in different jurisdictions. Such a duty should be elaborated upon in corporate law and corporate governance practices. Law and governance regulation cannot prescribe in detail what this responsibility would entail in the vast variety of corporate practice and reality. Regulation in corporate law could never be complete and anticipate all the dilemmas that come with the reality of dealing with different interests and concerns. Particularly as diverging considerations and interests will have to be balanced, we will have to rely on the people that lead corporations as directors to make judgments. Some would argue that it is impossible for directors to serve the interests of all stakeholders or even to balance them. It is true that there is no one predictable outcome of such exercise, no one right outcome. But the assumption that corporate decision-making is about taking the one and only correct decision was always illusory. Even in a strictly shareholder value-maximization context, decisions to invest, restructure, sell parts of the business, and so on have never been that clear-cut. Instead they require directors' judgment of various risks and opportunities, assessment of the corporation's own capabilities, and predictions about where markets, products, and innovation will move: all factors which are hard to get an absolute reading on and even harder to balance into an integrated decision. The shareholder value-maximization dogma only created an orientation for the outcome of the decision, not a measure that by some financial calculation miraculously produces the one and only correct outcome. Opening up to considerations other than the shareholders' financial interests does not require a fundamentally different cognitive skill-set for directors. They will have to apply their human ability to make judgments given the context of the corporation and the various interests that are at stake.[20] In driving for business success, the responsibility of the corporation in society will need to be taken into account.

4.14 Core principles of fair decision-making can be applied to give the duty of societal responsibility solid ground. One such principle is that in executing their duty of societal responsibility, directors should act as can reasonably be expected of directors in similar circumstances. This standard of behavior is often used by courts when conduct of directors is assessed. It allows for a mar-

20 Madsbjerg, Christian (2017), Sensemaking: What Makes Human Intelligence Essential in the Age of the Algorithm, Hachette Books.

ginal review of the decision-making or conduct in light of what is reasonable in the circumstances. The standard presumes that judgment and reason are indeed applied when balancing the interests and concerns for which responsibility exists.[21] A second principle is that in balancing the various interests, no relevant interest may be disproportionately harmed. Unnecessary harm, harm that can be avoided, is always disproportionate and therefore to be avoided. A third principle is that the board needs to apply procedural fairness. The concepts of reasonability, proportionality, and procedural fairness will help courts, who ultimately have to assess the conduct and decisions of boards and directors. A judicial assessment may lead to declaring decisions taken by the board null and void or to upholding a decision to dismiss a director who breached the duty. Under certain circumstances it may also lead to liability of individual directors.[22] Consequences of breaches of the duty of societal responsibility need to be thought through and standards need to be developed.

If a duty of societal responsibility of the board is introduced in corporate law, this should be further elaborated in corporate governance practices. I see at least five corporate governance elaborations. **4.15**

(a) *Corporate decision-making*: Boards should develop a decision-making practice to explicitly review how the decision furthers the purpose of the corporation or otherwise how the corporation in a responsible way addresses societal concerns, in particular how financial, human, social, and natural capital are used and affected. This will fundamentally change the deliberation and decision-making practices on boards. It will require very different information to be discussed on the board; information that not only sets out financial aspects of the decision, but also clarifies the impact of the decision on the well-being of employees, on the wider community in which the corporation operates, and on the environment and climate. It is likely that deliberations of this kind will also provide insights into heretofore unknown uncertainties. The shareholder primacy theory has led to a dominant corporate practice of simplification of reality by reducing it to measurable, predictable financial outcomes[23] (Ritzer calls this aspect of the rationalization process McDonaldization). This creates an illusion of control that ignores the role that unpredictability

21 Van Schilfgaarde, Peter (2019), Law and Life: Why Law? Springer.

22 See fn 14.

23 Ritzer, Georg (2007), The Weberian Theory of Rationalization and the McDonaldization of Contemporary Society, www.corwin.com/sites/default/files/upm-binaries/16567_Chapter_.pdf.

and chance play in a reality.[24] I would not be surprised if the new way of deliberating and decision-making, taking into account a much wider set of societal factors and challenges, were to bring us closer to the reality the corporation is actually faced with.

(b) *Board composition*: Because of the very different nature of board deliberation and decision-making, the composition of the board must change as well. Following the dot.com and financial crises of 2002 and 2008–9, the (regulatory) emphasis was put on directors, who should have a thorough understanding of financial reporting, control and risk. In recent years, understanding and experience of the digital world and opportunities has been in vogue. A board that is to seriously consider wider societal concerns needs to have the capability to understand and assess these wider aspects of the corporate reality. Concern may arise that boards will become too large to allow for effective deliberation and decision-making if all relevant forms of expertise have to be included in their composition. To avoid this, a new form of distributed leadership at board level could be developed. Built on the concept of X-teams,[25] an *X-board* could consist of a core group of members that comprises the formal board and additional members that can advise on specific matters. Additional members could be advisory members of the board, who participate in board meetings when their specific expertise or knowledge is required and who would not share in the collective responsibility of the board.

(c) *Executive remuneration*: A duty of societal responsibility must have consequences for the way in which executives are remunerated. The current practice of substantial short-term and long-term variable remuneration is a cornerstone of the shareholder primacy corporate practice. This practice must change if a duty of societal responsibility is to have any real effect. There is a widespread belief that variable remuneration based on target-setting in advance generates effective incentives for executives. I do not share that belief: substantial variable pay with target-setting in advance puts a complicated behavioral strain on people that is not effective and is potentially very damaging.[26] However, if variable pay is to

---

24 Winter, Jaap (2019), The Human Experience of Being-in-the-Board: A Phenomenological Approach, in: Levrau and Gobert (eds), Governance: The Art of Aligning Interests, Liber Amicorum Lutgart van den Berghe, Intersentia, pp.131–48, also available at https://ssrn.com/abstract=3319392.

25 Ancona, Deborah, Backman, Elaine and Bresman, Henrik (2008), X-Teams: New Ways of Leading in a New World, Ivey Business Journal, https://iveybusinessjournal.com/publication/x-teams-new-ways-of-leading-in-a-new-world/.

26 Winter, Jaap (2010), Corporate Governance Going Astray: Executive Remuneration Built to Fail, in: Festschrift Klaus Hopt, Walter de Gruyter 2010, pp.1521–35, also available at https://ssrn.com/abstract=1652137.

continue, then targets for short- and long-term remuneration must be set very differently, not only dealing with the financial interests that shareholders have but focusing instead on the achievement of the corporation's purpose in society and how the various sources of capital are used and affected by the corporation. That undoubtedly is going to be a complex affair, given how complicated remuneration schemes, target-setting, and measuring achievement have already become in the current context in which the incentives only seek to align with financial capital. There is a good case to be made for simplification of executive remuneration to fixed pay only, and for no longer using remuneration as a tool to stimulate responsible corporate behavior.

(d) *Governance of the organization*: Boards are ultimately responsible for the conduct of the corporation. In reality most corporate conduct arises through the acts of many employees in different roles throughout the organization. The board has the ultimate responsibility and authority to guide the actions of all employees toward the objectives of the corporation, whatever they may be. Over the past two decades we have seen this responsibility being strengthened in the directions of internal control and risk management. In practice this responsibility is typically formalized by building large compliance bureaucracies that seek to control people, which come at the cost of human inspiration, human morality, and human judgment.[27] Building new compliance bureaucracies to secure the exercise of the duty of societal responsibility will fail. If anything, societal responsibility requires human judgment at all levels of the organization. The board's role is to ensure that this judgment is not random, but adheres to general principles and values it has determined in light of its purpose and responsibility toward society. To ensure that the organizational conduct is in line with the stated principles and values, the board should install inspiration, discipline, and psychological safety in the organization and the people.[28] This requires different forms of leadership, at executive and non-executive levels, and often radically different ways of organizing.[29] This will require a strong focus on the collective, on collaboration. Trade-offs and negotiations at all levels of the organization

---

27 Winter, Jaap (2019), The Dehumanisation of the Large Corporation, published in Dutch in Ondernemingsrecht 2019/2, in English available at https://ssrn.com/abstract=3517492.

28 See on the difference between control and compliance on the one hand, and stretch and discipline on the other, the brilliant talk of Sumantra Goshal on the Smell of the Place at the World Economic Forum, https://youtu.be/UUddgE8rl0E.

29 Laloux, Frederic (2014), Re-inventing Organizations, Nelson Parker. See: https://www.reinventingorganizations.com/.

will have to be made explicit in order to generate a deliberative culture.[30] This is very different from the organizing and decision-making undertaken in the shareholder primacy paradigm that seeks to avoid and externalize multiple dimensions and considerations in order to serve one-sided effectiveness. True governance innovation throughout the organization requires becoming good at precisely this: inclusive, multi-dimensional reflection, deliberation, and decision-making.

(e) *Transparency*: Living up to a duty of societal responsibility entails transparency as to how the purpose of the corporation in society is served and how various sources of capital are used and affected by the corporation. Corporations should report on their impact in society and on the various sources of capital they use and affect. This will require new ways of measuring impact in society and on sources of capital beyond financial capital. It will take integrated reporting to another level. Reporting on societal impact and use of various sources of capital is still in its early days. So far, where it is practiced it is often an add-on to financial accounts geared to accounting for investor capital. Over time, as we learn more, we should expect this to become part of the regulated accounting process geared to accounting for the impact of corporations in society. Gathering and truly understanding information on the wider impact of the corporation in society will also be crucial for the board itself to be able to further the purpose of the corporation in society. To fulfill its duty of societal responsibility a board should be able to show how it has come to certain decisions, given the corporation's purpose in society and use of and impact upon various sources of capital.

4.16 When the duty of societal responsibility is anchored in corporate law and corporate governance elaborations such as these, this will bring to life a veritable and human commitment from within the corporation to act as a responsible corporate citizen in society.

30 Battilana, Julie, Fuerstein, Michael and Lee, Mike (2018), New Prospects for Organizational Democracy? In: Subramaniam (ed.), Capitalism Beyond Mutuality? Perspectives Integrating Philosophy and Social Science, Oxford University Press.

F. REGULATORY INITIATIVES TO INTRODUCE A DUTY OF SOCIETAL RESPONSIBILITY

A concrete proposal to amend Dutch corporate law was developed by a group of Dutch corporate law professors.[31] The proposal consists of three elements: **4.17**

- The current duty of executive and non-executive directors is to act in the interests of the corporation and its enterprise, suggesting a broader stakeholder approach. In practice, for many listed and private equity-owned corporations, this very general statement is implemented in particular to further financial results that are in the interests of shareholders. Also, the stakeholder concept that is embedded in Dutch corporate law appears to only include stakeholders who have some sort of connection with the corporation and its enterprises. External stakeholders, who have no relation with the corporation but can be negatively affected by its conduct, do not appear to be included in the approach.[32] The proposal is to extend the duty of executive and non-executive directors to ensure and monitor that the corporation acts as a responsible corporate citizen. This duty is a general duty for directors of all types of corporations and can be understood as a requirement which society imposes on directors and shareholders of corporations for enjoying the privilege of limited liability. The duty should primarily be understood to require directors to account for how they have balance the various interests, including interests and factors that are truly external to the corporation but are affected by the corporation's conduct.[33]
- Corporations can include in their articles of association a provision specifying its purpose. The purpose can provide the specific and concrete objectives of the particular corporation in light of the general responsibility to act as a responsible corporate citizen in society. Like the French provision in the Loi Pact,[34] this would be an option for corporations.
- Corporations who are subject to the full annual accounts regime (excluding small and medium-sized corporations) have to report how the directors

31 Winter, Jaap, De Jongh, Matthijs, Hijink, Steven, Timmerman, Vino, Van Solinge, Gerard and 20 co-authors (2020), Naar een zorgplicht voor bestuurders en commissarissen tot verantwoorde deelname aan het maatschappelijk verkeer, Ondernemingsrecht 2020/86, available at https:// phyleon .com/ wp-content/uploads/2020/05/Ondernemingsrecht-2020-86-2-Naar-een-zorgplicht-voor-bestuurders-en -commissarissen-tot-verantwoorde-deelname-aan-het-maatschappelijk-verkeer.pdf.

32 See the Dutch Supreme Court in Hoge Raad, 4 April 2014, NJ 2014, 286 (*Cancun*); ECLI:NL:HR:2014:797. See also Van Schilfgaarde, Winter, Wezeman, Schoonbrood (2022), Van de BV en de NV, Wolters Kluwer 2022, par. 5.

33 Van Schilfgaarde, Winter and Wezeman-Schoonbrood (2022) (fn 32).

34 Loi no 2019-486 du 22 mai 2019 relative à la croissance et la transformation des entreprises https://www .economie.gouv.fr/loi-pacte-croissance-transformation-entreprises#.

have ensured that the corporation has acted as a responsible corporate citizen, including its impact on human, social, and natural capital. This reporting duty would again be a general obligation for all corporations, not just those who have included a specific purpose in their articles of association.

4.18 The proposal led to a motion carried by a majority in the Dutch Parliament urging the government to investigate how a broader responsibility of boards can be ensured through regulation.[35] The responsible minister nonetheless later decided that it was not the appropriate time to introduce such a change in corporate law, as the need for it was not apparent and it should first be seen what the various initiatives at EU level will deliver. Also, the Dutch business community's response to the proposal has been strongly negative. Even proposals to strengthen the aspirational wording in the Dutch Corporate Governance Code have met with the same resistance.[36] Despite this resistance, the Dutch Corporate Governance Code as adopted in 2022 does provide in its first principle that the management board of the company is responsible for sustainable, long-term value creation by the company.[37] It should take into account the impact the actions of the company have on people and the environment. This core principle can have a stronger legal effect than mere aspiration. According to the case law of the Dutch Supreme Court, generally accepted principles of good corporate governance can be a source of legal obligations.[38] This first principle can be seen as such a generally accepted principle. In all likelihood, in new climate litigation, courts will also base their decision about the duties of companies and their boards and what they entail on this principle of the Code. Furthermore, the management board should develop a view on sustainable, long-term value creation by the company and formulate a strategy in line with that view (best practice provision 1.1.1).

4.19 At EU level, the EU Commission published a proposal for a directive on Corporate Sustainability Due Diligence (CSDD) in February 2022.[39] The

35 Tweede Kamer (Parliamentary proceedings of the Second Chamber) 2020/21, 35570 IX, No. 13; at: https://zoek.officielebekendmakingen.nl/kst-35570-IX-13.html.

36 The Dutch Corporate Governance Code contains principles and best practices. Listed companies are required to apply these or explain why they deviate. Available at: www.mccg.nl/english.

37 Corporate Governance Code, updated on 20 December 2022, at: www.mccg.nl/publicaties/codes/2022/12/20/dutch-corporate-governance-code-2022.

38 Hoge Raad (Dutch Supreme Court), judgment of 21 February 2003, NJ 2003, 182 (*HBG*); ECLI:NL:HR:2003:AF1486, Hoge Raad, judgment of 13 July 2007, NJ 2007, 34 (*ABN AMRO*); ECLI:NL:HR:2007:BA7972.

39 Document COM(2022) 71 final, available at: https://eur-lex.europa.eu/legal-content/EN/TXT/?uri=CELEX%3A52022PC0071; See also: https://ec.europa.eu/info/publications/proposal-directive-corporate-sustainable-due-diligence-and-annex_en.

directive introduces an obligation for certain large corporations in the EU to conduct human rights and environmental due diligence for their own operations and those of their subsidiaries and established business relationships in their value chain. In order to ensure that the duty of care that directors of a company owe to the company is understood and applied in a manner which is coherent and consistent with the due diligence obligations of the directive, Art. 25 of the proposed directive provides that Member States shall ensure that, when fulfilling their duty to act in the best interests of the company, directors of companies take into account the consequences of their decisions for sustainability matters, including, where applicable, human rights, climate change, and environmental consequences, in the short, medium, and long term. Member States must also ensure that their laws, regulations, and administrative provisions providing for a breach of directors' duty apply also to the provisions of Art. 25. Apart from the precise wording, Art. 25 seeks to clarify for the whole of the EU that directors of (at least certain large) corporations have some sort of societal duty when they seek to further the interests of the corporation.[40] Again, there is strong resistance to the adoption of such a duty of societal responsibility of directors. Legal scholars criticize the inclusion of Art. 25 in the proposal as going beyond the objectives of the directive, introducing language that does not seem to fit with the corporate law concepts of all Member States and without serious assessment of the consequences of Art. 25 in terms of effectiveness of director liability as a sanction.[41] This criticism comes on the back of sustained resistance from the business community. At the same time the business community claims to actively take responsibility for matters such as climate change: see for example the letter of the Alliance of CEO Climate Leaders to the world leaders at the COP 26 conference in Glasgow.[42] This paradox of claiming *to be responsible* but not wanting *to be held responsible* may be explained by the concept of learning anxiety. It may be that many business leaders do want to take responsibility for external effects such as climate change, but simply do not yet know how to build a successful business which takes into account these effects. Putting pressure on them ("it is not just

40 The CSDD directive introduces interesting further corporate law provisions. Art. 26 provides that directors are responsible for putting in place and overseeing the due diligence actions referred to in the directive, with due consideration for relevant input from stakeholders and civil society organizations. They must also take steps to adapt the corporate strategy to take into account the actual and potential adverse impact identified in the directive and measures taken to deal with them. Art. 15 introduces an obligation to adopt a plan to ensure that the business model and strategy of the company are compatible with the transition to sustainable economy and with the limiting of global warming to 1.5°C in line with the Paris Agreement; when setting variable remuneration this should duly be taken into account.

41 See for example the critical blog-post of the European Company Law Experts at https://ecgi.global/blog/proposed-due-diligence-directive-should-not-cover-general-duty-care-directors.

42 See www.weforum.org/agenda/2021/10/cop26/-ceo-climate-alliance-message-to-world-leaders.

your free choice to take some form of societal responsibility; you have to do it, and there may be consequences if you get it wrong") generates anxiety that leads to resistance to learning and experimenting. My fundamental concern is that we hesitate too much and too long to ensure that business truly takes responsibility for its substantial contribution to the transgression of planetary and social boundaries. The solution therefore should not be to renounce a duty of societal responsibility, but perhaps to provide for an exemption of liability of directors during the first five years, allowing them to learn without immediate personal consequences resulting from the new norm.[43]

4.20 If these proposals for a duty of societal responsibility are turned into national and EU law there will be a major shift in corporate law. Corporate law will continue to facilitate risk-taking and rewarding success to the extent that the corporation is conscious of the impact it has in society and includes concerns regarding this impact in its own decision-making. This can only truly happen if corporations are also engaging in a constructive dialogue with their stakeholders on the impact of the corporation for these stakeholders. Corporations may in this sense become open corporations, no longer shielded from society, but more integrated into society. As I said, this will generate a human commitment, a commitment of people to ensure the corporation acts responsibly in society. Some would argue that (corporate) law generally cannot achieve such a change in corporate conduct. I am myself deeply hesitant of piling detailed prescriptive rules on detailed rules in order to curb corporate behaviour. These detailed rules often lead to regulatory crowding-out effects.[44] But I do believe that corporate law can and must determine the core orientation with which corporations are directed. As government regulation cannot effectively guarantee that externalities threatening society and the world are dealt with appropriately, we need the corporation's directors to make these the corporation's own concerns. It is then for the directors to determine what the responsibility of the corporation in society in its specific context requires and involves.

4.21 If we truly address what is at stake across all these dimensions, it should be clear that we can no longer afford to close our eyes and pretend all is well, or at least well enough. Nor can we afford the cynical belief that a fundamental

43 Winter, Jaap, De Jongh, Matthijs, Hijink, Steven, Timmerman, Vino, Van Solinge, Gerard and 20 co-authors (2020), Naar een zorgplicht voor bestuurders en commissarissen tot verantwoorde deelname aan het maatschappelijk verkeer, Ondernemingsrecht 2020/86, available at https:// phyleon .com/ wp -content/ uploads/ 2020/ 05/ Ondernemingsrecht -2020 -86 -2 -Naar -een -zorgplicht -voor -bestuurders -en -commissarissen-tot-verantwoorde-deelname-aan-het-maatschappelijk-verkeer.pdf.

44 Winter, Jaap (2018), A Behavioural Perspective on Corporate Law and Corporate Governance, in: Gordon, Ringe (eds) The Oxford Handbook of Corporate Law and Corporate Governance, OUP.

reset will not work anyway. Undoubtedly there will be more ideas; perhaps better ideas, when we put our mind to it. Then let us work on them too. But doing nothing is relinquishing our responsibility for a humane future, for our children and our children's children. It should not be an option.

5

THE ROLE OF THE INVESTOR[1]

Ida Levine

5.001 Traditionally, investors made investment decisions based solely on financial factors with the goal of maximising risk-adjusted financial returns. But times have changed. Today, an ever-increasing number of investors are considering other environmental, social and governance ('ESG') factors in their investment decision-making. With the stark warning of the climate emergency coming from the 2023 final report of the United Nations Inter-Governmental Panel on Climate Change,[2] there is real urgency. Given market and regulatory trends, it is likely that ESG or 'sustainable' investing will no longer be consid-

1 As noted in the text, Sustainable Finance regulation is a rapidly changing area, although the direction seems clear. This chapter was submitted in April 2023, and there have been further developments since that date.

2 IPCC, 'Climate Change 2021: The Physical Science Basis' (October 2021) www.ipcc.ch/report/ar6/wg1/downloads/report/IPCC_AR6_WGI_SPM_final.pdf accessed 2 April 2023; IPCC, 'AR6 Synthesis Report: Climate Change 2023' www.ipcc.ch/report/ar6/syr/ accessed 2 April 2023.

ered a separate investment style, and that over time all investing will become sustainable.

ESG investing has been adopted by both institutional investors and retail savers. According to Bloomberg Intelligence, ESG assets surpassed $35 trillion in 2020, up from $30.6 trillion in 2018 and $22.8 trillion in 2016, reaching a third of total global assets under management.[3] In 2022, ESG assets were set to surpass $41 trillion and could exceed $50 trillion by 2025.[4] **5.002**

Moreover, 'sustainable finance' – the process of 'taking account of ESG considerations when making investment decisions in the financial sector, leading to increased longer-term investments into sustainable economic activities and projects'[5] – has become a pillar of economic policy, harnessing the power of investors to support environmental and social good. The European Union (with the United Kingdom as a member) has been a thought leader in this arena; it has continued to push the boundaries, as discussed below. The UK is following a separate path post-Brexit – and has shown its intention to be equally ambitious.[6] And in the US the Biden White House is taking climate seriously,[7] with regulators starting to focus on ESG – particularly in relation to disclosure and supervision.[8] **5.003**

At the beginning of the COVID-19 pandemic, there were questions about whether the focus on climate change and social considerations would endure. But the pandemic only seemed to reinforce the public's appetite for ESG **5.004**

3 Bloomberg, 'ESG Assets Rising to $50 Trillion Will Reshape $140.5 Trillion of Global AUM by 2025, Finds Bloomberg Intelligence' *Bloomberg* (London and New York, 21 July 2021) www.bloomberg.com/company/press/esg-assets-rising-to-50-trillion-will-reshape-140-5-trillion-of-global-aum-by-2025-finds-bloomberg-intelligence/ accessed 2 April 2023; Bloomberg, 'ESG May Surpass 41 Trillion Assets in 2022, But Not Without Challenges, Finds Bloomberg Intelligence' (24 January 2022) www.bloomberg.com/company/press/esg-may-surpass-41-trillion-assets-in-2022-but-not-without-challenges-finds-bloomberg-intelligence/ accessed 2 April 2023.

4 ibid.

5 Commission, 'Overview of Sustainable Finance' https://finance.ec.europa.eu/sustainable-finance/overview-sustainable-finance_en accessed 2 April 2023.

6 Jim Pickard, Daniel Thomas and Mathew Vincent, 'Rishi Sunak to Announce UK's First Green Gilts' *Financial Times* (London, 9 November 2020) www.ft.com/content/54a81c62-bcf7-431b-81ac-63ad22637363 accessed 2 April 2023; Financial Conduct Authority, 'CP22/20: Sustainability Disclosure Requirements (SDR) and Investment Labels' (29 March 2023) www.fca.org.uk/publications/consultation-papers/cp22-20-sustainability-disclosure-requirements-sdr-investment-labels accessed 29 March 2023.

7 Mathew Daly and Lisa Mascaro, 'On climate change, Biden $3.5T plan making up for lost time' *AP* (Washington, 29 September 2021) https://apnews.com/article/climate-change-joe-biden-business-environment-and-nature-environment-e9b976d57b1b8b35e459c9950b34fca0 accessed 2 April 2023.

8 US Securities and Exchange Commission (SEC), 'The Division of Examinations' Review of ESG Investing' (9 April 2021) www.sec.gov/exams/announcement/risk-alert-esg accessed 2 April 2023; *Modernization of Regulation S-K Items 101, 103, and 105*, Release Nos. 33-10825 (9 November 2020) [17 CFR 229 *et seq.* (9 November 2020)].

investing, with new emphasis on social alongside environmental issues – the new mantra is 'Build Back Better'.[9]

5.005 But sustainable investing is not without its challenges. There is growing regulatory scrutiny of so-called green-washing – environmental claims that are not reliable, giving the market a false impression of environmental impacts or benefits.[10] The topic has also become highly politicised in the United States, with political headwinds facing investment firms offering ESG products which take sustainability into account – particularly from the US Republican party.[11] Most recently, 21 Republican attorneys general sent a letter expressing concerns about asset managers pushing political ESG goals over maximising returns in the upcoming 2023 proxy season.[12]

5.006 In what follows, this chapter offers a discussion of the policy drivers of sustainable finance, with a focus on the EU, UK and US. It then reviews investment strategies and terminology in the fragmented world of ESG products and services. Next, it looks at the emerging global standards and regulatory consensus on sustainable investment – how EU/UK policy drivers have translated into rules and regulation, the renewed emphasis in the US and continuing work at the international level. Then it will briefly touch on the concept of fiduciary duty and how it can facilitate – or act as a block to – sustainable finance. Lastly, the chapter will close by taking stock of progress in the area and looking at complementary initiatives.

5.007 Given the volume of legislation and rule-making, and the rapid progress made in the area, the chapter necessarily represents a snapshot in time – but hopefully will give the reader a sense of the policy drivers and progress to date. It is clear at this juncture that global policymakers are putting most of their eggs in the 'transparency' basket – hoping that labelling and enhanced disclosure from investors, companies and other market participants and rules requiring integration of ESG into process will influence behaviours and drive a more sustainable approach to investment. This, in turn, is seen as a key to encour-

---

9 See Section 2 below.

10 Commission, 'Green Claims' https://environment.ec.europa.eu/topics/circular-economy/green-claims_en accessed 2 April 2023.

11 Ben Winck, 'Republicans Swim against Tide of ESG Money' *Reuters* (3 March 2023) www.reuters.com/legal/government/republicans-swim-against-tide-esg-money-2023-03-02/ accessed 2 April 2023.

12 Department of Justice, Open Letter dated March 30, 2023 https://content.govdelivery.com/attachments/MTAG/2023/03/30/file_attachments/2453301/2023-03-30%20Asset%20Manager%20letter%20Press%20FINAL.pdf accessed 15 April 2023.

aging market action supporting policy drivers. But will this approach have the desired result?[13]

A. POLICY DRIVERS

1. EU Green Deal

The European Commission ('Commission') announced the European Green Deal at the end of 2019.[14] The Green Deal[15] was meant to provide a growth strategy to transform the EU into an economy where: (i) there are no net emissions of greenhouse gases by 2050, following the Paris Agreement;[16] (ii) economic growth is decoupled from resource use; and (iii) no person and no place is left behind. The Commission's Action Plan[17] seeks to boost the efficient use of resources by moving to a clean, circular economy, restoring biodiversity and cutting pollution. It was updated in July 2021,[18] with the 'Fit for 55' package designed to support delivery of the EU's 2030 climate target of a 55 per cent reduction in carbon emissions. **5.008**

The Commission also noted the importance of a 'just and inclusive transition – highlighting social factors'.[19] Specific actions include: **5.009**

- investing in environmentally friendly technologies;
- supporting industry to innovate;
- rolling out cleaner, cheaper and healthier forms of private and public transport;
- decarbonising the energy sector;
- ensuring buildings are more energy efficient;

---

13 See Section 8 below, particularly footnote 207 and surrounding text.

14 Commission, 'A European Green Deal' https://ec.europa.eu/info/strategy/priorities-2019-2024/european-green-deal_en accessed 2 April 2023.

15 The EU Green Deal is discussed in more detail by Motani in Chapter 6 of this book.

16 United Nations Climate Change, 'The Paris Agreement' https://unfccc.int/process-and-meetings/the-paris-agreement/the-paris-agreement accessed 2 April 2023.

17 Commission, 'Communication from the Commission to the European Parliament, the European Council, the Council, the European Economic and Social Committee and the Committee of the Regions on The European Green Deal' (Communication) COM (2019) 640 final (Annex to the Communication on the European Green Deal).

18 Commission, 'Delivering the European Green Deal' https://ec.europa.eu/info/strategy/priorities-2019-2024/european-green-deal/delivering-european-green-deal_en#:~:text=Delivering%20the%20European%20Green%20Deal%20delivering_the_european_green_deal%20On%2014,step%20of%20the%20carbon%20neutrality%20set%20for%202050 accessed 2 April 2023.

19 More discussion on the concept of a 'Just Transition' is found in sub-section 1.2 below.

- working with international partners to improve global environmental standards.

5.010 Private investors have been within the Commission's sights. It has sought to use sustainable finance to deliver the Green Deal's objectives by channelling private investment into the transition to a 'climate-neutral, climate-resilient, resource-efficient and just economy', as a complement to public money.[20]

5.011 Sustainable finance is meant to support economic growth while reducing pressures on the environment and incorporating social and governance aspects. The Commission has prioritised transparency of ESG risks that may impact the environment, and mitigation of those risks through appropriate regulation of financial and corporate actors.[21]

2. Just Transition

5.012 The EU has also embraced the concept of a 'just transition',[22] recognising that the transition to a climate-neutral economy may have negative social and economic effects and seeking to have it happen in a fair way. The objective is that no one is left behind in the transition away from fossil fuels to more carbon-neutral alternatives. The just transition initiative seeks to provide financial and practical support to help workers and to look after the social welfare of those who stand to lose their jobs. And it also supports the socio-economic transformation of affected regions – providing funding for infrastructure, economic diversification and conversion of industry.

5.013 The EU has funded a Just Transition Mechanism, providing funding to Member States in their transition to a net-zero economy. The Just Transition Fund matches regional and member state funding; it provides targeted support to help mobilise at least €150 billion over the period 2021–7 in the most affected regions.[23] There is also an InvestEU and European Investment Bank ('EIB') public sector loan scheme. These two schemes seek to stimulate investment in the EU.

5.014 InvestEU builds on the model of the Investment Plan for Europe, which mobilised more than €500 billion from 2015 to 2020. The InvestEU Programme

---

20 Commission, Overview of Sustainable Finance (n 5).

21 ibid.

22 Commission, 'The Just Transition Mechanism: Making Sure No One Is Left Behind' https://ec.europa.eu/info/strategy/priorities-2019-2024/european-green-deal/finance-and-green-deal/just-transition-mechanism_en accessed 2 April 2023.

23 ibid.

aims to trigger a new wave – more than €372 billion – in investments using an EU budget guarantee to boost investment innovation and job creation in EU from 2021 to 2027.[24] The EIB public sector loan scheme provides loans starting at €25 million to public sector entities to finance a single large investment project or investment programme aligned with EIB priorities.[25] The funding supports SMEs, research and innovation, up-skilling and re-skilling programmes, job-search assistance, creation of green jobs, mobility and pension-bridging grants.

3. UK Green Finance Strategy

The UK Green Finance Strategy was announced in July 2019.[26] The strategy focuses on global and domestic climate and environmental objectives – and recognises the role of the financial sector. The strategy encompasses two objectives: (i) to align private sector financial flows with clean, environmentally sustainable and resilient growth supported by government action; and (ii) to strengthen the competitiveness of the UK financial sector. These objectives are translated into three pillars. **5.015**

The UK strategy's first pillar is 'Greening Finance' by ensuring that current and future financial risk and opportunities from climate and environmental factors are integrated into mainstream financial decision-making, and UK markets for green financial products are robust. The second pillar, 'Financing Green', aims to accelerate finance to support the delivery of the UK's carbon targets and clean growth, resilience and environmental ambitions, as well as international objectives. Finally, a third pillar ('capturing the opportunity') seeks to ensure that the UK financial services industry captures the domestic and international commercial opportunities from these first two strategic pillars.[27] **5.016**

4. Green Recovery and Green Industrial Revolution

With the COVID-19 pandemic, the EU Green Deal and UK Green Finance Strategy were translated into Green Recovery policies. Both the EU and the **5.017**

---

24 European Union, 'Response to the COVID-19 Pandemic with EU investment support' https://investeu.europa.eu/index_en accessed 2 April 2023.

25 European Investment Bank, 'Loans for the Public Sector' www.eib.org/en/products/loans/public-sector.htm accessed 2 April 2023.

26 HM Treasury and Department for Business, Energy and Industrial Strategy, 'Green Finance Strategy' (hereinafter 'UK Green Finance Strategy') (2 July 2019) https://assets.publishing.service.gov.uk/government/uploads/system/uploads/attachment_data/file/820284/190716_BEIS_Green_Finance_Strategy_Accessible_Final.pdf accessed 2 April 2023.

27 ibid at 7.

UK included a pledge on climate change in their recovery plans, with the EU devoting nearly €550 billion to green projects over the following seven years. This represents 30 per cent of a package including an EU budget of €1.074 trillion for 2021–7 and a €750 billion coronavirus recovery fund.[28] The EU has called this NextGenerationEU. It includes a Recovery and Resilience Facility providing loans and grants and is meant to help repair the immediate economic and social damage brought about by the coronavirus pandemic.[29] Part of the funding will consist of Green Bonds.

5.018 Former UK Prime Minister Boris Johnson announced a plan for a Green Industrial Revolution to transform life across the post-Brexit United Kingdom. This ten-point plan sought to mobilise £12 billion of government investment, and potentially three times as much from the private sector, to create and support up to 250,000 green jobs[30] – with a large role for sustainable finance and private investors in achieving environmental and social goals.

5.019 In November 2020, former UK Chancellor (and, at the time of writing, now Prime Minister) Rishi Sunak also confirmed a green investment package to create jobs and de-carbonise parts of the economy in the UK's COVID-19 recovery plan.[31] He announced the UK's intention to extend its global leadership in green finance and financial technology, including plans for a Sovereign Green Bond in 2021 and the introduction of more robust environmental disclosure standards so that investors and businesses could better understand the material financial impacts of their exposure to climate change, price climate-related risks more accurately and support the greening of the UK economy.[32]

5.020 The UK 'Green Gilt' was highly successful. Sales in September and October 2021 raised a total of £16 billion to help fund green projects, drive progress to

---

28 Kate Abnett and Mathew Green, 'EU makes world's biggest "green recovery pledge" – but will it hit its mark' *Reuters* (London, 22 July 2020) www.reuters.com/article/us-eu-summit-climate-change-idUSKCN24N231 accessed 2 April 2023.

29 Commission, 'Recovery plan for Europe' https:// ec .europa .eu/ info/ strategy/ recovery -plan -europe _en accessed 1 April 2023.

30 HM Government, 'The Ten Point Plan for a Green Industrial Revolution' (November 2020) https://assets.publishing.service.gov.uk/government/uploads/system/uploads/attachment_data/file/936567/10_POINT_PLAN_BOOKLET.pdf accessed 2 April 2023.

31 HM Treasury and The Rt Hon Rishi Sunak MP, 'Chancellor's Plan for Jobs to Help the UK's Recovery' (8 July 2020) www.gov.uk/government/news/rishis-plan-for-jobs-will-help-britain-bounce-back accessed 2 April 2023.

32 HM Treasury, 'Chancellor Sets Out Ambition for Future of UK Financial Services' (9 November 2020) www.gov.uk/government/news/chancellor-sets-out-ambition-for-future-of-uk-financial-services accessed 2 April 2023.

net zero and create jobs across the UK. The order book for the first sale was ten times oversubscribed and that for the second was 12 times oversubscribed, showing the large demand for green investment.[33] The Green Gilt also reflected the concept of a just transition, with its additional focus on 'social co-benefits'.[34]

The UK's leadership of the G7 and co-chair role, with Italy, of COP26 resulted in an extensive COP26 programme of events in Glasgow in November 2021, and the formation of a new Impact Investing Task Force ('Impact Task Force').[35] **5.021**

In addition to the meetings and agreements discussed below, the Glasgow COP26 saw unprecedented participation by the financial services sector, with a full programme of sustainable finance events. These included the Green Horizon Summit hosted by the Green Finance Institute and the City of London Corporation, which tackled key barriers to mobilising capital, how to finance transition and growth, how to build a global green finance playbook, how to price carbon and nature and how to meet the $100 billion international climate finance challenge.[36] **5.022**

The Impact Task Force delivered its reports in December 2021: the main report entitled 'Time to Deliver: mobilising private capital at scale for people and planet' (the 'ITF Report'), and related Workstream A and B reports on why 'Financing a better world requires impact transparency, integrity and harmonisation' and the importance of 'Mobilising institutional capital towards the SDGs and a just transition'.[37] **5.023**

33 HM Treasury, 'Second UK Green Gilt Raises Further £6 Billion for Green Projects' (21 October 2021) www.gov.uk/government/news/second-uk-green-gilt-raises-further-6-billion-for-green-projects accessed 2 April 2023.

34 Impact Investing Institute, 'Green+ Gilt' www.impactinvest.org.uk/project/green/ accessed 2 April 2023.

35 Impact Investing Institute, 'Press Release: UK Backs Impact Taskforce under Its G7 Presidency Led by the Impact Investing Institute and the Global Steering Group for Impact Investment' (12 July 2021) www.impactinvest.org.uk/press-release-uk-backs-impact-taskforce-under-its-g7-presidency-led-by-the-impact-investing-institute-and-the-global-steering-group-for-impact-investment/ accessed 2 April 2023; United Nations Climate Change, 'The UK–Italy Partnership' (UN Climate Change Conference 'COP26') https://ukcop26.org/pre-cop/ accessed 2 April 2023.

36 Green Finance Institute, 'Green Horizon Summit at COP 26' (2 November 2021) www.greenfinanceinstitute.co.uk/event/green-horizon-summit-cop26/ accessed 2 April 2023.

37 ITF Impact Taskforce, 'Accelerating the Scale of Private Capital for Public Good' www.impact-taskforce.com accessed 2 April 2023.

5.024 The UK has also set up a Transition Plan Taskforce tasked with developing a gold standard for transition plans from UK financial institutions and corporates, which will include a focus on the need for a just transition.[38]

5.025 Most recently, the UK government published its 2023 Green Finance Strategy (the 'UK Green Finance Strategy'), which sets out a policy blueprint for mobilising green finance and investment in the UK. The strategy underlines the UK commitment at COP26 to become the world's first net zero-aligned financial centre. It covers, among other topics, continuing work on the UK Green Taxonomy, transition plans, transmission channels, Scope 3 emissions reporting, the Taskforce on Nature-Related Financial Disclosures, voluntary carbon credits and reporting requirements for physical climate risks.[39]

5. US Green Legislation

5.026 During President Trump's administration, the US lagged behind the EU and UK, with no coherent plan for a federal (central) government Green Deal or Green Recovery plan. With President Biden's election, there was a change of direction in the US.

5.027 Initially, the President used Executive Orders to shift policy during his first 100 days. In January 2021, President Biden issued Executive Orders and a Memorandum addressing climate change policy (domestic and international) and scientific integrity, which included a moratorium on new oil and gas lease permits on federal lands and waters.[40] These steps were built on actions which President Biden took on his first day in office, such as rejoining the Paris Agreement,[41] revoking the permit for the Keystone XL pipeline and establishing a moratorium on federal leases in Arctic Wildlife Refuge.[42]

---

38 Gina Gambetta, 'UK government transition plan taskforce exploring Just Transition' *Responsible Investor* (8 August 2022)www.responsible-investor.com/uk-government-transition-plan-taskforce-exploring-just-transition/ accessed 2 April 2023.

39 HM Government, 'Mobilising Green Investment: 2023 Green Finance Strategy' (March 2023) https://assets.publishing.service.gov.uk/government/uploads/system/uploads/attachment_data/file/1149690/mobilising-green-investment-2023-green-finance-strategy.pdf accessed 15 April 2023.

40 The White House, 'FACT SHEET: President Biden Takes Executive Actions to Tackle the Climate Crisis at Home and Abroad, Create Jobs, and Restore Scientific Integrity Across Federal Government' (27 January 2021) www.whitehouse.gov/briefing-room/statements-releases/2021/01/27/fact-sheet-president-biden-takes-executive-actions-to-tackle-the-climate-crisis-at-home-and-abroad-create-jobs-and-restore-scientific-integrity-across-federal-government/ accessed 2 April 2023.

41 The Paris Agreement is discussed in Section 1.6 below. See The White House, 'Paris Climate Agreement' (20 January 2021) www.whitehouse.gov/briefing-room/statements-releases/2021/01/20/paris-climate-agreement/ accessed 2 April 2023.

42 The White House, 'Executive Order on Protecting Public Health and the Environment and Restoring Science to Tackle Climate Crisis' (20 January 2021) www.whitehouse.gov/briefing-room/presidential

These actions represented the President's first steps in tackling climate change domestically and internationally and implementing a federal climate plan. The Executive Orders have been subject to challenge in the courts[43] as well as in the US Congress. For example, Executive Order 13990 – which establishes an Interagency Working Group on the Social Cost of Green House Gases and directs the group to quantify in monetary values the social costs of carbon methane and nitrous oxide emissions – was challenged in a suit brought by the State of Missouri and 12 other states. This was dismissed by the US District Court, and an appeal is pending at the time of writing.[44] In addition, in November 2021 the US Supreme Court agreed to review the scope of the Environmental Protection Agency's authority to limit emissions from power plants – a move that also could hamper future climate action.[45] **5.028**

Much of President Biden's detailed green strategy has required legislation to be passed in the Congress with an equally divided Senate. In November 2021, the US Congress passed President Biden's flagship $1.2 billion Bipartisan Infrastructure Law which was signed into law by the President after months of haggling and negotiations.[46] The result was a spending programme that will funnel billions to states and local governments to upgrade outdated roads, bridges, transit systems and other public works. As part of the political compromise, most content on climate change was left to a companion social safety net and climate bill, known as the Build Back Better Act. **5.029**

The Build Back Better Act was amended to create the landmark Inflation Reduction Act which was signed into law by President Biden on 16 August 2022 after months of further negotiations.[47] Although not labelled as a climate bill, the Act will provide $369 billion for climate and clean energy provisions and is the most comprehensive climate investment ever taken by the US Congress. Commentators have underlined the importance of this historic Act.[48] According to a summary of the bill, the package aims to curb the country's **5.030**

-actions/2021/01/20/executive-order-protecting-public-health-and-environment-and-restoring-science-to -tackle-climate-crisis/ accessed 2 April 2023.

43 The subject of climate litigation is discussed by de Wit and Mills in Chapter 11 of this book.

44 *Missouri v Biden*, 4:21-cv-00287-AGF (E.D. Mo. Aug. 31, 2021).

45 Leslie Clark, Niina H. Farah and Pamela King, 'What the Supreme Court's move means for Biden in Glasgow' *E&E News* (1 November 2021) www.eenews.net/articles/what-the-supreme-courts-move-means -for-biden-in-glasgow/ accessed 2 April 2023.

46 The White House, 'President Biden's Bipartisan Infrastructure Law' www .whitehouse .gov/ bipartisan -infrastructure-law/ accessed 2 April 2023.

47 H.R.5376 – Inflation Reduction Act of 2022 www .congress .gov/ bill/ 117th -congress/ house -bill/ 5376 accessed 2 April 2023.

48 Paul Krugman, 'The Inflation Reduction Act is a huge deal for climate change' *The New York Times* (8 August 2022) www.nytimes.com/2022/08/08/opinion/climate-inflation-bill.html accessed 2 April 2023.

carbon emissions by roughly 40 per cent by 2030.[49] But there are some significant concessions to the oil and gas lobby that suggest political resistance to climate change legislation is far from over.

5.031 It is also important to note that many environmental issues are determined at the US state and local level. And there have been bright spots in many US states and cities. For example, the City of Los Angeles has pledged to meet the net-zero carbon targets in the Paris Agreement, and additional targets on recycling, diverting waste from landfills and renewable energy.[50]

6. International

5.032 There is also an international framework underpinning climate policy with the goal of bolstering regional economic and environmental policymaking encouraging sustainable finance. This started with the Paris Agreement in 2015. In order to tackle climate change and negative environmental impacts, 197 countries adopted the Paris Agreement at the COP21 in Paris on 12 December 2015.[51] It entered into force on 4 November 2016. The deal aims to substantially reduce global greenhouse gas emissions and to limit the global temperature increase in this century to 2 degrees Celsius while pursuing means to limit the increase even further to 1.5 degrees. It includes commitments from countries to reduce their emissions and work together to adapt to the impacts of climate change and calls on countries to strengthen their commitments over time.

5.033 The Agreement also provides a 'pathway for developed nations to assist developing nations in their climate mitigation and adaptation efforts', and a framework for monitoring and reporting countries' climate goals.[52] It is linked to the main UN convention on climate change.[53] Importantly, Article 2(1)(c) of the Paris Agreement emphasises the role of sustainable finance, stipulating

49 The White House, 'FACT SHEET: President Biden Sets 2030 Greenhouse Gas Pollution Reduction Target Aimed at Creating Good-Paying Union Jobs and Securing U.S. Leadership on Clean Energy Technologies' (22 April 2022) www.whitehouse.gov/briefing-room/statements-releases/2021/04/22/fact-sheet-president-biden-sets-2030-greenhouse-gas-pollution-reduction-target-aimed-at-creating-good-paying-union-jobs-and-securing-u-s-leadership-on-clean-energy-technologies/ accessed 2 April 2023.

50 LA, 'LA's Green New Deal, Sustainability Plan 2019' https://plan.lamayor.org accessed 2 April 2023.

51 The Paris Agreement (n 16).

52 United Nations, 'The Paris Agreement' www.un.org/en/climatechange/paris-agreement accessed 2 April 2023.

53 United Nations Framework Convention on Climate Change – Declarations, OJ L 33, 7.2. (1994) 13–28 https://eur-lex.europa.eu/eli/convention/1994/69/oj accessed 2 April 2023.

that the obligations include 'Making finance flows consistent with a pathway towards low greenhouse gas emissions and climate-resilient development'.[54]

In another international effort, in October 2019, at the time of the International Monetary Fund/World Bank annual meetings, the EU launched the International Platform on Sustainable Finance ('IPSF') together with Argentina, Canada, Chile, China, India, Kenya and Morocco. They have since been joined by Indonesia, New Zealand, Norway, Senegal, Singapore, Hong Kong, Switzerland and, following Brexit, the UK. Together, members of the IPSF represent 55 per cent of greenhouse gas emissions, 50 per cent of the world population and 55 per cent of global GDP.[55] **5.034**

The Paris Agreement was revisited at COP26 in November 2021. The Conference governmental meetings ended with global agreement to accelerate action on climate change, with nearly 200 countries agreeing the Glasgow Climate Pact to keep the goal of a 1.5 degree Celsius limit alive, and finalise outstanding elements of the Paris Agreement.[56] While this limit remains in sight, it will only be delivered with concerted efforts over the next year of all countries to revisit and strengthen their current emissions targets. **5.035**

Many commentators were disappointed at the lack of progress towards these goals at the Sharm el-Sheikh Climate Change Conference – COP27 – held in November 2022 in Egypt under the theme 'Together for Implementation'.[57] However, there was recognition of the historic decision to address the loss and damage associated with climate change and establish a fund for 'Loss and Damage' – a policy that supports vulnerable developing countries manage their loss and damage due to climate change. It acknowledges that the people and countries least responsible are being affected first, and most severely.[58] But, **5.036**

54 United Nations, 'Paris Agreement' (2015) https://unfccc.int/sites/default/files/english_paris_agreement.pdf accessed 2 April 2023.

55 Commission, 'International Platform on Sustainable Finance' https://ec.europa.eu/info/business-economy-euro/banking-and-finance/sustainable-finance/international-platform-sustainable-finance_en accessed 2 April 2023.

56 UN Climate Change Conference 2021, 'COP26 Keeps 1.5C Alive and Finalises Paris Agreement' (13 November 2021) https://ukcop26.org/cop26-keeps-1-5c-alive-and-finalises-paris-agreement/ accessed 2 April 2023.

57 See, e.g., William James, Kate Abnett and Valerie Volcovici, 'At COP27 climate talks, slow progress stokes worry over final deal' *Reuters* (13 November 2022) www.reuters.com/business/cop/cop27-climate-talks-slow-progress-stokes-worry-over-final-deal-2022-11-13/ accessed 15 April 2023; Adeline Stuart-Watt, 'Why COP27 will be remembered as the Loss and Damage COP and what to expect next' *LSE* (28 November 2022) www.lse.ac.uk/granthaminstitute/news/why-cop27-will-be-remembered-as-the-loss-and-damage-cop-and-what-to-expect-next/ accessed 2 April 2023.

58 ibid.

given the race against time to achieve net zero, there is substantial work left to do.

B. MARKET THEMES

5.037 Clearly, sustainable finance is an integral part of the solutions envisaged by policymakers to address the massive environmental and social challenges facing society. But what is ESG investing? And what are the market drivers?

5.038 As noted previously, ESG investing by institutional investors (including asset managers) and retail savers has grown significantly. What began as a niche area has rapidly become mainstream, with most investors embracing ESG investing in some shape or form. Part of this is driven by policy and regulation, but there are also market and societal influences leading to the popularity of the sustainability theme.

5.039 Thus, ESG investing has become a commercial proposition. More and more investors are looking to investment advisers and fund platforms to deliver ESG products and services – particularly millennials and younger savers.[59] People also are beginning to scrutinise their pensions, looking at ways to put their money to work in addressing social and environmental issues – from adapting to and mitigating climate change, to improving working conditions and diversity, to tackling inequality. They are starting to ask for investment and pension solutions that deliver both a financial return *and* a positive contribution to the environment or society.[60]

5.040 During the period of the COVID-19 pandemic, this trend was reinforced. There have been some studies showing that ESG has performed as well if not better than non-ESG investments, although the evidence is far from conclusive.[61] This focus on ESG is to some extent regional. A 2020 survey by RBC Asset Management of 800 institutional asset owners, consultants and managers showed that in most parts of the world the COVID-19 crisis left financiers with increased faith that ESG improves returns. Apparently, 97.5

---

59 RBC, 'The Shifting Landscape of Global Wealth' www.rbcwealthmanagement.com/en-asia/insights/the-shifting-landscape-of-global-wealth accessed 2 April 2023.

60 An example is the responsible investing activities of UK government pension fund NEST, which are based on engagement with its membership: see NEST, 'Paving the Way: Our Responsible Investment Activities in 2019' www.nestpensions.org.uk/schemeweb/dam/nestlibrary/paving-the-way-2019.pdf; See also 'Make My Money Matter' campaign https://makemymoneymatter.co.uk/ accessed 2 April 2023.

61 Financial Times, 'Moral Money' (London, 14 October 2020) www.ft.com/moral-money accessed 2 April 2023.

per cent of investors thought this in Canada, 96 per cent in Europe and 93 per cent in Asia – but only 74 per cent in the US.[62]

But do consumers know what they are getting? Is there clear differentiation and do ESG products and services deliver on their promise of both a financial return and benefits for people and planet? What about the risk of green-washing? And will these investments bring in a new era of sustainable finance and fulfil the objectives of policymakers and regulators? The truth is that the landscape is confusing and fragmented. With different approaches and conflicting terminology, there is a need for standard-setters and regulators to step in to bring some clarity – both at a local and a global level. **5.041**

C. DEVELOPING A COMMON LANGUAGE

1. Definitions and Standards

Given the confusion, organisations and firms have sought to define market terms and create ESG standards to provide a more coherent landscape. For example, the UN Principles for Responsible Investment ('PRI') organisation has identified key ESG issues, provided investment tools and framed definitions.[63] The CFA Institute has released voluntary global industry ESG Disclosure Standards to provide greater product transparency and comparability for investors by enabling asset managers to clearly communicate the ESG-related features of their investments.[64] **5.042**

In the UK, the BSI, the national standards body, also has a Sustainable Finance Standardization Programme to help define globally applicable standards for the finance sector.[65] At international level, the International Organisation for Standardization has compiled standards for Environmental Management.[66] **5.043**

62 ibid.

63 PRI, 'ESG Integration Techniques' www.unpri.org/listed-equity/esg-integration-techniques-for-equity-investing/11.article accessed 2 April 2023.

64 CFA Institute, 'CFA Institute Releases Global ESG Disclosure Standards for Investment Products' (1 November 2021) www.cfainstitute.org/en/about/press-releases/2021/cfa-institute-releases-global-esg-disclosure-standards-for-investment-products accessed 2 April 2023.

65 BSI, 'BSI Launches First Sustainable Finance Guide Setting Standards for Financial Institutions to Align to Global Sustainability Challenges' (20 January 2020) www.bsigroup.com/en-GB/about-bsi/media-centre/press-releases/2020/january/bsi-launches-first-sustainable-finance-guide-setting-standards-for-financial-institutions-to-align-to-global-sustainability-challenges/ accessed 2 April 2023.

66 ISO, 'ISO 14000 Family—Environmental Management' www.iso.org/iso-14001-environmental-management.html accessed 2 April 2023.

5.044 This also includes new frameworks for financial services organisations that wish to be sustainable and better aligned with global initiatives such as the United Nations' Sustainable Development Goals ('SDGs').[67] Industry associations such as the UK Investment Association have also built a Responsible Investment framework with categories and standard definitions.[68] Investment organisations and firms the world over are defining categories and terminology.[69] These uncoordinated efforts to bring clarity may have created more fragmentation for the time being.

5.045 There have been encouraging signs that global standard-setters are beginning to work together, such as the Impact Management Platform (now reinvented as Impact Frontiers), a collaboration between leading providers of public good standards and guidance for managing sustainability impacts.[70] And, finally, at COP26 held in Glasgow in November 2021, the IFRS Foundation announced a most welcome development - the establishment of a new International Sustainability Standards Board ('ISSB') to develop consensus on international sustainability standards.[71] The developments culminating in this important announcement are discussed more fully in section 7 below.

2. Spectrum of Capital

5.046 There is also the issue of 'green', 'ESG' or 'impact'-washing.[72] A common vocabulary and standards may emerge. But will standards and disclosure provide information to savers and other consumers about how financial products will impact people and planet? Will they have the right focus on environmental and social outcomes – positive or negative – that arise out of investments to meet public policy goals and investor expectations?

5.047 The Spectrum of Capital provides a different way to look at ESG investing. It is a tool used by many impact investors to differentiate impact investing from other types of sustainable finance. It views investments from the perspective of

67 United Nations, 'The 17 Goals' https://sdgs.un.org/goals accessed 2 April 2023; see also section 3.2 below.

68 See The Investment Association, 'The Responsible Investment Framework' (18 November 2019) www.theia.org/sites/default/files/2019-11/20191118-iaresponsibleinvestmentframeworkglossary.pdf accessed 2 April 2023.

69 See, for example, the sustainable investing glossary provided by Robeco, based in The Netherlands. www.robeco.com/uk/key-strengths/sustainable-investing/glossary/esg-definition.html accessed 2 April 2023.

70 Impact Management Platform https://impactmanagementplatform.org accessed 25 January 2022; Impact Management Norms https://impactfrontiers.org/norms/ accessed 2 April 2023.

71 IFRS, International Sustainability Standards Board www.ifrs.org/groups/international-sustainability-standards-board/ accessed 2 April 2023.

72 See the definition of 'greenwashing' in Cambridge Dictionary https://dictionary.cambridge.org/dictionary/english/greenwashing accessed 2 April 2023.

investor intention or purpose – with scrutiny of financial goals, impact goals and intentions.[73]

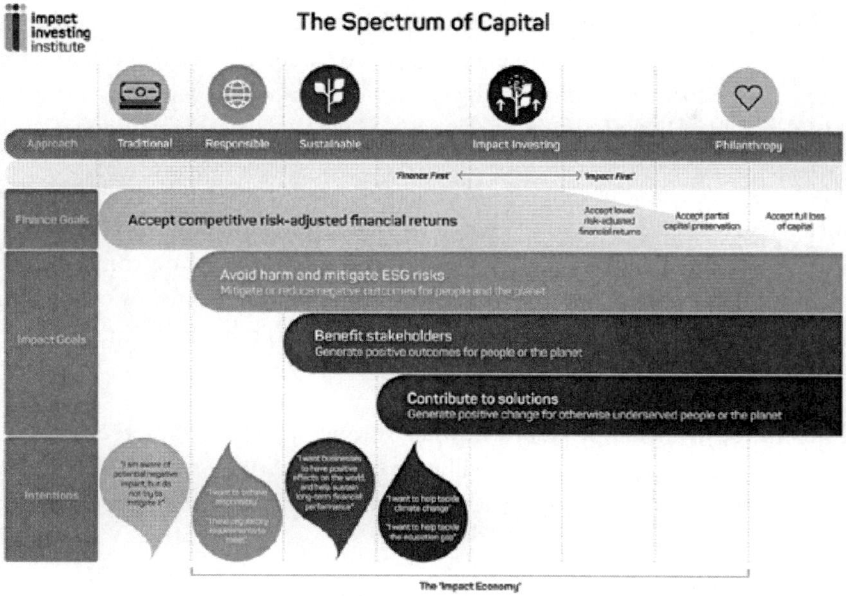

Source: Bridges Fund Management and Impact Management Project, www.bridgesfundmanagement.com/wp-content/uploads/2017/08/Bridges-Spectrum-of-Capital-print.pdf.

Figure 5.1 *The Bridges Spectrum of Capital*

The Spectrum begins with 'traditional' investment to maximise risk-adjusted returns. It then moves on to 'responsible' investing, where the investor wants to behave responsibly and mitigate risk by integrating ESG factors into investment decision-making, and to comply with regulatory obligations. 'Sustainable' investing moves to another level. Here an investor's mindset shifts to an interest in adopting progressive ESG practices expected to offer investment opportunities and enhance value. The sustainable investor wants to invest in businesses that have positive effects on the environment and society and help sustain long-term financial performance. **5.048**

The next step is 'impact investing'. This refers to investments 'made with the intention to generate positive, measurable social and environmental impact **5.049**

73 See Bridges Fund Management and Impact Management Project www .b ridgesfund management .com accessed 2 April 2023; a version of this chart is used in the Impact Task force Workstream A and B report, see ITF (n 37) 9, 16.

alongside a financial return'.[74] The focus on 'intentionality' differs from more traditional ESG analysis, which tends to be focused on how an organisation seeks to avoid harm, mitigate risk and manage its reputation. Impact investing is further divided into 'finance-first', which seeks to address societal challenges while achieving a competitive risk-adjusted financial return, where other impact investors are willing to accept lower risk-adjusted returns or accept a higher risk of loss of capital to achieve social or environmental impact.

5.050 There is also the concept of 'additionality' put forward by many impact investors and commentators – that 'a particular investment has impact only if it increases the quantity or quality of the enterprise's social outcomes beyond what would otherwise have occurred'.[75] This has been re-visited by others, who believe that the concept of investor 'contribution' is a better fit in the capital markets.[76]

5.051 Philanthropy (including venture philanthropy) is at the other end of the Spectrum; the philanthropist is willing to accept partial or full loss of capital to contribute to solutions to generate positive change for the environment or society.

D. SUSTAINABLE FINANCE REGULATION

1. Translating Policy into Regulation

5.052 There is a real need for policymakers to drill down and provide clear principles and rules to implement their policy objectives. This also may serve to provide greater clarity and convergence around ESG terminology and standards – and much-needed transparency about the impact and outcomes of investments to guard against 'green', 'ESG' or 'impact'-washing.

5.053 The EU has been the first out of the block on sustainable finance regulation. The Commission has formulated a comprehensive regulatory framework to create incentives and support its objectives under the EU Green Deal. Many of the new regulatory initiatives apply to the activities of investors.

---

74 Global Impact Investing Network (GIIN) https://thegiin.org/impact-investing accessed 2 April 2023.

75 Paul Brest and Kelly Born, 'Unpacking the Impact in Impact Investing' *SSIR* (14 August 2013) https://ssir.org/articles/entry/unpacking_the_impact_in_impact_investing accessed 2 April 2023; see also FCA, 'Sustainability Disclosure Requirements and investment labels' (July 2022) DP21/4 at 18–19: 'additionality can be defined in terms of whether a proposed activity will produce some "extra good" in the future relative to a baseline – typically the counter-factual in which the investment has not taken place.'

76 https://impactfrontiers.org/norms/investor-contribution/ accessed 2 April 2023.

The Commission released its Action Plan on Sustainable Finance ('Action Plan') in March 2018 stemming from the EU's commitment to channel private financial flows into investments supporting the Paris Agreement target of a carbon-neutral economy by 2050, and more broadly the United Nations Sustainable Development Goals (SDGs).[77] The Action Plan was based on the recommendations from the Commission's High-level Expert Group on Sustainable Finance ('HEG'). It sets out a comprehensive strategy to connect finance with sustainability. **5.054**

2. EU Regulatory Agenda

The EU followed through on its Action Plan with a detailed regulatory agenda including several initiatives that are relevant to investors and investment: **5.055**

- EU Taxonomy Regulation ('Taxonomy Regulation');[78]
- Regulation on sustainability-related disclosures in the financial services sector ('SFDR' or 'Disclosure Regulation');[79]
- Non-Financial Reporting Directive ('NFRD'),[80] which was replaced by the new Corporate Sustainability Reporting Directive ('CSRD');[81]
- Delegated acts amending the Alternative Investment Fund Managers Directive ('AIFMD'), the Undertakings for Collective Investment in Transferable Securities ('UCITS') Directive and Markets in Financial Instruments Directive, revised version ('MiFID 2' and, collectively, 'Delegated Acts');[82]

77 See, Commission, 'Action Plan on Financing Sustainable Growth' (Communication) COM (2018) 097 final. The SDGs formed part of the 2030 Agenda for Sustainable Development adopted by all United Nations Member States in 2015, which provides a shared blueprint for peace and prosperity for people and the planet, now and into the future. At its heart are the 17 Sustainable Development Goals (SDGs), which are an urgent call for action by all countries – developed and developing – in a global partnership. They recognise that ending poverty and other deprivations must go hand-in-hand with strategies that improve health and education, reduce inequality, and spur economic growth – all while tackling climate change and working to preserve our oceans and forests. See UN, The 17 Goals (n 67).

78 Council Regulation (EU) 2020/852 of 18 June 2020 on the establishment of a framework to facilitate sustainable investment, and amending Regulation (EU) 2019/2088 [2020] OJ L198/13.

79 Council Regulation (EU) 2019/2088 of 27 November 2019 on sustainability-related disclosures in the financial services sector [2019] OJ L317/1.

80 Council Directive (EU) 2014/95 of 22 October 2014 amending Directive 2013/34/EU as regards disclosure of non-financial and diversity information by certain large undertakings and groups [2014] OJ L330/1.

81 Council Directive (EU) 2022/2464 of 14 December 2022 amending Regulation (EU) No 537/2014, Directive 2004/109/EC, Directive 2006/43/EC and Directive 2013/34/EU, as regards corporate sustainability reporting, [2022] OJ L322/15.

82 On 2 August 2021, the following Level 2 measures were published in the Official Journal of the EU (the OJ): (i) Commission Delegated Regulation (EU) 2021/1255 of 21 April 2021 amending Delegated Regulation (EU) No 231/2013 as regards the sustainability risks and sustainability factors to be taken into account by Alternative Investment Fund Managers [2021] OJ L277/11; (ii) Commission Delegated Directive (EU) 2021/1270 of 21 April 2021 amending Directive 2010/43/EU as regards the sustainability risks and sustain-

- Regulation on EU Climate Transition Benchmarks, EU Paris-aligned benchmarks, and sustainability-related disclosures for benchmarks.[83]

5.056 As part of the EU, the UK made a significant contribution to the development of this regulatory regime. Post-Brexit, the UK has gone its own way. It took a body of existing legislation on board and is now separately scrutinising financial services regulation.[84] It has also started a regulatory programme of its own. This is discussed more fully in section 5 below.

3. Taxonomy Regulation

5.057 The EU Taxonomy Regulation became effective in July 2020. It provides a science-based framework for a comprehensive EU-wide classification system to enable financial firms to identify which economic activities and investments can be treated as 'environmentally sustainable'.[85]

(a) Green Taxonomy

5.058 Under the regulation, an activity is deemed to be environmentally sustainable if it:

- makes a substantial contribution to at least one of the six environmental objectives in the regulation or directly enables other activities to make a substantial contribution to one or more of these objectives;
- does not significantly harm any of these objectives;
- is carried out in compliance with minimum social standards (aligning with international guidelines, including the UN's Guiding Principles on Business and Human Rights); and
- complies with technical screening criteria which provide conditions under which an activity qualifies as contributing 'significantly' or causing 'significant harm' to environmental objectives.[86]

---

ability factors to be taken into account for Undertakings for Collective Investment in Transferable Securities (UCITS) [2021] OJ L277/141; and (iii) Commission Delegated Directive (EU) 2021/1269 of 21 April 2021 amending Delegated Directive (EU) 2017/593 as regards the integration of sustainability factors into the product governance obligations [2021] OJ L277/137.

83 Council Regulation (EU) 2019/2089 of 27 November 2019 amending Regulation (EU) 2016/1011 as regards EU Climate Transition Benchmarks, EU Paris-aligned Benchmarks, and sustainability-related disclosures for benchmarks [2019] OJ L317/17.

84 See UK European Union (Withdrawal) Act 2018; Financial Services (Miscellaneous Amendments) (EU Exit) Regulations 2020.

85 For a practical guide to understanding the EU taxonomy, see EU Taxonomy Navigator https://ec.europa.eu/sustainable-finance-taxonomy/ accessed 4 April 2023.

86 Council Regulation (EU) 2020/852 of 18 June 2020 on the establishment of a framework to facilitate sustainable investment, and amending Regulation (EU) 2019/2088 [2020] OJ L198/13.

This taxonomy relating to environmental objectives ('Green Taxonomy') is not a 'green' or 'eco-labelling' regime per se, but if an investment fund or product promotes environmental or social characteristics or has a sustainable investment objective,[87] then it must disclose the percentage of the investments underlying the financial fund or product that qualify as environmentally sustainable economic activities under the regulation. For other products, the Green Taxonomy requires the firm to include a statement that the investments underlying the financial product do not take into account the EU criteria for environmentally sustainable economic activities. **5.059**

BOX 5.1 THE EU TAXONOMY REGULATION'S ENVIRONMENTAL OBJECTIVES[88]

Article 9

Environmental objectives

For the purposes of this Regulation, the following shall be environmental objectives:

(a) climate change mitigation;
(b) climate change adaptation;
(c) the sustainable use and protection of water and marine resources;
(d) the transition to a circular economy;
(e) pollution prevention and control;
(f) the protection and restoration of biodiversity and ecosystems.

As noted previously, the Commission established the TEG to inform its work, including on the Green Taxonomy. Initially, the TEG was asked to provide recommendations for the technical screening criteria for economic activities that make a substantial contribution to climate change mitigation or adaptation, while avoiding significant harm to the four other stated environmental objectives: sustainable use and protection of water and marine resources; transition to a circular economy; pollution prevention control; and protection and restoration of biodiversity and ecosystems. **5.060**

87 See discussion of the Disclosure Regulation at sub-section 4.3 below.

88 Regulation (EU) 2020/852 of the European Parliament and of the Council of 18 June 2020 on the establishment of a framework to facilitate sustainable investment, and amending Regulation (EU) 2019/2088 (EU Taxonomy Regulation), [2020] OJ L 198/13. Available at: https://eur-lex.europa.eu/legal-content/EN/TXT/?uri=celex%3A32020R0852.

5.061 The TEG published its final report on 9 March 2020,[89] containing recommendations on its overarching design, as well as implementation guidance on how companies and financial institutions can use and disclose against the taxonomy, and a technical annex.[90] Other organisations, such as the PRI, have done further work with the industry to provide practical case studies applying the taxonomy.[91]

5.062 The Taxonomy Regulation is a relatively brief implementing Act which relies on hundreds of pages of detail in annexes and technical regulations. The Commission was tasked with establishing the list of environmentally sustainable activities by defining technical screening criteria for each environmental objective. A first delegated act on sustainable activities for climate change adaptation and mitigation objectives was approved in principle on 21 April 2021, and formally adopted on 4 June 2021 for scrutiny by the co-legislators (European Parliament and Member States).

5.063 The publication of the first delegated act was accompanied by the adoption of a Commission Communication on EU taxonomy, corporate sustainability reporting, sustainability preferences and fiduciary duties: '[D]irecting finance towards the European green deal that aimed at delivering key messages on how the sustainable finance toolbox facilitates access to finance for the transition.'[92] On 6 July 2021, the Delegated Act supplementing Article 8 of the Taxonomy Regulation was adopted by the Commission for scrutiny by the co-legislators. It specified the content, methodology and presentation of information to be disclosed by financial and non-financial undertakings concerning the proportion of environmentally sustainable economic activities in their business, investments or lending activities.[93] The Delegated Act was formally adopted in December 2021 after passing its period of scrutiny.[94]

5.064 Finally, most recently, in February 2022, the Commission proposed a second list of technologies to be included in the Green Taxonomy. The list found in

89 Commission, 'TEG Final Report on the EU Taxonomy' (9 March 2020) https://knowledge4policy.ec.europa.eu/publication/sustainable-finance-teg-final-report-eu-taxonomy_en accessed 2 April 2023.

90 Commission, 'Technical Annex to the TEG Final Report on the EU Taxonomy' (9 March 2020) https://finance.ec.europa.eu/system/files/2020-03/200309-sustainable-finance-teg-final-report-taxonomy-annexes_en.pdf accessed 2 April 2023.

91 PRI, 'EU Taxonomy Alignment Case Studies' www.unpri.org/policy/eu-sustainable-finance-taxonomy/eu-taxonomy-alignment-case-studies accessed 2 April 2023.

92 ibid.

93 ibid.

94 Kate Abnett, 'EU passes first chunk of green investment rules, contentious sectors still to come' *Reuters* (9 December 2021) www.reuters.com/markets/commodities/eu-passes-first-chunk-green-investment-rules-contentious-sectors-still-come-2021-12-09/ accessed 2 April 2023.

the Complementary Climate Delegated Act included natural gas and nuclear energy (if they meet certain strict conditions), which set off a vigorous debate about what should be considered a 'green investment'.[95] The list was subsequently approved and is now law.[96]

5.065 There is continuing controversy over the inclusion of gas and nuclear power in the EU Taxonomy list of 'green' investments, although the issue has been resolved politically and in legislation.[97] There have been several legal challenges[98] and requests for reviews, including from environmental groups such as Greenpeace.[99] In October 2022, Austria filed a suit against the Commission seeking an annulment of Regulation (EU) 2022/1214 of 9 March 2022 regarding certain economic activities (nuclear energy and fossil gas) and related disclosure requirements.[100] The crux of the case rests on the allegation that the contested regulation infringed on several existing procedural rules and regulations relating to the categorisation of certain economic activities as environmentally sustainable. It also remains to be seen how the market participants and companies will fare in complying with the Green Taxonomy, with its extensive, detailed disclosure requirements. It is certainly well-intentioned, and its role is accepted by market participants. Whether the metrics are workable and useful for investors and companies remains to be seen. There has been criticism from the investment community that the regulations comprised in the Green Taxonomy and SFDR are inconsistent and incomplete and will result in higher costs that are passed on to consumers; also that the timelines for implementation have been too short and unrealistic[101] and that there is insufficient guidance on social issues,[102] while a social taxonomy is still a work in progress.

95 Commission, 'EU Taxonomy: Complementary Climate Delegated Act to Accelerate Decarbonisation' (Last updated 11 July 2022) https://finance.ec.europa.eu/publications/eu-taxonomy-complementary-climate-delegated-act-accelerate-decarbonisation_en accessed 2 April 2023.

96 ibid.

97 European Parliament, 'Taxonomy: MEPs Do Not Object to the Inclusion of Gas and Nuclear Activities' (6 July 2022) www.europarl.europa.eu/news/en/press-room/20220701IPR34365/taxonomy-meps-do-not-object-to-inclusion-of-gas-and-nuclear-activities accessed 2 April 2023; Commission, 'EU Taxonomy for Sustainable Activities' https://finance.ec.europa.eu/sustainable-finance/tools-and-standards/eu-taxonomy-sustainable-activities_en#what accessed 4 April 2023.

98 See for example, Repasi v Commission (Case T-628/22) [2023] OJ C24/60.

99 Simmons+simmons, 'European Commission Faces Legal Challenge to EU Taxonomy' (13 October 2022) https://www.simmons-simmons.com/en/publications/cl96yg09s628w0a30jf7hywis/european-commission-faces-legal-challenge-to-eu-taxonomy accessed 4 April 2023.

100 Austria v Commission (Case T-625/22) [2023] OJ C24/59.

101 European Fund and Asset Management Association (EFAMA), 'EFAMA Calls for Consistency of Taxonomy KPI Metrics in EU Sustainable Finance Regime' (18 May 2021) www.efama.org/newsroom/news/efama-calls-consistency-taxonomy-kpi-metrics-eu-sustainable-finance-regime accessed 2 April 2023.

102 ibid.

(b) Social Taxonomy

5.066 The Taxonomy Regulation also provides for the creation of a Social Taxonomy.[103] Initially, the design of the EU Social Taxonomy is in the hands of the subgroup of the EU Platform for Sustainable Finance (the 'Platform'), which issued its initial report for public consultation in July 2021 (the 'Social Taxonomy Proposal').[104] It recognises that from the outset both environmental and social aspects have been part and parcel of the EU's sustainable finance strategy. This reflects the EU's recognition of the need for social investment to achieve the SDGs and to realise the social internal market envisaged in the Treaty on the European Union (Article 3)[105] and reflect global standards such as the UN Guiding Principles on Business and Human Rights ('UNGP').[106] Also, the Platform notes in its proposal that there are indications that investors see social investments as an opportunity, just as they acknowledge that it is risky not to take social factors into account in investments.

5.067 The proposal suggests a structure for a Social Taxonomy, bearing in mind the following: (1) what constitutes a substantial social contribution; (2) how to not do significant harm; and (3) what activities are harmful. The Platform group was also asked to consider the relationship between the social and environmental taxonomies. It identified four main differences between a social and an environmental taxonomy:

- Economic activities such as job creation are inherently socially beneficial. A Social Taxonomy must distinguish between these inherent benefits and added social benefits such as improving access to quality healthcare or ensuring decent jobs.
- Environmental objectives/criteria can be based on science, but a Social Taxonomy could be founded on international standards, such as the International Bill of Human Rights.
- The environmental taxonomy links criteria to economic activities. However, some social aspects, such as collective bargaining or tax transparency, cannot be linked to economic activities. Rather, they must be linked to the economic entity.

---

103 See art 26(2)(a) of the Taxonomy Regulation (n 79).

104 Platform on Sustainable Finance, 'Draft Report by Subgroup 4: Social Taxonomy' (July 2021) https://finance.ec.europa.eu/system/files/2021-07/sf-draft-report-social-taxonomy-july2021_en.pdf accessed 2 April 2023; Commission, 'Call for Feedback on the Draft Reports by the Platform on Sustainable Finance on a Social Taxonomy and on an Extended Taxonomy to Support Economic Transition' (last updated 6 September 2021) https:// ec .europa .eu/ info/ publications/ 210712 -sustainable -finance -platform -draft -reports _en accessed 2 April 2023.

105 Consolidated Version of the Treaty on the European Union [2012] OJ L326/13.

106 United Nations Guiding Principles Reporting Framework www.ungpreporting.org accessed 2 April 2023.

- For some social topics it might be more difficult to develop meaningful quantitative criteria.[107]

The development of the Social Taxonomy is at an early stage; this is a complex and ambitious piece of work. Importantly for climate, it is linked to the 'E' by the concept of a just transition. Progress on climate issues cannot come at the expense of massive social cost. **5.068**

It is clear that there will be significant challenges in navigating the subjective criteria included in a Social Taxonomy, given differences in cultural norms and standards in Member States on various issues. In Brussels, it appears that the Social Taxonomy will be put on hold until at least 2024 and the next Commission.[108] In the interim, there is an opportunity to focus on the social aspects of the transition to net zero and push for a just transition; for example, as contemplated by the UK government's recent Green Gilt.[109] **5.069**

4. Disclosure Regulation

The EU's Disclosure Regulation (also known as the SFDR)[110] entered into force in December 2019. It imposes transparency requirements in relation to the integration of sustainability into the investment decision-making and advisory processes. The SFDR applies broadly to all financial market participants ('FMPs'), including asset managers, insurance companies and pension funds; there are separate rules for investment advisory firms. Many of the disclosure requirements that cover asset managers started to apply from 10 March 2021. **5.070**

It is a ground-breaking piece of legislation setting ambitious disclosure requirements for investors based on a 'double-materiality' theme – requiring disclosure of both the *impact* of ESG factors on a firm and its activities, and the impact of a firm's investment decisions on the environment and society. Together with the Taxonomy Regulation, it begins to tackle the issue of terminology and 'green', 'ESG' or 'impact'-washing. And it requires disclosure on how a company's remuneration policies are consistent with the integration of sustainability risks. **5.071**

107 Platform on Sustainable Finance, 'Draft Report by Subgroup 4: Social Taxonomy' (n 104) 4.

108 Financial Post, 'EU puts key plank of ESG Rulebook on hold amid infighting' (31 July 2022) https://financialpost.com/pmn/business-pmn/europe-to-put-key-plank-of-esg-rulebook-on-hold-amid-infighting accessed 2 April 2023.

109 Impact Investing Institute, Green + Gilt (n 34).

110 Council Regulation (EU) 2019/2088 (n 80).

5.072 Specific disclosures are at the entity level and/or product level. They must be made (depending on the requirement) in pre-contractual information to investors, in periodic investor reports and/or publicly on firms' websites. Most significantly, at an entity level, an FMP over the size threshold[111] must disclose on its website information regarding the consideration (or not) of principal adverse impacts ('PAI') of its investment decisions on sustainability factors (environmental or social). There are also rules requiring remuneration policies to be consistent with the integration of sustainability risks (environmental and social).

5.073 There are additional detailed rules for sustainable investment products. The Disclosure Regulation provides a common framework for disclosure – but also acknowledges that there are sustainable products 'with various degrees of ambition' in the market. Requirements distinguish between financial products that promote environmental or social characteristics (known in the market as 'Article 8' or 'light green') and those financial products that have as an objective a positive impact on the environment and society (known as 'Article 9' or 'dark green').

5.074 The content, methodologies and presentation of the information required in relation to PAI and in relation to products that promote environmental or social characteristics or that have sustainable investment as their objective are set out in regulatory technical standards ('RTS') developed by the European Supervisory Authorities ('ESAs'), which were finally completed in September 2022 and became effective in January 2023 after much delay.[112]

5. Corporate Sustainability Reporting

5.075 The last of the disclosure measures is the CSRD. From 2018, EU law has required large companies to disclose information on the way they operate and manage environmental and social challenges pursuant to the NFRD requirements, which amended the EU Accounting Directive.[113]

5.076 At the end of 2019, the Commission committed to review the NFRD as part of the EU Green Deal. Many believe that the Disclosure Regulation and

---

111 FMPs with more than 500 employees *must* consider determine PAI in respect of both entity-level and product-level disclosures.

112 European Banking Authority (EBA), 'Joint Regulatory Technical Standards on ESG disclosure standards for financial market participants' www.eba.europa.eu/regulation-and-policy/transparency-and-pillar-3/joint-rts-esg-disclosure-standards-financial-market-participants accessed 2 April 2023.

113 Commission, Directive 2013/43/EU of 22 July 2013 https://eur-lex.europa.eu/LexUriServ/LexUriServ.do?uri=OJ:L:2013:201:0004:0006:en:PDF accessed 2 April 2023.

Taxonomy Regulation put the cart before the horse. FMPs will be subject to a demanding disclosure regime under the Disclosure Regulation and Taxonomy Regulation before parallel company disclosure is available. Thus, the objectives of the Commission's review are two-fold: (i) to improve disclosure of climate and environmental data by companies to investors about the sustainability of their investments; and (ii) to make changes consistent with these other regulations.

In particular, the Commission noted that disclosure under the NFRD did not adequately reflect the double-materiality perspective by providing information on how non-financial issues (and sustainability issues in particular) impact companies and their business model, and how companies and their activities impact the environment and society.[114] This important concept is at the heart of a more robust disclosure of environmental and social impacts. The Commission intends to use the 'best and most widely accepted elements' of existing international non-financial/ESG reporting standards as its starting point. **5.077**

On 21 April 2021, the Commission adopted a proposal for a CSRD following its consultations. It introduced detailed reporting requirements and embraced a 'double materiality standard'.[115] It also required the audit (assurance) of reported information and provided for machine-readable reporting that feeds into the European single access point envisaged in the Capital Markets Union Action Plan. **5.078**

The EU Council and European Parliament reached a provisional political agreement on the CSRD in June 2022; the European Financial Reporting Advisory Group ('EFRAG') was responsible for establishing European standards, following technical advice from a number of European agencies.[116] On 5 January 2023 the Corporate Sustainability Reporting Directive (CSRD) entered into force.[117] This new directive modernises and strengthens the rules **5.079**

114 Commission, 'Consultation Document – Review of the Non-financial Reporting Directive' (11 June 2020) www.eba.europa.eu/sites/default/documents/files/document_library/Publications/Other%20publications/2020/885448/European%20Commission%20Public%20Consultation%20%20on%20NFRD%20%28EBA%20answer%29.pdf accessed 2 April 2023.

115 Commission, 'Sustainable Finance Package' (4 June 2021) https://ec.europa.eu/info/publications/210421-sustainable-finance-communication_en#csrd accessed 2 April 2023.

116 European Council, 'New Rules on Corporate Sustainability Reporting: Provisional Political Agreement between the Council and the European Parliament' (21 June 2022) www.consilium.europa.eu/en/press/press-releases/2022/06/21/new-rules-on-sustainability-disclosure-provisional-agreement-between-council-and-european-parliament/ accessed 2 April 2023.

117 Council Directive (EU) 2022/2464 of 14 December 2022 amending Regulation (EU) No 537/2014, Directive 2004/109/EC, Directive 2006/43/EC and Directive 2013/34/EU, as regards corporate sustainability reporting, [2022] OJ L322/15.

about the social and environmental information that companies have to report. A broader set of large companies, as well as listed SMEs, is now required to report on sustainability – approximately 50.000 companies in total. The first companies will have to apply the new rules for the first time in financial year 2024, for reports published in 2025.[118]

5.080 Once again, the EU has implemented an ambitious package on sustainability reporting which provides transparency and disclosure using a clearly articulated double-materiality standard. The UK is fulfilling a promise of equal ambition, at least with respect to climate reporting, as discussed below.[119]

6. Regulation of Investors and Funds

5.081 After a long gestation period, on 2 August 2021 the Delegated Acts were finally published, requiring AIFMs, UCITS management companies and EU MiFID investment firms to integrate sustainability risk and factors into their policies and procedures. These amend the previous Level 1 legislation.[120]

5.082 The Delegated Acts do not propose new organisational rules or conduct rules. They are brief, providing text to amend existing organisational/governance and conduct-of-business rules under the three EU regimes. The amendments generally require firms to integrate sustainability risks and factors as part of compliance with the existing rules in relation to risk management, due diligence on investments, product governance, suitability determinations and organisational requirements.

5.083 These include long-awaited ESG rules on product governance and suitability, requiring MiFID firms to reach out to clients to determine their sustainability preferences in determining suitability and fulfilling product governance responsibilities. These changes require substantial process and system changes by MiFID firms, and are viewed by many as a game-changer in developing the

---

118 Commission, 'Corporate Sustainability Reporting' https://finance.ec.europa.eu/capital-markets-union-and-financial-markets/company-reporting-and-auditing/company-reporting/corporate-sustainability-reporting_en accessed 2 April 2023.

119 Commission, 'Questions and Answers: Corporate Sustainability Reporting Directive Proposal' (21 April 2021) https://ec.europa.eu/commission/presscorner/detail/en/qanda_21_1806 accessed 2 April 2023.

120 On UK and international developments, see HM Treasury, 'A Roadmap towards Mandatory Climate-Related Disclosures' (November 2020) https:// assets .publishing .service .gov .uk/ government/ uploads/ system/ uploads/ attachment_data/ file/ 933783/ FINAL_TCFD_ROADMAP .pdf#: ~: text = 1 .5 %20The %20UK %20Government %20was %20one %20of %20the ,in %20line %20with %20the %20Green %20Finance %20Strategy%20recommendations accessed 2 April 2023; US SEC, 'Agency Rule List – Spring 2021' (June 2021) https://d16yj43vx3i1f6.cloudfront.net/uploads/2021/06/Sec.Reg_.Agenda.2021.pdf accessed 2 April 2023.

European market for sustainable/ESG products. Asset managers and advisers have been required to review their client take-on procedures and their product ranges to reflect these new requirements, and to consider client preferences on ESG investing and sustainable investment. Best practice will develop over time, as the rules themselves are fairly simple. Although not all clients will be interested, the industry anticipates more attention and investment discussion with clients about sustainability and ESG products – only heightening the current interest in ESG investing.

7. Other Tools: Green Claims criteria, Benchmarks, Ecolabel, Green Bond Standard

The EU is also looking at other tools to encourage more sustainable investment by institutions and retail savers, and to protect against negative practices such as green, ESG or impact-washing. **5.084**

Most recently, on 22 March 2023, the EU Commission published its proposal for a common criteria against green-washing and misleading environmental claims.[121] By this proposal, when companies make explicit green claims about their products and services, they will be obliged to respect minimum norms on how the claims are substantiated and communicated.[122] Consumers are expected to gain more clarity and stronger reassurance as to the quality of information provided by companies on their environmentally friendly products and services. **5.085**

Another tool is to provide a blueprint for robust and consistent sustainable benchmarks. The regulatory work on this is at an early stage, but there is a proliferation of different ESG benchmarks in the market. Moreover, organisations such as the World Benchmarking Alliance ('WBA') make the case for a coherent range of global sustainable benchmarks.[123] The WBA has set out to develop benchmarks comparing companies' performance on the SDGs backed by science and leveraging international norms and standards. The WBA has launched an Oil and Gas Benchmark alongside partners the Carbon Disclosure Project and ADEME (Agence de la Transition Ecologique). It **5.086**

121 European Commission, Proposal for a Directive of the European Parliament and of the Council on substantiation and communication of explicit environmental claims (Green Claims Directive), COM/2023/166 final, 22 March 2023.

122 Commission, 'Consumer Protection and Sustainable Finance: Enabling Sustainable Choices and Ending Greenwashing' https://ec.europa.eu/commission/presscorner/detail/en/ip_23_1692 accessed 5 April 2023.

123 World Benchmarking Alliance (WBA) www.worldbenchmarkingalliance.org/ accessed 2 April 2023.

assesses 100 keystone listed and state-owned oil and gas companies' targets and performance against the Paris Agreement goals.

5.087 So far, the EU has finalised two types of climate benchmark: the Paris-Aligned Benchmark ('PAB'), where underlying assets are selected so that the resulting benchmark portfolio's GHG emissions are aligned with the long-term global warming target of 1.5 degrees Celsius in the Paris Climate Agreement; and the Climate Transition Benchmark ('CTB'), where the portfolio is on a transitional decarbonisation trajectory of 2.0 degrees Celsius.

5.088 Following the legislative process, a Regulation on EU Paris-aligned Benchmarks and sustainability-related disclosures for benchmarks was published in the Official Journal on 9 December 2019. It entered into force on 30 April 2020.[124]

5.089 The EU has also implemented a new Green Bond Standard.[125] The EU Green Deal underlined the need for long-term signals to direct financial and capital flows to green investments. On 1 March 2023, the EU Commission welcomed a political agreement on the European Green Bond Standards.[126] Accordingly, Green Bonds are likely to play an increasingly important role in financing assets needed for the low-carbon transition.

5.090 Finally, the EU Ecolabel for Financial Products includes ongoing work on a label for retail financial products. The objective is to allow retail investors concerned with the environmental impact of their investment to rely upon a trusted and verified label to make informed investment decisions while incentivizing financial markets to develop more products with reduced or positive environmental impacts.[127] Work remains ongoing.

---

124 Council Regulation (EU) 2019/2089 (n 84).

125 European Commission, Proposal for a regulation of the European Parliament and of the Council on European green bonds, COM (2021) 391 final, 6 July 2021; Commission, 'European Green Bond Standard' https://finance.ec.europa.eu/sustainable-finance/tools-and-standards/european-green-bond-standard_en accessed 2 April 2023.

126 Commission, 'Sustainable Finance: Commission Welcomes Political Agreement on European Green Bond Standard' https://ec.europa.eu/commission/presscorner/detail/en/mex_23_1301 accessed 4 April 2023.

127 European Environmental Bureau (EEB), 'Progress towards an EU Ecolabel for Retail Financial Products' (23 April 2020) https://eeb.org/library/progress-towards-an-eu-ecolabel-for-retail-financial-products/ accessed 2 April 2023.

8. UK and Brexit

(a) Impact of Brexit

There is a substantial body of sustainable finance legislation being developed in Brussels. Prior to Brexit, the UK played a significant role in the formulation of this EU legislation. Thus, before the Brexit withdrawal date of December 2020 (the 'Withdrawal Date'), the question arose: how would this law become part of UK law?[128] The EU sustainable finance rules create significant obligations for financial firms, but also present opportunities to showcase green and other sustainable products and to put sustainability at the heart of investment. They are complex, and their success depends on financial service firms undertaking detailed strategic, investment, technical and operational analysis and making systems and process changes. **5.091**

EU legislation includes both regulations that are directly applicable in Member States and directives that must be implemented. There are also EU sustainable finance standards, benchmarks and labels in development. The two primary 'in-flight' EU regulations on the Withdrawal Date were the Disclosure Regulation and the Taxonomy Regulation, and there was ongoing work at Level 2 (implementing regulations, delegated regulations, technical standards). Under the Withdrawal Act,[129] direct EU legislation, *so far as it was operative immediately before the Withdrawal Date*, became part of UK law on or after that date. **5.092**

Because the disclosure obligations under the Disclosure Regulation and the Taxonomy Regulation came into effect after the Withdrawal Date, they did not become part of UK law under these onshoring provisions. There was an encouraging letter from John Glen, Economic Secretary to the Treasury, stating that the government would be addressing any deficiencies in the retained law to ensure that it was fully operable from the end of the implementation period. As he noted, promoting globally consistent standards is a key ingredient to strengthen the UK's status as a global hub for the growing area of sustainable finance.[130] **5.093**

128 See generally, Jonathan Herbst and Simon Lovegrove (eds), *Brexit and Financial Regulation* (OUP 2020).

129 UK European Union (Withdrawal) Act 2018.

130 HM Treasury Letter to Chair of European Scrutiny Committee, '9355/18: Proposal for a Regulation of the European Parliament and of the Council on the establishment of a framework to facilitate sustainable investment' (28 May 2020) https://europeanmemoranda.cabinetoffice.gov.uk/files/2020/06/EST_letter_to_Sir_William_Cash_MP_.pdf accessed 2 April 2023.

5.094 Since then, the UK Treasury has consulted on a new Future Regulatory Framework ('FRF') Review. The FRF was established to explore how the UK financial services regulatory framework should adapt to Brexit – and ensure that the new framework would be fit for the future. The UK Treasury also consulted with relevant stakeholders and the results of the consultation were published in July 2022.[131] The consultation has included questions on financial regulation and climate and the transition to net zero.

(b) UK Post-Brexit Regulation

5.095 There has also been a particular focus on green issues. The UK government published a Ten-Point Plan for a Green Industrial Revolution, setting out an approach to 'build back better', support green jobs and accelerate the UK's path to net zero.[132] As previously noted, the UK's ambitions to extend its global leadership in green finance and financial technology have included becoming the first country to mandate climate-related disclosures for companies, pension funds and insurance companies, and developing a Green Taxonomy with scientific metrics using the EU Taxonomy as its basis.[133]

5.096 The UK government announced its intention to make disclosures aligned to the Task Force on Climate-Related Financial Disclosures ('TCFD')[134] mandatory across the economy by 2025, with a significant proportion of mandatory requirements in place by 2023. The UK Taskforce's Interim Report and accompanying Roadmap[135] set out a pathway to achieving that ambition, taking a global lead on TCFD. The Taskforce was composed of the Bank of England, Financial Conduct Authority ('FCA'), Department of Work and Pensions ('DWP'), Department for Business, Energy and Industrial Strategy ('BEIS') and Pensions Regulator.

5.097 In October 2021, in advance of COP26, the UK government released 'Greening Finance: A Roadmap to Sustainable Investing', with concrete plans

131 HM Treasury, 'Financial Services Future Regulatory Framework Review: Proposals for Reform' (July 2022) https://assets.publishing.service.gov.uk/government/uploads/system/uploads/attachment_data/file/1092499/FRF_Review_-_Proposals_for_Reform__Government_Response_-_July_2022_.pdf accessed 2 April 2023.

132 See HM Government, 'The Ten Point Plan for a Green Industrial Revolution' (n 30).

133 See HM Treasury, 'Chancellor Sets Out Ambition for Future of UK Financial Services' (n 32).

134 Nathan Reiff, 'Task Force on Climate-Related Financial Disclosures (TCFD)' *Investopedia* (6 August 2021) www.investopedia.com/what-is-the-tcfd-task-force-on-climate-related-financial-disclosures-4771379 accessed 2 April 2023. See also accompanying text in Section 7.

135 HM Treasury, 'A Roadmap towards Mandatory Climate-Related Disclosures' (n 120).

to roll out TCFD disclosure across the financial and pensions sectors.[136] The paper is a call to action, and states that:

- Products will need to set out their impact, and justify their sustainability claims.
- Asset managers will need to set out how they incorporate sustainability into their investment strategies.
- There will be expectations around the publication of transition plans to net zero.
- Financial firms and pension schemes will be expected to use this information to shift financial flows to align with a net-zero economy.

It also outlined plans for TCFD-aligned Listing Rules for UK-listed issuers and for Sustainability Disclosure Requirements ('SDR'), including entity- and product-level disclosures by asset managers and asset owners and in respect of investment products. By the end of December 2021, the FCA had put in place climate-related disclosure requirements reflecting a 'double-materiality' approach and aligned with the TCFD's recommendations for the following regulated firms: **5.098**

- premium listed companies;
- issuers of standard listed shares and global depositary receipts (GDRs);
- asset managers;
- life insurers;
- FCA-regulated pension providers.[137]

In Primary Market Bulletin 36, the FCA set out its disclosure expectations and supervisory strategy for its TCFD-aligned Listing Rules; it is working on further technical guidance.[138] The rule for premium listed companies came into effect for accounting periods beginning on or after 1 January 2021. The rule for standard listed companies applied for accounting periods beginning on or after 1 January 2022. **5.099**

The FCA set out the rules for investors in its policy statement entitled 'Enhancing climate-related disclosures by asset managers, life insurers, and **5.100**

136 HM Government, 'Green Finance: A Roadmap to Sustainable Investing' (October 2021) https:// assets .publishing .service .gov .uk/ government/ uploads/ system/ uploads/ attachment _data/ file/ 1031805/ CCS0821102722-006_Green_Finance_Paper_2021_v6_Web_Accessible.pdf accessed 2 April 2023.

137 FCA, 'Climate-Related Reporting Requirements' (last updated 6 October 2022) www.fca .org.uk/ firms/ climate-change-sustainable-finance/reporting-requirements accessed 2 April 2023.

138 FCA, 'Primary Market Bulletin No. 36' (15 November 2021) www.fca .org .uk/ publications/ newsletters/ primary-market-bulletin-36 accessed 2 April 2023.

FCA-regulated pension providers'.[139] It also set up a Disclosures and Labels Advisory Group ('DLAG'), an expert advisory group made up of key financial market stakeholders and subject matter experts, to provide independent advice to FCA on the development and implementation of new sustainability-related financial disclosure requirements and a sustainable classification and labelling system for investment products (or 'labels') aligned with the Roadmap.[140] At the end of 2022, FCA issued a policy statement with proposed labels and disclosure rules.[141] Part of this work has been considering how the new UK SDR will sit with the EU SFDR, which is a parallel body of legislation. These measures promise to address 'green', 'ESG' or 'impact'-washing by setting clear criteria for sustainability labels, including a sustainable impact label. We expect final rules sometime during Q3 2022.[142] The rules could have a profound effect on the market for sustainable investment products,[143] and lead the way globally.

5.101 The UK has also embedded the recommendations of the TCFD into UK pensions law.[144] The relevant regulations came into force on 1 October 2021 and impose requirements on certain UK pension schemes for the identification, assessment and management of climate-related risks and opportunities effective from dates in 2021/22. These include requirements relating to governance, strategy and risk management, and requirements to select and calculate climate-related metrics and to set and measure performance against targets.

5.102 These developments have been instructive because there was concern as to the fate of pre-Brexit EU laws on sustainability and their continued application in the UK.[145] According to the UK's Retained EU Law (Revocation and Reform) Bill,[146] most retained EU laws would be automatically revoked by December

---

139 FCA, 'PS21/24: Enhancing Climate-Related Disclosures by Asset Managers, Life Insurers and FCA-Regulated Pension Providers' (December 2021) www.fca.org.uk/publication/policy/ps21-24.pdf accessed 2 April 2023.

140 FCA, 'Disclosures and Labels Advisory Group (DLAG) Terms of Reference' www.fca.org.uk/publication/fca/dlag-terms-of-reference.pdf accessed 2 April 2023.

141 See FCA (n 6).

142 FCA, 'FCA updates on its Sustainability Disclosure Requirements (SDR) and investment labels consultation' (last updated 29 March 2023) www.fca.org.uk/news/news-stories/fca-updates-sustainability-disclosure-requirements-and-investment-labels-consultation accessed 2 April 2023.

143 Sally Hickey, 'IA urges FCA to re-think sustainable fund labels proposals' *FT ADVISER* (23 February 2023) www.ftadviser.com/Articles3/2023/02/22/IA-urges-FCA-to-re-think-sustainable-fund-labels-proposals accessed 2 April 2023.

144 The Occupational Pension Schemes (Climate Change Governance and Reporting) Regulations 2021.

145 Osborne Clarke, 'The UK Retained EU Law Bill: Legislative Havoc or Promised Post-Brexit Deregulation' (6 February 2023) www.osborneclarke.com/insights/uk-retained-eu-law-bill-legislative-havoc-or-promised-post-brexit-deregulation accessed 4 April 2023.

146 Retained EU Law (Revocation and Reform) Bill, HL Bill 117 (as amended in Committee).

2023 as part of a 'sunset clause'. The only exception to this revocation relates to retained EU laws that already form part of UK's domestic primary legislation.[147]

Finally, no discussion of UK standards and rules applicable to investors would be complete without a mention of the UK Stewardship Code.[148] The UK Stewardship Code is aligned with UK company law and contains principles for institutional investors to follow in engaging with companies. It is a voluntary code for asset managers, asset owners and service providers and comprises a set of 'apply or explain' principles for asset managers and owners and a separate set for service providers.[149] The code provisions have significant similarities with the Code for Responsible Investing in South Africa (CRISA).[150] The first version of the UK Stewardship Code was released in 2010. The most recent revision of the Stewardship Code called out environmental (in particular, climate change) and social factors, in addition to governance, as material issues for investors to consider when making investment decisions and undertaking stewardship. It took effect from 1 January 2020, and firms were required to submit a final Stewardship Report to the UK Financial Reporting Council by 31 March 2021 to be included in the first list of signatories. **5.103**

E. US REGULATORY ACTION

Under President Trump, the US took a very different course than the EU and UK on sustainable finance and climate change. President Trump withdrew the US from the Paris Agreement,[151] and the administration stepped away from developing a meaningful green policy agenda or setting goals to address climate change and environmental issues in regulation. **5.104**

The position on the Paris Agreement has now been reversed by President Biden, as discussed above. A start has also been made on agency action adopting a more friendly attitude to ESG and green investing. **5.105**

147 The Law Society, 'Retained EU Law' (23 February 2023) www.lawsociety.org.uk/topics/brexit/retained-eu-law#:~:text=Overview,be%20renamed%20as%20assimilated%20law accessed 5 April 2023.

148 Financial Reporting Council (FRC), 'The UK Stewardship Code' (2020) www.frc.org.uk/getattachment/5aae591d-d9d3-4cf4-814a-d14e156a1d87/Stewardship-Code_Final2.pdf accessed 2 April 2023.

149 Financial Reporting Council (FRC), 'The UK Stewardship Code' (2020) www.frc.org.uk/getattachment/5aae591d-d9d3-4cf4-814a-d14e156a1d87/Stewardship-Code_Final2.pdf accessed 2 April 2023.

150 The similarities between the UK Stewardship Code and CRISA are further elaborated in Chapter 9 by Jonathan Maphosa.

151 Matt McGrath, 'Climate change: US formally withdraws from Paris agreement' *BBC News* (4 November 2020) www.bbc.com/news/science-environment-54797743 accessed 2 April 2023.

1. ERISA

5.106 The regulatory agenda of the US SEC and DOL during President Trump's administration reflected its negativity towards ESG and sustainability. Most notable were the Department of Labor ('DOL') fiduciary proposals under the US Employee Retirement Income Security Act of 1974 ('ERISA'), which strictly interpreted existing principles making it more difficult for US retirement (pension) funds to take ESG factors into account in their investing.[152]

5.107 The Trump DOL prohibited consideration of ESG concerns in making investment decisions unless they presented economic risk or opportunities that investment professionals 'would treat as material economic considerations under generally accepted investment theories'. The DOL stated in its original release that 'ESG investing raises heightened concerns under ERISA' and that plan assets could not be enlisted to pursue social and environmental objectives apart from financial gains.[153] The rule proposal was subject to a 30-day comment period that ended on 30 July 2020. A majority of the 1,100 comments submitted were opposed to the DOL's proposal.[154] The DOL unveiled its final rule on 30 October 2020. It required ERISA plan fiduciaries to select investments based on pecuniary factors, described as any factor that a fiduciary prudently determines is expected to have a material effect on risk and return. Under the rule, fiduciaries could consider ESG issues but only when relevant to financial analysis.[155]

5.108 The Trump DOL also made changes to ERISA's proxy voting requirements. These limited an ERISA-covered pension plan fiduciary's ability to vote on certain proxy proposals, including on ESG issues, unless the fiduciary 'prudently determines that the matter has an economic impact on the plan'.[156]

5.109 As expected, President Biden has revisited these DOL rules. On 20 May 2021, he issued an Executive Order that, among other things, directs the Labor Secretary to reconsider the Trump administration rules. The Executive

152 US Department of Labour, 'Financial Factors in Selecting Plan Investments' (30 June 2020) www.dol.gov/agencies/ebsa/laws-and-regulations/rules-and-regulations/public-comments/1210-AB95 accessed 2 April 2023.

153 Karina Karakulova, 'DOL Finalizes Rule on ESG Investing: Is "Nonpecuniary" a Synonym for "ESG"?' *CFA Institute* (2 December 2020) https://blogs.cfainstitute.org/marketintegrity/2020/12/02/dol-finalizes-rule-on-esg-investing-is-nonpecuniary-a-synonym-for-esg/ accessed 2 April 2023.

154 Sarah Minn, 'DOL, Dubious About ESG Pension Investing, Cuts It a Bit of Slack in Final Rule' *Chief INVESTMENT Officer* (2 November 2020) www.ai-cio.com/news/dol-dubious-esg-pension-investing-cuts-bit-slack-final-rule/ accessed 2 April 2023.

155 US Department of Labour, 'Financial Factors in Selecting Plan Investments' (n 152).

156 ibid at 39115.

Order on Climate-Related Financial Risk directs the Secretary to 'consider suspending, revising, or rescinding any rules from the prior administration that would have barred investment firms from considering environmental, social and governance factors, including climate-related risks, in their investment decisions related to workers' pensions'.[157] The order is clearly intended to address the two final rules published in 2020 by the Trump administration that undermined consideration of environmental, societal and governance issues by ERISA fiduciaries.

Under the heading 'Bolster the Resilience of Life Savings and Pensions', the order also asks the Labor Department to report on other measures that can be implemented to protect the life savings and pensions of US workers and families from climate-related financial risk, and to assess how the Federal Retirement Thrift Investment Board has taken ESG factors, including climate-related risk, into account. On 22 November 2022, the DOL released a final rule – Prudence and Loyalty in Selecting Plan Investments and Exercising Shareholder Rights ('Final Rule') – under ERISA that 'clarif[ied] that fiduciaries may consider climate change and other environmental, social, and governance (ESG) factors when they make investment decisions and when they exercise shareholder rights, including voting on shareholder resolutions and board nominations'.[158] This was subsequently challenged in the US Congress, but was left in force after President Biden's 20 March 2023 veto of the relevant legislation.[159] **5.110**

2. Climate Order: Other Measures

The 20 May 2021 Executive Order also directed the US National Climate Advisor and the Director of the National Economic Council to develop a comprehensive government-wide climate-risk strategy to identify and disclose **5.111**

157 The White House, 'FACT SHEET: President Biden Directs Agencies to Analyze and Mitigate the Risk Climate Change Poses to Homeowners and Consumers, Businesses and Workers, and the Financial System, and Federal Government Itself' (20 May 2021) www.whitehouse.gov/briefing-room/statements-releases/2021/05/20/fact-sheet-president-biden-directs-agencies-to-analyze-and-mitigate-the-risk-climate-change-poses-to-homeowners-and-consumers-businesses-and-workers-and-the-financial-system-and-federal-government/ accessed 2 April 2023.

158 US Department of Labour, 'Final Rule on Prudence and Loyalty in Selecting Plan Investments and Exercising Shareholder Rights' (22 November 2022) www.dol.gov/agencies/ebsa/about-ebsa/our-activities/resource-center/fact-sheets/final-rule-on-prudence-and-loyalty-in-selecting-plan-investments-and-exercising-shareholder-rights accessed 2 April 2023.

159 The White House, 'Message to the House of Representatives – President's Veto of H.J. Res 30' 920 March 2023) www.whitehouse.gov/briefing-room/presidential-actions/2023/03/20/message-to-the-house-of-representatives-presidents-veto-of-h-j-res-30/; Reuters, 'Biden uses first veto to defend rule on ESG investing' (21 March 2023) www.reuters.com/business/sustainable-business/biden-vetoes-resolution-block-labor-dept-rule-esg-investing-2023-03-20/ accessed 2 April 2023.

climate-related financial risk to government programmes, assets and liabilities. This would include identifying the public and private financing needed to reach economy wide net-zero emissions by 2050, while advancing economic opportunity, worker empowerment and environmental mitigation, especially in disadvantaged communities and communities of colour.

5.112 Further, it encouraged Treasury Secretary Janet Yellen, in her role as chair of the Financial Stability Oversight Council ('FSOC'), to work with its members to assess climate-related financial risk to the stability of the federal government and of the US financial system. These include the Chairs of the Board of Governors of the Federal Reserve System (the 'Fed'), Securities and Exchange Commission ('SEC'), Office of the Comptroller of the Currency ('OCC') and Commodity Futures Trading Commission, among others. She is also asked to consider issuing a report on actions to reduce risks to financial stability, including plans that member agencies are taking to improve climate-related disclosures and other sources of data, and to incorporate climate-related financial risk into regulatory and supervisory practices.

5.113 It is interesting to note that the Fed and OCC had already joined the Network for Greening the Financial System, an organisation of central banks and supervisors who come together on a voluntary basis to strengthen the global response required to meet the goals of the Paris Agreement and to enhance the role of the financial system in managing risks and mobilising capital for green and low-carbon investments in the broader context of environmentally sustainable development.[160]

3. SEC Agency Action

5.114 On 28 May 2021, the SEC responded to investor demand on ESG with 'an all-agency approach' including a number of recent actions,[161] including, among others:

- a Statement directing the Corporation Finance Division to enhance its focus on climate-related disclosure in public company filings;
- the creation of a Climate and ESG Task Force in the Division of Enforcement;[162] and

160 Network for Greening the Financial System (NGFS) www.ngfs.net/en accessed 2 April 2023.

161 US SEC, 'SEC Response to Climate and ESG Risks and Opportunities' (26 October 2021) www.sec.gov/sec-response-climate-and-esg-risks-and-opportunities accessed 2 April 2023.

162 US SEC, 'SEC Announces Enforcement Task Force Focused on Climate and ESG Issues' (4 March 2021) www.sec.gov/news/press-release/2021-42 accessed 2 April 2023.

- a Risk Alert to highlight observations from recent exams of investment advisers, registered investment companies, and private funds offering ESG products and services which highlighted deficiencies and control weaknesses as well as good practice.[163]

Finally, on 21 March 2022, the SEC proposed rule changes that would require registrants to include climate-related disclosures in their registration statements and periodic reports, including information about climate-related risks that are reasonably likely to have a material impact on their business, results of operations or financial condition, and certain climate-related financial statement metrics in a note to their audited financial statements. The required information about climate-related risks also would include disclosure of a registrant's greenhouse gas emissions, which have become a commonly used metric to assess a registrant's exposure to such risks.[164] Following the recent Supreme Court case *West Virginia v Environmental Protection Agency*, related to the Clean Air Act and the ability of the Environmental Protection Agency (EPA) to regulate carbon dioxide emissions related to climate change, some commentators have questioned whether the proposed changes will be subject to challenge in the US courts.[165] **5.115**

F. FIDUCIARY DUTY

The term 'fiduciary duty' is used as a shorthand to describe a bundle of duties which are expressed differently in common law and civil law systems and formulated in various ways under the law of jurisdictions across the globe. It is based in case law and more general statutes and must be viewed alongside more recent sustainable finance legislation and regulations. **5.116**

In the investment context, the concept is described in the landmark 2015 report 'Fiduciary Duty in the 21st Century' as 'duties (or equivalent obligations) which exist to ensure that those who manage other people's money act in the interests of beneficiaries, rather than serving their own interests'.[166] It is **5.117**

163 US SEC, 'The Division of Examinations' Review of ESG Investing' (n 8).

164 US SEC, 'SEC Proposes Rules to Enhance and Standardize Climate-Related Disclosures for Investors' (21 March 2022) www.sec.gov/news/press-release/2022-46 accessed 2 April 2023.

165 Jonathan D. Uslaner and Will Horowitz, 'Will the SEC's proposed climate risk disclosure rules survive Supreme Court scrutiny?' *Reuters* (5 August 2022) www.reuters.com/legal/legalindustry/will-secs-proposed-climate-risk-disclosure-rules-survive-supreme-court-scrutiny-2022-08-05/ accessed 2 April 2023.

166 See PRI, 'Fiduciary in the 21st Century' (2015) www.unpri.org/download?ac=1378 accessed 2 April 2023: this 2015 report followed a 2005 report written by Freshfields commissioned by a group of investment managers organised under the United Nations Environment Programme Finance Initiative (UNEP FI) (commonly referred to as the 'Freshfields report'); see UNEPFI, 'A Legal Framework for the Integration of

defined more simply in the ITF Report as 'the legal duty of a trustee (or other) to act in the best financial interests of their beneficiaries'.[167]

5.118 The most important of the duties are:

- *Loyalty*: Fiduciaries should act in good faith in the interests of their beneficiaries, should impartially balance the conflicting interests of different beneficiaries, should avoid conflicts of interest and should not act for the benefit of themselves or a third party.
- *Prudence*: Fiduciaries should act with due care, skill and diligence, investing as an 'ordinary prudent person' would.[168]

5.119 Traditionally, 'fiduciary duty' has been seen as requiring investment managers and pension fund trustees to take only financial factors into account in investing, rather than ethical concerns or quality of life factors. Thus, the issue has come up in sustainable finance as a potential obstacle or blocker to ESG investing (responsible, sustainable or impact) because environmental or social factors are viewed as non-financial factors. Despite the conclusions of the 2005 Freshfields Report and the views of other commentators,[169] this misconception persists to this day. The world and public opinion have changed, but the law has been relatively static. Many investors continue to point to their fiduciary duties and the need to deliver financial returns to their beneficiaries as reasons why they cannot invest integrating environmental and social factors.

5.120 This is a complex and rapidly evolving area deserving of a separate chapter. There are initiatives which seek to re-examine fiduciary duty and make it clear that investors not only may take environmental and social factors into account alongside financial factors in investing for beneficiaries, but may also provide options available to policymakers to facilitate investing to resolve sustainability challenges as an end in itself.[170] Notably, in the UK Green Finance Strategy, there is mention of ongoing work to clarify fiduciary duty as part of the discus-

---

Environmental, Social and Governance Issues into Institutional Investment' (October 2005) www.unepfi.org/fileadmin/documents/freshfields_legal_resp_20051123.pdf. It has been followed by a more recent 2021 report commissioned by PRI, Generation Foundation and UNEP Finance Initiative, and written by Freshfields (the 'Legal Framework for Impact'). See PRI, 'A Legal Framework for Impact' (2021) www.unpri.org/download?ac=13902 accessed 2 April 2023.

167 See ITF Report (n 37) 27.

168 PRI, 'Fiduciary in the 21st Century' (n 166); see also Freshfields, a-legal-framework-for-impact.pdf.

169 Impact Investing Institute, 'Impact Investing by Pension Funds – Fiduciary duty-legal context' (October 2020) www.impactinvest.org.uk/wp-content/uploads/2020/11/Impact-investing-by-pension-funds-Fiduciary-duty---the-legal-context.pdf accessed 2 April 2023.

170 PRI, 'A Legal Framework for Impact' (n 166) 7 and Part C; ITF Report (n 37) 15.

sion of pension scheme regulation.[171] This subject should be watched closely over the next few years given the ongoing changes in regulation requiring disclosure at the product and entity level, and stewardship codes and other actions requiring investors to integrate ESG into their investment process and operations.

G. GLOBAL DEVELOPMENTS

With more US support and increasing interest in Asia and Africa,[172] the development of global consensus on sustainable finance standards and regulation is becoming more of a possibility. Until now, at the global level, the area has been dominated by soft law initiatives led by the United Nations and other supranational organisations such as the UNPRI,[173] the SDGs,[174] the United Nations Global Compact,[175] the OECD Guidelines for Multinational Enterprises[176] and the International Labour Standards.[177] **5.121**

Many of these organisations have joined the mainstream investment world. Since it was founded in 2006, UNPRI has grown into an organisation with collective assets under management represented by PRI signatories standing at US$103.4 trillion as at 31 March 2020, representing 3,038 signatories.[178] Set out in 2015 by the UN General Assembly, the SDGs – a collection of 17 interlinked goals designed to be a 'blueprint to achieve a better and more sustainable future for all'[179] – have been implemented in measurement and reporting frameworks such as the United Nations Development Programme ('UNDP').[180] **5.122**

The SDGs are goals, not legally binding rules or regulations. But they have had a profound influence. They have been described as a 'Rosetta Stone' to connect business, government, academia and civil society to align around **5.123**

171 See UK Green Finance Strategy (n 26) 56.

172 Developments in Africa are discussed by Maphosa in Chapter 6.

173 PRI www.unpri.org accessed 2 April 2023.

174 See United Nations, 'The 17 Goals' (n 69).

175 UN Global Compact, www.unglobalcompact.org/ accessed 2 April 2023.

176 Organisation for Economic Co-operation and Development (OECD), 'Guidelines for Multinational Enterprises' www.oecd.org/corporate/mne/ accessed 2 April 2023.

177 International Labour Organisation (ILO), 'Introduction to International Labour Standards' www.ilo.org/global/standards/introduction-to-international-labour-standards/lang--en/index.htm accessed 2 April 2023.

178 PRI, 'Annual Report 2020: Foreword' www.unpri.org/annual-report-2020/foreword accessed 2 April 2023.

179 United Nations, 'Sustainable Development Goals' www .un .org/ sus tainablede velopment/ sustainable -development-goals/ accessed 2 April 2023.

180 UNDP, www.undp.org/content/undp/en/home.html accessed 2 April 2023.

sustainability priorities and contribute towards progress.[181] UNDP is working with the EU and financial firms to put them at the heart of sustainable finance. They are already being used by many companies and financial firms as a way of benchmarking their activities and reporting to the public.[182] The 17 goals were originally designed for governments and policy action, but many – for example, Good Health and Well-being (SDG 3), Quality Education (SDG 4), Gender Equality (SDG 5), Clean Water and Sanitation (SDG 6), Affordable and Clean Energy (SDG 7), Decent Work and Economic Growth (SDG 8), Responsible Consumption and Production (SDG 12) and Climate Action (SDG 13) – are used to invest and map out ESG disclosure by many investment and other financial firms.[183]

5.124 Also formed in 2015, TCFD – established by the Financial Stability Board – is another important global initiative.[184] The Task Force consists of 32 members from across the G20, representing both preparers and users of financial disclosures. It is chaired by Michael R. Bloomberg, founder of Bloomberg L.P. As a Taskforce, it has developed a reporting framework based on a set of consistent disclosure recommendations for use by companies and other organisations to provide transparency about their climate-related risk exposures to investors, lenders, insurance underwriters and the public.

5.125 TCFD sets expectations and provides guidance on climate-related risks. It has shifted the focus from historical reporting to a forward-looking assessment of future risks and opportunities, aligned with stress testing and scenario analysis by companies. Conceived as a voluntary disclosure framework, it is rapidly finding its way into regulation. As noted above, the UK recently announced its intention to make TCFD-aligned disclosures mandatory across the economy by 2025, with a significant portion of mandatory requirements in place by

---

181 Anthony F. Pipa, Max Bouchet and Krista Rasmussen, 'American Leadership in Advancing the SDGs to Achieve Equity and Sustainability' *Brookings* (12 November 2020) www.brookings.edu/blog/up-front/2020/11/12/american-leadership-in-advancing-the-sdgs-to-achieve-equity-and-sustainability/ accessed 2 April 2023.

182 KPMG, 'How to Report on the SDGs' (February 2018) https://assets.kpmg.com/content/dam/kpmg/xx/pdf/2018/02/how-to-report-on-sdgs.pdf accessed 2 April 2023.

183 See also PRI, 'The SDG Investment Case' (12 October 2017) www.unpri.org/sustainable-development-goals/the-sdg-investment-case/303.article accessed 2 April 2023.

184 Nathan Reiff, 'Task Force on Climate-Related Financial Disclosures (TCFD)' *Investopedia* (6 August 2021) www.investopedia.com/what-is-the-tcfd-task-force-on-climate-related-financial-disclosures-4771379 accessed 2 April 2023.

2023.[185] TCFD was also considered by the Commission in the context of its work on the CSRD.[186]

Over the years, several other influential international standard-setting groups have addressed ESG metrics and reporting, including the SASB Foundation ('SASB'), the World Economic Forum ('WEF'), the Global Reporting Initiative ('GRI'), the International Integrated Reporting Council ('IIRC', the Carbon Disclosure Project ('CDP') and the Climate Disclosure Standards Board ('CDSB'). These organisations set out frameworks and standards for sustainability, including climate-related reporting, that sit alongside the TCFD recommendations. SASB and the IIRC subsequently merged to form the Value Reporting Foundation ('VRF').[187] **5.126**

A new concept that originally came out of the work of SASB, WEF and others is that of 'dynamic materiality', which further develops the EU standard of 'double materiality'. This recognises that the materiality of E&S factors is dynamic and will unfold over time – with some triggers, such as the acceleration of climate change, making this happen very rapidly. This perspective is based on the premise that 'what appears financially immaterial today can quickly prove to be business-critical tomorrow' – as we are seeing more than ever in today's COVID-aware economic landscape.[188] **5.127**

The collective vision of these global organisations was of multi-stakeholder standard-setting that would reduce the reporting burden on reporting organisations while facilitating analysis, interpretation and action by users of information.[189] **5.128**

On 30 September 2020, the International Financial Reporting Standards Foundation ('IFRS'), the global accounting standard-setter, launched a consultation paper seeking to assess demand for global ESG standards.[190] The **5.129**

185 See section 4.7 above.

186 Commission, 'Questions and Answers: Corporate Sustainability Reporting Directive Proposal' (21 April 2021) https://ec.europa.eu/commission/presscorner/detail/en/qanda_21_1806 accessed 2 April 2023.

187 Value Reporting Foundation (VRF), www.valuereportingfoundation.org accessed 2 April 2023.

188 Donato Calace, 'Double and Dynamic: Understanding the Changing Perspectives on Materiality' *SASB STANDARDS* (2 September 2020) www.sasb.org/blog/double-and-dynamic-understanding-the-changing-perspectives-on-materiality/ accessed 2 April 2023.

189 CDP, 'Five global organisations, whose frameworks, standards and platforms guide the majority of sustainability and integrated reporting, announce a shared vision of what is needed for progress towards comprehensive corporate reporting – and the intent to work together to achieve it' (11 September 2020) www.cdp.net/en/articles/media/comprehensive-corporate-reporting accessed 2 April 2023.

190 IFRS, 'Consultation Paper on Sustainability Reporting' (September 2020) https://cdn.ifrs.org/content/dam/ifrs/project/sustainability-reporting/consultation-paper-on-sustainability-reporting.pdf accessed 2 April 2023.

paper asked whether the Foundation should expand its current remit of developing financial reporting standards and use its experience in international standard-setting to guide sustainability reporting and establish a new standard-setter on sustainability. This consultation was a watershed moment, with a recognition of the important role that sustainability plays in the enterprise value of companies. On April 2021, the IFRS Trustees published two documents on sustainability-related reporting. The first, a Feedback Statement,[191] summarised the significant matters raised by respondents to their consultation paper. The second is an Exposure Draft that outlined targeted amendments to the IFRS Foundation Constitution to accommodate an International Sustainability Standards Board ('ISSB') to set IFRS sustainability standards.[192]

5.130 As noted above, at the COP26 in November 2021 the IFRS Foundation Trustees finally announced the creation of a new standard-setting board, the ISSB, which will be chaired by Emmanuel Faber, former Chief Executive Officer of Danone. It sits beside the International Accounting Standards Board (IASB). The intention is for the ISSB to deliver a comprehensive global baseline of sustainability-related disclosure standards that provide investors and other capital market participants with information about companies' sustainability-related risks and opportunities to help them make informed decisions.[193] The ISSB promises to be a significant force in developing consensus on a baseline of international sustainability standards – with a recognition that there also may be regional enhancements.

5.131 In March 2022, the ISSB launched a consultation on two proposed standards. One sets out general sustainability-related disclosure requirements and the other specifies climate-related disclosure requirements.[194] The exposure drafts

191 IFRS, 'IFRS Foundation Trustee's Feedback Statement on the Consultation Paper on Sustainability Reporting' (April 2021) www .ifrs .org/ content/ dam/ ifrs/ project/ sustainability -reporting/ sustainability -consultation-paper-feedback-statement.pdf accessed 2 April 2023.

192 IFRS, 'Exposure Draft: Proposed Targeted Amendments to the IFRS Foundation Constitution to Accommodate an International Sustainability Standards Board to Set IFRS Sustainability Standards' (April 2021) www .ifrs .org/ content/ dam/ ifrs/ project/ sustainability -reporting/ ed -2021 -5 -proposed -constitution -amendments-to-accommodate-sustainability-board.pdf accessed 2 April 2023.

193 IFRS, 'International Sustainability Standards Board' www .ifrs .org/ groups/ international -sustainability -standards-board/ accessed 2 April 2023.

194 IFRS, '[Draft] IFRS S1 General Requirements for Disclosure of Sustainability-related Financial Information' (March 2022) www .ifrs .org/ content/ dam/ ifrs/ project/ general -sustainability -related -disclosures/ exposure -draft -ifrs -s1 -general -requirements -for -disclosure -of -sustainability -related -financial -information .pdf; IFRS, '[Draft] IFRS S2 Climate-related Disclosures' (March 2022) www.ifrs.org/content/dam/ifrs/project/ climate -related -disclosures/ issb -exposure -draft -2022 -2 -climate -related -disclosures .pdf accessed 2 April 2023.

build on TCFD and incorporate industry-based disclosure requirements derived from SASB standards. The consultation period ended on 29 July 2022. When the ISSB issues the final requirements, they will form a comprehensive global baseline of sustainability disclosures designed to meet the information needs of investors in assessing enterprise value. The ISSB is working closely with other international organisations and jurisdictions to support the inclusion of the global baseline into jurisdictional requirements. The ISSB has further plans to consult on its standard-setting priorities.[195]

Finally, the Chair of the International Organization of Securities Commissions ('IOSCO') has reconfirmed its role in supporting global sustainability reporting standards, working together with the ISSB. It has also set up IOSCO work streams to coordinate the international regulatory response on this issue.[196] **5.132**

H. TAKING STOCK

The area of sustainable finance is changing rapidly at the national, regional and international levels. As noted in the Introduction, it is moving so quickly that any chapter will soon be out of date because of the lightning speed of development of this area of law and regulation. There are important initiatives emerging from global standard-setters seeking to create a common language and standards, and from regional and local policymakers and regulators around the globe who seem willing to support that effort. There seems to be some appetite to coordinate an international response around sustainable finance – at least in relation to sustainability disclosure. **5.133**

At the global level, there is a commitment from the ISSB on an integrated, cohesive sustainability baseline reporting framework. The ISSB, IOSCO, regional regulators and standard-setters are also looking at accounting standards with a focus on how sustainability factors affect a company's enterprise value and sit within the broader topic of public interest reporting on the impact of the company's activities on people and planet (the second prong of double materiality). Jurisdictions such as the EU and UK are already building on **5.134**

195 IFRS, 'ISSB Delivers Proposals that Create Comprehensive Global Baseline of Sustainability Disclosures' (31 March 2022) www.ifrs.org/news-and-events/news/2022/03/issb-delivers-proposals-that-create-comprehensive-global-baseline-of-sustainability-disclosures/ accessed 2 April 2023.

196 Deloitte, 'Chair of the IOSCO Task Force on Sustainable Finance reconfirms that IOSCO stands ready to support global sustainability reporting standards' (29 October 2020) www.iasplus.com/en/news/2020/10/chair-of-the-iosco-task-force-on-sustainable-finance-reconfirms-that-iosco-stands-ready-to-support-global-sustainability-reporting-standards accessed 2 April 2023.

TCFB and the ISSB global approach, and embracing the concept of double materiality in their new disclosure regimes.

5.135 The EU sustainable finance regulatory agenda set out to support the Green Deal and Green Recovery and implement the Paris Agreement. The UK has maintained net-zero carbon and other targets consistent with the Paris Agreement, and its commitment to a robust sustainable finance regulatory framework. The US under President Biden has changed course to an environmental policy in line with the Paris Agreement and more. And the COP26 and COP27 agreements are a step forward, although there is much more work to be done.

5.136 Thus, there are encouraging signs of greater global policy and regulatory coherence supporting a net-zero economy. Likewise, the COVID-19 pandemic has only highlighted the need for a parallel transition to a more just and equal economy with an emphasis on social criteria. For the moment, the regulatory lynchpins are transparency and process. The hope is that this will create behavioural change and drive more private investment into well-defined and understood sustainable products and better investment and risk-management practices to support the growing global sustainability paradigm, with a view towards positive outcomes for people and planet.

5.137 Policymakers and regulators will be watching closely to see whether these prompts yield the desired outcomes. There are still no mandatory measures impacting the investment process or incentives such as remuneration. But the European Banking Authority has recommended that ESG indicators and ESG risk-related objectives and/or limits are reflected in the design of remuneration policies – including considering the implementation of a remuneration policy that links the variable remuneration of certain staff to the successful achievement of ESG objectives, subject to green-washing and excessive risk-taking concerns.[197]

5.138 There is also the new area of sustainable governance.[198] An initiative from the Commission aims to improve the EU regulatory framework on company law

197 European Banking Authority (EBA), 'EBA Report on Management and Supervisions of ESG Risks for Credit Institutions and Investment Firms' (2021) EBA/REP/2021/18 www.eba.europa.eu/sites/default/documents/files/document_library/Publications/Reports/2021/1015656/EBA%20Report%20on%20ESG%20risks%20management%20and%20supervision.pdf accessed 2 April 2023.

198 This new EU initiative is discussed in more detail by Winter in Chapter 4 of this book.

and corporate governance.[199] It would create a new body of company law and re-cast directors' duties to enable companies to focus on long-term sustainable value creation rather than short-term benefits. It aims to better align the interests of companies; their shareholders, managers and stakeholders; and society by adopting a multi-stakeholder approach – helping companies integrate sustainability into their own operations and value chains.

We are at a tipping point, with much of the ambitious regulatory programme of the EU and UK coming into effect and a global framework for sustainability disclosure starting to emerge. The jury is still out on whether this approach will produce the desired investment to support environmental and social outcomes. Some voices from the investment industry, such as that of Tariq Fancy, the former chief investment officer for sustainability at Blackrock, criticise the ESG project, saying it is damaging to the important causes it purports to support.[200] **5.139**

The world will be watching to see whether the desired investor actions follow in line with the programme's policy underpinnings – providing private funding and support for the critical move to a global net-zero carbon economy and other environmental transitions, and a fairer, just society with more equal benefits for all. **5.140**

199 Commission, 'Sustainable Corporate Governance' https://ec.europa.eu/info/law/better-regulation/have-your-say/initiatives/12548-Sustainable-corporate-governance accessed 2 April 2023.

200 Robert Armstrong, 'The ESG investing industry is dangerous' *Financial Times* (24 August 2021) www.ft.com/content/ec02fd5d-e8bd-45bd-b015-a5799ae820cf accessed 2 April 2023.

6

THE EUROPEAN GREEN DEAL

Habib Motani

6.01 In December 2019, a then relatively new European Commission leadership published a Communication[1] announcing a 'European Green Deal' (EGD), presenting it as a bold roadmap[2] for achieving a sustainable, carbon neutral economy for the EU by 2050. This chosen name, with its echoes of Roosevelt's New Deal, was intended to convey a sense of the transformative nature of the proposal and indeed, the Communication described it as 'a new growth strategy that aims to transform the EU into a fair and prosperous society, with a modern resource-efficient and competitive economy where there are no net emissions of greenhouse gases in 2050 and where economic growth is decoupled from resource use'. A bold and ambitious vision indeed, and, importantly, one focused not simply on responding to the climate crisis but on doing so in a positive and fair way, seizing the opportunities presented and dedicated to approaching the challenge of achieving net carbon neutrality, both as an objective in its own right and, as importantly, as a once-in-a-generation opportunity for promoting well-being and quality of life for the citizens of the EU. The proposal recognised that the journey proposed would be hard and, for some,

1 Communication from the Commission on the European Green Deal (December 2019). https://eur-lex.europa.eu/legal-content/EN/TXT/HTML/?uri=CELEX:52019DC0640&from=EN.

2 'Roadmap' contained in the Annex to the Communication on the European Green Deal (December 2019). https://eur-lex.europa.eu/legal-content/EN/TXT/?qid=1596443911913&uri=CELEX:52019DC0640#document2.

particularly difficult. Hence, a stated desire for a 'just and inclusive' transition that delivers for all the EU's citizens.

6.02 Almost five years on, this chapter outlines some of the important milestones reached so far on the road towards bringing the objectives of the EGD into reality and reflects on some of the issues that have arisen. It looks forward to the next steps on the journey and goes on to consider how 'real life events' might prove to be obstacles in the road towards a successful outcome. First it recaps the roadmap set out by the Commission in December 2019, identifying the steps proposed in the EGD in respect of the eight elements set out in Figure 6.1 below.

A. THE EGD ROADMAP

6.03 The EGD provides a 'roadmap', comprising numerous initiatives aimed at making Europe the first climate-neutral continent by 2050. It is organised around eight elements designed to transform the European economic model by making it less reliant on resource use and covers all sectors of the economy, notably transport, energy, agriculture, buildings and industries such as steel, cement, ICT, textiles and chemicals. The emphasis is on the actions needed to boost efficient use of resources by moving to a clean, circular economy, as well as halting climate change, reversing biodiversity loss and cutting pollution. The EGD outlines the investments needed and financing tools to be made available and explains how to ensure a just and inclusive transition.

6.04 In the EGD, the Commission is attempting to 're-set' EU environmental, energy, economic and social policy, making consistent use of all policy levers to ensure that *all* EU policy contributes to the overall objectives of the ECD. In addition, the Commission will work with EU member states to increase efforts to ensure that existing legislation and policies relevant to the EGD are enforced and effectively implemented. This will mean that, in addition to new proposals, such as the European Climate Law[3] which was adopted in June 2021, existing legislation and policies relevant to the EGD will be reviewed and adjusted as necessary, in furtherance of the objectives of the EGD.

3 Regulation (EU) 2021/1119 of the European Parliament and of the Council of 30 June 2021 establishing the framework for achieving climate neutrality and amending Regulations (EC) No 401/2009 and (EU) 2018/1999 ('European Climate Law'). OJ L 243, 9.7.2021. https://eur-lex.europa.eu/legal-content/EN/TXT/?uri=CELEX:32021R1119.

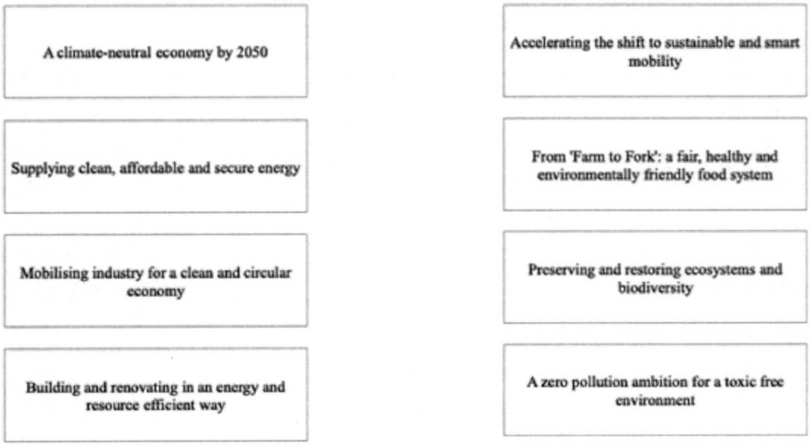

Source: Based on Figure 1: The European Green Deal, in: The European Green Deal, Communication from the Commission to the European Parliament, the European Council, the Council, the European Economic and Social Committee and the Committee of the Regions, Brussels, 11.12.2019 COM(2019) 640 final, at: https://eur-lex.europa.eu/resource.html?uri=cellar:b828d165-1c22-11ea-8c1f-01aa75ed71a1.0002.02/DOC_1&format=PDF.

Figure 6.1 The European Green Deal: eight key elements

6.05 Aligned with the objectives of the Paris Agreement, particularly Article 2(1)(c) to make 'finance flows consistent with a pathway towards low greenhouse gas emissions and climate-resilient development',[4] the EGD seeks to fulfil its objectives by ensuring a flow of investment to meet increased climate and energy targets, both through EU funding and through facilitation of private sector funding. The focus is on ensuring that there is a socially 'just transition' to these more stringent goals, doing more to mobilise research and facilitate innovation, encourage greener national budgets and implement environmentally positive price signals, such as through eradicating tax advantages for fossil fuels. The EU seeks to ensure that its policies 'do no harm' (a so-called green oath) by ensuring that the burden falls fairly on all parts of society. Indeed, although fighting climate change and environmental degradation is a common endeavour, not all regions and member states start from the same point. A 'Just Transition Mechanism'[5] will support those regions that rely heavily on

4 Council Decision (EU) 2016/1841 of 5 October 2016 on the conclusion, on behalf of the European Union, of the Paris Agreement adopted under the United Nations Framework Convention on Climate Change, at: https://eur-lex.europa.eu/legal-content/EN/TXT/?uri=OJ%3AL%3A2016%3A282%3ATOC.

5 The Just Transition Mechanism: making sure no one is left behind. European Commission. https://ec.europa.eu/info/strategy/priorities-2019-2024/european-green-deal/finance-and-green-deal/just-transition-mechanism_en.

carbon-intensive activities, supporting those most vulnerable to the transition, providing access to reskilling programmes and employment opportunities in new economic sectors.

B. THE ROADMAP: WHERE ARE WE NOW?

In the period since the EGD was first announced, progress has been made in several key areas, despite delays due to the COVID-19 pandemic. There are now numerous legislative and non-legislative measures in progress,[6] with more to follow. **6.06**

Table 6.1 below gives a snapshot of the status as at 1 August 2022. **6.07**

C. KEY MILESTONES

1. A New European Climate Law for EU Net-zero Emissions by 2050

In the EGD Communication, the Commission acknowledges that then existing policies would reduce greenhouse gas emissions by only 60 per cent by 2050 (compared to 1990 levels). It therefore proposed enactment of a Climate Law enshrining the commitment to carbon net neutrality by 2050 and a plan to increase the reduction in greenhouse gas emissions (compared to 1990 levels) to at least 50 per cent and towards 55 per cent by 2030. To achieve these targets, the Commission envisaged review and, as appropriate, revision to all climate-related policies, including the EU Emissions Trading System, which the Commission foresaw expanding to cover additional sectors. **6.08**

A new European Climate Law was duly introduced by the Commission and adopted by the Parliament and the Council. It came into force in July 2021. In addition to setting a legally binding target for the EU to achieve net-zero greenhouse gas emissions by 2050, there are important provisions on interim targets for the period up to 2030 and 2040, adaptation to climate change and assessments of progress made. It 'establishes a framework for the irreversible and gradual reduction of anthropogenic greenhouse gas emissions by sources and enhancement of removals by sinks regulated in Union law' by 'set[ting] out a binding objective of climate neutrality in the Union by 2050 in pursuit of **6.09**

6 'A European Green Deal' Legislative Train Schedule. European Parliament. https://www.europarl.europa.eu/legislative-train/theme-a-european-green-deal/file-european-green-deal.

the long-term temperature goal set out in point (a) of Article 2(1) of the Paris Agreement'[7] and 'provides a framework for achieving progress in pursuit of the global adaptation goal established in Article 7 of the Paris Agreement'.[8] Article 4 of the Law is an important Article in looking at the interim period leading up to 2050. It resets the target for net reduction in greenhouse gas emissions by 2030 to at least 55 per cent (compared to 1990 levels), reflecting an increased ambition on the part of the Commission subsequent to the original announcement of the EGD. It also provides for the adoption of an intermediate target in 2040.

2. The 'Fit for 55' Package

6.10 The EGD Communication emphasised the importance of ensuring that existing legislation and policies be reviewed and adjusted if required to meet the new, stricter emissions targets. The European Climate Law therefore required the European Commission to consider amending other EU legislation as necessary. In September 2020, the Commission published the 2030 Climate Target Plan,[9] which identified the key legislative changes that would be needed to meet the revised emissions reduction target. On 14 July 2021, the Commission published a Communication and its 'Fit for 55' package[10] of legislative proposals to overhaul climate and energy legislation to align with the EU 2030 targets; this was followed by an additional four proposals on 15 December 2021. All are still going through the EU legislative process and agreement on these proposals is a key objective in 2023.

6.11 An important part of the Commission's 'Fit for 55' package relates to carbon trading, one of the EU's key climate initiatives. The Commission has proposed

7 Which requires '[h]olding the increase in the global average temperature to well below 2 °C above pre-industrial levels and pursuing efforts to limit the temperature increase to 1,5 °C above pre-industrial levels'.

8 Which refers to 'the global goal on adaptation of enhancing adaptive capacity, strengthening resilience and reducing vulnerability to climate change, with a view to contributing to sustainable development and ensuring an adequate adaptation response in the context of the temperature goal referred to in Article 2'.

9 The 2020 Climate Target Plan. Communication from the Commission to the European Parliament, the Council, the European Economic and Social Committee and the Committee of the Regions: 'Stepping up Europe's 2030 climate ambition' (September 2020). https://knowledge4policy.ec.europa.eu/publication/communication-com2020562-stepping-europe%E2%80%99s-2030-climate-ambition-investing-climate_en#:~:text=Publication%20%7C%202020-,Communication%20COM%2F2020%2F562%3A%20Stepping%20up%20Europe's%202030%20climate,the%20benefit%20of%20our%20people&text=With%20the%202030%20Climate%20Target,below%201990%20levels%20by%202030.

10 Communication from the Commission to the European Parliament, the Council, the European Economic and Social Committee and the Committee of the Regions: 'Fit for 55': Delivering the EU's 2030 Climate Target on the way to climate neutrality (July 2021). https://eur-lex.europa.eu/legal-content/EN/TXT/?uri=CELEX:52021DC0550.

to revise and expand the EU Emissions Trading System[11] (ETS) comprehensively, for example by expanding it to emissions from maritime transport or by creating a new separate (upstream) emissions trading system for emissions from fuels used in road transport and building. The Council adopted its general approach on 29 June 2022, maintaining the overall ambition proposed by the Commission and trilogue discussions commenced in July 2022. Another core proposal is the introduction of a Carbon Border Adjustment Mechanism (CBAM) adopted by the Council in March 2022[12], the aim of which is to equalise the price of carbon between domestic products and imports to prevent the risk of carbon leakage[13]. Trilogue meetings on the CBAM began in July 2022.

D. FINANCING THE EUROPEAN GREEN DEAL

To achieve the goals set by the EGD in 2019, the Commission pledged to mobilise at least €1 trillion in sustainable investments by the end of the decade, from both public and private sectors. In January 2020 the Commission presented a European Green Deal Investment Plan[14] (also known as the Sustainable Europe Investment Plan), which is the investment pillar of the EGD, designed to facilitate the necessary finance, either directly through the EU budget or by creating an 'enabling framework' for private investors and the public sector to make sustainable investments. **6.12**

One of the most important elements of the EGD Investment Plan is the Just Transition Mechanism, aimed at providing financial support to the areas in the European Union most affected by the transition to carbon neutral. This is to be financed in a number of ways, including via a dedicated Just Transition Scheme under InvestEU[15] and loans from the European Investment Bank that **6.13**

11 Based on Directive 2003/87/EC of the European Parliament and of the Council of 13 October 2003 establishing a system for greenhouse gas emission allowance trading within the Union Consolidated text: Directive 2003/87/EC of the European Parliament and of the Council of 13 October 2003 establishing a system for greenhouse gas emission allowance trading within the Union and amending Council Directive 96/61/EC (Text with EEA relevance). https://eur-lex.europa.eu/legal-content/EN/TXT/?uri=CELEX%3A02003L0087-20210101&qid=1658158483982.

12 Draft regulation of the European Parliament and of the Council establishing a carbon border adjustment mechanism – General approach (March 2022). https://data.consilium.europa.eu/doc/document/ST-7226-2022-INIT/en/pdf.

13 Carbon leakage explained here: European Commission: https://climate.ec.europa.eu/eu-action/eu-emissions-trading-system-eu-ets/free-allocation/carbon-leakage_en; European Parliament: www.europarl.europa.eu/RegData/etudes/ATAG/2022/729462/EPRS_ATA(2022)729462_EN.pdf.

14 The European Green Deal Investment Plan and Just Transition Mechanism explained. European Commission (January 2020) https://ec.europa.eu/commission/presscorner/detail/en/qanda_20_24.

15 InvestEU and recovery. European Commission. https://investeu.europa.eu/investeu-and-recovery_en.

are backed by the EU budget and from a new Just Transition Fund. The Just Transition Fund will primarily provide grants to regions where many people work in coal, lignite, oil shale and peat production or to regions with greenhouse gas-intensive industries, for example to support workers in developing skills for jobs in other, clean energy sectors and to support investments in clean energy transition. The legislation[16] required to establish the Just Transition Fund came into force on 1 July 2021.

6.14 As well as public funding at EU and Member State level, private capital is seen as key to funding the transition to a sustainable economy. In July 2021 the Commission launched its Renewed Sustainable Finance Strategy,[17] a package of measures designed to improve the flow of money towards financing the transition. The Renewed Sustainable Finance Strategy builds upon the EU Sustainable Finance Action Plan, which has led to significant developments, including the EU Taxonomy, Green Bond Standards and Sustainability Benchmarks, discussed elsewhere in this book. There is an emphasis on inclusion, to support SMEs and individuals, by providing the tools and incentives to access transition finance and also by exploring how to exploit the opportunities digital technologies offer for sustainable finance. It also highlights the necessity for the financial system to become more resilient to the risks posed by climate change and environmental degradation and the steps needed to achieve this. The Commission will report on this strategy's implementation by the end of 2023.

E. SUSTAINABLE CORPORATE GOVERNANCE

6.15 The Commission has included an initiative on sustainable corporate governance among the deliverables of various aspects of the EGD, including the Action Plan on a Circular Economy,[18] the Biodiversity Strategy,[19] the Farm to

16 Regulation (EU) 2021/1056 of the European Parliament and of the Council of 24 June 2021 establishing the Just Transition Fund (June 2021) https://eur-lex.europa.eu/legal-content/EN/TXT/?uri=uriserv%3AOJ.L_.2021.231.01.0001.01.ENG&toc=OJ%3AL%3A2021%3A231%3ATOC.

17 European Commission. Strategy for financing the transition to a sustainable economy (July 2021) https://finance.ec.europa.eu/publications/strategy-financing-transition-sustainable-economy_en.

18 Circular Economy Action Plan 2020 summary for business. World Business Council for Sustainable Development (October 2020). https://docs.wbcsd.org/2020/11/WBCSD_Circular_Economy_Action_Plan_2020%E2%80%93Summary_for_business.pdf.

19 Biodiversity strategy for 2030. European Commission. https://environment.ec.europa.eu/strategy/biodiversity-strategy-2030_en#:~:text=The%20EU's%20biodiversity%20strategy%20for,contains%20specific%20actions%20and%20commitments.

Fork Strategy,[20] the Chemicals Strategy,[21] the 2020 New Industrial Strategy[22] and the Strategy for Financing the Transition to a Sustainable Economy,[23] illustrating how the rationale behind the EGD permeates all aspects of EU policy. To further the objectives of these various strategies, on 23 February 2022 the Commission proposed a Corporate Sustainability Due Diligence Directive,[24] including mandatory human rights and environmental due diligence ('mHREDD'), which, if implemented, would establish far-reaching requirements for large companies operating in the EU.

One of the aims of the Corporate Sustainability Due Diligence Directive **6.16**
is to foster sustainable and responsible corporate behaviour and to anchor human rights and environmental considerations in companies' operations and corporate governance, discussed in other chapters in this book. The Directive establishes a corporate due diligence duty, the core elements of this being identifying, bringing to an end, preventing, mitigating and accounting for negative human rights and environmental impacts in the company's own operations, those of their subsidiaries and the value chain operations carried out by entities with whom the company has an established 'business relationship'. In addition, certain large companies need to have a plan to ensure that their business strategy is compatible with limiting global warming to 1.5°C in line with the Paris Agreement. Directors are incentivised to contribute to sustainability and climate change mitigation goals. The Directive also introduces duties for the directors of in-scope EU companies. These duties include setting up and overseeing the implementation of the due diligence processes and integrating due diligence into the corporate strategy. In addition, when fulfilling their duty to act in the best interest of the company, directors must take into account the human rights, climate change and environmental consequences of their decisions. The provisions of the proposed Directive are complex and raise interpretational questions around scope and mode of application, as well as significant civil liability issues.

20 Farm to Fork Strategy. European Commission. https:// food .ec .europa .eu/ horizontal -topics/ farm -fork -strategy_en.

21 Chemicals Strategy for Sustainability. European Chemicals Agency. https:// echa .europa .eu/ hot -topics/ chemicals-strategy-for-sustainability.

22 European industrial strategy. European Commission. https:// ec .europa .eu/ info/ strategy/ priorities -2019 -2024/ europe -fit -digital -age/ european -industrial -strategy _en #: ~: text = The %202020 %20Industrial %20Strategy%20included,and%20scale%20of%20this%20transformation.

23 Strategy for financing the transition to a sustainable economy. European Commission (July 2021). https:// finance.ec.europa.eu/publications/strategy-financing-transition-sustainable-economy_en.

24 Corporate sustainability due diligence: fostering sustainability in corporate governance and management systems. European Commission. (February 2022) https://ec.europa.eu/info/business-economy-euro/doing -business-eu/corporate-sustainability-due-diligence_en.

6.17 The Commission's proposal has been vigorously debated in the European Parliament and Council, and political agreement was reached in July 2022. The indicative plenary vote is expected to be in November 2022. Once adopted by the European Parliament and the Council, the Directive must be transposed into national laws. Member States will have two years from the date the Directive enters into force to implement the requirements relating to large companies, and four years for mid-sized companies.

F. WHAT NEXT?

6.18 Most of the measures key to delivering the European Green Deal are now in progress. While some are in force, most are making their way through the EU legislative process (see Table 6.1) and the Commission hopes that agreement will be reached on these by the end of the current parliamentary term in May 2024. Further new legislation and revisions to existing legislation are expected to be announced in the coming months. The Commission is expected to adopt packages of further climate and environment measures, including with regard to transport emissions and carbon removal certification, proposals to improve ambient air and water quality and key initiatives in the circular economy addressing, in particular, the sustainability of packaging and plastics, the growing challenge of microplastics pollution, the 'right to repair' and end-of-life vehicles.

G. OBSTACLES IN THE ROAD?

6.19 Notwithstanding delays due to the COVID-19 pandemic, progress has been made across most elements of the EGD, despite criticism in some quarters that decarbonisation is still not happening fast enough. However, there are undoubtedly further obstacles in the road. The transition from fossil fuels to clean energy, one of the central pillars of the EGD, was never going to be easy, necessitating expensive trade-offs between combating climate change and economic and political considerations. Russia's invasion of Ukraine has made energy transition more difficult, as energy security becomes a major problem for EU member states dependent on oil and gas imports from Russia. This raises the question whether the energy crisis could potentially derail the EGD. In the immediate short term, there is real potential that EU member states will delay phasing out coal or nuclear plants and boost domestic or alternative fossil fuel supplies and it is interesting to note that the Taxonomy Complementary

Climate Delegated Act[25] on gas and nuclear activities, which applies from 1 January 2023, includes specific nuclear and gas energy activities (under certain conditions) in the list of environmentally sustainable economic activities covered by the EU Taxonomy. Inclusion of gas and nuclear within the EU Taxonomy is controversial[26] and may face legal challenge. Nevertheless, many, including within the leadership of the Commission, are determined to accelerate efforts to decarbonise, redoubling efforts to bring renewable supplies online more quickly.[27] Thus, although the energy crisis may be an obstacle in the road towards a successful implementation of the objectives of the EGD in the short term, in the longer term it may provide a strong impetus towards a faster green energy transition.

25 Commission Delegated Regulation (EU) 2022/1214 of 9 March 2022 amending Delegated Regulation (EU) 2021/2139 as regards economic activities in certain energy sectors and Delegated Regulation (EU) 2021/2178 as regards specific public disclosures for those economic activities. https://eur-lex.europa.eu/legal-content/EN/TXT/PDF/?uri=CELEX:32022R1214&from=EN.

26 Response to the Complementary Delegated Act. EU Platform on Sustainable Finance (January 2022) https://ec.europa.eu/info/sites/default/files/business_economy_euro/banking_and_finance/documents/220121-sustainable-finance-platform-response-taxonomy-complementary-delegated-act_en.pdf.

27 REPowerEU: Joint European action for more affordable, secure and sustainable energy. European Commission (March 2022). https://ec.europa.eu/commission/presscorner/detail/en/ip_22_1511.

Table 6.1 Key actions in the EGD: Status

Actions	Status
Climate ambition	
Proposal on a European 'Climate Law' enshrining the 2050 climate neutrality objective	Adopted June 2021[i]
Comprehensive plan to increase the EU 2030 climate target to at least 50% and towards 55% in a responsible way	Adopted Sep 2020[ii]
Proposals for revisions of relevant legislative measures to deliver on the increased climate ambition, following the review of Emissions Trading System Directive; Effort Sharing Regulation; Land use, land use change and forestry Regulation; Energy Efficiency Directive; Renewable Energy Directive; CO_2 emissions performance standards for cars and vans	Adopted July 2021[iii]
Proposal for a revision of the Energy Taxation Directive	Adopted July 2021[iv]
Proposal for a carbon border adjustment mechanism for selected sectors	Adopted July 2021[v]
New EU Strategy on adaptation to Climate Change	Adopted February 2021[vi]
Review of EU rules on fluorinated greenhouse gases	Launched in July 2020, proposal for a new Regulation adopted April 2022[vii]
EU Framework for harmonised measurement of transport and logistics emissions	Expected Q4 2022
Review of the CO_2 emission standards for heavy-duty vehicles	Expected Q4 2022
Carbon removal certification	Expected Q4 2022
Clean, affordable and secure energy	
Assessment of the final National Energy and Climate Plans	Published Sep 2020[viii]
Strategy for smart sector integration	Adopted July 2020[ix]
'Renovation wave' iniative for the building sector	Adopted October 2020[x]
New European Bahaus	Adopted September 2021[xi]
Evaluation and review of the Trans-European Network – Energy Regulation	Commission adopted proposed revision December 2020[xii]
Strategy on offshore wind (now referred to as 'offshore renewable energy')	Adopted November 2020[xiii]
Industrial strategy for a clean and circular economy	
EU Industrial strategy	Adopted March 2020[xiv], updated May 2021[xv]
Circular Economy Action Plan, including a sustainable products initiative and particular focus on resource-intense sectors such as textiles, construction, electronics and plastics	Adopted March 2020[xvi]
Initiatives to stimulate lead markets for climate-neutral and circular products in energy intensive-industrial sectors	From 2020
Proposal to support zero carbon steel-making processes by 2030	Published July 2020[xvii]

Actions	Status
Legislation on batteries in support of the Strategic Action Plan on Batteries and the circular economy	Adopted December 2020[xviii]
Propose legislative waste reforms A number of measures, including review of the Packaging and Packaging Waste Directive REFIT[xix] and revision of the waste framework to reduce waste and the environmental impact of waste management[xx] In 'A European Green Deal'	From 2020
Initiative on the right to repair	Expected Q3 2022
Sustainable and smart mobility	
Strategy for sustainable and smart mobility	Adopted December 2020[xxi]
Funding call to support the deployment of public recharging and refuelling points as part of alternative fuel infrastructure	From 2020
Assessment of legislative options to boost the production and supply of sustainable alternative fuels for the different transport modes	Q&As published July 2021[xxii]
Revised proposal for a Directive on Combined Transport	2017 proposal was withdrawn in September 2020[xxiii], new proposal expected in 2022[xxiv]
Review of the Alternative Fuels Infrastructure Directive and the Trans-European Network – Transport Regulation	Adopted July 2021[xxv] and December 2021[xxvi]
Initiatives to increase and better manage the capacity of railways and inland waterways	From 2021
Proposal for more stringent air pollutant emissions standards for combustion-engine vehicles	Delayed.
Greening the Common Agricultural Policy/'Farm to Fork' Strategy	
Examination of the draft national strategic plans, with reference to the ambitions of the European Green Deal and the Farm to Fork Strategy	New CAP regulations entered into force December 2021.[xxvii] EU countries were given until 31 December 2021[xxviii] to submit their national CAP strategic plans. Following this, the Commission had six months to approve the plans ahead of their implementation in January 2023. By the end of May 2022, the Commission had sent observation letters[xxix] relating to all 28 draft CAP strategic plans that were submitted by EU countries, but approval has been delayed.
A 'Farm to Fork' Strategy	Adopted May 2020[xxx]
An Action Plan of an overall 27 legislatives and non-legislative measures accompanies the strategy	From 2020
Sustainable use of pesticides – revision of EU rules	Adopted June 2022[xxxi]
Preserving and protecting biodiversity	
EU Biodiversity Strategy for 2030	Adopted May 2020[xxxii]
Measures to address the main drivers of biodiversity loss	Proposal adopted June 2022[xxxiii]
New EU Forest Strategy for 2030	Adopted July 2021[xxxiv]
Measures to support deforestation-free value chains	Council adopted negotiating position June 2022[xxxv]

Actions	Status
Towards a zero-pollution ambition for a toxic free environment	
Chemicals strategy for sustainability	Adopted October 2020[xxxvi]
Zero-pollution action plan for water, air and soil	Adopted May 2021[xxxvii]
Revision of measures to address pollution from large industrial installations	Proposal adopted April 2022[xxxviii]
Revision of Regulation on classification, labelling and packaging (EC 1272/2008)	Expected Q2 2022[xxxix]
Integrated Water Management – revised lists of surface and ground water pollutants	Expected Q3 2022[xl]
Review of Ambient air quality legislation	Expected Q3 2022 [xli]
Mainstreaming sustainability in all EU policies	
Proposal for a Just Transition Mechanism, including a Just Transition Fund, and a Sustainable Europe Investment Plan	Adopted 2020[xlii]; Regulation (EU) 2021/1056 establishing the JFT [xliii] in force since June 2021
Renewed sustainable finance strategy	Adopted July 2021[xliv]
Review of the Non-Financial Reporting Directive	Proposal adopted April 2021[xlv]
Initiatives to screen and benchmark green budgeting practices of the Member States and of the EU	EU Green Budgeting Reference Framework (GBRF)[xlvi] published January 2022; Webpage[xlvii]
Various initiatives	
Review of the relevant State aid guidelines, including the environment and energy State aid guidelines	Revised guidelines adopted January 2022[xlviii]
Align all new Commission initiatives in line with the objectives of the Green Deal and promote innovation	From 2020
Stakeholders to identify and remedy incoherent legislation that reduces the effectiveness in delivering the European Green Deal	From 2020
Integration of the Sustainable Development Goals in the European Semester	From 2020
The EU as a global leader	
EU to continue to lead the international climate and biodiversity negotiations, further strengthening the international policy framework	From 2019
Strengthen the EU's Green Deal Diplomacy in cooperation with Member States	From 2020
Bilateral efforts to induce partners to act and to ensure comparability of action and policies	From 2020
Green Agenda for the Western Balkans	Adopted October 2020[xlix]
Working together – a European Climate Pact	
Launch of the European Climate Pact	Launched December 2020
Proposal for an 8th Environmental Action Programme	Adopted April 2022[l]

Notes: For reference purposes only. Position as at 1 August 2022. Reproduced from the Annex to the 'European Green Deal', COM(2019) 640 final. Amended based on the Commission's Work Programmes 2020, 2021 and 2022 and information available from the official websites of the European Union. This publication does not necessarily deal with every important topic or cover every aspect of the topics with which it deals. It is not intended to provide legal or other advice.

i. Regulation (EU) 2021/1119 of the European Parliament and of the Council of 30 June 2021 establishing the framework for achieving climate neutrality and amending Regulations (EC) No 401/2009 and (EU) 2018/1999 ('European Climate Law'). (July 2021) https://eur-lex.europa.eu/legal-content/EN/TXT/?uri=CELEX:32021R1119
ii. Communication from the Commission to the European Parliament, the Council, the European Economic and Social Committee and the Committee of the Regions Stepping up Europe's 2030 climate ambition Investing in a climate-neutral future for the benefit of our people (September 2020) https://eur-lex.europa.eu/legal-content/EN/TXT/?uri=CELEX:52020DC0562
iii. European Green Deal: Commission proposes transformation of EU economy and society to meet climate ambitions (July 2021) https://ec.europa.eu/commission/presscorner/detail/en/IP_21_3541
iv. Proposal for a Council Directive restructuring the Union framework for the taxation of energy products and electricity (recast) (July 2021) https://eur-lex.europa.eu/legal-content/en/TXT/?uri=CELEX%3A52021PC0563
v. Proposal for a Regulation of The European Parliament and of the Council establishing a carbon border adjustment mechanism (July 2021) https://eur-lex.europa.eu/legal-content/en/TXT/?uri=CELEX%3A52021PC0564
vi. Communication from the Commission to the European Parliament, the Council, the European Economic and Social Committee and the Committee of the Regions Forging a climate-resilient Europe - the new EU Strategy on Adaptation To Climate Change (February 2021) https://eur-lex.europa.eu/legal-content/EN/TXT/?uri=COM:2021:82:FIN
vii. EU legislation to control F-gases https://climate.ec.europa.eu/eu-action/fluorinated-greenhouse-gases/eu-legislation-control-f-gases_en
viii. Communication from the Commission to the European Parliament, the Council, the European Economic and Social Committee and the Committee of the Regions an EU-wide assessment of National Energy and Climate Plans Driving forward the green transition and promoting economic recovery through integrated energy and climate planning (September 2020) https://eur-lex.europa.eu/legal-content/EN/TXT/?qid=1600339518571&uri=COM%3A2020%3A564%3AFIN
ix. Communication from the Commission to the European Parliament, the Council, the European Economic and Social Committee and the Committee of the Regions Powering a climate-neutral economy: An EU Strategy for Energy System Integration (July 2020) https://eur-lex.europa.eu/legal-content/EN/TXT/?qid=1603122220757&uri=CELEX:52020DC0662
x. Communication from the Commission to the European Parliament, the Council, the European Economic and Social Committee and the Committee of the Regions A Renovation Wave for Europe - greening our buildings, creating jobs, improving lives (October 2020) https://ec.europa.eu/energy/sites/ener/files/eu_renovation_wave_strategy.pdf
xi. Communication from the Commission to the European Parliament, the Council, the European Economic and Social Committee and the Committee of the Regions New European Bauhaus (September 2021) https://new-european-bauhaus.europa.eu/system/files/2021-09/COM(2021)_573_EN_ACT.pdf
xii. Commission proposes revised rules for cross-border energy infrastructure in line with the European Green Deal (December 2020) https://ec.europa.eu/commission/presscorner/detail/en/ip_20_2394
xiii. Communication from the Commission to the European Parliament, the Council, the European Economic and Social Committee and the Committee of the Regions An EU Strategy to harness the potential of offshore renewable energy for a climate neutral future (November 2020) https://eur-lex.europa.eu/legal-content/EN/TXT/?uri=COM:2020:741:FIN&qid=1605792629666
xiv. Communication from the Commission A New Industrial Strategy for Europe (March 2020) https://eur-lex.europa.eu/legal-content/EN/TXT/?qid=1593086905382&uri=CELEX%3A52020DC0102
xv. Updating the 2020 Industrial Strategy: towards a stronger Single Market for Europe's recovery (May 2021) https://ec.europa.eu/commission/presscorner/detail/en/IP_21_1884
xvi. Communication from the Commission to the European Parliament, the Council, the European Economic and Social Committee and the Committee of the Regions A new Circular Economy Action Plan for a cleaner and more competitive Europe (March 2020) https://eur-lex.europa.eu/legal-content/EN/TXT/?qid=1583933814386&uri=COM:2020:98:FIN
xvii. Proposal for a European Partnership under Horizon Europe Clean Steel - Low Carbon Steelmaking (July 2020) - https://ec.europa.eu/info/sites/default/files/research_and_innovation/funding/documents/ec_rtd_he-partnerships-for-clean-steel-low-carbon-steelmaking.pdf
xviii. Green Deal: Sustainable batteries for a circular and climate neutral economy (December 2020) https://ec.europa.eu/commission/presscorner/detail/en/ip_20_2312
xix. https://environment.ec.europa.eu/topics/waste-and-recycling/packaging-waste_en

xx. Revision of the waste framework to reduce waste and the environmental impact of waste management in "A European Green Deal" https://www.europarl.europa.eu/legislative-train/theme-a-european-green-deal/file-revision-of-the-eu-waste-framework
xxi. Communication from the Commission to the European Parliament, the Council, the European Economic and Social Committee and the Committee of the Regions Sustainable and Smart Mobility Strategy – putting European transport on track for the future (December 2020) https://eur-lex.europa.eu/legal-content/EN/TXT/?uri=CELEX%3A52020DC0789
xxii. Questions and Answers - Sustainable transport, infrastructure and fuels (July 2021) https://ec.europa.eu/commission/presscorner/detail/en/qanda_21_3525
xxiii. Withdrawal of Commission proposals 2020/C 321/03 (September 2020) https://eur-lex.europa.eu/legal-content/EN/TXT/?uri=uriserv:OJ.C_.2020.321.01.0037.01.ENG
xxiv. Communication from the Commission to the European Parliament, the Council, the European Economic and Social Committee and the Committee of the Regions Sustainable and Smart Mobility Strategy – putting European transport on track for the future (December 2020) https://eur-lex.europa.eu/legal-content/EN/TXT/?uri=CELEX%3A52020DC0789
xxv. Proposal for a Regulation of the European Parliament and of the Council on the deployment of alternative fuels infrastructure, and repealing Directive 2014/94/EU of the European Parliament and of the Council (July 2021) https://ec.europa.eu/info/sites/default/files/revision_of_the_directive_on_deployment_of_the_alternative_fuels_infrastructure_with_annex_0.pdf
xxvi. Proposal for a Regulation of the European Parliament and of the Council on Union guidelines for the development of the trans-European transport network, amending Regulation (Eu) 2021/1153 and Regulation (EU) No 913/2010 and repealing Regulation (EU) 1315/2013 (December 2021) https://eur-lex.europa.eu/legal-content/EN/ALL/?uri=COM:2021:812:FIN
xxvii. New CAP regulations enter into force (December 2021) https://agriculture.ec.europa.eu/news/new-cap-regulations-enter-force-2021-12-07_en
xxviii. CAP Strategic Plans https://agriculture.ec.europa.eu/cap-my-country/cap-strategic-plans_en
xxix. Observation letters on CAP strategic plans https://agriculture.ec.europa.eu/cap-my-country/cap-strategic-plans/observation-letters_en
xxx. Communication from the Commission to the European Parliament, the Council, the European Economic and Social Committee and the Committee of the Regions A Farm to Fork Strategy for a fair, healthy and environmentally-friendly food system https://eur-lex.europa.eu/legal-content/EN/TXT/?uri=CELEX:52020DC0381
xxxi. Pesticides – sustainable use (updated EU rules) https://ec.europa.eu/info/law/better-regulation/have-your-say/initiatives/12413-Pesticides-sustainable-use-updated-EU-rules-_en
xxxii. Communication from the Commission to the European Parliament, the Council, the European Economic and Social Committee and the Committee of the Regions EU Biodiversity Strategy for 2030 Bringing nature back into our lives (May 2020) https://eur-lex.europa.eu/legal-content/EN/TXT/?qid=1590574123338&uri=CELEX:52020DC0380
xxxiii. Proposal for a Nature Restoration Law (June 2022) https://environment.ec.europa.eu/publications/nature-restoration-law_en
xxxiv. Communication from the Commission to the European Parliament, the Council, the European Economic and Social Committee and the Committee of the Regions New EU Forest Strategy for 2030 (July 2021) - https://eur-lex.europa.eu/legal-content/EN/TXT/?uri=CELEX:52021DC0572
xxxv. Council agrees on new rules to drive down deforestation and forest degradation globally (June 2022) https://www.consilium.europa.eu/en/press/press-releases/2022/06/28/council-agrees-on-new-rules-to-drive-down-deforestation-and-forest-degradation/
xxxvi. Communication from the Commission to the European Parliament, the Council, the European Economic and Social Committee and the Committee of the Regions Chemicals Strategy for Sustainability Towards a Toxic-Free Environment (October 2020) https://eur-lex.europa.eu/legal-content/EN/TXT/?uri=COM%3A2020%3A667%3AFIN
xxxvii. https://environment.ec.europa.eu/strategy/zero-pollution-action-plan_en
xxxviii. Green Deal: Modernising EU industrial emissions rules to steer large industry in long-term green transition (April 2022) https://ec.europa.eu/commission/presscorner/detail/en/IP_22_2238
xxxix. Revision of EU legislation on hazard classification, labelling and packaging of chemicals https://ec.europa.eu/info/law/better-regulation/have-your-say/initiatives/12975-Revision-of-EU-legislation-on-hazard-classification-labelling-and-packaging-of-chemicals_en
xl. Integrated water management – revised lists of surface and groundwater pollutants https://ec.europa.eu/info/law/better-regulation/have-your-say/initiatives/12662-Integrated-water-management-revised-lists-of-surface-and-groundwater-pollutants_en
xli. Air quality - revision of EU rules https://ec.europa.eu/info/law/better-regulation/have-your-say/initiatives/12677-Air-quality-revision-of-EU-rules_en

xlii. The Just Transition Mechanism: making sure no one is left behind https://ec.europa.eu/info/strategy/priorities-2019-2024/european-green-deal/finance-and-green-deal/just-transition-mechanism_en
xliii. Regulation (EU) 2021/1056 of the European Parliament and of the Council of 24 June 2021 establishing the Just Transition Fund (June 2021) https://eur-lex.europa.eu/eli/reg/2021/1056/2021-06-30
xliv. Communication from the Commission to the European Parliament, the Council, the European Economic and Social Committee and the Committee of the Regions Strategy for Financing the Transition to a Sustainable Economy (July 2021) https://eur-lex.europa.eu/legal-content/EN/TXT/?uri=CELEX:52021DC0390
xlv. Proposal for a Directive of the European Parliament and of the Council amending Directive 2013/34/EU, Directive 2004/109/EC, Directive 2006/43/EC and Regulation (EU) No 537/2014, as regards corporate sustainability reporting (April 2021) https://eur-lex.europa.eu/legal-content/EN/TXT/?uri=CELEX:52021PC0189
xlvi. European Commission Green Budgeting Reference Framework https://ec.europa.eu/info/sites/default/files/economy-finance/european_commission_green_budgeting_reference_framework.pdf
xlvii. Green budgeting in the EU https://economy-finance.ec.europa.eu/economic-and-fiscal-governance/green-budgeting-eu_en
xlviii. Legislation (Energy & Environment) https://competition-policy.ec.europa.eu/sectors/energy-environment/legislation_en
xlix. Communication from the Commission to the European Parliament, the Council, the European Economic and Social Committee and the Committee of the Regions An Economic and Investment Plan for the Western Balkans (October 2020) https://eur-lex.europa.eu/legal-content/EN/TXT/?uri=CELEX%3A52020DC0641
l. Environment action programme to 2030 https://environment.ec.europa.eu/strategy/environment-action-programme-2030_en

7

EU CLIMATE LAW

David Brinkman

A. INTRODUCTION

7.01 European Climate Law (or 'Climate Law')[1] can be thought of as revolutionary to a certain extent. Although it is not the first climate-neutrality law,[2] it is one of the most ambitious laws to combat climate change. It is a framework law. That means that it sets overarching objectives which need to be operationalised by other legal acts to be achieved.

7.02 The explanatory memorandum to the original proposal[3] explains the concept of a framework law in the meaning that it

> aims to provide a direction by setting the EU on a path to climate neutrality, certainty on the EU's commitment and for transparency and accountability by setting out a process of assessment and reporting. It requests Member States to take the necessary measures

1 Regulation (EU) 2021/1119 of the European Parliament and of the Council of 30 June 2021 establishing the framework for achieving climate neutrality and amending Regulations (EC) No 401/2009 and (EU) 2018/1999 ('European Climate Law'), [2021] OJ L 243, pp.1–17.

2 See for instance the UK Climate Change Act 2008, which was amended in 2019 to introduce the net-zero objective, or the Canadian Net-Zero Emissions Accountability Act, which came into force 29 June 2021, S.C. 2021, c. 22.

3 COM(2020) 80, dated 4 March 2020.

> to enable the collective achievement of the climate-neutrality objective but it does not prescribe specific policies or measures [...] It sets a mechanism for reviewing existing policies and Union legislation or taking additional measures, but does not included the detailed proposals yet.

What makes the Climate Law significant is its binding nature on the entire EU. On its own, the impact might not be apparent. However, the measures that aim to achieve climate neutrality will likely affect every part of the EU economy as well as everyday life. **7.03**

B. HISTORY

The Climate Law was adopted on 30 June 2021 and writes into law the EU's goal, as set in the European Green Deal[4] of 11 November 2019, to become climate-neutral by 2050. To fully understand its meaning and scope, it is worth looking at its history. **7.04**

Many of the EU climate ambitions can be traced back to the United Nations Framework Convention on Climate Change (UNFCCC).[5] This convention was approved by the EU in 1993[6] and entered into force on 21 March 1994. The purpose of this convention is to promote the stabilisation of the concentration of greenhouse gases in the atmosphere at a level at which would prevent dangerous anthropogenic interference (that is, interference caused by humans) with the climate system. Such a level should be achieved within a time frame that allows ecosystems to adapt naturally to climate change, to ensure that food production is not threatened and to enable economic development to proceed in a sustainable manner. The parties to the UNFCCC are referred to as Annex I countries and non-Annex I countries. Annex I countries constitute developed countries, including the then European Economic Community. According to Article 4(2) of the convention, Annex I countries must take the lead, in an international context, in counteracting climate change and its negative consequences. Apart from having committed to reducing greenhouse gas emissions, Annex I countries must periodically report on the measures they have taken. **7.05**

---

4 See Commission's website at: https://ec.europa.eu/clima/eu-action/european-green-deal/european-climate-law_en, accessed 9 May 2023.

5 UNFCCC, 1992: United Nations Framework Convention on Climate Change. United Nations, FCCC/INFORMAL/84 GE. 05-62220 (E) 200705, Secretariat of the United Nations Framework Convention on Climate Change, Bonn, Germany. https://unfccc.int/files/essential_background/background_publications_htmlpdf/application/pdf/conveng.pdf.

6 Council Decision of 15 December 1993 concerning the conclusion of the United Nations Framework Convention on Climate Change, [1994] OJ L 33/11, pp.11–28.

7.06 Article 7 UNFCCC provides for the Conference of the Parties ('COP'). The COP is the highest decision-making body within the UNFCCC. The COP meets annually at climate conferences. Resolutions passed by the COP are generally not legally binding.

7.07 At the climate conference in Kyoto in 1997 (COP 3), the Kyoto Protocol[7] was agreed upon between a number of Annex I countries, including the European Union.[8] This protocol records the reduction targets for the period 2008–12. The Kyoto Protocol focused on cutting the emissions of six specific greenhouse gases, not all anthropogenic greenhouse gases. According to this protocol, the then Member States of the EU were obliged to achieve a reduction target of 8 per cent compared to 1990.

7.08 The Paris Agreement[9] was concluded at the climate conference in Paris in 2015 (COP 21).[10] The Paris Agreement constitutes a treaty within the meaning of the Vienna Convention on the Law of Treaties[11] – that is, an agreement between States in written form governed by international law. The Paris Agreement therefore goes beyond being a mere COP decision. The reason to choose a treaty was the push by a large coalition, which included the EU, to conclude a new legal agreement to extend or replace the Kyoto Protocol.[12] To align the Paris Agreement with the UNFCC and its subsidiary bodies, a partially binding COP decision, adopting the Paris Agreement, was nonetheless taken.[13] The binding aspects of the COP 21 decision are decisions to give effect to the Paris Agreement.[14]

---

7 Kyoto Protocol to the United Nations Framework Convention on Climate Change, 10 Dec. 1997, 2303 UNTS 162.

8 Ratified by Council Decision of 25 April 2002 concerning the approval, on behalf of the European Community, of the Kyoto Protocol to the United Nations Framework Convention on Climate Change and the joint fulfilment of commitments thereunder, [2002] OJ L 130, pp.1–3.

9 Paris Agreement to the United Nations Framework Convention on Climate Change, 12 Dec. 2015, TIAS No. 16-1104.

10 Ratified by the EU by Council Decision (EU) 2016/1841 of 5 October 2016 on the conclusion, on behalf of the European Union, of the Paris Agreement adopted under the United Nations Framework Convention on Climate Change, [2016] OJ L 282, pp.1–3.

11 Vienna Convention on the Law of Treaties (Vienna, 23 May 1969; in force 27 January 1980), Article 2.1(a).

12 Daniel Bodansky, 'The Legal Character of the Paris Agreement', Review of European Community & International Environmental Law, [2016] 25(2), p.144.

13 UNFCCC, Decision 1/CP.21, Adoption of the Paris Agreement (UN Doc. FCCC/CP/2015/10, Add.1, 29 January 2016). See for more background Daniel Bodansky, 'The Legal Character of the Paris Agreement', Review of European Community & International Environmental Law, [2016] 25(2), p.148.

14 Article 14(9) of the Paris Agreement even refers to the COP21 decision: 'Each Party shall communicate a nationally determined contribution every five years in accordance with decision 1/CP.21.'

The Paris Agreement sets out a long-term temperature goal of holding the increase in the global average temperature to below 2°C above pre-industrial levels, while pursuing efforts to limit the temperature increase to 1.5°C above pre-industrial levels. Second, it aims to strengthen the global response to the threat of climate change by increasing the ability to adapt to the adverse impacts of climate change; third, it seeks to make finance flows consistent with a pathway towards low greenhouse gas emissions and climate-resilient development.[15] 7.09

According to the Paris Agreement, parties to it 'are to undertake [...] ambitious efforts [...] with the view to achieving the purpose of this Agreement'.[16] Each party is expected to set a 'nationally determined contribution' ('NDC') regarding their greenhouse gas emission reduction and other climate-related policies.[17] In addition, all parties should strive to formulate and communicate long-term low greenhouse gas emission development strategies.[18] Parties, including regional economic integration organizations and their Member States, may also jointly submit NDCs.[19] To date, the European Union and its Member States are the only parties to the Paris Agreement that have a joint NDC.[20] 7.10

As is the case in many treaties, the Paris Agreement consists of a mix of recommendations, expectations and legal requirements.[21] The Paris Agreement contains strong procedural obligations when it comes to NDCs. Each party to the agreement needs to prepare, communicate and maintain successive NDCs that it intends to achieve.[22] NDCs must be updated every five years[23] and each successive NDC is expected to be more ambitious.[24] Also, the form is important. Each party shall provide the information necessary for clarity, transparency and understanding the NDC.[25] All NDCs communicated by parties are recorded 7.11

15 Article 2(1) of the Paris Agreement.
16 Article 3 of the Paris Agreement.
17 Article 3 and 4 of the Paris Agreement.
18 Article 4(19) of the Paris Agreement.
19 Article 4(16) to (18) of the Paris Agreement.
20 According to the UN's website, 193 States and one regional economic integration organisation, the EU, have joined the Paris Agreement. See: www.un.org/en/climatechange/paris-agreement#:~:text=Today%2C%20194%20Parties%20(193%20States,strengthen%20their%20commitments%20over%20time.
21 Daniel Bodansky, 'The Legal Character of the Paris Agreement', Review of European Community & International Environmental Law, [2016] 25(2), p.145.
22 Article 4(2) of the Paris Agreement.
23 Article 4(9) of the Paris Agreement.
24 Article 4(3) of the Paris Agreement.
25 Article 4(8) of the Paris Agreement.

in a public registry.[26] And finally, each party is required to provide information to track progress in implementing and achieving its NDC.[27]

7.12 So are these NDCs binding? Here the treaty text becomes ambiguous, as can be seen in Article 4(2) of the Paris Agreement. On the one hand, each party has an obligation to take the necessary measures at their national level following their NDC: 'parties shall pursue domestic mitigation measures.' However, the outcome of the NDC is an expectation rather than an obligation: 'with the aim of achieving the objectives of such contributions.'

7.13 The same can be seen in one of the important substantive provisions in the agreement. The collective aim to reach global peaking of emissions as soon as possible and to undertake rapid reductions thereafter, so as to achieve net zero emissions in the second half of this century (Article 4.1), is formulated as a recommendation or expectation rather than a legal obligation.[28] An explanation[29] for the softness of certain provisions is that the US would be able to enter into the Paris Agreement on the basis of ratification by its President without requesting advice and consent of the Senate. The obligations that do arise out of the agreement would nonetheless be acceptable because they were procedural in nature, because they reiterated obligations the Senate had already approved in the UNFCCC or because they reflected and complemented existing US law.

7.14 Of course, there are other explanations as well. Without being legally bound by a certain minimum threshold, more parties might have been convinced to accede to the agreement. In addition, political pressure from the NDCs could prove to be just as effective as a legally binding nature. Moreover, the extensive reporting process of the NDCs and the obligation of stepping up each NDC are legally binding. Therefore, parties cannot row back on the commitments they have made.

7.15 Whether certain provisions of the Paris Agreement can be applied by domestic courts may vary from jurisdiction to jurisdiction, depending on its doctrines regarding judicial application of treaties. Even non-binding provisions in combination with, for instance, the European Convention on Human Rights

---

26 Article 4(12) of the Paris Agreement. The registry is accessible online via: https://unfccc.int/NDCREG.

27 Article 13(7)(b) of the Paris Agreement.

28 Daniel Bodansky, 'The Legal Character of the Paris Agreement', Review of European Community & International Environmental Law, [2016] 25(2), p.146.

29 Daniel Bodansky, 'The Legal Character of the Paris Agreement', Review of European Community & International Environmental Law, [2016] 25(2), pp.149 and 150.

lead to an enforceable national commitment. One such example is the Dutch *Urgenda* case,[30] in which a non-profit foundation sought a court order directing the State to reduce emissions of greenhouse gases in line with the Paris Agreement and the UNFCCC objective. The Dutch Supreme Court ruled that pursuant to Articles 2 (right to life) and 8 (right to respect for private and family life) ECHR, the Dutch State was obliged to achieve a certain reduction, due to the risk of dangerous climate change that could have a severe impact on the lives and welfare of the residents of the Netherlands.

The commitments under the Paris Agreement apply not only at country level but also at EU level. First of all, the EU itself is a signatory to the Paris Agreement; second, the Paris Agreement creates special requirements relating to regional economic integration organisations such as the European Union.[31] **7.16**

On 6 March 2020 the Union submitted its long-term low greenhouse gas emission development strategy, and on 17 December 2020 its NDC, to the UNFCCC. The subsequent Climate Law is the overall framework for the Union's contribution to the Paris Agreement.[32] **7.17**

The Climate Law builds, at least in part, on the regulatory framework which was already in place for achieving the 2030 greenhouse gas emission reduction target. Before the Climate Law, the EU's overarching objective was a 40 per cent greenhouse gas emission reduction compared to 1990 levels.[33] The framework to achieve this target covers the main sources of greenhouse gas emissions, as well as setting up a monitoring system. Under the Climate Law, we see that all these initiatives are updated and bolstered to align with growing ambition in reduction targets. Below the most important legislation is highlighted. **7.18**

- The Governance Regulation,[34] introduced in 2018, is the Union's main legal instrument used to monitor progress regarding the Union's overall greenhouse gas reduction objective as well as progress towards the objectives in the areas of renewable energies and energy efficiency.[35] This regu-

30 See for instance in the Netherlands the *Urgenda* case (Supreme Court, *Dutch State v Stichting Urgenda*, dated 20 December 2019, ECLI:NL:HR:2019:2006).

31 Article 4(16) to 4(18) of the Paris Agreement.

32 Recital 8 of the Climate Law.

33 European Council, Conclusions, 2030 Climate and Energy Policy Framework of 23, 24 October 2014, EUCO 169/14.

34 Regulation (EU) 2018/1999 on the Governance of the Energy Union and Climate Action, [2018] OJEU L328/1.

35 Sabine Schlacke, Helen Wentzien, Eva-Maria Thierjung and Miriam Köster, 'Implementing the EU Climate Law via the "Fit for 55" Package', Oxford Open Energy, 2022, p.3.

lation is a key measure of the energy union strategy[36] and at the time part of the 'Clean energy for all Europeans package'.[37] It requires EU Member States to develop integrated national energy and climate plans (NECPs) based on a common template. The Climate Law amends the Governance Regulation to align the scope of the Governance Regulation with that of the Climate Law.[38]

- The EU Emissions Trading Scheme (EU EUTS), laid down in the ETS Directive,[39] establishes the framework of the European carbon market. It operationalises the emission reduction target via economic incentives. The directive sets a cap on the total amount of certain greenhouse gases that can be emitted by the installations covered by the system. The cap is reduced over time so that total emissions fall. If an operator of an installation remains below its cap, it can keep the spare allowances to cover his future needs or else sell them to another installation that is short of allowances.[40] This trading system aims to ensure an efficient allocation of financial resources for reduction.
- The Effort Sharing Decision[41] had established binding national targets for emission reductions for the period 2013–20. These targets concern emissions from sectors not currently included in the EU ETS, such as transport, buildings, agriculture and waste. Its successor, the Effort Sharing Regulation,[42] sets binding annual greenhouse gas emission targets for Member States for the period 2021–30.
- Regarding energy, two important directives have been in place. Since 2009, the Renewable Energy Directive is in force. This directive sets, *inter alia*, the overarching European target for renewable energy. From its original EU target of 20 per cent renewables by 2020, the target was revised in

36 COM/2015/080, see also: https://energy.ec.europa.eu/topics/energy-strategy/energy-union_en.

37 https://energy.ec.europa.eu/topics/energy-strategy/clean-energy-all-europeans-package_en.

38 Article 13(1) of the Climate Law.

39 Directive 2003/87/EC of the European Parliament and of the Council of 13 October 2003 establishing a system for greenhouse gas emission allowance trading within the Union and amending Council Directive 96/61/EC [2003] OJEU L 275/32.

40 https://climate.ec.europa.eu/eu-action/eu-emissions-trading-system-eu-ets_en, accessed 9 May 2023.

41 Decision No 406/2009/EC of the European Parliament and of the Council of 23 April 2009 on the effort of Member States to reduce their greenhouse gas emissions to meet the Community's greenhouse gas emission reduction commitments up to 2020 [2009] OJEU L140/136.

42 Regulation (EU) 2018/842 on binding annual greenhouse gas emissions reductions by Member States from 2021 to 2030 contributing to climate action to meet commitments under the Paris Agreement, [2018] OJEU L156/26.

2018[43] to 32 per cent for 2023, and a proposal[44] is pending to raise the target for 2030 to 45 per cent.

- In the same vein, the Energy Efficiency Directive[45] was introduced in 2012. This directive established a set of binding measures to help the EU reach its 20 per cent energy efficiency target by 2020. In 2018, the amending Directive on Energy Efficiency was agreed to update the policy framework to 2030 and beyond, setting an energy efficiency target for 2030 of at least 32.5 per cent. To achieve the 2030 greenhouse gas emission targets, this directive is being revised[46] with an increased and binding energy efficiency target of 36 per cent reduction for final energy consumption and 39 per cent for primary energy consumption by 2030.
- The Regulation on the inclusion of greenhouse gas emissions and removals from land use, land use change and forestry land use, land use change and forestry (or LULUCF Regulation),[47] adopted in 2018, requires Member States to balance greenhouse gas emissions and removals from land use, land use change and forestry.[48] This means that EU Member States have to ensure that greenhouse gas emissions accounted[49] from land use, land use change or forestry are balanced by at least an equivalent accounted removal of CO_2 from the atmosphere in the period 2021 to 2030. As of 2021, a revision of this regulation was pending.[50] The proposed regulation lays out a process on how to determine, by 2025, binding targets for Member States from 2031 onwards.

After the conclusion of the Paris Agreement, and as illustrated by the legisla- **7.19**
tive proposals above, the EU became increasingly aware that efforts to combat climate change had to be stepped up. The European Parliament declared a climate and environment emergency in a resolution of 28 November 2019.[51]

43 Directive (EU) 2018/2001 on the promotion of the use of energy from renewable sources (recast), [2018] OJEU L328/82.

44 COM(2021) 557.

45 Directive (EU) 2018/2002 amending Directive 2012/27/EU on energy efficiency, [2018] OJEU L328/210.

46 COM(2021) 558.

47 Regulation (EU) 2018/841 of the European Parliament and of the Council of 30 May 2018 on the inclusion of greenhouse gas emissions and removals from land use, land use change and forestry in the 2030 climate and energy framework, and amending Regulation (EU) No 525/2013 and Decision No 529/2013/EU [2018] OJEU L 156/1.

48 See also: Beatriz Perez de las Heras, 'European Climate Law(s): Assessing the Legal Path to Climate Neutrality' (2021) 21 Romanian J Eur Aff 19, p.25.

49 Under the methodology of Article 5 of this regulation.

50 COM(2021) 554.

51 European Parliament resolution of 28 November 2019 on the climate and environment emergency (2019/2930(RSP)) [2021] OJ C 232/28.

It has also repeatedly called on the Union to increase its 2030 climate target, and for that increased target to be part of the Climate Law.[52]

7.20 In its announcement of the Green Deal in December 2019,[53] the Commission expressed the intention for the EU to become a global leader promoting ambitious environment, climate and energy policies. The Commission also spoke of the need to increase the EU's climate ambition for 2030 and 2050.

7.21 The European Council made a similar statement in December 2020:

> To meet the objective of a climate-neutral EU by 2050 in line with the objectives of the Paris Agreement, the EU needs to increase its ambition for the coming decade and update its climate and energy policy framework. To that end, the European Council endorses a binding EU target of a net domestic reduction of at least 55% in greenhouse gas emissions by 2030 compared to 1990. It calls on the co-legislators to reflect this new target in the European Climate Law proposal and to adopt the latter swiftly.[54]

C. WHAT IS THE CLIMATE LAW ABOUT?

1. Ambition and Rationale

7.22 The Climate Law is an EU Regulation which entered into force on 29 July 2021. As a regulation it is directly applicable in all Member States without requiring any transposition into national law.[55] Its preamble contains an extensive explanation of its rationale and ambition.

7.23 It sets out that climate change is an existential threat which requires enhanced ambition and increased climate action by the Union and its Member States.[56] It also commemorates the action which the Union has taken so far[57] and that 'the Union is a global leader in the transition towards climate neutrality, and it is determined to help raise global ambition and to strengthen the global response to climate change, using all tools at its disposal, including climate diplomacy'.[58]

---

52 Recital 19 of the Climate Law.

53 See the Commission Communication COM(2019) 640 final at https://eur-lex.europa.eu/legalcontent/EN/TXT/?qid=1576150542719&uri=COM%3A2019%3A640%3AFIN. See also: https://ec.europa.eu/info/strategy/priorities-2019-2024/european-green-deal_en.

54 www.consilium.europa.eu/media/47296/1011-12-20-euco-conclusions-en.pdf.

55 Article 288 TFEU.

56 Recital 1 to the Climate Law.

57 Recitals 12–15 to the Climate Law.

58 Recital 16 to the Climate Law.

Addressing growing climate risks is – according to the Climate Law – not merely a matter of increasing costs. Climate action should be an opportunity for all sectors of the economy in the Union to help secure industry leadership in global innovation.[59] The law emphasises that it is possible to decouple economic growth from greenhouse gas emissions, as it seems to have been the case so far. Between 1990 and 2019, greenhouse gas emissions were reduced by 24 per cent while the economy grew by 60 per cent over the same period.[60] The Commission is also encouraged to facilitate sector-specific climate dialogues and partnerships by bringing together key stakeholders, to encourage sectors to draw up voluntary roadmaps and to plan their transitions towards the climate-neutrality objective. **7.24**

The objective can not only be achieved by addressing greenhouse gas emissions but also by removal by sinks. Sinks include natural and technological solutions based on carbon capture and storage (CCS) and carbon capture and use (CCU) technologies. Carbon sinks can play an important role in agriculture, forestry and land use sectors.[61] **7.25**

The key elements of the law are: (1) the objective of climate neutrality by 2050 for the EU as a whole with intermediate milestones, (2) the qualitative objective to improve adaptation to climate change, (3) a monitoring and review system on the progress and (4) the establishment of a European Scientific Advisory Board on Climate Change. **7.26**

2. The Main Objective of the Law

According to Article 1 of the Climate Law, this Regulation 'establishes a framework for the irreversible and gradual reduction of anthropogenic greenhouse gas emissions by sources and enhancement of removals by sinks regulated in Union law.' The Climate Law is explicitly linked to the Paris Agreement, as explained by Article 1 paragraph 2: **7.27**

> This Regulation sets out a binding objective of climate neutrality in the Union by 2050 in pursuit of the long-term temperature goal set out in point (a) of Article 2(1) of the Paris Agreement, and provides a framework for achieving progress in pursuit of the global adaptation goal established in Article 7 of the Paris Agreement.

---

59 Recital 7 to the Climate Law.

60 Recital 7 to the Climate Law.

61 Recitals 20 and 21 to the Climate Law.

7.28 The climate-neutrality objective is enshrined in Article 2(1) of the Law, stating that 'Union-wide greenhouse gas emissions and removals regulated in Union law shall be balanced within the Union at the latest by 2050, thus reducing emissions to net zero by that date, and the Union shall aim to achieve negative emissions thereafter'.

7.29 Article 4 of the Law provides for an intermediate Union climate target of a net reduction of greenhouse gas emissions by at least 55 per cent by 2030 compared to 1990 levels. The original proposal[62] did not contain the intermediate target of 55 per cent. Under this proposal, the Commission would 'explore options' for a new 2030 target of 50–55 per cent emission reductions when reviewing the reduction target of – at the time – 40 per cent set by the Governance Regulation. In the amended Commission proposal[63] the 55 per cent reductions target was set. The European Parliament wanted to go a step further, and, unsuccessfully, proposed a reductions target of 60 per cent.[64]

7.30 Article 4, paragraphs (3)–(6) of the Climate Law lays down the obligation to set a Union-wide climate target for 2040. This provision was the subject of debate between the co-legislators. In the original Commission proposal, the Commission was empowered to adopt delegated acts to supplement the Climate Law by setting out a trajectory at Union level to achieve the 2050 climate-neutrality objective. This meant that the Commission would have a significant amount of discretion to impose additional measures. Both the European Parliament and the Council[65] reduced the role of the Commission to its current form as set out in Article 4(3). Under the current text, the Commission needs to make a legislative proposal within six months of the first global stocktake of the Paris Agreement for a 2040 Union climate target.

7.31 Perhaps the Council and Parliament were hesitant to give the Commission this mandate due to the significant scope and ambition of the proposal. After all, according to the Climate Law the transition to climate neutrality requires changes across the entire policy spectrum and a collective effort of all sectors

62 COM(2020) 80 final.

63 COM(2020) 563 final.

64 Amendments adopted by the European Parliament on 8 October 2020 on the proposal for a regulation of the European Parliament and of the Council establishing the framework for achieving climate neutrality and amending Regulation (EU) 2018/1999 (European Climate Law) (COM(2020)0080 – COM(2020)0563 – C9-0077/2020 – 2020/0036(COD)).

65 Council of the European Union, Outcome of Proceedings, Proposal for a Regulation of the European Parliament and of the Council establishing the framework for achieving climate neutrality and amending Regulation (EU) 2018/1999 (European Climate Law) – general approach, p.16.

of the economy and society, as highlighted in the European Green Deal.[66] All relevant Union legislation and policies need to be consistent with, and contribute to, the fulfilment of the climate-neutrality objective.

3. Adaptation to Climate Change

Relevant Union institutions and Member States are required to 'ensure continuous progress in enhancing adaptive capacity, strengthening resilience and reducing vulnerability to climate change'.[67] This obligation was also laid down in Article 7 of the Paris Agreement, whereby parties agreed to 'establish the global goal on adaptation of enhancing adaptive capacity, strengthening resilience and reducing vulnerability to climate change'. **7.32**

On 24 February 2021 the Commission published the Union strategy plan on adaptation to climate change, called 'Forging a climate-resilient Europe: The new EU Strategy on Adaptation to Climate Change'.[68] The strategy sets out how the Union can adapt to the unavoidable impacts of climate change and become climate-resilient by 2050. This action plan builds on a previous version, the 2013 EU Adaptation Strategy.[69] The strategy plan was endorsed by the Council on 10 June 2021.[70] **7.33**

The strategy plan sums up what has already been achieved under the 2013 strategy: all Member States now have a national adaptation strategy or plan; adaptation has been mainstreamed into the EU's policies and long-term budget; and the Climate-ADAPT platform,[71] launched in 2012 as an online knowledge hub, has become a key reference for knowledge on adaptation. **7.34**

Under the 2021 strategy plan the Commission sets out the vision for the EU to be a climate-resilient society, fully adapted to the unavoidable impacts of climate change, by 2050. This should be achieved via the following key policy areas:[72] **7.35**

- *To make adaptation smarter*: Improving knowledge and availability of data, regarding climate impacts and resilience; securing more and better data on

66 https://ec.europa.eu/info/strategy/priorities-2019-2024/european-green-deal_en, accessed 9 May 2023.
67 Article 5 of the Climate Law.
68 COM(2021) 82.
69 'An EU Strategy on adaptation to climate change', COM(2013), 216 final.
70 www .consilium .europa .eu/ en/ press/ press -releases/ 2021/ 06/ 10/ council -endorses -new -eu -strategy -on -adaptation-to-climate-change/, accessed 9 May 2023.
71 https://climate-adapt.eea.europa.eu/, accessed 9 May 2023.
72 See for a summary the Commission press release dated 24 February 2021: https://ec.europa.eu/commission/presscorner/detail/en/qanda_21_664, accessed 9 May 2023.

climate-related risk and losses, and updating and expanding the knowledge hub Climate-ADAPT as a source of knowledge on climate impacts and adaptation.

- *To make adaptation more systemic*: Supporting policy development at all levels of governance, society and the economy and in all sectors by improving national adaptation strategies and plans; integrating climate resilience in macro-fiscal policy, and promoting and providing financial incentives for nature-based solutions for adaptation. Examples of nature-based solutions are protecting and restoring local ecosystems, developing urban green spaces and installing green roofs and walls. According to the Commission, inland solutions can boost the supply of clean, fresh water and reduce risks of flooding. In coastal and marine areas, nature-based solutions can enhance coastal defence and reduce the risk of algal blooms.
- *Speeding up adaptation across the board*: The Commission acknowledges that so far, adaptation planning remains slow, and physical solutions for adaptation are lagging behind. This is despite the fact that the EU increased the spending target for climate action to 30 per cent in its long-term budget for 2021–7, with adaptation as a key component. Therefore, the development and rollout of adaptation solutions need to be accelerated and climate-related risk needs to be reduced. The Commission highlights certain areas of attention; for instance, Europe's building stock and the need to withstand the impacts of climate change. The Commission will explore options to better predict climate-induced stress on buildings and to integrate climate resilience considerations into the construction and renovation of buildings. It will also encourage water efficiency and savings to ensure the availability and sustainability of fresh water.

7.36 The Climate Law, which entered into force 20 days after the Council approved the 2021 strategy plan on adaptation to climate change, aligns with that strategy. This means that Union institutions and Member States need to ensure that policies on adaptation are coherent and mutually supportive, provide co-benefits for sectoral policies and work towards better integration of adaptation to climate change in a consistent manner in all policy areas.[73] For Member States, these actions need to be captured in national adaptation strategies and plans, keeping in mind the Union strategy and the most recent scientific evidence.[74] In their policymaking as well as in their national adaptation strategies, Member States need to pay particular attention to the vulnerability of relevant sectors and the most impacted and vulnerable parts of the population.

73 Article 5(3) of the Climate Law.

74 Article 5(4) of the Climate Law.

4. Review and Monitoring

The Climate Law tasks the European Commission with reviewing and monitoring progress. It does so in three instances. **7.37**

- *Review what was there*: Under Article 4(2) the Commission has reviewed relevant Union legislation and legislative procedures to assess the feasibility of the objectives of the Climate Law, by a deadline of 30 June 2021. In case this legislation does not contribute to achieving these aims, the Commission should consider taking measures, including amending that legislation. As a result, among others, the Effort Sharing Regulation[75] has been amended and revisions of the LULUCF Regulation,[76] the Energy Efficiency Directive[77] and the Renewable Energy Directive[78] are pending.
- *Review what is coming*: The Commission needs to assess the consistency of any draft measure or legislative proposal, including budgetary proposals, with the climate-neutrality objective.[79] Here a type of 'comply or explain' principle applies. This means that any new measure or proposal needs to be in line with the climate-neutrality objective to the extent reasonably possible. If not, the Commission needs to provide the reasons for the non-alignment.
- *Monitor progress*: As of 30 September 2023, the Commission shall assess every five years the consistency of all Union measures as well as the individual and collective progress of all Member States towards climate neutrality and progress on adaptation.[80] If the Commission finds that a Member State's measure is inconsistent with the climate-neutrality objective, it may issue recommendations to that Member State. These recommendations will be made publicly available. The Member State involved needs to inform the Commission within six months of receipt of the recommendations on how it intends to take due account of the recommendations 'in a spirit of solidarity between Member States and the Union and between Member States'.[81] Moreover, individual Member States need to report on their progress on the achievement of the climate-neutrality objective in

---

75 Regulation (EU) 2018/842 on binding annual greenhouse gas emissions reductions by Member States from 2021 to 2030 contributing to climate action to meet commitments under the Paris Agreement, [2018] OJEU L156/26.

76 COM(2021) 554.

77 COM(2021) 558.

78 COM(2021) 557.

79 Article 6(4) of the Climate Law.

80 Article 6(1) and (2) and 7(1) of the Climate Law.

81 Article 7(3)(a) of the Climate Law.

their national energy and climate plans,[82] which they are required to submit under the Governance Regulation.[83] These progress reports are used by the Commission to set the NDC for the Union under the Paris Agreement.

5. European Scientific Advisory Board on Climate Change

7.38 To strengthen the EU's scientific knowledge relating to climate change and to ensure informed policies are adopted, the Climate Law sets up a European Scientific Advisory Board on Climate Change.[84] This Advisory Board is composed of 15 senior scientific experts covering a broad range of relevant disciplines. Among other tasks, the Advisory Board provides scientific advice on the consistency of proposed and existing EU measures in relation to the Climate Law and the Union's international commitments under the Paris Agreement. It also identifies actions and opportunities needed to successfully achieve the Union climate targets. Member States are invited via the Climate Law to establish their own national climate advisory body.

7.39 The Advisory Board is established through an amendment of the founding Regulation[85] of the European Environment Agency (the EEA). The management board of the EEA designates the members of the Advisory Board for a term of four years, which is renewable once. The Advisory Board adopts its own work programme independently but consults the management board of the EEA when doing so. The work programme for each year[86] can be found on the website of the EEA.

7.40 In the original proposal[87] for the Climate Law, there was no mention of any advisory board. This triggered criticism, for instance that experience in Member States had shown that an independent scientific body can support consistency between long-term goals and short-term action.[88] The Scientific

---

82 The progress reports are not submitted yet at the date of drafting this chapter but the national energy and climate plans for 2021 to 2030 can be found at https://commission.europa.eu/energy-climate-change-environment/ implementation -eu -countries/ energy -and -climate -governance -and -reporting/ national -energy-and-climate-plans_en, accessed 9 May 2023.

83 Regulation (EU) 2018/1999 of the European Parliament and of the Council on the Governance of the Energy Union and Climate Action [2018] OJ L 328/1.

84 www.eea.europa.eu/about-us/climate-advisory-board/european-scientific-advisory-board-on, accessed 9 May 2023.

85 Regulation (EC) No 401/2009 of the European Parliament and of the Council on the European Environment Agency and the European Environment Information and Observation Network, [2009] OJ L 126/13.

86 See for 2023: www.eea.europa.eu/about-us/climate-advisory-board/2023-work-programme-of-the/view, accessed 9 May 2023.

87 COM(2020) 80 final.

88 See: Nils Meyer-Ohlendorf, 'A European Climate Law, Analysis of the European Commission Proposal', 6 April 2020, Ecologic Institute, Berlin.

Advisory Board was added by an amendment proposed by the European Parliament.[89]

The Advisory Board reinforces the Climate Law by making available high-quality expertise and separating the analytical advice from politics. In fulfilling their objectives, independent advisory bodies enhance the credibility and acceptability of climate change policy in the eyes of the general public, businesses, civil society and politicians. They can also provide cover and reinforcement to governments in case of political resistance to the adoption of the required targets and policies.[90] Even more, an independent body like the Advisory Board can hold governments accountable for policy enactment. Such bodies have also been shown to increase transparency and legitimacy of policymaking.[91] All this is important since achieving the objectives of the Climate Law will require policy consistency and constant calibration of targets over several decades. **7.41**

D. RELEVANT INSTITUTION?

The Climate Law is binding on 'relevant Union institutions and the Member States', who are required to take the necessary measures at Union and national level to enable the collective achievement of the climate-neutrality objective.[92] In doing so, they need to take into account the importance of promoting both fairness and solidarity among Member States and cost-effectiveness in achieving this objective (Article 2(2) of the Climate Law). **7.42**

In general, Union institutions are also the addressees of regulations. Union institutions are therefore bound by the provisions in the same manner as other addressees. However, reference to 'Union institution' is qualified by the word 'relevant' throughout the text of the law; that is, the obligations only refer to 'relevant Union institutions'. The law does not define what 'relevant Union institution' means. The question arises whether this means that some Union **7.43**

89 Amendments adopted by the European Parliament on 8 October 2020 on the proposal for a regulation of the European Parliament and of the Council establishing the framework for achieving climate neutrality and amending Regulation (EU) 2018/1999 (European Climate Law), 2020/0036(COD).

90 Alina Averchenkova and Lara Lazaro [2020], 'The Design of an Independent Expert Advisory Mechanism under the European Climate Law: What Are the Options?' London: Grantham Research Institute on Climate Change and the Environment and Centre for Climate Change Economics and Policy, London School of Economics and Political Science, p.9.

91 Carlos Abreu Amorim and Ana Cardoso, 'European Climate Law – Real Changes or Postponed Future?' EU Law Journal, July 2021 7(1), p.145.

92 Articles 2(2), 4(1), 5(1) and (3) of the Climate Law.

institutions are excluded. In other words, are relevant Union institutions those institutions that have a competence to adopt legislation or policy relevant for the Climate Law, or should all Union institutions act within their competence, *where relevant*?

7.44 The answer to this question is not straightforward.[93] In any case, all Union institutions are bound by the Paris Agreement, of which the Climate Law is largely an implementation. This follows from Article 216(2) of the Treaty on the Functioning of the EU (TFEU), which deals with international treaties signed by the EU: 'Agreements concluded by the Union are binding upon the institutions of the Union and on its Member States.' According to Kuijper, '[t]hey are obliged to take all measures necessary for the effective implementation of international agreements concluded by the [EU] and to abstain from acts which could hinder the proper implementation of agreements'.[94]

7.45 With regard to the Paris Agreement, both the Commission and the European Parliament[95] have said, for instance, that the European Central Bank, as a Union institution, is bound by the Agreement.[96] The ECB President at the time, Mario Draghi, supported this view on 26 February 2018 during a hearing with the European Parliament.[97]

7.46 However, in a speech, executive board member of the ECB Frank Elderson has said that 'there are a number of strong indications that the ECB is not

---

93 This ambiguity is reflected in the different language versions of the text of the Climate Law, with some of them referring to equivalents of the word 'relevant' (such as the Spanish, Dutch, Danish, Swedish, Romanian and Maltese versions) while others refer to the equivalent of the word 'competent' (such as the Italian, French, Portuguese, Greek, Bulgarian and German versions). The words 'relevant' and 'competent' are therefore used interchangeably.

94 'Thereby it also enables the [then] Community to fulfil its international responsibilities': Pieter Jan Kuijper, 'Introduction to the Symposium on Responsibility of International Organizations and of (Member) States: Attributed or Direct Responsibility or Both?' International Organizations Law Review (2010) 7(9), p.134.

95 See EP resolution on the ECB Annual Report 2017 (2019): '25. Recalls that the ECB *as an EU institution* is bound by the Paris agreement; invites the ECB, in full respect of its mandate, its independence and the risk management framework, to integrate the commitment to the Paris agreement and [...] ESG principles into its policies' (emphasis added) and EP, Committee on Economic and Monetary Affairs, 'Report on the [ECB] Annual Report 2020' (2021) A9-0002/202: '18. [...] recalls that the ECB, *as a European institution*, is bound by the Paris Agreement' (emphasis added). In the context of sustainable finance see EP, Committee on Economic and Monetary Affairs, 'Report on Sustainable Finance' (2018) A8-0164/2018, para 23.

96 Caoimhe Cotter, 'The European Central Bank and Climate Change: A Public International Law Perspective' (LLM thesis, University of Leiden 2022).

97 EP, Committee on Economic and Monetary Affairs, 'Monetary Dialogue with Mario Draghi [...]' (Brussels, 26 February 2018): '[the ECB is] party to the Paris climate agreement, and the ECB supports the general economic policies and the aims of the Union.' This representation, however, is not fully accurate: rather, the EU is party to the Paris Agreement, and the ECB, as an institution, is therefore bound indirectly.

a relevant institution under the Climate Law'.[98] His argument is – among others – that the requirements under the Climate Law require further environmental policymaking which is outside the remit of the ECB's competence.[99]

It may turn out that the question which institutions are 'relevant Union institutions' for the Climate Law is more academic than practical. There is a general requirement to ensure consistency between policies and activities in the Union, taking all of its objectives into account (Article 7 TFEU). This consistency requirement is limited by the principle of conferral of powers, where each Union institution can act only within its mandate and the powers that were conferred upon it. In practical terms this means that a Union institution acting within its mandate should refrain from making decisions that counter policies promoted by other institutions and, on the other hand, should positively consider those policies in the design of its own policies.[100] **7.47**

It does not stop there. According to Article 11 TFEU, environmental protection requirements must be integrated into the definition and implementation of the Union's policies and activities, in particular with a view to promoting sustainable development. Measures which seek to combat or mitigate the impact of climate change clearly serve the environment policy objective of Article 191(1) TFEU and can therefore be understood as 'environmental protection requirements' for the purposes of Article 11 TFEU.[101] Article 11 TFEU is significant since it is formulated as an *obligation*. In addition, it applies across the board for the Union without being limited to certain competences. **7.48**

The question remains as to what can be expected of Union institutions that are not co-legislators. In this respect, there are two aspects of the integration principle which are important to highlight. First, Article 11 TFEU does not comprise an additional competence of the EU. Rather, it is a primary law requirement to carry out a strategic environmental impact assessment, which extends to all individual measures, policies, programmes, plans and laws.[102] **7.49**

98 Speech held in Amsterdam at 1 December 2022, to be found at: www.ecb.europa.eu/press/key/date/2022/html/ecb.sp221201_1~435e6ea81a.en.html, accessed 9 May 2023.

99 This view is also put forward by Chiara Zilioli and Michael Ioannidis in 'Climate Change and the Mandate of the ECB: Potential and Limits of Monetary Contribution to European Green Policies', [2022] Common Market Law Review 59.

100 Chiara Zilioli and Michael Ioannidis, 'Climate Change and the Mandate of the ECB: Potential and Limits of Monetary Contribution to European Green Policies', Common Market Law Review, [2022] 59, p.380.

101 Chiara Zilioli and Michael Ioannidis, 'Climate Change and the Mandate of the ECB: Potential and Limits of Monetary Contribution to European Green Policies', Common Market Law Review, [2022] 59, p.379 and Jan H. Jans, 'Stop the Integration Principle?' (2011) 33 Fordham International Law Journal 1533, at p.1542.

102 Christian Calliess and Ebru Tuncel, 'Greening the Euro? The Impact of the Environmental Integration Clause (Art. 11 TFEU) on the European Central Bank (ECB) Primary and Secondary Objectives', Berliner Online-Beiträge zum Europarecht, (2022) 136, p.12.

Second, the Court of Justice of the EU (CJEU) has consistently affirmed that 'integrating' environmental protection requirements in other Union policies and activities means incorporating the objectives of the EU environmental policy.[103]

7.50 The Climate Law requires the Union to reduce greenhouse gas emissions according to certain milestones but does not flesh out how these reductions are to be achieved, nor does it contain a clear allocation of responsibilities. On a political level, both at Union and Member State, further policy choices need to be made to come to specific requirements. Apart from perhaps supporting the Commission in its reporting on the progress, the main requirement to integrate seems the overall objective of climate neutrality. It will be up to Union institutions to carry out a strategic environmental impact assessment, which extends to all individual measures, policies and programmes, and plans how they can support this objective within their own competence and powers.[104]

E. ENFORCEMENT VIA THE INFRINGEMENT PROCEDURE

7.51 If a Member State[105] fails to meet its obligations under the Climate Law or its related EU laws, the Commission is empowered to take action against that Member State on the basis of Article 258 TFEU. This is usually referred to as the infringement procedure.

7.52 The infringement procedure begins with a request for information (a letter of formal notice) to the Member State concerned, which must be answered within a specified period of time, usually two months. If the Commission is not satisfied with the information and concludes that the Member State in question is failing to fulfil its obligations under EU law, the Commission may then send a formal request to comply with EU law (a reasoned opinion), calling on the Member State to inform the Commission of the measures taken

103 Javier Solana, 'The Power of the Eurosystem to Promote Environmental Protection', European Business Law Review, [2019] 30(4), p.558 and the case-law cited therein.

104 An example of this are the policies of the ECB to incorporate climate considerations, an overview of which can be found at: www.ecb.europa.eu/ecb/climate/green_transition/html/index.en.html#:~:text=Cutting%20carbon%20emissions%20is%20the,net%2Dzero%20economy%20by%202050, accessed 9 May 2023.

105 In the case of failure to act not on the part of a Member State but on that of a Union institution, a failure to act procedure can be initiated. Under Article 265 of the Treaty on the Functioning of the European Union, should the European Parliament, the European Council, the Council of the European Union, the European Commission or the European Central Bank, in infringement of the treaties, fail to act, the EU Member States and the other Union institutions may bring an action before the Court of Justice of the European Union to have the infringement established. Similarly to the infringement procedure, the failure to act procedure is only admissible if the institution, body, office or agency concerned has first been called upon to act.

to comply within a specified period of time, usually two months.[106] This phase is generally referred to as the pre-judicial part. The objective of this phase is to clarify the facts of the case and allow the Member State to defend itself, eventually to rectify the situation, and to avoid litigation before the CJEU.[107] If the alleged infringement is not satisfactorily resolved, the Commission may then turn to the CJEU (the judicial phase).

The Climate Law, however, 'aims to provide a direction [...] to climate neutrality [...] but it does not prescribe specific policies or measures'.[108] There are certainly enforceable requirements that stem from it but the Commission would likely base its infringement proceedings on more specific EU law. For instance, the requirement for Member States to adopt, implement and update national adaptation strategies is laid down in Article 5(4) of the Climate Law but any failure to do so would more likely be pursued via the Governance Regulation. The reason is the simple fact that the Climate Law lays down high-level obligations, which are operationalised in more granular requirements in specific laws. **7.53**

F. CONCLUSION

In 2018, the UN International Panel on Climate Change (IPCC) highlighted the unprecedented scale of the challenge required to keep warming to 1.5°C. Its Sixth Assessment Report, dated 19 March 2023, is even more dire. Based on the current NDCs by parties to the Paris Agreement, that objective will not be met. According to the IPCC: 'For mitigation, global [greenhouse gas] emissions in 2030 implied by NDCs announced by October 2021 would make it likely that warming will exceed 1.5°C during the 21st century and would make it harder to limit warming below 2°C.'[109] **7.54**

These findings stress the importance of the European Climate Law. This law does not exist in isolation, however. It is part of a larger package in which the EU is trying to tackle climate change, covering energy and emission reduction and climate change adaptation. The Climate Law binds the Union and its **7.55**

106 See Commission Q&A at https://ec.europa.eu/commission/presscorner/detail/en/MEMO_12_12, accessed 9 May 2023.

107 Ludwig Krämer, 'EU Enforcement of Environmental Laws: From Great Principles to Daily Practice – Improving Citizen Involvement', Environmental Policy and Law, [2014] 44(1–2).

108 Explanatory Memorandum from the original Commission proposal, COM(2020) 80, dated 4 March 2020.

109 Synthesis report of the IPCC Sixth Assessment Report (AR6), Longer Report, dated 19 March 2023, p.23, to be found at: https://report.ipcc.ch/ar6syr/pdf/IPCC_AR6_SYR_LongerReport.pdf, accessed 9 May 2023.

Member States and is, to some extent, in its requirements even more specific and tangible than the Paris Agreement. Instead of a best effort obligation, the Climate Law sets a hard requirement of greenhouse gas reductions by 2035 and 2040[110] and climate neutrality as of 2050.

7.56 However, the impact – and therefore the success – of the Climate Law is still dependent on further action by legislators at Union and Member State level. Given the findings of the IPCC so far, it is likely that the current measures to reach the Climate Law targets need to be stepped up.

110 Still to be determined at the time of writing. The Commission launched a public consultation, to run from 31 March 2023 until 23 June 2023, to 'allow evidence and feedback to be collected from stakeholders on the EU's future climate ambition and its challenges and opportunities for all sectors of the economy'. See the consultation website at https://ec.europa.eu/info/law/better-regulation/have-your-say/initiatives/13793-EU-climate-target-for-2040/public-consultation_en, accessed 9 May 2023.

8

THE ECB'S MANDATE IN THE FACE OF CLIMATE CHANGE AND BIODIVERSITY LOSS[1]

René Smits

1 Research and editorial support by Maurice Lenz and Nils Beijeman is gratefully acknowledged. I owe a special debt of gratitude to Diederik van den Bogaerde for his research and editing support.

A. INTRODUCTION

1. Defining 'Sustainable Finance'

8.001 When discussing sustainable finance, one needs to express a view on the meaning of the term. An insightful exposition on what supervisors understand was provided by Andrea Enria, Chair of the Supervisory Board of the European Central Bank (ECB), as he then was.[2] Enria defined sustainability in two different ways. In the first perspective, 'sustainability' means that banks are capable to withstand shocks and stay in business over the long term. The second definition relates to 'being sustainable on a larger scale, at the level of society', where 'climate change is one of the key issues'. This approach sees sustainable finance as incentivizing banks to invest more capital into green project and assets. This chapter takes this second view as its starting point. It asks the question whether, from a legal perspective, the mandate of the ECB authorizes it to take climate change and biodiversity loss into account in its policies and activities, or even requires it to do so.

2 *Regulation, Proportionality and the Sustainability of Banking*, speech by Andrea Enria, Chair of the ECB's Supervisory Board, at the Retail Banking Conference 'Creating sustainable financial structures by putting citizens first' of European Savings Bank Group, Brussels, 21 November 2019; at: www.bankingsupervision.europa.eu/press/speeches/date/2019/html/ssm.sp191121_1~a65cdec01d.en.html.

2. Broad Outline of this Chapter

In the context of climate change and biodiversity, discussions of the mandate of the European System of Central Banks (ESCB)[3] often focus on its monetary policy brief and its prudential supervisory tasks, the two mainstays of activities of the Frankfurt-based euro-area central bank. Beyond environmental concerns, the scope of the Eurosystem's[4] mandate has been the subject of litigation emanating from constitutional complaints from Germany – leading to the *Gauweiler* (OMT)[5] and *Weiss* (PSPP)[6] cases and to the stand-off between the German Constitutional Court and the European Court of Justice (CJEU)[7] – and from the United Kingdom, leading to a judgment on the limitation of the ECB's mandate in the area of payments.[8] This chapter is concerned with the scope of the ESCB's mandate in the face of climate change and biodiversity. **8.002**

The focus will first be on monetary policy, then extend to prudential supervision and, finally, will briefly touch upon other elements of the mandate, including payment systems oversight and the issuance of banknotes. **8.003**

It is submitted that core elements of the line of reasoning developed below apply to the entire mandate. For ease of reading, in the following sections I will refer to monetary policy and only occasionally mention supervision – the reader is invited to consider the other elements of the mandate included in the reasoning. **8.004**

Similarly, to facilitate understanding, I discuss the mandate of the ECB in full acknowledgement of the legal situation that it is the European *System of* Central Bank*s* that is entrusted with this mandate. While recognizing the statutory injunction to operate in a decentralized manner,[9] I focus on the central entity in the system.[10] Since the ESCB is governed by the decision-making **8.005**

---

3 The ESCB consists of the ECB and the NCBs of all Member States. References to the ESCB in EU law may refer to either the system in its entirety or to the 'Eurosystem', that is, the monetary policy authority for the Euro Area (Article 282(1) TFEU).

4 The Eurosystem consists of the ECB and the National Central Banks (NCBs) of the Member States that have adopted the euro: Article 282, second sentence, TFEU.

5 Case C-62/14 *Peter Gauweiler and Others v Deutscher Bundestag*: ECLI:EU:C:2015:400.

6 Case C-493/17 *Weiss and Others*: ECLI:EU:C:2018:1000.

7 Judgment of the *Bundesverfassungsgericht* (*BVerfG*, German Constitutional Court, Second Senate, of 5 May 2020; English translation at: www.bundesverfassungsgericht.de/SharedDocs/Entscheidungen/EN/2020/05/rs20200505_2bvr085915en.html.

8 Case T-496/11, *UK v ECB*: ECLI:EU:T:2015:133. See, also: Case T-45/12 *UK* v. *ECB*: ECLI:EU:T:2015:289 and Case T-93/13 *UK v ECB*: ECLI:EU:T:2015:290.

9 Article 12.1, third paragraph, ESCB Statute Responsibilities of the decision-making bodies.

10 This also applies in the context of the ECB's prudential supervisory tasks: the Single Supervision Mechanism (SSM) consists of the ECB and National Competent Authorities (NCAs), with the ECB positioned

bodies of the ECB,[11] it is in the ECB's Governing Council that the fulfilment of the Eurosystem's mandate is ultimately decided, subject to judicial review and democratic control. The reader is invited to read the arguments as applying to the ESCB or the Eurosystem.[12] Likewise, references to the Statute of the European System of Central Banks and of the European Central Bank, Protocol No. 4 attached to the Treaty on the Functioning of the European Union (TFEU), will be short-handed as 'ESCB Statute'. Finally, in order to avoid unnecessary repetition, this chapter will speak about climate change when climate change and loss of biodiversity are meant,[13] as both developments produce risks for central banks and for the financial system, beyond threatening our economies and the survival of mankind on our planet.

B. HISTORY OF THE INTERPETATION OF THE MANDATE

1. Primacy of Price Stability

8.006 The ECB's overriding objective is price stability: 'The primary objective of the [ESCB[14]] shall be to maintain price stability', Article 127(1) TFEU proclaims.[15] Price stability is also the first of the three guiding principles underlying Economic and Monetary Union (EMU), compliance with which Article 119(3) TFEU requires.[16] Price stability is further mentioned as an objective to

---

centrally. See the *L-Bank* judgment: Case C-450/17 P *Landeskreditbank Baden-Württemberg – Förderbank v European Central Bank* ECLI:EU:C:2019:372.

11 Article 8 ESCB Statute General Principle.

12 Similarly, in respect of the SSM and the prudential supervision mandate.

13 Only differentiating between the two issues when there is a need to so, such as in respect of international norms.

14 See the explanation above on the ECB, ESCB and Eurosystem.

15 This is repeated in Article 282(2) TFEU and in Article 2 ESCB Statute.

16 'These activities of the Member States and the Union shall entail compliance with the following guiding principles: stable prices, sound public finances and monetary conditions and a sustainable balance of payments.' The 'activities' to which this provision refers concern the establishment of an economic (first paragraph) and a monetary (second paragraph) union. Article 119(1) calls for 'the adoption of an economic policy which is based on the close coordination of Member States' economic policies, on the internal market and on the definition of common objectives, and conducted in accordance with the principle of an open market economy with free competition', while Article 119(2) specifies as follows: 'these activities shall include a single currency, the euro, and the definition and conduct of a single monetary policy and exchange-rate policy the primary objective of both of which shall be to maintain price stability and, without prejudice to this objective, to support the general economic policies in the Union, in accordance with the principle of an open market economy with free competition.'

be achieved in Article 3(3) TEU.[17] The CJEU emphasized the importance of price stability in its *Gauweiler* judgment:[18]

> The Protocol on the ESCB and the ECB is thus characterised by *a clear mandate, which is directed primarily at the objective of ensuring price stability*. The *tightly drawn nature of that mandate* is further reinforced by the procedures for amending certain parts of the Statute of the ESCB and of the ECB. [italics added]

2. Secondary Mandate and Other Relevant Provisions

It is only in a secondary fashion that other objectives are relevant for the ECB's mandate. These further considerations, having to do with 'support [of] the general economic policies in the Union with a view to contributing to the achievement of the objectives of the Union as laid down in Article 3 of the Treaty on European Union',[19] are discussed in sections E and F below. Further provisions of relevance for the interpretation of what the ECB is mandated to undertake are the integration provisions of the TFEU,[20] notably Article 11, discussed in section G below, and the provision on the binding nature of international agreements (Article 216(2) TFEU), in relation to the Paris Agreement,[21] a matter for discussion in section H below. Finally, as will be discussed in section I below, the principle of an open market economy favouring an efficient allocation of resources,[22] often conflated with a principle of 'market neutrality', is also invoked as relevant for the interpretation of the ECB's mandate in the context of climate change and biodiversity. **8.007**

17 The second sentence of Article 3(3) TEU reads as follows: 'It [the European Union] shall work for the sustainable development of Europe based on balanced economic growth *and price stability*, a highly competitive social market economy, aiming at full employment and social progress, and a high level of protection and improvement of the quality of the environment' (*italics added*). In its previous incarnation as Article 2 of the EC Treaty, price stability was mentioned as 'non-inflationary growth': 'The Community shall have as its task, by establishing a common market and an economic and monetary union and by implementing the common policies or activities referred to in Articles 3 and 3a [currently: Article 119 TFEU], to promote throughout the Community a harmonious and balanced development of economic activities, sustainable and *non-inflationary* growth respecting the environment, a high degree of convergence of economic performance, a high level of employment and of social protection, the raising of the standard of living and quality of life, and economic and social cohesion and solidarity among Member States' (*italics added*).

18 Paragraph 44.

19 Article 127(1) TFEU, language which is repeated in Article 282(2) TFEU and in Article 2 ESCB Statute.

20 See Box 2 – integration provisions in the TFEU.

21 See the United Nations Framework Convention on Climate Change ELI: http:// data .europa .eu/ eli/ convention/1994/69/oj [1994] OJ L33/13; and the Paris Agreement [2016] OJ L282/4.

22 Article 127(1), third sentence, TFEU; Article 2, third sentence, ESCB Statute; Article 119(1) and (2) TFEU.

3. The ECB's Initial Approach: Solely Primary Mandate

8.008 Ever since its inception, the ECB has emphasised the twin characteristics of being an *independent* central bank and being entrusted with *delivering price stability* as its primary mandate. Insofar as support of economic policies in the European Union played any role, it was, at best, auxiliary. Most of the time, the reasoning the ECB followed was that a faithful implementation of its primary task constituted full execution of its secondary mandate, as well: providing price stability allowed the achievement of economic policy goals and contributed to the variety of objectives of the Union set out in Article 3 TEU. As Yolaine Fischer has set out,[23] 'ensuring price stability is considered to be instrumental in contributing to the achievement of the general economic policies of the EU, by supporting non-inflationary growth and a high level of employment'.

8.009 It is noteworthy that, in its very first communication on the monetary policy strategy it would pursue,[24] the ECB states: 'As mandated by the Treaty establishing the European Community, the maintenance of price stability will be the primary objective of the ESCB. Therefore, the ESCB's monetary policy strategy *will focus strictly on this objective*' [italics added].

8.010 The secondary objective is not even mentioned. In a similar vein, the first President of the ECB made clear, in a speech in Dublin seven weeks ahead of the launch of the euro,[25] that the serious concerns of the Governing Council about unemployment in the euro area would not diminish its commitment to price stability alone; only by working towards that ultimate goal would reducing unemployment be served. A longer quote will make this perspective clear:

> [L]et me emphasise that the Governing Council of the ECB is very concerned about the unacceptably high rate of unemployment in the euro area. However, an inflationary monetary policy would not solve Europe's serious unemployment problem. On the contrary, an inflationary policy would not only unacceptably flout the Maastricht Treaty; a Treaty, let me remind you, that has been ratified by all the Member States of the European Union and endorsed by the public in referenda in several countries, including Ireland. *An inflationary monetary policy would almost certainly lead to higher unemployment in the medium run, as long-term interest rates would rise and the benefits of price stability*

---

23 Yolaine Fischer, *Global warming: does the ECB mandate legally authorise a 'green monetary policy'?*, in Sustainability and Financial Markets, pp.163–98, notably at p.172.

24 *A stability-oriented monetary policy strategy for the ESCB*, press release, 13 October 1998, at: www.ecb.europa.eu/press/pr/date/1998/html/pr981013_1.en.html.

25 *The ESCB's stability-oriented monetary policy strategy*, speech by the President of the European Central Bank, Dr Willem F. Duisenberg, at the Institute of European Affairs on 10 November 1998 in Dublin, at: www.ecb.europa.eu/press/key/date/1998/html/sp981110.en.html.

> *would be lost*. Such a policy would therefore be entirely counterproductive. Let me be very clear: *in the interest of all European citizens, the Governing Council is determined to protect price stability*. The ESCB's independence is a means to facilitate the achievement of this goal. *Only by preserving price stability and thereby creating the stable environment required for continued higher employment and growth, can the European System of Central Banks (ESCB) serve the public and address the public's understandable concerns*. [italics added]

We see here that any consideration of other policy objectives (in this case, employment) is seen as undermining the primary mandate, as if including high unemployment in the considerations would automatically lead the ECB to pursue an inflationary monetary policy.[26] **8.011**

We saw the same emphasis on the first leg of the mandate when, in 2003, the ECB's first monetary policy strategy review was announced[27] – the secondary objective was not even mentioned.[28] It was only in the monetary policy strategy review of 2020–1 that the introductory words to its conclusion[29] mentioned the secondary mandate and even highlighted several elements of the Union's objectives:[30] 'These objectives include balanced economic growth, a highly competitive social market economy aiming at full employment and social progress, and a high level of protection and improvement of the quality of the environment.' **8.012**

By then, the thinking of the ECB had developed such that climate change formed part of the considerations for the achievement of its *primary* mandate. **8.013**

---

26 How different it is on the other side of the Atlantic Ocean, where the US central bank, the Federal Reserve System, takes unemployment more seriously, in pursuit of its mandate 'to promote effectively the goals of maximum employment, stable prices, and moderate long-term interest rates': Section 2A, Monetary policy objectives, Federal Reserve Act (see Ben Winck, 'The government is pursuing "maximum employment" for the first time. Here's how it differs from "full employment" and the risks it brings'. *Business Insider*. See: www.businessinsider.com/what-is-maximum-employment-full-employmentlabor-market-federal-reserve-risks-2021-6?international=true&r=US&IR=T#:~:text=The%20Fed%20is%20targeting%20%22maximum,inflationary%20spiral%20is%20set%20off.

27 *The ECB's monetary policy strategy*, press release, 8 May 2003, at: www.ecb.europa.eu/press/pr/date/2003/html/pr030508_2.en.html.

28 *The ECB's monetary policy strategy after the evaluation and clarification of May 2003*, Speech by Jean-Claude Trichet, President of the European Central Bank, delivered at the Center for Financial Studies' key event, Frankfurt am Main, 20 November 2003, at www.ecb.europa.eu/press/key/date/2003/html/sp031120.en.html.

29 *The ECB's monetary policy strategy statement*, at: www.ecb.europa.eu/home/search/review/html/ecb.strategyreview_monpol_strategy_statement.en.html. See, also, *ECB's Governing Council approves its new monetary policy strategy*, press release, 8 July 2021, at: www.ecb.europa.eu/press/pr/date/2021/html/ecb.pr210708~dc78cc4b0d.en.html.

30 While also referring to the further mandate in respect of financial stability: 'The Eurosystem shall also contribute to the smooth conduct of policies pursued by the competent authorities relating to the prudential supervision of credit institutions and the stability of the financial system.'

4. Secondary Mandate Held Primary Place When (Re-)interpreting Mandate

8.014 Until recently, then, the arguments proffered to explain why the ECB could (or could not) adopt policies or take measures which take climate change into account related mostly to the secondary mandate, to the incidence of the integration provision on the environment or to the binding nature of the Paris Agreement.[31] Stronger realisation of the impact of climate change on the fulfilment of the price stability mandate has lately shifted the focus in the debate to the ECB's primary mandate. Economists have argued that the shocks resulting from climate change and the transition risks entailed may affect price stability and may undermine traditional methods of trying to achieve price stability to such an extent that there is no need to solely rely on the secondary objective and additional arguments for the advocacy of climate change consciousness.[32] This change in the current of thinking also affects the approach I take here.

8.015 Below, I will first undertake a more inclusive interpretation of the primary and secondary objectives and then enter into the further arguments for a climate-conscious approach to the mandate of the ECB. Before doing so, let me explain the development of my own thinking.

5. Development of My Own Thinking

8.016 In my PhD thesis on the ECB, I wrote that[33]

> if two courses of action are open to the [Euro-]System, one of which is clearly more favourable to stable prices than the other, the choice should be for those measures which are most conducive to price stability. If there is no material difference in effect on price stability, the ESCB is free to choose a course of action on different grounds

8.017 and, referring to the objectives of Article 2 EC Treaty (now Article 3 TEU):[34] 'Indirectly, therefore, these objectives also bind the ESCB.'

---

31 See footnote 20 above.

32 See Franziska Bremus, Geraldine Dany-Knedlik and Thore Schlaak (2020). Price stability and climate risks: Sensible measures for the European Central Bank. *DIW Weekly Report*, *10*(14), 206–13.

33 *The European Central Bank – Institutional Aspects*, 1997, p.187.

34 *The European Central Bank – Institutional Aspects*, 1997, p.190. In 1997, I added that '[i]t can certainly be argued, even in the absence of such a reference [to the Community's objectives], the ESCB were bound by Article 2's enumeration of objectives. After all, the ESCB is fully embedded in the Community legal order'. This was before the CJEU confirmed, also basing itself on the reference to the Community's objectives, in the *OLAF* case that 'the ECB, pursuant to the EC Treaty, falls squarely within the Community framework'. Judgment of 10 July 2003 in Case C-11/00 (*Commission v ECB*), ECLI:EU:C:2003:395.

My initial basic approach to the requirement to support economic policies[35] emphasized the absence of a single Community economic policy and the legal requirement of such (largely national) economic policies as themselves being bound by the overall Treaty objectives. This finding is based on Article 102A EC Treaty,[36] currently Article 120 TFEU, the most ignored[37] of the economic union provisions in the EMU chapter, which reads: **8.018**

> Member States shall conduct their economic policies with a view to contributing to the achievement of the objectives of the Union, as defined in Article 3 of the Treaty on European Union, and in the context of the broad guidelines referred to in Article 121(2). The Member States and the Union shall act in accordance with the principle of an open market economy with free competition, favouring an efficient allocation of resources, and in compliance with the principles set out in Article 119.

I also noted the possibility for the Community to adopt economic policy measures based on Article 103A of the European Community Treaty (TEC),[38] currently Article 122 TFEU, as a route through which the Ecofin Council could adopt EU-wide policies which the ECB is required to support.[39,40] The recent use of this provision for the SURE mechanism[41] and the Recovery and Resilience Facility (RFF) funded by European Union Recovery Instrument[42] makes this reference more topical again. Article 122 TFEU has also been invoked as the legal basis for the (voluntary and possibly mandatory) **8.019**

35 *The European Central Bank – Institutional Aspects*, 1997, pp.187–90.

36 *The European Central Bank – Institutional Aspects*, 1997, pp.188 and 190.

37 In view of often divergent, domestically focused and inward-looking economic policies of the Member States and the observed major deviations from EU economic policy recommendations (see Konstantinos Efstathiou and Guntram Wolff, 'What Drives National Implementation of EU Policy Recommendations' [2019] Bruegel).

38 See for its text: www.cvce.eu/content/publication/2002/4/9/2c2f2b85-14bb-4488-9ded-13f3cd04de05/publishable_en.pdf. It is remarkable that this document is not found at the EurLex site.

39 *The European Central Bank – Institutional Aspects*, 1997, p.188.

40 In this context, I noted the distinction between EC-wide and Euro Area-specific measures and the possibility that economic policy coordination for the latter may become stricter than for the Community (now Union).

41 SURE was the temporary mechanism to support unemployment benefits in the Member States in the COVID-19 pandemic. See Council Regulation (EU) 2020/672 of 19 May 2020 on the establishment of a European instrument for temporary support to mitigate unemployment risks in an emergency (SURE) following the COVID-19 outbreak, OJ L 159/1, 20.5.2020.

42 The RRF is a combined loan/grant facility within the Union's multi-annual budgetary framework. See Regulation (EU) 2021/241 of the European Parliament and of the Council of 12 February 2021 establishing the Recovery and Resilience Facility, OJ L 57/17, 18.2.2021. Disbursements for the RRF are undertaken on the basis of the European Union Recovery Instrument, based on Article 122 TFEU; see the references in recital 19 of the preamble to, and in Article 6 of, Council Regulation (EU) 2020/2094 of 14 December 2020 establishing a European Union Recovery Instrument to support the recovery in the aftermath of the COVID-19 crisis, OJ L 433I/23, 22.12.2020.

Union-wide demand reduction for natural gas, to counter diminishing gas supplies from Russia in the context of its full-scale invasion of Ukraine.[43]

8.020 In my thesis, I declared the question whether the ESCB would be bound directly by the objectives of the Treaty 'a matter of theoretical interest' as 'the reference to Article 2 EC Treaty [now Article 3 TEU] makes abundantly clear that the ESCB is to support economic policies with a view to contributing to the achievement of the Community's goals'. I continued: '[i]t can certainly be argued that, even in the absence of such a reference, the ESCB were bound by Article 2's enumeration of objectives', because 'the ESCB is fully embedded in the Community legal order'.[44]

8.021 I still stand behind most of what I wrote in 1997, but have shifted towards a more comprehensive view of the relevance and pertinence of the secondary objective. I would no longer agree with the implication that Carel van den Berg[45] inferred from my insistence that the ECB is to support the *general* economic policies finding,[46] namely 'that the ESCB can be measured not in terms of support of a specific course of action conducted by Member States or the Community, but rather by the support of *underlying trends* in economic policy' [italics added].

6. Schedule of the Remainder of this Chapter

8.022 As will become clear below, I deem the ECB's support for the EU's climate policies and the adoption of climate-friendly measures and operations in furtherance of the Union's Green Deal[47] to be squarely within its mandate.

---

43 Council Regulation (EU) 2022/1369 of 5 August 2022 on coordinated demand-reduction measures for gas, OJ L 206/1, 8.8.2022.

44 A prelude to the subsequent finding of the CJEU, also basing itself on the reference to the Community's objectives, in the *OLAF* case that 'the ECB, pursuant to the EC Treaty, falls squarely within the Community framework'. Judgment of 10 July 2003 in Case C-11/00 (*Commission v ECB*), ECLI:EU:C:2003:395. The ECB has only been an EU institution since the Reform Treaty of Lisbon; the ECB is now mentioned among the institutions in Article 13(1) TEU. See Article 1 sub 14), Treaty of Lisbon amending the Treaty on European Union and the Treaty establishing the European Community, signed at Lisbon, 13 December 2007, OJ C 306/1, 17.12.2007.

45 C.C.A. van den Berg, The Making of the Statute of the European System of Central Banks – An Application of Checks and Balances, PhD, 2004, p.55. Van den Berg's finding that '[i]t is very difficult to make this secondary objective operational' and his sole focus on the level of interest rate set by the ECB as relevant for assessing compliance constitute a reading with which I would beg to differ.

46 *The European Central Bank – Institutional Aspects*, 1997, p.188.

47 See the 11 December 2019 announcement by the European Commission of the European Green Deal. This should enable Europe to become the first carbon-neutral continent in the world by 2050. See the Commission Communication COM(2019) 640 final at https://eur-lex.europa.eu/legal-content/EN/TXT/?qid=1576150542719&uri=COM%3A2019%3A640%3AFIN. See, also, https://ec.europa.eu/info/strategy/priorities-2019-2024/european-green-deal_en.

Also, furtherance of other economic policies and wider Union goals may be considered to be part of the ECB's mandate; but that issue is beyond the scope of this chapter.

The question I endeavour to answer in the following is whether the ECB's mandate *allows* or even *requires* it to include climate change and biodiversity loss considerations in exercising its functions and, if either is the case, what this might mean for its main areas of activity. **8.023**

In order to do so, the recent development of thinking within the ECB is first set out. **8.024**

7. Development of ECB Thinking on its Primary Mandate

At first sight, there seems to be not much scope to include considerations of climate change in understanding the ECB's mandate. As referred to above, recently, ECB officials have started to mention the risks which climate change poses for the fulfilment of the primary mandate. ECB President Christine Lagarde clearly mentioned climate change as an element to be included in policy-setting in an interview with the *Financial Times* published on 8 July 2020: 'as we have this price stability mandate that I described for you early on, climate change actually has an impact on price stability.'[48] Nine days later, ECB Executive Board member Isabel Schnabel, citing 'material risks to price stability in the medium to long term' posed by climate change, underlined the need to include climate change considerations in the execution of the central bank's core mandate.[49] She mentioned two paths along which climate change may diminish the effectiveness of monetary policy: 'large and persistent shocks to output inflation' as a result of delayed policy action against climate change, and impairment of the central bank's ability to address such shocks in case **8.025**

48 *Interview with Financial Times*, video interview with Christine Lagarde, President of the ECB, conducted by Roula Khalaf on 7 July 2020 and posted on 8 July 2020, at: www.ecb.europa.eu/press/inter/date/2020/html/ecb.in200708~8418847210.en.html. Ms Lagarde specified: 'even without changing our mandate, climate change has an impact. I'll tell you, it has an impact on how we model the economy going forward, how we forecast, how we measure risk, how we stress test institutions, how we value the collaterals that we receive, how we link and join forces with other national central banks to explore together what policies can actually have a decisive impact on fighting climate change. This clearly will be part of our strategy.' See Financial Times, 8 July 2020: *Lagarde puts green policy top of agenda in ECB bond buying – President wants central bank to 'explore every avenue' in fight against climate change*, at: www.ft.com/content/f776ea60-2b84-4b72-9765-2c084bff6e32.

49 *Never waste a crisis: COVID-19, climate change and monetary policy*, speech by Isabel Schnabel, Member of the Executive Board of the ECB, at a virtual roundtable on 'Sustainable Crisis Responses in Europe' organised by the INSPIRE research network, 17 July 2020, at: www.ecb.europa.eu/press/key/date/2020/html/ecb.sp200717~1556b0f988.en.html.

'[r]ising temperatures and an increased frequency of natural disasters [...] further suppress potential output growth and hence the real equilibrium interest rate around which central banks have to calibrate their policies'.[50]

8.026 This line of reasoning concerns the primary (that is, price stability) mandate, as Schnabel made clear: 'Importantly, this argument is not about weighing secondary objectives, which may provide additional justifications for monetary policy taking into account climate change. It is about protecting the primary objective.'[51]

8.027 It is noteworthy that, around the time that the ECB's Board members were openly discussing the need to include climate change in preparation and execution of the central bank's primary function, the ECB started a consultation on a draft guide on this matter for supervisory purposes.[52] Also, Supervisory Board Chair Andrea Enria, who had already foreshadowed climate concerns in an earlier speech,[53] spoke about the need to take climate risks fully into account for prudential supervision. This was also reflected in public utterances in the ECB's banking supervision Newsletter.[54]

8.028 Six weeks after her aforementioned speech, Isabel Schnabel made the same argument in favour of an ECB contribution to tackling climate change.[55] Focusing on the urgency of strong policy responses from a variety of public and private actors, arguing that 'there have been few instances in the past where society and policymakers have faced such a clear and significant threat to lives, jobs and prosperity' and citing 'broad agreement that climate risks continue to be mispriced in financial markets', she concluded that 'current market prices are unlikely to yield the needed transition towards a carbon-neutral economy at the pace required to stimulate investment and innovation and safeguard a sustainable growth path with stable prices'. This led her to call for 'collective and concerted action by all stakeholders, first and foremost by legislators and

---

50 Ibid.

51 Ibid.

52 See the draft *ECB Guide on climate-related and environmental risks – Supervisory expectations relating to risk management and disclosure,* at: www.bankingsupervision.europa.eu/legalframework/publiccons/pdf/climate-related_risks/ssm.202005_draft_guide_on_climate-related_and_environmental_risks.en.pdf.

53 See n 2 above.

54 *Ramping up climate-related and environmental risk supervision*, ECB Supervision Newsletter, 18 November 2020, at: www.bankingsupervision.europa.eu/press/publications/newsletter/2020/html/ssm.nl201118_4.en.html.

55 *When markets fail – the need for collective action in tackling climate change*, speech by Isabel Schnabel, Member of the Executive Board of the ECB, at the European Sustainable Finance Summit, Frankfurt am Main, 28 September 2020, at: www.ecb.europa.eu/press/key/date/2020/html/ecb.sp200928_1~268b0b672f.en.html.

national governments' and to state that '[t]he Eurosystem, for its part, cannot be a bystander in the transition towards a carbon-neutral economy'.

She identified 'three dimensions of support': as prudential supervisor (on which more in section M below), as large-scale investor and 'as independent guardian of the single currency', where 'we are investigating if and how our *monetary policy operations and portfolios* could be adjusted to reflect the fact that climate change, if not addressed swiftly, may affect the economy in ways that pose potentially material risks to price stability in the medium to long term'.[56] Schnabel mentioned *collateral*, which the ECB may decide to accept only 'if it is able to fully assess climate-related risks' or which the ECB may subject to haircuts representing the (climate-related) risks involved. Reassessing the benchmark allocation for *asset purchasing programmes* was a second method mentioned, requiring disclosure of climate-related risks involved in the assets and perhaps extending to 'excluding certain bonds – based on clear and transparent rules – that are used to finance projects that conflict with the decarbonisation objectives of the EU'.[57] Implicitly acknowledging the effects on mis-pricing and fostering a 'non-green' economy that the then current asset programmes were alleged to have,[58] Schnabel mentioned that, by thus changing course on monetary policy, the ECB 'could avoid a scenario in which [its] monetary policy contributes to locking in investments in sectors and technologies that are more acutely exposed to the disruptive effects of the transition to a carbon-neutral economy'. All the issues mentioned by Christine Lagarde and Isabel Schnabel were to be reflected upon in the ECB's monetary policy review.[59] This exercise in reassessing whether the ECB's monetary policy set-up is apt for the second decade of the twenty-first century has been affected,[60] as so much in Europe's economy and politics, by the outbreak of Covid-19 in 2020. In a speech of 30 September 2020, the ECB President summed up the challenges: **8.029**

> [W]e have to factor in a renewed focus on mitigating climate change, too, which could have an impact on inflation through progressive changes in the energy mix as we transition towards a carbon-neutral economy. *Climate change affects all aspects of monetary*

56 Bold in original.

57 Isabel Schnabel; see footnote 55 above.

58 Sini Matikainen, Emanuele Campiglio and Dimitri Zenghelis, 'The climate impact of quantitative easing', *Centre for Climate Change Economics and Policy*, May 2017, 1–36, at: www.lse.ac.uk/granthaminstitute/wp-content/uploads/2017/05/ClimateImpactQuantEasing_Matikainen-et-al-1.pdf.

59 See the Q&As on this exercise at: www.ecb.europa.eu/home/search/review/html/questions.en.html; and the *ECB Listens* portal at: www.ecb.europa.eu/home/search/review/html/form.en.html.

60 ECB Press Release, *ECB extends review of its monetary policy strategy until mid-2021*, 2 April 2020, at: www.ecb.europa.eu/press/pr/date/2020/html/ecb.pr200402~942a1358ee.en.html.

> *policy: output and inflation, long-term interest rates and policy transmission.* That is why we are carefully studying the implications of climate change for our primary objective as part of our strategy review.[61]

8.030 A general contribution on the ECB's legal mandate by four authors from the institution does not mention climate change but is relevant in this context as they give their interpretation as a contribution to the monetary policy review.[62] In their exhaustive treatment and prudent approach, their arguments are based on an analogy with the case law that accepts measures *indirectly* supporting price stability (by protecting the transmission mechanism of monetary policy: see the cases of *Gauweiler* and *Weiss*). The authors stipulate that monetary policy measures aiming at price stability 'may therefore take into account other considerations'. They mention 'full employment, a high level of protection and improvement of the quality of the environment, or financial stability', subject to these measures being necessary for price stability and embedded in decision-making that respects certain parameters, including proportionality. They emphasize the ECB's discretion in taking the necessary elements into account when devising monetary policy measures. When discussing the ECB's secondary objective, the authors distinguish between support for the general economic policies in the Union, which is a direct obligation, and contributing to the objectives of the Union, which is indirect as it works through the support of economic policies. It is up to the authorities responsible for these economic policies to take the specific decisions thereto; such policy-making is not for the ECB. Transparency is required: the authors argue that the ECB should identify the relevant economic policies in the Union which it seeks to support.

8.031 I agree with these authors' reading of the secondary objective as a self-standing source of competence: 'most plausible seems the interpretation according to which the ECB could rely on the secondary objective as an alternative legal basis for a monetary policy measure, provided this is without prejudice to price stability', footnoting as follows: 'This could suggest, for example, that the ECB could take action related to the protection of the environment if the action is covered by its competence to pursue the primary or secondary objectives'.[63]

---

61 *The monetary policy strategy review: some preliminary considerations*, speech by Christine Lagarde, President of the ECB, at the 'ECB and Its Watchers XXI' conference, Frankfurt am Main, 30 September 2020, at: www.ecb.europa.eu/press/key/date/2020/html/ecb.sp200930~169abb1202.en.html (italics added).

62 Michael Ioannidis, Sarah Jane Hlásková and Chiara Zilioli, *The Mandate of the ECB: Legal Considerations in the ECB's Monetary Policy Strategy Review* (September 2021). ECB Occasional Paper No. 2021/276, at https://papers.ssrn.com/sol3/papers.cfm?abstract_id=3928298.

63 Ibid. This is not the place to criticise the authors for not including the Commission among the economic policy setters at EU level.

Their contribution is further relevant for the parameters it identifies for fulfilling the secondary objective.

The development of the thinking at the ECB reflects the collective reflections of the central banks[64] and supervisors who have gathered to exchange views and best practices on the green transition. Before expressing my own views on the preferred interpretation of the ECB's primary mandate, it is time to make an excursion to this relevant recent grouping. **8.032**

C. NETWORK FOR GREENING THE FINANCIAL SECTOR

1. Origins and Objective

The emerging awareness of the need to tackle climate change and to include the risks emanating from climate change in supervision of the financial industry and in devising monetary policy has brought central banks and supervisors together in a dedicated association. In humble beginnings,[65] the Network of Central Banks and Supervisors for Greening the Financial System (NGFS) brought together eight central banks and supervisors in 2017, with the intention of exchanging best practices in this area on a voluntary basis, thus contributing to the development of financial-sector risk management related to climate and environmental threats and 'to mobilise mainstream finance to support the transition towards a sustainable economy'.[66] The purpose of the NGFS is now described more forcefully as follows:[67] **8.033**

> The Network's purpose is to help strengthening the global response required to meet the goals of the Paris agreement and to enhance the role of the financial system to manage risks and to mobilize capital for green and low-carbon investments in the broader context of environmentally sustainable development. To this end, the Network defines and promotes best practices to be implemented within and outside of the Membership of the NGFS and conducts or commissions analytical work on green finance.

The renewed July 2020 Charter of the NGFS describes its objective as follows: **8.034**

---

64 An excellent overview of the challenges and central banks' methods of facing them can be found here: Fred Pearce, *As Disasters Mount, Central Banks Gird Against Threat of Climate Change*, 18 August 2021, at: https://e360.yale.edu/features/as-disasters-mount-central-banks-gird-against-threat-of-climate-change.

65 An intriguing account of how climate change became an accepted topic of discourse among central bankers, and an explanation of the development of such advocacy among 'first movers' (the Bank of England, the Banque de France and De Nederlandsche Bank), can be found in Katrijn Siderius (2022), *An unexpected climate activist: central banks and the politics of the climate-neutral economy*, Journal of European Public Policy, at: https://doi.org/10.1080/13501763.2022.2093948.

66 See www.ngfs.net/en.

67 See www.ngfs.net/en/about-us/governance/origin-and-purpose.

> The [NGFS] is a group of Central Banks and prudential supervisory authorities willing, on a voluntary basis, to exchange experiences, share best practices, contribute to the development of environment and climate risk management in the financial sector, and to mobilize mainstream finance to support the transition toward a sustainable economy. Its purpose is to define, promote and contribute to the development of best practices to be implemented within and outside of the Membership of the NGFS and to conduct or commission analytical work on green finance.[68]

8.035 By 14 June 2022, the network of original eight agencies[69] had grown to 116 members and 19 observers.[70] Membership is geographically and institutionally diverse, with central banks and supervisory agencies spanning the continents, and including European Supervisory Authorities (ESAs)[71] and the central banks of monetary unions (the ECB and the *Banque Centrale des Etats de l'Afrique de l'Ouest* (BCEAO)).[72] It is noteworthy that several jurisdictions have a variety of agencies represented: both their central bank and their financial sector or market supervisor. The NGFS was initially energetically chaired by then DNB Director Frank Elderson, one of the world's two leading central bank protagonists of action against climate change, the other being Mark Carney. As Governor of the Bank of England,[73] this Canadian–British economist delivered a key speech[74] setting the issue of climate change squarely on the agenda in the City.[75] The current chair is Ravi Menon, Managing Director of the Monetary Authority of Singapore.

68 At: www.ngfs.net/sites/default/files/media/2020/09/03/ngfs_charter_final.pdf. The 2023 charter is similarly worded; see https://www.ngfs.net/sites/default/files/media/2023/04/27/ngfs_charter_-27_april_2023.pdf.

69 Banco de Mexico, the Bank of England, the Banque de France and Autorité de Contrôle Prudentiel et de Résolution (ACPR), De Nederlandsche Bank, the Deutsche Bundesbank, Finansinspektionen (the Swedish FSA), the Monetary Authority of Singapore and the People's Bank of China; see the Joint statement by the Founding Members of the Central Banks and Supervisors Network for Greening the Financial System – One Planet Summit at: www.banque-france.fr/en/communique-de-presse/joint-statement-founding-members-central-banks-and-supervisors-network-greening-financial-system-one.

70 See www.ngfs.net/en/about-us/membership. By end 2023, it had grown to 134 members and 21 observers.

71 The European Banking Authority (EBA), the European Securities and Markets Authority (ESMA) and the European Insurance and Occupational Pensions Authority (EIOPA). These authorities are entrusted with the coordination of supervision of financial services in the single market and have been given specific supervisory powers. They also play a role in the implementation of the EU's green taxonomy.

72 See www.bceao.int/. The Banque des Etats de l'Afrique Centrale (BEAC; (www.beac.int/beac/la-beac/) and the Eastern Caribbean Central Bank (ECCB; www.eccb-centralbank.org/) are not members (yet).

73 Mark Carney is currently the UN Secretary-General's Special Envoy on Climate Action and Finance; see: www.un.org/sg/en/content/sg/personnel-appointments/2019-12-01/secretary-general-appoints-mark-joseph-carney-of-canada-special-envoy-climate-action-and-finance.

74 'Breaking the tragedy of the horizon – climate change and financial stability', speech by Mr Mark Carney, Governor of the Bank of England and Chairman of the Financial Stability Board, at Lloyd's of London, London, 29 September 2015, at: www.bis.org/review/r151009a.pdf.

75 See also 'A new horizon', speech given by Mark Carney, Governor Bank of England at the European Commission Conference: A global approach to sustainable finance, 21 March 2019, at: www.bis.org/review/r190322a.pdf.

2. Main Deliverables

The key products of the NGFS, beyond the activation of mutual cooperation and inspiration on the global theme of climate change and the financial sector, have been a succession of reports and the guidance on its website. Among these are climate scenarios, assisting central banks and supervisors to design and analyse scenarios underpinning their preparations, and those of the financial-sector agents, for the green transition.[76] Exploring the ways in which central banks can remain resilient to climate change and how they can protect their balance sheets, a March 2021 report sets out a host of options to factor in climate change into their operations.[77] The guidance given always alludes to the central bank's specific mandate and acknowledges that while '[t]here is a broad consensus among members of the NGFS that, at the very least, central banks should carefully assess, and where appropriate adopt, additional risk management measures to protect their balance sheets against the financial risks brought about by climate change', 'there is as of yet no consensus among central banks as to what climate-related adjustments would be optimal', 'reflecting the diversity of existing central bank operational frameworks'. The inventory of options, the provision of criteria to assess the menu of options and the sketching of the strategic choices faced by central banks enable well-reasoned decision-making and thereby pave the way to operational choices. I have no doubt that the NGFS' work has prepared the ground for the choices made by the ECB, to be discussed in section L below.[78] **8.036**

The NGFS has also issued a number of recommendations, both to the members of its own grouping and to policy makers. The former include integrating climate-related risks into financial stability monitoring and micro-supervision (a prudential issue), integrating sustainability as a factor in central banks' own portfolios and bridging data gaps.[79] On this issue, the NGFS calls for 'convergence towards a common and consistent set of global sustainability disclosure standards' and a global taxonomy. More forward-looking data and more granular data are required upon which to base business decisions and **8.037**

---

76 See www.ngfs.net/ngfs-scenarios-portal/, and the (second) NGFS Climate Scenarios for central banks and supervisors, June 2021, at: www.ngfs.net/en/ngfs-climate-scenarios-central-banks-and-supervisors-june-2021.

77 *Adapting central bank operations to a hotter world: reviewing some options*, at: www.ngfs.net/sites/default/files/media/2021/06/17/ngfs_monetary_policy_operations_final.pdf.

78 For an overview of the NGFS' work and of climate-related measures taken by European central banks, see Clara Isabel González Martínez, The role of central banks in combating climate change and developing sustainable finance, *Banco de España* Economic Bulletin 3/2021; at: https://ssrn.com/abstract=3937139.

79 See the *Progress report on bridging data gaps*, May 2021, at: www.ngfs.net/sites/default/files/medias/documents/progress_report_on_bridging_data_gaps.pdf.

policy-making. A survey[80] on whether their mandates would provide an opportunity for central banks to reflect climate change in their operational framework provided insights into the diverse legal positions on the interlinkage of climate goals with the primary objective of central banks, again preparing the ground for well-founded decision-making. The *Guide on Climate-related Disclosure for Central Banks* provides guidance for central banks on how to produce climate-related disclosures, covering central banks' governance, strategy and risk management, in line with recommendations on financial disclosures issued by the Task Force on Climate-related Financial Disclosures (TCFD).[81]

3. Wider Context

8.038 The Network, as a dedicated association, works within a wider context of bodies engaged in the promotion of financial stability. The Financial Stability Board,[82] once headed by Mark Carney,[83] has dedicated work on the impact of climate change on financial stability,[84] including stocktaking of the experience of financial authorities to take physical and transition risk into account,[85] and made an inventory of the implications of climate change for financial stability.[86] The FSB's main impact has been its proposal to the G20 in 2015 to establish an 'industry-led disclosure task force on climate-related risks'.[87] This TCFD has issued Recommendations[88] which focus on governance, strategy, risk management and metrics and targets. It keeps track of adherence to its Recommendations, and has issued further guidance.[89]

---

80 *Survey on monetary policy operations and climate change: key lessons for further analyses*, December 2020, at: www.ngfs.net/sites/default/files/medias/documents/survey_on_monetary_policy_operations_and_climate_change.pdf.

81 Guide on climate-related disclosure for central banks, December 2021, at: www.ngfs.net/sites/default/files/medias/documents/guide_on_climate-related_disclosure_for_central_banks.pdf.

82 See www.fsb.org/.

83 See his Arthur Burns Memorial Lecture, given as Governor of the Bank of England, in Berlin on 22 September 2016: *Resolving the climate paradox*, at: www.fsb.org/wp-content/uploads/Resolving-the-climate-paradox.pdf.

84 See www.fsb.org/work-of-the-fsb/financial-innovation-and-structural-change/climate-related-risks/.

85 *Stocktake of financial authorities' experience in including physical and transition climate risks as part of their financial stability monitoring*, 22 July 2020, at: www.fsb.org/2020/07/stocktake-of-financial-authorities-experience-in-including-physical-and-transition-climate-risks-as-part-of-their-financial-stability-monitoring/.

86 *The Implications of Climate Change for Financial Stability*, 23 November 2020, at: www.fsb.org/wp-content/uploads/P231120.pdf.

87 *Proposal for a disclosure task force on climate-related risks*, 9 November 2015, at: www.fsb.org/wp-content/uploads/Disclosure-task-force-on-climate-related-risks.pdf.

88 *Recommendations of the Task Force on Climate-related Financial Disclosures, Final Report*, 15 June 2017, at: www.fsb.org/wp-content/uploads/P290617-5.pdf.

89 See: *Guidance on Risk Management Integration and Disclosure*, October 2020, at: www.fsb.org/wp-content/uploads/P291020-2.pdf. See also *Guidance on Scenario Analysis for Non-Financial Companies*, October 2020, at: www.fsb.org/wp-content/uploads/P291020-3.pdf. After its 2023 status report, the TCFD has fulfilled its

The central banks' central bank, the Basel-based Bank for International Settlement (BIS), is also active in this area. It undertakes research,[90] with a notable publication introducing the concept of the Green Swan and highlighting[91] 8.039

> radical uncertainty associated with a physical, social and economic phenomenon that is constantly changing and involves complex dynamics and chain reactions. Traditional backward-looking risk assessments and existing climate-economic models cannot anticipate accurately enough the form that climate-related risks will take. These include what we call 'green swan' risks: potentially extremely financially disruptive events that could be behind the next systemic financial crisis.

The Basel Committee on Banking Supervision (BCBS) has issued guidelines.[92] 8.040
The BIS has a 'green finance' section of its Innovation Hub[93] and has even issued three green bonds: one in US dollars, one in euros and an Asian Green Bond Fund, in compliance with private green bond standards ('green bond fund initiative').[94] For more BCBS initiatives on green finance, see section M below.

It is against the backdrop of these global initiatives and activities that the ECB 8.041
has been reflecting on its mandate, to the interpretation of which we now return.

D. PRIMARY MANDATE: THE PREFERRED INTERPRETATION

I consider the previously quoted views of the Executive Board members 8.042
relevant for the interpretation of the ECB's primary mandate. This is not because economists[95] should have precedence when interpreting the law, and certainly not because the ECB board would be able to give an authoritative

remit and disbanded, with the FSB requesting the IFRS Foundation to take over monitoring of companies' climate-related disclosures.

90 See www.bis.org/topic/green_finance/research.htm. And: *Guidance on Metrics, Targets, and Transition Plans*, October 2021, at: https://assets.bbhub.io/company/sites/60/2021/07/2021-Metrics_Targets_Guidance-1.pdf.

91 *The green swan – Central banking and financial stability in the age of climate change*, Patrick Bolton, Morgan Despres, Luiz Awazu Pereira Da Silva Frédéric Samama and Romain Svartzman, January 2020, at: www.bis.org/publ/othp31.pdf.

92 See www.bis.org/topic/green_finance/cooperation.htm.

93 See www.bis.org/about/bisih/topics/green_finance.htm.

94 *BIS launches green bond fund for central banks*, press release, 26 September 2019, at: www.bis.org/press/p190926.htm; *BIS launches second green bond fund for central banks*, press release, 25 January 2021, at: /www.bis.org/press/p210125.htm; *BIS launches Asian Green Bond Fund*, press release, 25 February 2022, at: www.bis.org/press/p220225.htm.

95 Isabel Schnabel is an economist by training; Christine Lagarde has a legal professional background.

interpretation unchecked by the courts and academic critique, but because an acknowledgement of climate change effects on the pursuit of the price stability mandate is especially relevant in the context of a multidisciplinary approach to interpreting the law. This is, again, no abdication of responsibility on the part of lawyers but rather an acknowledgement of the necessity to rely on other disciplines when it comes to society's, or nature's, effects on human behaviour and the regulation thereof. Just as economics needs to rely on (climate) science when assessing the likely impact of climate change on economic variables, so are lawyers dependent on economists' assessments of developments and relationships when interpreting an 'economic' mandate, such as that of the ECB.[96] And both depend on climate change scientists to assess the future of the planet and the actions needed to save it from its most dominant inhabitants: human animals.[97] Assuming the validity of the assessment of the impact of climate change on economic variables and on the ECB's pursuit of price stability, I consider an interpretation that not only *allows* but actually *requires* the central bank to take climate change and biodiversity into account when devising and implementing monetary policy to be a valid and compellingly convincing interpretation of the ECB's mandate.[98] This is my preferred interpretation of the relevant provisions.[99]

8.043 The question then is to what extent the ECB may or should take climate change into account in setting and executing monetary policy. This will be the subject of section K below. First, I turn to a weighing of secondary objectives in the context of the issue of climate change.

---

96 The word 'economic' is in quotation marks because in the law of the EMU a distinction is made between 'economic' and 'monetary', with the latter an exclusive Union competence and the former primarily within the purview of Member States and, in any case, in the hands of the (State and Union) governments and not the central banks. See Articles 3(1)(c), 2(3), 5(1) and (2) and 136 TFEU. Here, I use the word 'economic' in the wide, non-legal sense of the word as encompassing monetary union matters. I recall paragraph 60 of the CJEU's judgment in the *Weiss* Case (judgment of 11 December 2018 in Case C-493/17, ECLI:EU:C:2018:1000): 'the authors of the Treaties did not intend to make an absolute separation between economic and monetary policies."'

97 See the August 2021 report by the Intergovernmental Panel on Climate Change (IPCC): *Climate Change 2021: The Physical Science Basis*, at: www.ipcc.ch/report/ar6/wg1/#FullReport.

98 Shared by Banque de France Governor François Villeroy de Galhau: 'the financial stability and monetary policy mandates of central banks impose the obligation and also give them the tools to respond to the climate imperative'; see his:'Climate change: central banks are taking action', Banque de France Financial Stability Review No. 23, June 2019 (Greening the financial system: the new frontier), at: https://entreprises.banque-france.fr/sites/default/files/media/2019/08/27/financial_stability_review_23.pdf#page=8. Most recently, see *Climate Change 2022 Mitigation of Climate Change Working Group III Contribution to the Sixth Assessment Report of the Intergovernmental Panel on Climate Change*, October 2021, at: www.ipcc.ch/report/ar6/wg3/.

99 Recalling Article 127(1), first sentence; Article 282(2), second sentence, TFEU; and Article 2 ESCB, first sentence, ESCB Statute.

E. THE ECB'S SECONDARY OBJECTIVE

1. Price Stability Takes Precedence

When addressing the issue of climate change as relevant for the interpretation of the ECB's mandate, attention has hitherto largely focused on the secondary objective, which was discussed in the paragraphs on the history of the interpretation approach. As stated previously, this requires the ECB to 'support the general economic policies in the Union with a view to contributing to the achievement of the objectives of the Union as laid down in Article 3 of the Treaty on European Union'.[100] The secondary objective clearly has a subordinate role as the relevant provisions begin: 'Without prejudice to the objective of price stability, the ESCB shall support [...]'. **8.044**

The Treaty's insistence on the precedence of price stability is made abundantly clear in the provisions governing the euro's external relations. Article 219 in Title V on international agreements of Part Five of the TFEU (relating to the Union's external action) sets out how exchange-rate arrangements may be made in respect of the euro. Both in the case of 'formal' exchange-rate agreements (Article 219(1) TFEU)[101] – unlikely in the present-day context of floating exchange rates[102] – and when adopting 'general orientations for exchange rate policy' (Article 219(2) TFEU),[103] the precedence of price stability is crystal **8.045**

100 Article 127(1) TFEU; language which is repeated in Article 282(2) TFEU and in Article 2 ESCB Statute.

101 Article 219 (1) TFEU reads: 'By way of derogation from Article 218, the Council, either on a recommendation from the European Central Bank or on a recommendation from the Commission and after consulting the European Central Bank, in an endeavour to reach a consensus consistent with the objective of price stability, may conclude formal agreements on an exchange-rate system for the euro in relation to the currencies of third States. The Council shall act unanimously after consulting the European Parliament and in accordance with the procedure provided for in paragraph 3. The Council may, either on a recommendation from the European Central Bank or on a recommendation from the Commission, and after consulting the European Central Bank, in an endeavour to reach a consensus consistent with the objective of price stability, adopt, adjust or abandon the central rates of the euro within the exchange-rate system. The President of the Council shall inform the European Parliament of the adoption, adjustment or abandonment of the euro central rates.'

102 Which came about 50 years ago at the time of writing of the first version of this chapter: on 15 August 1971, US President Nixon announced the severing of the link between gold and the US dollar, which had underpinned the post-Second World War Bretton Woods system of fixed but adjustable parities between the main western currencies. See Barry Eichengreen, *The Big Float*, 11 June 2021, Project Syndicate, at: www.project-syndicate.org/onpoint/nixon-shock-bretton-woods-collapse-fifty-years-later-by-barry-eichengreen-2021-06?barrier=accesspaylog.

103 Article 219(2) TFEU reads: 'In the absence of an exchange-rate system in relation to one or more currencies of third States as referred to in paragraph 1, the Council, either on a recommendation from the Commission and after consulting the European Central Bank or on a recommendation from the European Central Bank, may formulate general orientations for exchange-rate policy in relation to these currencies. These general orientations shall be without prejudice to the primary objective of the ESCB to maintain price stability.'

clear. When the ECB is consulted on a formal agreement,[104] this consultation is to endeavour 'to reach a consensus [between the Council and the ECB] consistent with the objective of price stability'. Similarly, when determining the euro's rate in an exchange-rate system, that is in applying a 'formal' agreement on the relation of the euro with the currencies of third countries, the Council's consultations with the ECB[105] are to strive for a consensus to reach price stability. In the absence of formal arrangements for exchange-rate policy, the Council may adopt (but has refrained from doing so until now) 'general orientations' which 'shall be without prejudice to the primary objective of the ESCB to maintain price stability'. In the previous section, an interpretation of this overriding primary mandate to maintain price stability which *permits*, nay even *requires*, the ECB to take climate change and biodiversity into account has been presented as compellingly convincing.

2. Interpreting the Wording of the Secondary Mandate

8.046 Having thus established that the priority for price stability in the ECB's mandate is omnipresent in the Treaty,[106] one may start to interpret the words devoted to the secondary objective. Before exploring what they say about the relevance of climate change for the European Union's central bank, it may be useful to explain some of the peculiarities of the language used.

8.047 There is no obligation to support 'the' EU's 'economic policy' because there is no such thing. When EMU was established, the conduct of monetary policy was centralised, but economic policy remained largely an affair of the individual states. This is borne out by Articles 2(3)[107] and 5 TFEU[108] that grant coordinating powers to the Union in respect of the Member States' economic policies. Beyond prohibitions – of monetary financing of the public sector (Article 123 TFEU), of privileged access of the public sector to the financial

---

104 This consultation is prescribed when the Council acts on a recommendation of the Commission. Alternatively, the ECB itself can submit a recommendation to the Council for a formal exchange-rate agreement.

105 Again, such consultations are mandated in case the adoption, adjustment or abandonment of a central rate for the euro in relation to a third currency emanates from the Commission. Alternatively, the ECB itself can submit a recommendation to the Council for determining or abandoning the euro's central rate in an agreement.

106 And in the ESCB Statute, where Article 2 mirrors Articles 127(1) and 282(2) TFEU on the ESCB's mandate.

107 Which reads: 'The Member States shall coordinate their economic and employment policies within arrangements as determined by this Treaty, which the Union shall have competence to provide.'

108 Paragraph 1 of which reads: 'The Member States shall coordinate their economic policies within the Union. To this end, the Council shall adopt measures, in particular broad guidelines for these policies. Specific provisions shall apply to those Member States whose currency is the euro.' Paragraph 2 concerns the coordination of employment policies and the right of initiative to coordinate social policies.

sector (Article 124 TFEU) and of mutual liability or debt assumption (the 'no bail-out clause' of Article 125 TFEU)[109] – and rather generally phrased obligations,[110] the economic union provisions largely provide for coordination. Both general economic policy coordination (Article 121) and specific and ultimately intrusive rules on budgetary constraints (Article 126, the so-called Excessive Deficits Procedure) are provided for. Even though these Treaty provisions have been 'topped up' by the Stability & Growth Pact[111] and elaborated in economic governance rules,[112] which have been vastly expanded since the great financial crisis and the subsequent sovereign debt crisis, the underlying approach is one of Member State competences in the area of economic policy. This explains the reference to supporting '*general* economic policie*s*': both the 'general' and the plural (polic*ies*) imply that there is, as yet, no EU (or euro-area) economic policy, except as a result of coordination and market pressure[113] towards convergence.

---

109 Case C-370/12 *Pringle*: ECLI:EU:C:2012:756.

110 Such as in Article 120(1), first sentence, cited above.

111 Resolution of the European Council on the Stability and Growth Pact Amsterdam, 17 June 1997 [1997] OJ C236/1. Elaborated in Council Regulations of 7 July 1997: No 1466/97 on the strengthening of the surveillance of budgetary positions and the surveillance and coordination of economic policies, and No 1467/97 on speeding up and clarifying the implementation of the excessive deficit procedure, [1997] OJ L 209/1 and L209/6.

112 Reference is made to the 'six-pack' of legislation adopted in 2011 and the 'two-pack' which followed in 2013, and to the 'Fiscal Compact Treaty'. See Regulation (EU) No 1173/2011 of the European Parliament and of the Council of 16 November 2011 on the effective enforcement of budgetary surveillance in the euro area [2011] OJ L306/1; Regulation (EU) No 1174/2011 of the European Parliament and of the Council of 16 November 2011 on enforcement measures to correct excessive macroeconomic imbalances in the euro area [2011] OJ L306/8; Regulation (EU) No 1175/2011 of the European Parliament and of the Council of 16 November 2011 amending Council Regulation (EC) No 1466/97 on the strengthening of the surveillance of budgetary positions and the surveillance and coordination of economic policies [2011] OJ L306/12; Regulation (EU) No 1176/2011 of the European Parliament and of the Council of 16 November 2011 on the prevention and correction of macroeconomic imbalances [2011] OJ L306/25; Council Regulation (EU) No 1177/2011 of 8 November 2011 amending Regulation (EC) No 1467/97 on speeding up and clarifying the implementation of the excessive deficit procedure [2011] OJ L306/33; Council Directive 2011/85/EU of 8 November 2011 on requirements for budgetary frameworks of the Member States [2011] OJ L306/41 [the 'six-pack']; Regulation (EU) No 472/2013 of the European Parliament and of the Council of 21 May 2013 on the strengthening of economic and budgetary surveillance of Member States in the euro area experiencing or threatened with serious difficulties with respect to their financial stability [2013] OJ L140/1; Regulation (EU) No 473/2013 of the European Parliament and of the Council of 21 May 2013 on common provisions for monitoring and assessing draft budgetary plans and ensuring the correction of excessive deficit of the Member States in the euro area [2013] OJ L140/11 [the 'two-pack']; and the Treaty on Stability, Coordination and Governance in the Economic and Monetary Union, at: www.consilium.europa.eu/media/20399/st00tscg26_en12.pdf.

113 The idea underlying the Maastricht concept of EMU was that, when national governments acted within the rather loose confines of the economic union provisions, markets would also induce proper (budgetary) behaviour. The 2008–12 crisis proved that concept to be unsustainable. This is not the place to elaborate further on the 'unbalanced nature' of EMU (a well-developed monetary arm next to an underdeveloped economic union arm), or on how to redress this condition.

8.048 Additionally, Article 122 TFEU (already referred to above) provides for the adoption of 'measures appropriate to the economic situation' and allows for EU financial assistance in case events beyond a Member State's control lead to severe difficulties. As indicated before, this provision underlies common storage of strategic material and supported the temporary support mechanism in the sovereign debt crisis.[114] It has since been used again in the context of the pandemic crisis[115] – the European Union Recovery Instrument[116] is based on it – as well as for joint demand reduction for natural gas. Furthermore, Article 136 TFEU provides for strengthened economic policy cooperation in respect of the euro-area Member States, but even this article does not provide for a common euro-area economic policy.

3. The Need for Economic Policy Clarity at EU Level

8.049 This state of affairs has made the required support of economic policies a rather flimsy secondary objective: without a clear, single policy to follow, all the ECB could do was ensure its monetary policy did not undermine the general trend of these policies. At the least, the ECB is to take into consideration the thrust of the economic policy recommendations to individual governments issued by the Council under the preventive arm of the SGP,[117] or the euro-area specific broad economic policy guidelines (BEPGs) issued by the Council.[118] It would be recommendable for such BEPGs to be more specific in their requirements for greening the economy and fostering the transition to a CO_2-free economy than the latest versions are.[119] Although the 'green and digital transitions' are

114 Council Regulation (EU) No 407/2010 of 11 May 2010 establishing a European financial stabilisation mechanism [2010] OJ L118/1.

115 Council Regulation (EU) 2020/672 of 19 May 2020 on the establishment of a European instrument for temporary support to mitigate unemployment risks in an emergency (SURE) following the COVID-19 outbreak [2020] OJ L159/1.

116 Council Regulation (EU) 2020/2094 of 14 December 2020 establishing a European Union Recovery Instrument to support the recovery in the aftermath of the COVID-19 crisis, OJ L 433 I/23, 22.12.2020.

117 Article 5(2) Regulation 1466/97, as amended. These annual Council recommendations concern a Member State's National Reform Programme and simultaneously deliver an opinion on their Stability Programme. For the 2020 recommendations annex opinions, see https://ec.europa.eu/info/publications/2020-european-semester-country-specific-recommendations-commission-recommendations_en. See the Broad Economic Policy Guidelines issued in 2015: Council Recommendation (EU) 2015/1184 of 14 July 2015 on broad guidelines for the economic policies of the Member States and of the European Union, OJ L 192, 18.7.2015, p.27.

118 Council Recommendation of 13 July 2021 on the economic policy of the euro area, OJ C 283/1, 15.7.2021, Council Recommendation of 5 April 2022 on the economic policy of the euro area (2022/C 153/01), OJ C 153/1, 7.4.2022, and Council Recommendation of 16 May 2023 on the economic policy of the euro area, [2023] OJ C180/1.

119 This point is in line with a recent Bruegel policy contribution. Its authors posit that 'it is very likely that climate change will lead to increasing economic divergence between member states' and note that 'binding, measurable targets are absent and not demanded from member states', concluding with a call for 'binding

mentioned and climate change and climate mitigation occur in the text, the ambition of the 2021 guidelines falls far short of the European Climate Law,[120] adopted around the same time. While the 2022 guidelines are more explicit in their references to the green and digital transitions, and refer to the RRF as inducing structural transformation in the context of these transitions, they lack focus and specificity on 'green' economic policy-making.[121] For the ECB to derive guidance from EU policy makers, clarity of language and specificity of measures expected would be helpful.[122]

Despite this lack of specificity, the ECB has shown its willingness to underpin EU politicians' economic policy decision-making. Its newly introduced Transmission Protection Instrument (TPI) may be activated depending on the pursuit of 'sound and sustainable fiscal and macroeconomic policies' by the jurisdiction whose public bonds it would purchase in order 'to support the effective transmission of monetary policy'.[123] Thus, the ECB is making a monetary policy instrument supportive of the EU's fiscal and economic policy framework[124] – a clear example of application of its secondary objective.[125] **8.050**

4. Preferred Interpretation of the Secondary Objective

As set out above in section B, the ECB itself has held in the past that proper implementation of its primary mandate sufficed where its secondary objective is concerned: ensuring price stability would allow the achievement of the other objectives.[126] This approach to Article 127(1), second sentence, TFEU (since **8.051**

adaptation plans'. Although they do not relate this to the BEPGs, I consider this a useful instrument for binding national governments and, thereby, influencing regional and local governments. Klaas Lenaerts, Simone Tagliapietra and Guntram Wolf, *How can the European Union adapt to climate change while avoiding a new fault line?*, Policy Contribution Issue no 11/22, June 2022, at: www.bruegel.org/sites/default/files/2022-06/PC%2011%202022.pdf.

120 See the section below on this EU regulation.

121 And, shockingly for a document dated 5 April 2022, fail to mention the war in Ukraine as relevant for the 'surge in energy prices' (which is twice mentioned and considered 'linked to the post-lockdown adjustment process') while, again, not specifying what policy action is to be taken beyond the labour market.

122 The EU green taxonomy is a case in point: it assists the ECB in making 'green' investment choices.

123 Press Release, *The Transmission Protection Instrument*, 21 July 2022, at: www.ecb.europa.eu/press/pr/date/2022/html/ecb.pr220721~973e6e7273.en.html.

124 The ECB refers to the Excessive Deficit Procedure (Article 126 TFEU); the Excessive Imbalance Procedure (Article 121 TFEU); debt sustainability analyses by the Commission; the European Stability Mechanism; and the IMF, and to the commitments undertaken in the recovery and resilience plans for the RFF as four constituent elements for TPI eligibility of Member States' public debt to be purchased on the secondary market.

125 This was remarked by Martin Sandbu in his comments on the TPI: *The ECB reminds everyone who really has the authority*, Financial Times, 21 July 2022, at: www.ft.com/content/3f1e6cb3-1a63-412e-bb1f-a8624760fd86.

126 Yolaine Fischer, *Global warming: does the ECB mandate legally authorise a 'green monetary policy'?*, in Sustainability and Financial Markets, pp.163–98, at p.172.

given up by the ECB itself) deprives this provision of '*effet utile*' and makes it senseless as the secondary objective is read as subsumed in the primary objective.

8.052 It is submitted that, in the context of climate change, biodiversity and perhaps beyond,[127] the ECB's secondary objective and the reference to Article 3 TEU contained therein are solid bases for changing course and including climate change considerations in setting and implementing monetary policy. Even without the reference to Article 3 TEU, the clear adoption of climate change policies by the Union mandates the ECB to heed these economic policies and to adjust its monetary policy to adapt to them. Again, I recall what I wrote in 1997:[128] 'in case of such a material choice [between measures which are more and those which are less supportive of the economic policies in the EC], the [Euro-]System is to opt for measures which support the policies adopted by the Community [Union].'

8.053 The EU Climate Law is a clear signal of the course of EU economic policies for the coming decades.

5. The EU Climate Law

8.054 General economic policies in the Union now clearly reflect the intention to steer Europe towards a CO_2-free economy, even the first carbon-free[129] economy in the world. The European Climate Law[130] makes the intentions of the legislator abundantly clear.[131] Providing 'a framework for the irreversible

---

127 A case can be made for more attention to be given, in setting and implementing monetary policy, to employment or other social factors based on the reference to Article 3 TEU, or on the so-called integration provisions on consistency with other policy objectives (Articles 7–13 TFEU). As already mentioned above, this goes beyond the scope of this chapter. For the incidence of Article 11 TFEU, see section G below.

128 *The European Central Bank – Institutional Aspects*, 1997, p.189.

129 In line with Dirk Schoenmaker, the term 'carbon-free' stands for the absence of 'all greenhouse gas emissions, which include carbon dioxide (CO_2), methane (CH_4) and nitrous oxide (N_2O)'. See Dirk Schoenmaker, 'Greening monetary policy' (2021) *Climate Policy*, vol. 21, no. 4, 581–92, https://doi.org/10.1080/14693062.2020.1868392.

130 Regulation (EU) 2021/1119 of the European Parliament and of the Council of 30 June 2021 establishing the framework for achieving climate neutrality and amending Regulations (EC) No 401/2009 and (EU) 2018/1999 ('European Climate Law'), OJ L 243/1, 9.7.2021.

131 With the initiation, on 14 July 2021, of a host of implementing proposals, the European Commission has made its resolve to 'deliver the European Green Deal' crystal-clear. See, among many others, 'Fit for 55': delivering the EU's 2030 Climate Target on the way to climate neutrality, COM/2021/550 final, and proposals on land use, energy efficiency and adapting the Emissions Trading System, at: https://ec.europa.eu/info/strategy/priorities-2019-2024/european-green-deal/delivering-european-green-deal_en#documents. (See the consolidated text of Directive 2003/87/EC of the European Parliament and of the Council of 13 October 2003 establishing a system for greenhouse gas emission allowance trading within the Union and amending

and gradual reduction of anthropogenic greenhouse gas emissions by sources and enhancement of removals by sinks regulated in Union law', Article 1 reads:

> This Regulation sets out a *binding objective of climate neutrality in the Union* by 2050 in pursuit of the long-term temperature goal set out in point (a) of Article 2(1) of the Paris Agreement, and provides a framework for achieving progress in pursuit of the global adaptation goal established in Article 7 of the Paris Agreement. This Regulation also sets out *a binding Union target of a net domestic reduction in greenhouse gas emissions for 2030.* [italics added]

Article 2 is even more specific and addresses the Member States *and* the EU's institutions: **8.055**

> Climate-neutrality objective
> 1. Union-wide greenhouse gas emissions and removals regulated in Union law shall be balanced within the Union at the latest by 2050, thus reducing emissions to net zero by that date, and the Union shall aim to achieve negative emissions thereafter.
> 2. The relevant Union institutions and the Member States shall take the necessary measures at Union and national level, respectively, to enable the collective achievement of the climate-neutrality objective set out in paragraph 1, taking into account the importance of promoting both fairness and solidarity among Member States and cost-effectiveness in achieving this objective.

To this author it is clear that the ECB, with its balance sheet[132] equal to 60 per cent of the euro-area GDP,[133] is among the 'relevant' institutions addressed in this provision. **8.056**

In the light of the above, an obligation to support these policies and adapt monetary policy towards carbon neutrality can be derived from the ECB's secondary objective. There is no compelling reason for the ECB to avoid a judgment on environmental, social and governance (ESG) performance and transition preparedness in pursuing a green monetary policy as Schoenmaker posits, based on the need to avoid 'specific policies on the environment'. I consider such specific involvement of central bankers in choosing between 'green' and 'non-green' a valid mechanism for realising the mandate as contained in the secondary objective, not a steering of monetary policy towards a specific policy. **8.057**

Council Directive 96/61/EC , OJ L 275/32, 25.10.2003, at: https://eur-lex.europa.eu/legal-content/EN/TXT/?uri=CELEX%3A02003L0087-20210101.

132 See https://thetradable.com/charts/european-central-bank-balance-sheet-is-equal-to-64-of-eurozone-gdp.

133 And its central role in banking supervision: see below.

8.058 Rather, as the central bank for the euro area which is clearly steering towards a carbon-free economy, the ECB is expected to serve the general economic policies adopted; this may well encompass making value judgements, naturally based on adequate research and appropriate reasoning (motivation); requirements which also derive from the case law on the discretion Union institutions have in complex economic assessments.[134]

8.059 The reference to the objectives of the Union enshrined in Article 3 TEU make this obligation only more strict, as will be explained in the next section.

BOX 8.1 TREATY PROVISIONS RELATING TO THE ECB'S MANDATE IN THE CONTEXT OF CLIMATE CHANGE [RELEVANT ELEMENTS UNDERLINED][135]

Article 127(1) TFEU

The primary objective of the European System of Central Banks (hereinafter referred to as 'the ESCB') shall be to maintain price stability. Without prejudice to the objective of price stability, the ESCB shall support the general economic policies in the Union with a view to contributing to the achievement of the objectives of the Union as laid down in Article 3 of the Treaty on European Union. The ESCB shall act in accordance with the principle of an open market economy with free competition, favouring an efficient allocation of resources, and in compliance with the principles set out in Article 119.

Article 11 TFEU

Environmental protection requirements must be integrated into the definition and implementation of the Union's policies and activities, in particular with a view to promoting sustainable development.

Article 3 TEU

1. The Union's aim is to promote peace, its values and the well-being of its peoples.[136]

---

134 See paragraph 69 of the judgment of 16 June 2015 in Case C-62/14 (*Peter Gauweiler and Others v Deutscher Bundestag*), ECLI:EU:C:2015:400: 'Nevertheless, where an EU institution enjoys broad discretion, a review of compliance with certain procedural guarantees is of fundamental importance. Those guarantees include the obligation for the ESCB to examine carefully and impartially all the relevant elements of the situation in question and to give an adequate statement of the reasons for its decisions', with references to the discretion of the EU legislature in areas of environmental policy(!): judgments in *Afton Chemical*, C-343/09, EU:C:2010:419, paragraph 28, and *Billerud Karlsborg and Billerud Skärblacka*, C-203/12, EU:C:2013:664, paragraph 35.

135 Reproduced from my study 'SSM and the SRB accountability at European level: room for improvements?' Banking Union, prepared for European Parliament's Economic Governance Support Unit (EGOV), April 2020, at: www.europarl.europa.eu/RegData/etudes/STUD/2020/645726/IPOL_STU(2020)645726_EN.pdf.

136 Protection against climate change would contribute to the well-being of Europeans.

2. […]
3. The Union shall establish an internal market. It shall work for the sustainable development of Europe based on balanced economic growth and price stability, a highly competitive social market economy, aiming at full employment and social progress, and a high level of protection and improvement of the quality of the environment. It shall promote scientific and technological advance. It shall combat social exclusion and discrimination, and shall promote social justice and protection, equality between women and men, solidarity between generations and protection of the rights of the child.[137] […]
4. The Union shall establish an economic and monetary union whose currency is the euro.
5. In its relations with the wider world, the Union shall uphold and promote its values and interests and contribute to the protection of its citizens. It shall contribute to peace, security, the sustainable development of the Earth, solidarity and mutual respect among peoples, free and fair trade, eradication of poverty and the protection of human rights, in particular the rights of the child,[138] as well as to the strict observance and the development of international law, including respect for the principles of the United Nations Charter.
6. The Union shall pursue its objectives by appropriate means commensurate with the competences which are conferred upon it in the Treaties.

F. CONTRIBUTION TO THE OBJECTIVES OF THE UNION

The indirect reference to the Union's ultimate objectives in the mandate of the ECB provides an eloquent case for including climate change and biodiversity in the ECB's remit. A number of these objectives are clearly connected to the challenges of climate change. The Union strives for 'the *sustainable development of Europe* based on *balanced economic growth* and price stability';[139] both the element of 'sustainability' and the 'balance' in the growth objective are evident indications of the relevance of climate change related issues. Similarly, '*a high level of protection and improvement of the quality of the environment*'[140] is a clear indication of the 'green' objectives the Union seeks to achieve – again an obvious indication for the ECB to observe this aspect in pursuing monetary policy.[141] **8.060**

137 Future generations will bear the brunt of climate change, so solidarity with our offspring is imperative.

138 Human rights include the right to life (Article 2) and environmental protection (Article 37) under the Charter of Fundamental Rights of the European Union ('EU Charter').

139 Article 3(3), second sentence, TEU (italics added).

140 Article 3(3), second sentence, TEU (italics added).

141 A strong plea for honouring its secondary mandate, arguing – as I do – that the ECB is legally required to incorporate climate change considerations into its monetary policy framework, came from Martin Sandbu: *The ECB should follow the Fed's embrace of a second mandate*, Financial Times, 31 August 2020, at: www.ft.com/content/380e6290-ded1-4050-aa5f-9c3d1b9ed2bd.

8.061 Two elements of the EU's objectives relate to intergenerational issues, which climate change clearly is – if the present generation in charge does not take adequate action it may be too late for the next generation to save the world as we know it, or even to sustain human habitation across the globe. The Union strives for '*solidarity between generations and protection of the rights of the child*'[142] and, in the context of 'its relations with the wider world', it is 'to contribute to [...] *the protection of human rights, in particular the rights of the child*'.[143] Even though the latter objective was situated by the Treaty authors in the global context, it may be assumed that the protection of human rights, which include social and economic rights,[144] is also intended to address those of its own citizens. Furthermore, the interests of European citizens and those of other jurisdictions coincide when it comes to combating climate change[145] so that addressing human rights in the context of extra-Union situations still underscores the relevance of taking climate change into account for the central bank. Again, a reference to children is a clear indication of the forward-looking, inter-generational approach of the Treaty when it comes to the Union's objectives. I take these references as clearly validating taking into account climate change in the conduct of monetary policy. This also holds true for the objective of 'contribut[ing] to the *protection of its citizens*',[146] which must be understood as encompassing their right to life and to development[147] – aspects which are seriously threatened by climate change. It is '*the sustainable development of the Earth*'[148] which most obviously concerns a global issue such as climate change. Because the ECB's mandate indirectly refers to this objective as well, there is no doubt in my mind that there is an obligation to support policies that help to preserve the Earth, and to adopt policies in the ECB's own fields of competence that help the Earth to develop in a sustainable manner. A final reference is of a legal nature: 'the strict observance and *the development of international law*, including respect for the principles of the United Nations Charter'[149] would seem to imply that the Union will uphold its obligations under the Paris Agreement and any other international agreement in the area of climate

---

142 Article 3(3), fourth sentence, TEU (italics added).

143 Article 3(5), second sentence, TEU (italics added).

144 Article 34 EU Charter.

145 Even though one evidently has to admit that the effects of climate change will affect inhabitants of jurisdictions with less economic development more harshly and will affect the poor worse than the rich. Also, inhabitants of unprotected low-lying jurisdictions, such as several Pacific Ocean islands, Bangladesh or the Maldives, are more at risk than those of geographically higher-situated, or better protected, human beings.

146 Article 3(5), first sentence, TEU (italics added).

147 Article 2 EU Charter.

148 Mentioned as an objective of the Union in Article 3(5), second sentence, TEU (italics added).

149 Article 3(5), second sentence, final words, TEU (italics added).

change and biodiversity,[150] and that, consequently, the ECB has to abide by these as well. This argument is a prelude to the reasoning in respect of Article 216(2) TFEU, to be expounded in section H.

G. INTEGRATION PROVISIONS

1. The Incidence of Article 11 TFEU (Integration Provision relating to Environmental Protection)

Even though, on the basis of the reasoning set out above, I conclude that the ECB has a clear mandate to green its monetary policy (and remember: the reasoning followed here also applies to other fields of competence, subject to their specificities, as it is only for the sake of easy reading that these sections focus on monetary policy), it is worthwhile to further explore additional arguments. One such argument, which has been strongly made by Javier Solana,[151] is the incidence of Article 11 TFEU on the environment.[152] **8.062**

Article 11 reads as follows: 'Environmental protection requirements must be integrated into the definition and implementation of the Union's policies and activities, in particular with a view to promoting sustainable development.' The provision forms part of a Title[153] in the Treaty that instructs the Union to be consistent in its policies and activities (Article 7), highlighting six aspects which need to be observed: equal treatment, especially between men and women (Article 8); employment and social aspects (Article 9); non-discrimination (Article 10); environmental protection (Article 11); consumer protection (Article 12); and animal welfare (Article 13).[154] **8.063**

---

150 UN Framework Convention on Climate Change; UN Convention on Biological Diversity; Council Directive 92/43/EEC Habitats Directive (Council Directive 92/43/EEC of 21 May 1992 on the conservation of natural habitats and of wild fauna and flora); European Parliament and Council Directive 2009/147/EC Birds Directive (Directive 2009/147/EC of the European Parliament and of the Council of 30 November 2009 on the conservation of wild birds, OJ L 20/7, 26.1.2010); the Convention on International Trade in Endangered Species of Wild Fauna and Flora; the Bonn Convention on Migratory Species (CMS); the Bern Convention on the Conservation of European Wildlife and Natural Habitats (www .coe .int/ en/ web/ conventions/full-list/-/conventions/treaty/104?module=treaty-detail&treatynum=104).

151 Javier Solana, 'The power of the Eurosystem to promote environmental protection' (2019) *European Business Law Review* 30, no. 4: 547–76.

152 The use of the term 'environment' reveals a perception of reality as humans standing aloof from, rather than being part of, a whole including nature.

153 Title II (Provisions having general application) of Part One (Principles) of the TFEU.

154 The remaining provisions of this Title concern services of general economic interest (Article 14), transparent governance (Article 15), data protection and privacy (Article 16) and respect for religious and non-confessional organizations (Article 17).

8.064 As a 'horizontal' or 'cross-sectional' clause, Article 11 intends to ensure that environmental concerns are integrated in all policies, which must include monetary policy. Moreover, the reference to 'sustainable development' in Article 11 may be taken to include the Sustainable Development Goals (SDGs).[155]

8.065 The SDGs are objectives for the achievement by 2030 of a global society in which hunger and extreme poverty have been eradicated; adequate health and quality education, clean water and sanitation, affordable clean energy and decent work are available; climate action is undertaken; gender discrimination has ended; and good governance is provided. The 17 goals have been adopted in a Resolution of the General Assembly of the United Nations (UNGA).[156] As a UNSG resolution is not a legally binding instrument, the SDGs derive their power from the vision of a better world for all and should inspire public authorities, private actors and non-governmental organizations (NGOs) alike. As it is written on a UN website: 'While the Global Goals are not legally binding, governments are expected to take ownership and establish national frameworks for the achievement of the 17 Goals.'[157] Because of their interdependency, the SDGs provide a fitting framework for a sustainable and equitable world.

2. General Consistency Clause (*Article 7*)

8.066 Beyond the specific instruction contained in Article 11 TFEU, the general consistency clause of Article 7 TFEU, which instructs the EU to 'ensure consistency between its policies and activities',[158] is a strong argument for the ECB to ensure its policies and activities are congruent with those of the EU at large,

155 A statement on the European Commission's website ('We are committed to implement the SDGs in all our policies and encourage EU countries in doing the same'), at https://ec.europa.eu/international-partnerships/sustainable-development-goals_en, may not be legally convincing but is an indication of the commitment by the EU's executive to the SDGs.

156 *Transforming our world: the 2030 Agenda for Sustainable Development*, Resolution A/RES/70/1, adopted on 25 September 2015; see: https://sustainabledevelopment.un.org/index.php?page=view&type=111&nr=8496&menu=35.

157 At: www.globalgoals.org/faq.

158 Fischer argues that 'specific attention must also be given to Article 7 TFEU': Yolaine Fischer, *Global warming: does the ECB mandate legally authorise a 'green monetary policy'?*, in Sustainability and Financial Markets, at p.173.

where the Commission,[159] the Parliament[160] and the European Council[161] have endorsed the Green Deal and the transition towards a carbon-free economy by 2050.

3. Application to the CSPP

Solana's contribution emphasizes the Corporate Sector Purchasing Programme (CSPP), part of the ECB's Asset Purchasing Programme (APP). Solana's central question is formulated as follows: 'The indirect effect that the CSPP is having on climate change raises an evident question: is the Eurosystem bound by an obligation to protect the environment?' Relying on case law in respect of the integration principle for environmental protection in other fields,[162] Solana convincingly argues[163] that the ECB, in devising monetary policy, must likewise adhere to Article 11, while correctly conceding that 'absolute priority of environmental protection would be untenable'.[164] He argues that 'failure to comply with [Article 11 TFEU] could raise serious doubts about the validity of monetary policy measures',[165] although he expects a 'lenient standard of compliance with Art. 11 TFEU' should the CJEU be confronted with a ques- **8.067**

159 See footnote 47 above.

160 See the references to 'the impact of climate change on inflation dynamics and transmission risks in monetary policy' and to 'the ECB, as a European institution, [being] bound by the Paris Agreement' and the '[calls] on the ECB to align its collateral framework with climate change-related risks and to disclose its level of alignment with the Paris Agreement, as well as examining such alignment in the banking sector' and 'for a proactive and qualitative risk management approach which integrates climate change-related systemic risks' in the European Parliament's resolution of 10 February 2021 on the European Central Bank – annual report 2020; at: www.europarl.europa.eu/doceo/document/TA-9-2021-0039_EN.html.

161 See the European Council conclusions of 20 June 2019, at: www.consilium.europa.eu/media/39922/20-21-euco-final-conclusions-en.pdf. Notable quotes: 'The EU can and must lead the way, by engaging in an in-depth transformation of its own economy and society to achieve climate neutrality' and 'to ensure a transition to a climate-neutral EU in line with the Paris Agreement' and 'The EU and its Member States remain committed to scaling up the mobilisation of international climate finance from a wide variety of private and public sources'. The European Council conclusions of 12 December 2019 stated: 'the European Council endorses the objective of achieving a climate-neutral EU by 2050, in line with the objectives of the Paris Agreement' (with Poland resisting this conclusion); see: www.consilium.europa.eu/media/41768/12-euco-final-conclusions-en.pdf. The 11–12 December 2020 European Council conclusions were even more explicit: 'To meet the objective of a climate-neutral EU by 2050 in line with the objectives of the Paris Agreement, the EU needs to increase its ambition for the coming decade and update its climate and energy policy framework. To that end, the European Council endorses a binding EU target of a net domestic reduction of at least 55% in greenhouse gas emissions by 2030 compared to 1990. It calls on the co-legislators to reflect this new target in the European Climate Law proposal and to adopt the latter swiftly'; see: www.consilium.europa.eu/media/47296/1011-12-20-euco-conclusions-en.pdf.

162 Solana mentions the common agricultural policy, the common transport policy, the internal market and the common commercial policy.

163 Solana, p.558.

164 Solana, p.559.

165 Solana, p.549.

tion about the legality of monetary policy measure in the context of Article 11 TFEU.[166]

8.068 The value of Javier Solana's contribution lies in his insistence that the Eurosystem 'take into account horizontal objectives of environmental protection when designing and implementing the policy measures that aim at its primary objective of price stability', in what he calls 'the procedural obligation laid down in Art. 11 TFEU' beyond the 'substantive dimension' of the provision. Moreover, by citing rather formalistic answers by ECB President Mario Draghi to questions on the environmentally adverse effects of the CSPP,[167] Solana drew attention to the lack of engagement on the issue of climate change that appeared in Frankfurt as recently as 2017. How times have changed.

4. Integration Provisions: My Approach

8.069 My own approach to Article 11 TFEU in relation to the mandate of the ECB is that, even if there were no convincing arguments derived from the primary mandate, or from the secondary mandate and the references to the Union's ulterior objectives (which there are plenty, as argued above), Article 11 TFEU clearly obliges the European Union's central bank to take the environment seriously into account when devising monetary policy.[168] This obligation concerns the *procedural* steps towards devising monetary policy (that is, research, options of measures, and so on) *and* the *substantive* contribution to environmental protection: whenever price stability may be maintained in manners conducive to protection of the environment, the opportunity to adopt such 'green' measures may not be foregone.

BOX 8.2 TREATY INTEGRATION PROVISIONS[169]

Article 7 TFEU

The Union shall ensure consistency between its policies and activities, taking all of its objectives into account and in accordance with the principle of conferral of powers.

Article 8 TFEU

166 Solana, p.561.

167 See the Committee on Economic and Monetary Affairs, 'Transcript of the Monetary Dialogue with Mario Draghi, President of the ECB, Held on 25 September 2017', p.11 at: www.ecb.europa.eu/press/key/date/2017/html/ecb.sp170925_2_transcript.en.pdf.

168 This is also supported by the general consistency clause of Article 7 TFEU.

169 Provisions of the Treaty on European Union and the Treaty on the Functioning of the European Union.

In all its activities, the Union shall aim to eliminate inequalities, and to promote equality, between men and women.

Article 9 TEU

In defining and implementing its policies and activities, the Union shall take into account requirements linked to the promotion of a high level of employment, the guarantee of adequate social protection, the fight against social exclusion, and a high level of education, training and protection of human health.

Article 10 TEU

In defining and implementing its policies and activities, the Union shall aim to combat discrimination based on sex, racial or ethnic origin, religion or belief, disability, age or sexual orientation.

Article 11 TEU

Environmental protection requirements must be integrated into the definition and implementation of the Union's policies and activities, in particular with a view to promoting sustainable development.

H. APPLICATION OF ARTICLE 216(2) TFEU: BINDING THE ECB TO 'PARIS'

A further argument to consider 'greening' of the ECB's activities legally imperative derives from Article 216(2) TFEU. This provides that '[a]greements concluded by the Union are binding upon the institutions of the Union and on its Member States'. With the EU a signatory to the Paris Agreement, which is has ratified,[170] the 2016 convention binds all EU institutions, including the ECB. Without elaborating on the scope and nature of the Paris Agreement,[171] it is useful to recall its objective, as set out in Article 2(1): **8.070**

(a) Holding the increase in the global average temperature to well below 2 °C above pre-industrial levels and pursuing efforts to limit the temperature increase to 1,5 °C above pre-industrial levels, recognizing that this would significantly reduce the risks and impacts of climate change;

(b) Increasing the ability to adapt to the adverse impacts of climate change and foster climate resilience and low greenhouse gas emissions development, in a manner that does not threaten food production; and

170 See n 21.

171 On which others have contributed widely: see Jennifer,Jacquet and Dale Jamieson, 'Soft but significant power in the Paris Agreement' (2016) *Nature Climate Change*, vol. 6, no. 7, 643–6 and Kayla Clark, 'The Paris Agreement: its role in international law and American jurisprudence' (2018) *Notre Dame J. Int'l Comp. L.* vol. 8, 107.

(c) Making finance flows consistent with a pathway towards low greenhouse gas emissions and climate-resilient development.

8.071 In the context of finance, the following provision[172] seems of particular relevance:

> 3. As part of a global effort, developed country Parties should continue to take the lead in mobilizing climate finance from a wide variety of sources, instruments and channels, noting the significant role of public funds, through a variety of actions, including supporting country-driven strategies, and taking into account the needs and priorities of developing country Parties. Such mobilization of climate finance should represent a progression beyond previous efforts.' [underlining added, RS]

8.072 As an EU institution, the ECB should ensure that, in implementing its mandate in an independent fashion, its activities are in line with the EU's global commitments to 'reduce the risks and impacts of climate change' and help 'mobilis[e] climate finance'. Since Eurosystem financing (of banks, also to support their role in providing credit to the real economy) can be characterised as 'public funds', Article 9(3) of the Paris Agreement may be considered to be addressed to the euro area's central banks.

8.073 In the context of Article 216 TFEU, it may be recalled that the European Parliament has reminded the ECB on several occasions of its being bound by the Paris Agreement. It did so in its reports on the ECB's annual reports for 2017,[173] 2018,[174] 2019[175] and 2020.[176] In its feedback to the European Parliament on the resolution on its 2018 annual report, the ECB explained

---

172 Article 9(3) Paris Agreement.

173 Paragraph 25 of the European Parliament resolution of 16 January 2019 on the ECB Annual Report 2017 (2018/2101(INI)) reads as follows: '25. Recalls that the ECB as an EU institution is bound by the Paris agreement; invites the ECB, in full respect of its mandate, its independence and the risk management framework, to integrate the commitment to the Paris agreement and economic, social and governance principles (ESG principles) into its policies.' Available at: www.europarl.europa.eu/doceo/document/TA-8-2019-0029_EN.html.

174 Paragraph 19 of the European Parliament resolution of 12 February 2020 on the European Central Bank Annual Report for 2018 (2019/2129(INI)) reads as follows: '19. Recalls that, as an EU institution, the ECB is bound by the Paris Agreement on climate change and that this should be reflected in its policies, while fully respecting its mandate and its independence; welcomes the emergence of a discussion about the role of central banks and supervisors in supporting the fight against climate change; calls on the ECB to implement the environmental, social and governance principles (ESG principles) into its policies, while fully respecting its mandate and its independence.' Available at: www.europarl.europa.eu/doceo/document/TA-9-2020-0034_EN.html.

175 European Parliament resolution of 10 February 2021 on the European Central Bank Annual Report 2020 [what is meant is 2019], at: www.europarl.europa.eu/doceo/document/A-9-2021-0002_EN.html#title1.

176 Paragraph 22 of the European Parliament resolution of 16 February 2022 on the European Central Bank – annual report 2021 (2021/2063(INI), at: www.europarl.europa.eu/doceo/document/TA-9-2022-0029_EN.html.

how it takes climate change into account.[177] After first pointing at the measures governments can take – they are said to have 'a broad spectrum of policy options available to them to tackle climate change, including carbon pricing through fiscal measures' – the ECB acknowledges that central banks can 'support and complement the collective endeavour of governments by focusing on their areas of competence'. It specifies that, in the monetary policy review, 'the ECB will closely examine the risks that climate change poses to the conduct of monetary policy and how climate change considerations can be included in the Eurosystem's monetary policy framework'; mentions[178] that it is 'already contributing to the transition to a low-carbon economy' by holding 20 per cent of the 'eligible green bond universe' under its corporate bond purchasing programme, the CSPP;[179] announces that its micro- and macroprudential frameworks may incorporate climate-related risks; and recalls further involvement. This includes membership of the NGFS and technical input into the work of the Technical Expert Group on Sustainable Finance[180] which assisted the European Commission in the development of an EU Taxonomy for green finance. Furthermore, the ECB stated that it was 'exploring how to further incorporate climate change concerns in its own operations' (staff pension fund portfolio,[181] own funds portfolio[182]) and that it was 'stepping up its analytical and research capabilities on climate change'. Two years later, in feedback to the European Parliament's resolution on the ECB Annual Report 2019,[183] the ECB set out the many steps it had undertaken (inauguration of

177 ECB, Feedback on the input provided by the European Parliament as part of its resolution on the ECB Annual Report 2018, 7 May 2020 at: www.ecb.europa.eu/pub/pdf/other/ecb.20200507_feedback_on_the_input_provided_by_the_european_parliament~4d3f01294d.en.pdf.

178 Adding 'following the principle of market neutrality', on which more below.

179 On the green bonds purchases by the Eurosystem under the CSPP, see *Purchases of green bonds under the Eurosystem's asset purchase programme*, prepared by Roberto A. De Santis, Katja Hettler, Madelaine Roos and Fabio Tamburrini and published as part of the ECB Economic Bulletin, Issue 7/2018, at: www.ecb.europa.eu/pub/economic-bulletin/focus/2018/html/ecb.ebbox201807_01.en.html. See also FAQ on sustainability-linked bonds, at: www.ecb.europa.eu/paym/coll/standards/marketable/html/ecb.slb-qa.en.html.

180 See https://ec.europa.eu/info/publications/sustainable-finance-technical-expert-group_en.

181 Which works with 'a selective exclusion list' and whose investment managers as 'signatories of the United Nations Principles for Responsible Investment must apply proxy voting guidelines incorporating environmental, social and governance considerations'. On the UNPRI, see: www.unpri.org/pri/.

182 Where 'the ECB is investigating if and how climate-related considerations can be integrated'.

183 The relevant paragraphs in the European Parliament's resolution of 10 February 2021 on the European Central Bank Annual Report 2020 (2020/2123(INI)) read as follows: 'Actions against climate change [...] 18. Notes, respecting the independence of the ECB, the impact of climate change on inflation dynamics and transmission risks in monetary policy; recalls the impact of the ECB in maintaining price stability; recalls that the ECB, as a European institution, is bound by the Paris Agreement; [...] 19. Takes note of President Lagarde's commitment to examine climate-friendly changes to ECB's operations and 'to explore every avenue available in order to combat climate change'; calls on the ECB to align its collateral framework with climate change-related risks and to disclose its level of alignment with the Paris Agreement, as well as examining such alignment in the banking sector; [...] 20. Welcomes the fact that the purchases of green bonds and their share of the ECB's portfolio continue to increase; [...] 21. Encourages efforts to increase research capabilities

the climate change centre, acceptance of certain sustainability-linked bonds as collateral and for asset purchases, the announcement of annual climate-related disclosures for Eurosystem euro-denominated non-monetary policy portfolios, incorporating environmental standards in the own funds and pension fund portfolios, integrating climate risk into stress-testing, publication of the *Guide on Climate-related and Environmental Risks*) and mentioned the monetary policy strategy review in which it was 'assessing further steps'.[184]

8.074 In the context of the binding nature of international agreements, it should be recalled that such norms are also in existence, or in preparation, for biodiversity. The 1993 Convention on Biological Diversity,[185] ratified by the European Union,[186] was scheduled to be followed with a convention in 2022 at the Kunming Biodiversity Conference, an event postponed four times due to the Covid pandemic;[187] the 15th UN biodiversity conference (COP15) was held in December 2022 in Montreal, Canada. In a resolution[188] of January 2020, the European Parliament called for this follow-up agreement to contain 'legally binding targets'. The EU's own Biodiversity Strategy[189] for 2030 is part of the European Green Deal, which shows the close connection between the climate change and biodiversity objectives.

I. OPEN MARKET ECONOMY PRINCIPLE

1. The Open Market Principle: A Novelty in EU Law

8.075 The 'principle of an open market economy with free competition, favouring an efficient allocation of resources' was inserted into primary EU law as guiding

---

regarding the impact of climate change on financial stability and the euro area.' See www.europarl.europa.eu/doceo/document/A-9-2021-0002_EN.html#title1.

184 ECB, Feedback on the input provided by the European Parliament as part of its resolution on the ECB Annual Report 2019, 14 April 2021, at: www.ecb.europa.eu/pub/pdf/other/ecb.20210414_feedback_on_the_input_provided_by_the_european_parliament~7d4de6f4c2.en.pdf.

185 OJ L 309/3, 13.12.1993, ELI: http://data.europa.eu/eli/convention/1993/626/oj. See, also: www.cbd.int/doc/legal/cbd-en.pdf.

186 See www.cbd.int/information/parties.shtml.

187 See https://en.wikipedia.org/wiki/2022_Kunming_Biodiversity_Conference.

188 European Parliament resolution of 16 January 2020 on the 15th meeting of the Conference of Parties (COP15) to the Convention on Biological Diversity, at: www.europarl.europa.eu/doceo/document/TA-9-2020-0015_EN.pdf. Parliament 'calls on the Commission and the Member States to strengthen the implementation mechanisms of the CBD and to actively pursue the development of ambitious legally binding targets, detailed timelines, clear performance indicators, tracking instruments and peer review/reporting mechanisms based on common standards – ideally in cooperation with sub-national governments – to ensure full transparency and accountability for the Parties and the overall effectiveness of the next Global Biodiversity Strategy plan'.

189 See https://ec.europa.eu/environment/strategy/biodiversity-strategy-2030_en.

the functioning of EMU. The injunction can be found in Article 119(1) and (2) TFEU and thus includes the economic union 'pillar' of EMU, to which the first paragraph is devoted just as much as the monetary 'pillar' which the second paragraph of Article 119 specifies. The principle is mentioned twice, and ahead of Article 119(3), where the 'guiding principles' for the entire enterprise are specified.[190] The principle of an open market economy is repeated[191] in the second sentence of Article 127(1) TFEU, where the ESCB specifically is addressed: 'The ESCB shall act in accordance with the principle of an open market economy with free competition, favouring an efficient allocation of resources, and in compliance with the principles set out in Article 119.'

The principle has been reformulated from the draft that the Committee of Governors had proposed[192] which was a mere injunction 'to act consistently with free and competitive markets'.[193] Even though the insertion of the open market principle was an innovation and an explicit confirmation that the EEC project was one of free markets, as many had held before the Maastricht Treaty[194] specified so, this principle is not an effective hindrance to a 'green' tilt of the Eurosystem's activities, as will be explained below. At the outset of EMU, I wrote that '[t]his admonition may make it difficult for the ESCB to adopt monetary control measures which are contrary to free competition between financial institutions or which contain an element of subsidy'.[195] The Eurosystem should endeavour to avoid measures which evidently count as a subsidy provided to one market participant over another, or to one clearly delineated class of market participants over a competing category. In this perspective, the principle seeks to extend to the financial sector's engagements with the central bank the prohibition of state aid (Article 107 TFEU). The principle cannot be read as requiring the central bank to treat all classes of assets similarly: distinctions on the basis of creditworthiness are a clear example of permitted differentiation between assets and, hence, issuers. This already indicates that taking the risks ensuing from climate change into **8.076**

190 The guiding principles are: stable prices; sound public finances and monetary conditions; and a sustainable balance of payments.

191 The TEU, in Article 3(3), also refers to 'a highly competitive social market economy' in the context of the internal market. This paragraph mentions this objective as one of many; it contains – in the same sentence – other objectives including 'a high level of protection and improvement of the quality of the environment'.

192 See the draft statute and the accompanying commentary of 16 November 1990, at: www.ecb.europa.eu/ecb/access_to_documents/document/cog_pubaccess/shared/data/ecb.dr.parcg2019_0109draftstatute19901115.en.pdf?2a924dc4462ce1045313d1acd5d00949.

193 *The European Central Bank – Institutional Aspects*, 1997, p.181.

194 The Treaty of Maastricht established the European Union and amended the Treaty establishing the European Economic Community (EEC Treaty), inter alia with provisions on EMU.

195 *The European Central Bank – Institutional Aspects*, 1997, p.191.

account in distinguishing between assets does not infringe the principle of an open market economy.

2. Market Neutrality Argument

8.077 Yet, an often-cited rebuke to calls for the ECB to include climate change considerations in its non-standard monetary policy measures is that this would run counter to the principle of market neutrality. The ECB itself, in its response to the European Parliament in the context of its accountability vis-à-vis Europe's parliamentarians, recalls the principle of market neutrality.[196] Often, reference is made to the principle of an open market economy favouring an efficient allocation of resources that was, as indicated, introduced when the EMU provisions were adopted in the Treaty of Maastricht. These two principles, although closely related, should be distinguished. The first (market neutrality)[197] is a self-imposed rule that central banks apply to their operations, whereas the second is a public law injunction to the European central banking system. Moreover, as will be argued below, the second rule does not stand in opposition to an interpretation of the ECB's mandate as requiring it to actively operate in a manner which helps diminish climate change and loss of biodiversity.

8.078 As early as 2006, the ECB announced that, in its portfolio operations, it would follow the market neutrality principle.[198] In an exposé on managing its foreign reserves, own funds and pension fund portfolios, the ECB stated: 'The ECB's portfolio management activities are subject to strict rules which ensure market neutrality, ethical behaviour and a strict separation between portfolio management and policy-making', explaining 'market neutrality' as follows: '[The ECB] endeavours, in its portfolio management activities, not to cause any undue distortion in market prices. In practice, this means that the ECB's portfolio management activities are only conducted in markets that are deep and liquid enough to ensure that portfolio management transactions are easily absorbed at market-determined prices.'[199]

---

196 See the ECB, Feedback on the input provided by the European Parliament as part of its resolution on the ECB Annual Report 2018, n 177.

197 See Jens van 't Klooster, *The Myth of Market Neutrality: A Comparative Study of the European Central Bank's and the Swiss National Bank's Corporate Security Purchases*, DOI: https://doi.org/10.1080/13563467.2019.1657077, 18 September 2020.

198 Portfolio management at the ECB, Monthly Bulletin April 2006, at: www.ecb.europa.eu/pub/pdf/other/pp75-86_mb200604en.pdf?b9a17c47ba3fa4e5313bc0b8345d3a1e.

199 Ibid.

In explaining its CSPP, the ECB also explained its adherence to 'market neutrality', again with reference to the principle of an open market economy.[200] More generally, for all the asset purchasing programmes, the ECB confesses that it 'adheres to the principle of market neutrality'.[201] **8.079**

The 'principle of market neutrality' is only a rule when emanating from the ECB itself, as can be read in its Guideline on NCBs' asset and liabilities management.[202] Although the ECB has presented 'market neutrality' as the operational concept which serves the principle of an open market economy,[203] it is submitted that there is no legal requirement to operate market neutrality under the Treaty-given principle. **8.080**

3. Open Market Principle Does Not Require ECB to Act in Line with Dysfunctional Markets

First and foremost, the principle of an open market economy does not oblige the ECB to act in conformity with markets that are dysfunctional. The additional words 'favouring an effective allocation of resources' in the injunction to follow the market-conformity principle make clear what the Treaty authors intended: they had in mind that monetary policy should not undermine freely functioning markets to bring about an efficient allocation of resources. After all, that's what free markets are supposed to do: ensure that resources are allocated through the price mechanism resulting from demand and supply in **8.081**

---

200 The ECB's corporate sector purchase programme: its implementation and impact, in: ECB Economic Bulletin, Issue 4/2017, at: www.ecb.europa.eu/pub/pdf/ecbu/eb201704.en.pdf. The reasoning is as follows: 'In pursuing its objective of maintaining price stability, the ECB is mandated to act in accordance with the principle of an open market economy with free competition, favouring an efficient allocation of resources. Consequently, the ECB aims for a market-neutral implementation of the APP, and therefore CSPP purchases are conducted according to a benchmark that reflects proportionally the market value of eligible bonds.'

201 See the explanation of the APP on its website: www.ecb.europa.eu/mopo/implement/omt/html/index.en.html.

202 In Guideline (EU) 2019/671 of the European Central Bank of 9 April 2019 on domestic asset and liability management operations by the national central banks (recast) (ECB/2019/7), OJ L 113/11, 29.4.2019, ELI: http://data.europa.eu/eli/guideline/2019/671/oj, the ECB imposes the following limitation on remuneration: 'The remuneration of non-monetary policy deposits other than government deposits shall take into account the principles of proportionality, market neutrality and equal treatment.' Article 4(2) Limitations on the remuneration of non-monetary policy deposits.

203 In a reply to a written question from an MEP relating to sustainability considerations, President Lagarde wrote, as recently as 21 November 2019: 'In the implementation of monetary policy, the operational concept of market neutrality has been considered the most appropriate concept to, on the one hand, ensure the effectiveness of the ECB's monetary policy measures from a price stability perspective and, on the other hand, respect the principle of an open market economy.' Letter from the ECB President to Mr Ernest Urtasun, MEP, on monetary policy, at: www.ecb.europa.eu/ecb/access_to_documents/document/correspondence/shared/data/ecb.dr.cor20191121Urtasun.en.pdf; the MEP's question (Z-045/2019) can be found here: www.europarl.europa.eu/doceo/document/ECON-QZ-641438_EN.pdf.

an as efficient manner as possible. There is widespread agreement that current market mechanisms do not lead to an efficient allocation of resources when the effects on climate change are included in the assessment. When prices do not reflect the true costs or benefits of an instrument for society as a whole, markets do not lead to Pareto efficiency. The European CO_2-emission scheme has been introduced precisely to ensure that the carbon effects of production are 'priced in'.[204] Should monetary policy adopt the outcome of current markets as a given which the central bank feels bound to accept and follow, this policy would effectively go *against* an efficient allocation of resources by prolonging the financing of 'non-green' production factors.

8.082 It is, therefore, submitted that the principle of an open market economy with free competition favouring an effective allocation of resources does not stand in the way of a 'greening' of the ECB's activities.[205] This principle is even considered to require the opposite: a recalibration of the ECB's operations to reflect a truly efficient and market-conforming outcome. Of course, this raises issues of taxonomy (which assets can be considered 'green'?) and requires an assessment that needs to be underpinned by adequate reasoning (why the central bank opts for certain operations or classes of assets rather than blindly following the current market outcomes). Such issues do not amount to an adequate rebuttal of the legal assessment that the market-conformity principle does not stand in the way of a 'greening' of operations; indeed, that it requires such greening. This author reads the principle not as *opposing* a 'greening' but as *requiring* it.

4. Bank of England on Market Neutrality

8.083 In this context it is interesting to note that another central bank seems to embrace a perspective under which its own 'market neutrality principle' operates in a novel fashion. Bank of England Governor Andrew Bailey suggested[206] becoming 'climate change consistent neutral': to distinguish between assets in their climate-related effects and then not to make a distinction among such

---

204 Directive 2003/87/EC of the European Parliament and of the Council of 13 October 2003 establishing a scheme for greenhouse gas emission allowance trading within the Community and amending Council Directive 96/61/EC [2003] OJ L275/32.

205 Contrary to the stance taken by then Bundesbank President Jens Weidmann, *How central banks should address climate change*, Financial Times, 19 November 2020, at: www.ft.com/content/ed270eb2-e5f9-4a2a-8987-41df4eb67418.

206 How to Build Back Greener after the Pandemic, Bloomberg podcast by Stephanie Flanders and Lucy Meakin, 29 October 2020, at: www.bloomberg.com/news/articles/2020-10-29/how-to-build-back-greener-after-the-pandemic. The statement was brought to my attention by a tweet from Positive Money of 29 October 2020, at: https://twitter.com/positivemoneyuk/status/1321819698007281670?s=11.

'green' assets.[207] I consider this a valid approach, also for other central banks that are (self-)bound to market neutrality.

5. Open Market Principle Not Enforceable

As a further consideration on the principle of an open market economy, it is recalled that, admittedly in another (internal market) context, the Court has ruled[208] that Articles 3a, 102a and 103 EC Treaty (currently Articles 119, 120, 126 TFEU) 'do not impose on the Member States clear and unconditional obligations which may be relied on by individuals before the national courts. What is involved is a general principle whose application calls for complex economic assessments which are a matter for the legislature or the national administration.' Yolaine Fischer, whose writing[209] drew my attention to this, also refers to the Opinion of the Advocate General[210] in this reference for a preliminary ruling on the compatibility with EU law of the French system of fixed book prices. The Advocate General opines that the articles cited are 'rather principles which, on their own, have no binding legal effect but which are to be viewed in conjunction with the other provisions of Community law which define their content more closely'[211] and concludes: 'obligations may arise for Member States only from provisions of Community law which are worded in a sufficiently specific, precise and clear manner. However, that specifically is not so in the case of the abovementioned general principles of an open market economy with free competition and economic policy.'[212] **8.084**

I agree with Fischer that this assessment of the effect of the principle of an open market economy also applies to EU institutions, such as the ECB. The ECB is free to act within its discretion in the complex economic assessments it is bound to make in pursuing its price stability mandate and carrying out its functions, having due regard to the principle without this prescribing a fixed outcome, irrespective of the circumstances the ECB faces. **8.085**

---

207 The Bank of England's vanguard role in taking climate change into consideration in its monetary and prudential policies becomes clear from its third TCFD aligned disclosure: *The Bank of England's climate-related financial disclosure 2022*, 22 June 2022, at: www.bankofengland.co.uk/prudential-regulation/publication/2022/june/the-bank-of-englands-climate-related-financial-disclosure-2022.

208 Judgment of 3 October 2000 in Case C-9/99 (*Échirolles Distribution SA* v *Association du Dauphiné and Others*), ECLI:EU:C:2000:532.

209 Yolaine Fischer, *Global warming: does the ECB mandate legally authorise a 'green monetary policy'?*, in Sustainability and Financial Markets, pp.163–98.

210 Opinion of Advocate General Alber of 6 June 2000; ECLI:EU:C:2000:299.

211 Opinion, paragraph 49.

212 Opinion, paragraph 50.

J. FURTHER ARGUMENT: EMERGENCY RATIONALE AND CLIMATE STABILITY PRECONDITIONS AS A FALLBACK

8.086 For the sake of completeness, reference should be made to other arguments that may be advanced for the conclusion that climate change and biodiversity loss are to be included in the setting of monetary policy. A first such reasoning relates to the emergency nature of the impending global disaster should climate change not be countered and halted, or biodiversity loss stopped and reversed. For the central bank of a region representing 16 per cent of global output[213] not to take climate change into account would amount to a gross neglect of its duties. This approach can be likened to the perspective taken in 2012 when the ECB, faced with widespread lack of belief in the continuity of the single currency and with actual preparations for its demise across business, acted with President Mario Draghi's famous statement in London: 'Within our mandate, the ECB is ready to do whatever it takes to preserve the euro. And believe me, it will be enough.'[214] This statement preceded the announcement of a set of monetary policy measures, announced but never implemented, that were intended to dispel market speculation on the end of the euro.[215] Faced with existential threats, this time to the continuity of society and the economy as we know it, interpreting one's mandate by stretching it to the limits may be considered justified.

8.087 A slightly different perspective is that taken by Yolaine Fischer, who argues that climate stability is a precondition for obtaining price stability,[216] or even that 'the survival of the euro is a prerequisite [for] the Eurosystem's mandate', and that 'the preservation of the existence of the euro [...] is an essential – or existential – part of the Eurosystem's primary objective, i.e. the preservation of price stability'.[217] Her argument is, essentially, that in worst-case scenarios which would unfold if no climate action is taken, there is no single currency to be the guardian of, or price stability to be maintained, as EMU may be considered at risk in economic and political upheavals triggered by climate change.

---

213 See www.statista.com/statistics/253512/share-of-the-eu-in-the-inflation-adjusted-global-gross-domestic-product/.

214 Verbatim of the remarks made by Mario Draghi, speech by Mario Draghi, President of the European Central Bank at the Global Investment Conference in London, 26 July 2012, at: www.ecb.europa.eu/press/key/date/2012/html/sp120726.en.html.

215 The so-called 'Outright Monetary Transactions (OMT); press release, Technical features of Outright Monetary Transactions, 6 September 2012, at: www.ecb.europa.eu/press/pr/date/2012/html/pr120906_1.en.html. For the currently relevant TPI, see the text accompanying n 123 above.

216 Yolaine Fischer, at p.174.

217 Yolaine Fischer, at p.177.

These additional interpretative routes, relying on 'emergency' powers, provide ammunition to the new reading of the ECB's mandate that I present here. I consider the arguments based on the primary and secondary objective, on the consistency clauses and on the binding nature of international agreements adequate for this reading without a need to rely on 'emergency' powers. **8.088**

Finally, a word on the precedence of central banking action and its appropriateness when other actors fail to act. Here, a quote from a UNEP study[218] is worth citing: **8.089**

> The case for central banks to pursue sustainability objectives beyond their traditional core mandates of maintaining monetary and financial stability can be seen as an application of the theory of the second best. If first best policies for fixing the misallocation of capital cannot be implemented, then the government may resort to a second best policy and mandate the central bank or financial supervisor to address negative environmental externalities by using the tools they have at their disposal. Thus, it is important to initially consider if other actors can adopt first best policies that make a policy engagement of the central bank redundant. If first best policies are impossible because of political deadlock or the weakness of the institutions that should pursue them, possible second best policies by other agents – including the central bank – and their potential distortions need to be considered.

In this chapter, the argument is that governments may mandate central banks to act when other (political) action fails. I would argue that this 'second-best' option may also be applicable when the mandate is already, implicitly 'green', as I have argued, and primary decision-making is inadequate. **8.090**

K. IMPLICATIONS OF THE REASONING

What does the approach to the mandate as set out above imply for monetary policy? Before going into this, a look at the EU Taxonomy is in order, since the ECB may have to rely on classification of activities as ESG-conforming. **8.091**

1. EU Taxonomy

The EU is developing a taxonomy for ESG activities and assets. Various legal acts set out the requirements for labelling items as in conformity with ESG standards. They also impose transparency requirements. This legislation is further meant to assist in avoiding 'greenwashing'. Central to these standards **8.092**

218 Ulrich Volz, *On the Role of Central Banks in Enhancing Green Finance*, Inquiry Working Paper 17/01, February 2017, at: http://unepinquiry.org/wp-content/uploads/2017/02/On_the_Role_of_Central_Banks_in_Enhancing_Green_Finance.pdf.

is the Taxonomy Regulation,[219] which defines what can count as an 'environmentally sustainable investment'. It defines environmental objectives: climate change mitigation and adaptation, the transition to a circular economy, the sustainable use and protection of water and marine resources, the transition to a circular economy, pollution prevention and control and the protection and restoration of biodiversity and ecosystems.[220] It sets out what a substantial contribution to any of these objectives entails[221] and which activities substantially harm environmental objectives.[222] Technical screening criteria will be specified in delegated acts adopted by the Commission.[223] The first of such legal acts, the EU Taxonomy Climate Delegated Act,[224] defines these criteria for economic activities substantially contributing to climate change mitigation or adaptation. The lengthy detailed descriptions,[225] not yet including the agricultural sector, require navigation, for which an EU Taxonomy Compass has been devised.[226] Further delegated acts specify elements of the taxonomy, including reporting requirements[227] and how to treat natural gas and nuclear power under the taxonomy[228] – an issue that created a lot of political discourse,[229] with court action against the Commission announced.[230]

---

219 Regulation (EU) 2020/852 of the European Parliament and of the Council of 18 June 2020 on the establishment of a framework to facilitate sustainable investment, and amending Regulation (EU) 2019/2088, OJ L 198/13, 22.6.2020.

220 Article 9, Taxonomy Regulation.

221 Articles 10–16, Taxonomy Regulation.

222 Article 17, Taxonomy Regulation.

223 Articles 19 and 23, Taxonomy Regulation.

224 Commission Delegated Regulation (EU) 2021/2139 of 4 June 2021 supplementing Regulation (EU) 2020/852 of the European Parliament and of the Council by establishing the technical screening criteria for determining the conditions under which an economic activity qualifies as contributing substantially to climate change mitigation or climate change adaptation and for determining whether that economic activity causes no significant harm to any of the other environmental objectives, [2021] OJ L442/1.

225 The delegated act contains a mere 7 pages but its annexes run to 50 pages: see https://ec.europa.eu/info/law/sustainable-finance-taxonomy-regulation-eu-2020-852/amending-and-supplementary-acts/implementing-and-delegated-acts_en.

226 See: https://ec.europa.eu/sustainable-finance-taxonomy/.

227 Commission Delegated Regulation (EU) 2021/2178 of 6 July 2021 supplementing Regulation (EU) 2020/852 of the European Parliament and of the Council by specifying the content and presentation of information to be disclosed by undertakings subject to Articles 19a or 29a of Directive 2013/34/EU concerning environmentally sustainable economic activities, and specifying the methodology to comply with that disclosure obligation, [2021] OJ L 443/9. Directive 2013/34/EU, the EU's annual statements directive ([2013] OJ L182/19), requires certain companies to publish a (consolidated) non-financial statement.

228 Commission Delegated Regulation (EU) 2022/1214 of 9 March 2022 amending Delegated Regulation (EU) 2021/2139 as regards economic activities in certain energy sectors and Delegated Regulation (EU) 2021/2178 as regards specific public disclosures for those economic activities, [2022] OJ L 188/1.

229 This legal act could have been rejected by the Council or the Parliament as co-legislators, but was not.

230 The Luxembourg Minister for Energy tweeted on 6 July 2022: 'I deeply regret that today @Europarl_EN failed to object to the delegated act under the #EUTaxonomy, allowing #gas & #nuclear to be part of the EU sustainable finance policy' and announced joint court action together with Austria against the act; see https://twitter.com/ClaudeTurmes/status/1544630232388444160.

Further main legal acts in the EU Taxonomy are the Sustainable Finance Disclosures Regulation (SFDR),[231] the Non-Financial Reporting Directive (NFRD),[232] the Benchmark Regulation[233] and the Benchmark Regulation Amendment.[234] These are all further implemented in technical standards, including by the ESAs.[235,236] The taxonomy is a sign of the implementation of the SDGs and the Paris Agreement, to which the preamble of several of the legal acts specifically refer.[237] A Corporate Sustainability Reporting Directive, proposed by the Commission and in the course of begin adopted by the Council and Parliament, extends and details sustainability reporting[238] and the Corporate Sustainability Due Diligence Directive (CSDDD).[239] **8.093**

The EU Taxonomy therefore is another clear indication of the legislative intent to 'green' the economy, to encourage the transition to a carbon-neutral economy and to re-direct financial flows to sustainable investments. This is a further clear indicator of the desirable direction of the economy in the eyes of the legislator. Also, the criteria and benchmarks resulting from the taxonomy will be guidance for the ECB when re-directing its own portfolios and activities towards sustainable finance. This is made clear in the ECB's latest reporting on its climate-related actions.[240] **8.094**

231 Regulation (EU) 2019/2088 of the European Parliament and of the Council of 27 November 2019 on sustainability-related disclosures in the financial services sector, [2019] OJ L 317/1.

232 Directive 2014/95/EU of the European Parliament and of the Council of 22 October 2014 amending Directive 2013/34/EU as regards disclosure of non-financial and diversity information by certain large undertakings and groups [2014] OJ L 330/1.

233 Regulation (EU) 2016/1011 of the European Parliament and of the Council of 8 June 2016 on indices used as benchmarks in financial instruments and financial contracts or to measure the performance of investment funds and amending Directives 2008/48/EC and 2014/17/EU and Regulation (EU) No 596/2014, [2016] OJ L 171/1; consolidated text at: https://eur-lex.europa.eu/legal-content/EN/TXT/?uri=CELEX%3A02016R1011-20191210.

234 Regulation (EU) 2019/2089 of the European Parliament and of the Council of 27 November 2019 amending Regulation (EU) 2016/1011 as regards EU Climate Transition Benchmarks, EU Paris-aligned Benchmarks and sustainability-related disclosures for benchmarks, [2019] OJ L 317/17.

235 By way of example, see EBA, ESMA, EIOPA, Final Report on draft Regulatory Technical Standards with regard to the content, methodologies and presentation of disclosures pursuant to [Articles of the SFDR], JC 2021 03, 2 February 2021, at: www.esma.europa.eu/sites/default/files/library/jc_2021_03_joint_esas_final_report_on_rts_under_sfdr.pdf.

236 See www.esma.europa.eu/policy-activities/sustainable-finance/climate-related-benchmarks.

237 See recitals 2 and 3 of the preamble to the Taxonomy Regulation, and recitals 1–3 of the SFDR.

238 Directive (EU) 2022/2464 of the European Parliament and of the Council of 14 December 2022 amending Regulation (EU) No 537/2014, Directive 2004/109/EC, Directive 2006/43/EC and Directive 2013/34/EU, as regards corporate sustainability reporting, [2022], OJ L 322/15.

239 Corporate sustainability due diligence: Council and Parliament strike deal to protect environment and human rights, press release, 14 December 2023, at: https://www.consilium.europa.eu/en/press/press-releases/2023/12/14/corporate-sustainability-due-diligence-council-and-parliament-strike-deal-to-protect-environment-and-human-rights/.

240 See the text accompanying n 305 below.

2. Taking a Longer-term Perspective?

8.095 Taking a brief look at what a new reading of the ECB's mandate might entail in the area of monetary policy,[241] the very first change to expect might be the inclusion of a longer-term perspective into the ECB's monetary policy stance. This might mean introducing into the expectations of business and households an element of long-term prediction, namely that the transition to a CO_2-free economy will be accompanied by sufficient measures on the central bank side to maintain price stability. Thus, the scenario planning that central banks and supervisors expect banks subject to their supervision to undertake is an activity that central banks must engage in themselves. The research and planning undertaken by central banks can be expected to be influenced by climate change in any reading of their mandates. A clear presentation of how climate change would affect monetary policy, in either a doom scenario or one of addressing the climate change challenge, was given by Benoît Coeuré in 2018.[242] He identified the shocks, their distribution and their persistence that would affect the devising of monetary policy, while discussing options to change course in respect of monetary policy portfolios, where his analysis shied away from a more robust interpretation of the mandate.

3. Including Climate Change Variables and Risks Into Account in Policy-Setting

8.096 Such scenario planning would then spill over from research into policy. Where transition risks and physical risks undermine the goal of price stability, one would expect the central bank to incorporate such variables in its monetary policy stance – as the ECB is doing, to be elaborated in section L below.

4. The ECB's Own Funds

8.097 A quick win in greening a central bank's activities concerns the bank's own funds, that is, its capital, and its own pension fund's investments. Provided there is a sufficiently clear taxonomy on which to base its investment decisions, the central bank can start playing its part by ensuring these are 'greened'. Again, this underscores the importance of a proper taxonomy. It is these examples that ECB President Christine Lagarde gave in her press conference

---

241 Other areas of activity will be the subject of sections below.

242 *Monetary policy and climate change,* speech by Benoît Cœuré, Member of the Executive Board of the ECB, at a conference on 'Scaling up Green Finance: The Role of Central Banks', organized by the Network for Greening the Financial System, the Deutsche Bundesbank and the Council on Economic Policies, Berlin, 8 November 2018, at: www.ecb.europa.eu/press/key/date/2018/html/ecb.sp181108.en.html.

on 23 January 2020. She referred to the ECB Pension Fund and its paid-up capital and reserves, and, furthermore, mentioned the CSPP and collateral. She also recalled the elements described in the previous section: having climate risk embedded in risk assessment, models and forecasts, and including it in the financial stability approach in the ESRB: stress-testing and pilot.[243]

5. Favouring or Requiring Green Collateral?

Ensuring that 'climate-related financial risks are given due consideration in their own risk management' is an element of greening that even long-term (former) sceptics such as Jens Weidmann favour.[244] The ESCB Statute requires lending by the Eurosystem to be effected 'based on adequate collateral' (Article 18.1, second indent, *in fine*). Thus, even without giving climate considerations the role welcomed by this author, a case can be made for working towards a system in which collateral is only acceptable if it will not be tainted by deterioration due to climate change. Accepting securities issued by industries which engage in economic activities that will become redundant, or bonds representing companies whose assets become stranded, is not a wise policy for any financial market operator. It is forbidden territory for a central banking system working under the injunction of collateral adequacy, such as the Eurosystem. Should the taxonomy for financial products be insufficient to make a distinction between 'adequate' and 'inadequate' collateral, the ECB will have to undertake its own research to establish the level of risk it can run when accepting collateral in an economy that is transitioning. An interesting suggestion by Jens Weidmann is for the Eurosystem to 'consider only purchasing securities or accepting them as collateral for monetary policy purposes if their issuers meet certain climate-related reporting obligations',[245] thus relying on adequate disclosure by the market to weigh the risk profile of its portfolio of assets purchased or of collateral accepted. A slightly different angle was already taken on this point by then-Executive Board member Benoît Coeuré in his 2018 speech on climate change and the Eurosystem,[246] where he alluded to the effect of the introduction of a green taxonomy which, 'once adopted, [would] automatically be reflected in our collateral framework. That is, once **8.098**

243 Press conference by Christine Lagarde, President of the ECB, Frankfurt am Main, 23 January 2020, at: www.ecb.europa.eu/press/pressconf/2020/html/ecb.is200123~0bc778277b.en.html. Ms Lagarde did not make mention of the Public Sector Purchasing Programme (PSPP) share for marketable debt instruments issued by international or supranational institutions located in the Euro Area, or of 'green' T-LTROs (*targeted* long-term refinancing operations, that is, 'linked to [the banks'] loans to non-financial corporations and households'.

244 The quote is from his contribution to the *Financial Times* cited in n 205.

245 This quote also is from his contribution to the *Financial Times* cited in n 205.

246 *Monetary policy and climate change*, Benoît Cœuré, cited in n 242.

markets and credit risk agencies price climate risks properly, the amount of collateralised borrowing counterparties can obtain from the ECB will be adjusted accordingly.'

8.099 Beyond its own risk measurement requirements, the obligation to support the economic policies in the Union would also provide a valid legal argument for greening collateral. In this context, mention may be made of the argument put forward during the hearing before the Committee on economic and monetary affairs of the European Parliament by Frank Elderson, as a candidate for the function of Executive Director at the ECB.[247] In his view, the mandate and the requirement of adequate collateral necessitate that climate change risk (physical risk, transition risk) are taken into account.

6. Greening Asset Purchasing Programmes

8.100 As already intimated, working towards a 'green threshold' for the purchasing of assets would be another step the central bank could take to ensure its observance of climate-related risk management and support of climate policies. Here, the same instruments that would apply for the greening of collateral can be put to good use: an adequate green taxonomy, ratings based on disclosures by financial market participants and own research into the measure of contribution to a CO_2-neutral economy or to transitioning towards such an economy. Taking the carbon intensity of assets into account in the context of monetary policy has been proposed by Dirk Schoenmaker: 'a tilting approach to steer or tilt the allocation of the Eurosystem's assets and collateral towards low-carbon sectors, which would reduce the cost of capital for these sectors relative to high-carbon sectors.'[248]

7. Greening Bank Lending: Green TLTROs?

8.101 As a final example of the kind of changes that can be brought about in the monetary policy sphere once the central banks heed their mandate in a climate change-relevant manner, Targeted Long-Term Refinancing Operations (TLTROs) may be mentioned.[249] Such operations serve to finance the banks in the euro area with the specific intention of ensuring that such financing results

247 As he then was. Public hearing on 9 November 2020, at: www.youtube.com/watch?v=CWam9__AL4Y&ab_channel=PositiveMoneyEurope. See, also, Mr Elderson's opening statement, at: www.dnb.nl/actueel/algemeen-nieuws/speeches-oud/opening-statement-by-frank-elderson-to-the-economic-and-monetary-affairs-committee-of-the-european-parliament/

248 Dirk Schoenmaker, *Greening monetary policy*, Bruegel Working Paper, Issue 02, 19 February 2019. Also available in a 6 November 2020 version at: https://papers.ssrn.com/sol3/papers.cfm?abstract_id=3242814.

249 See www.ecb.europa.eu/mopo/implement/omo/tltro/html/index.en.html.

in on-lending to the real economy (hence 'targeted'). When banks report on their on-lending activities they will receive an extra advantageous interest rate on their borrowing, in current circumstances, which will be paid by the ECB for on-lending. Greening of such operations would entail that the criteria for the ECB's subsidy are widened to include an element of sustainability: solely on-lending which supports activities that are considered 'green' or that contribute to the transition to a CO_2-free economy will be subsidized.

Such green TLTROs have been proposed by Jens van 't Klooster and Rens van Tilburg,[250] who advocate a selective approach to the ECB's refinancing of banks' lending activities, based on the EU's green taxonomy. Commercial banks should prove the taxonomy compliance of individual loans to households and firms for construction, renovation and energy-saving measures for such lending to count in the context of a Green TLTRO. The authors argue that the ECB should 'start a limited pilot programme today targeted on funding for building and renovations in accordance with the Taxonomy requirement for real estate'. **8.102**

It is clear that such a programme relies more heavily on the appraisal capacity of the ECB than on ratings of 'greenness' of securities based on the taxonomy, as here the ECB needs to validate the reporting by banks of their 'green' on-lending. Yet, this is not different *in principle* from the task it has set itself by engaging in unconventional central banking operations with TLTROs, which is based on banks reporting their on-lending to the real economy. Again, as with other greening operations, green TLTROs rely on the existence of an appropriately developed taxonomy. **8.103**

8. Greening Foreign Reserve Management

Hardly covered thus far is the issue of greening foreign reserves, whose management is one of the basic tasks of the ECB.[251] Uncharted thus far, the issue of making foreign reserves compatible with green standards seems a relevant avenue to explore.[252] **8.104**

250 Jens van 't Klooster and Rens van Tilburg, *Targeting a sustainable recovery with Green TLTROs*, September 2020 (*Positive Money Europe* & *Sustainable Finance Lab*), at: www.positivemoney.eu/wp-content/uploads/2020/09/Green-TLTROs.pdf. Note that this was written when the ECB was fighting possible deflation; targeted lending is not an instrument to combat inflation.

251 Article 127(2), third indent: 'to hold and manage the official foreign reserves of the Member States.'

252 Strong support for a wide array of climate-mitigating monetary policy instruments, including greening foreign reserve management, is expressed by Lena Boneva, Gianluigi Ferrucci and Francesco Paolo Mongelli in 'Climate change and central banks: what role for monetary policy?' *Climate Policy*, vol. 22, no. 6, 770–87 at: https://doi.org/10.1080/14693062.2022.2070119.

L. WHAT THE ECB HAS DECIDED

1. Monetary Policy Review Results: Climate Action Plan

8.105 After this already lengthy discussion of the history of the interpretation of the ECB's mandate in the context of EU policy preferences including on climate change and biodiversity loss, and of my preferred interpretation of the mandate, both primary and secondary and embedded in other Treaty provisions, it is time to have a look at the ECB's projected climate change measures, and their first year of implementation. These were announced at the end of the monetary policy review, on 8 July 2021. The press release[253] and comprehensive action plan[254] make the ECB's commitment crystal clear. The first lines read as follows:

> The ECB's Governing Council is strongly committed:

- to further incorporating climate change considerations into its monetary policy framework;
- to expanding its analytical capacity in macroeconomic modelling, statistics and monetary policy with regard to climate change;
- to including climate change considerations in monetary policy operations in the areas of disclosure, risk assessment, collateral framework and corporate sector asset purchases;
- to implementing the action plan in line with progress on the EU policies and initiatives in the field of environmental sustainability disclosure and reporting.[255]

Before elaborating on the action plan, the communiqué states that

> the Governing Council underlines its commitment to more systematically reflect environmental sustainability considerations in its monetary policy. The decision follows the conclusion of the strategy review of 2020–21, in which the reflections on climate change and environmental sustainability were of central importance.[256]

8.106 A clear reference to the political primate – 'Addressing climate change is a global challenge and a policy priority for the European Union. While governments and parliaments have the primary responsibility to act on climate

253 *ECB presents action plan to include climate change considerations in its monetary policy strategy*, press release, 8 July 2021, at: www.ecb.europa.eu/press/pr/date/2021/html/ecb.pr210708_1~f104919225.en.html.

254 Detailed roadmap of climate change-related actions, at: www.ecb.europa.eu/press/pr/date/2021/html/ecb.pr210708_1_annex~f84ab35968.en.pdf.

255 See the ECB press release of 8 July 2021.

256 Ibid.

change, within its mandate, the ECB recognises the need to further incorporate climate considerations into its policy framework'[257] – is followed by an eloquent explanation of the reasons why climate change affects price stability:

> Climate change and the transition towards a more sustainable economy affect the outlook for price stability through their impact on macroeconomic indicators such as inflation, output, employment, interest rates, investment and productivity; financial stability; and the transmission of monetary policy. Moreover, climate change and the carbon transition affect the value and the risk profile of the assets held on the Eurosystem's balance sheet, potentially leading to an undesirable accumulation of climate-related financial risks.[258]

Even the legal obligation to incorporate climate change into its policies is highlighted: 'With this action plan, the ECB will increase its contribution to addressing climate change, *in line with its obligations under the EU Treaties*'[259] (italics added). **8.107**

On the measures in the action plan, it is stated that '[t]he design of these measures will be *consistent with the price stability objective* and should take into account the implications of climate change for *an efficient allocation of resources*'[260] (italics added). This wording makes clear that price stability and the efficiency injunction will be prevalent: the two main elements of discussion on what the ECB can or must do, as set out above. **8.108**

The areas of climate change action announced by the ECB are:[261] **8.109**

1. *Macroeconomic modelling and assessment of implications for monetary policy transmission*: developing models and analyses on the impact of climate change and 'related policies'[262] on the economy and corporates and citizens.[263]
2. *Statistical data for climate change risk analyses*: developing 'experimental indicators' on 'green financial instruments and the carbon footprint of financial institutions' and the latter's exposure to physical risk. Again, this element relates to EU policy-making and legislation as the development

257 Ibid.
258 Ibid.
259 Ibid.
260 Ibid.
261 Formatting taken over from the ECB communication.
262 The policies adopted to address climate change for which governments and parliaments have the primary responsibility, as the ECB stated. Of course, these public actors include the EU's political institutions: Parliament, Council, European Council.
263 In ECB parlance: 'households and firms'.

is to be 'in line with progress on the EU policies and initiatives in the field of environmental sustainability disclosure and reporting'.

3. *Disclosures as a requirement for eligibility as collateral and asset purchases*: by 2022, the ECB is to detail plans on requiring disclosure for private assets[264] to include this 'as a new eligibility criterion or as a basis for a differentiated treatment for collateral and asset purchases'. Here, too, EU policy-making on sustainability disclosure is dominant. Also, proportionality – the crucial element in the judicial assessment of central bank measures[265] – is mentioned as a means to take account of SMEs.
4. *Enhancement of risk assessment capabilities*: developing climate stress tests to the Eurosystem's balance sheet, based on the already existing climate stress methodology for the economy as a whole. Credit rating agencies (CRAs) will face scrutiny as to whether they adequately incorporate climate change risks into their credit ratings.
5. *Collateral framework*: climate risks are to be included in the assessment of the adequacy of collateral posted; monitoring 'structural market developments in sustainability products' and, surprisingly, a readiness 'to support innovation in the area of sustainable finance within the scope of its mandate', in the context of which reference is made to the 20 September 2020 press release on acceptance of sustainability-linked bonds as collateral.[266]
6. *Corporate sector asset purchases*: corporate bond purchases by the ECB will 'incorporate climate change criteria, in line with its mandate'. This means there needs to be 'alignment of issuers with, at a minimum, EU legislation implementing the Paris agreement through climate change-related metrics or commitments of the issuers to such goals'. Disclosure of climate-related information of the CSPP will begin in 2023. Such disclosures are already undertaken for the non-monetary policy portfolios.[267] Based on a 'common stance for climate change-related sustainable and responsible investment principles for euro-denominated non-monetary policy portfolios', the ECB and the NCBs of the euro area are preparing climate-related disclosures by 2023, starting on the basis of the 'recommendations of the Task Force on Climate-related Financial Disclosures

264 Note: not for public assets, thus keeping the PSPP out of focus.

265 The case law on the OMT and the PSPP; see nn 5, 6 and 7.

266 *ECB to accept sustainability-linked bonds as collateral*, press release, 22 September 2020, at: www.ecb.europa.eu/press/pr/date/2020/html/ecb.pr200922~482e4a5a90.en.html.

267 *Eurosystem agrees on common stance for climate change-related sustainable investments in non-monetary policy portfolios*, press release, 4 February 2021, at: www.ecb.europa.eu/press/pr/date/2021/html/ecb.pr210204_1~a720bc4f03.en.html.

(TCFD) as the initial framework'. The TCFD[268] was mandated by the Financial Stability Board (FSB) to develop standards for transparent climate-related disclosures.[269] Among the four categories of disclosures (Governance, Strategy, Risk Management, Metrics and Targets, graphically depicted as shown in Figure 8.1), the Eurosystem will be 'reporting, as a minimum, in the category of metrics and targets'.

Source: Figure 2 of the TCFD's June 2017 Recommendations.

Figure 8.1 *Core elements of recommended climate-related financial disclosures*

268 See www.fsb-tcfd.org/.

269 See the *Recommendations of the Task Force on Climate-related Financial Disclosures*, 15 June 2017, at: https://assets.bbhub.io/company/sites/60/2020/10/FINAL-2017-TCFD-Report-11052018.pdf.

2. Assessment

8.110 A fair assessment needs to await actions and follow-up; developments in the first year are indicated under sub-section 3 below, and assessed there. The following remarks concern the announcement only.

8.111 The European Parliament welcomed the ECB's inclusion of climate change in its monetary policy, in a resolution[270] mentioning 'climate' 29 times (as against 9 times the year before[271]), and, in the monetary dialogue with Parliament, the ECB President explained what the central bank is undertaking.[272] Parliament is crystal clear in its assessment of the ECB's legal obligations:[273]

> Recalls that the ECB, as an EU institution, is bound by the EU's commitments under the Paris Agreement; emphasises that tackling the climate and biodiversity emergency requires the ECB to take an integrated approach that should be reflected in all its policies, decisions and operations, together with adhering to its mandate of supporting the general economic policies of the Union, specifically, in this case, the achievement of a climate-neutral economy by 2050 at the latest, as outlined in the European Climate Law; considers that the ECB needs to use all the tools at its disposal to fight and mitigate climate-related risks.

8.112 My own view is that the ECB has come a long way in acknowledging the issue of climate change and addressing it in its policies and activities: it is at the forefront of central banks' action. Its example is likely to move other central banks. And, while governments, including the legislative and executive institutions at EU level, are still the main agents that need to move on climate change, a clear direction from the central banks may spur the public authorities to do their part.

8.113 Greening of portfolios and collateral will of necessity be undertaken gradually, as ECB board member Isabel Schnabel made clear in an interview.[274] Also,

---

270 European Parliament resolution of 16 February 2022 on the European Central Bank – annual report 2021 (2021/2063(INI), at: www.europarl.europa.eu/doceo/document/TA-9-2022-0029_EN.html.

271 European Parliament resolution of 10 February 2021 on the European Central Bank – annual report 2020 (2020/2123(INI)), at: www.europarl.europa.eu/doceo/document/TA-9-2021-0039_EN.html.

272 European Parliament plenary debate on the ECB Annual Report, Introductory statement by Christine Lagarde, President of the ECB, at the plenary session of the European Parliament, Strasbourg, 14 February 2022, at: www.ecb.europa.eu/press/key/date/2022/html/ecb.sp220214_1~ec87ef8c3a.en.html.

273 European Parliament resolution of 16 February 2022, paragraph 22.

274 In her interview with *FOCUS Magazin*, conducted by Carla Neuhaus on 17 August and published on 20 August 2021, at: www.ecb.europa.eu/press/inter/date/2021/html/ecb.in210821~186713780d.en.html, Isabel Schnabel said, on re-directing the CSPP, that 'it would not make sense to completely exclude climate offenders' because 'We have to focus on accelerating the transition to a climate-neutral economy. Excluding certain sectors or firms from our asset purchase programme would be counterproductive. In order to lower emissions, firms with high levels of carbon emissions are extremely important because they offer scope for making the

drawing up criteria to select bonds will take time: '[W]e need to draw up new criteria for selecting bonds. For example, we could in the future buy more bonds from firms that commit to the goals of the Paris climate agreement and thus show that they are willing to adapt their business model.' So, making progress will take time.

There is an obvious lacuna in the action plans: the public sector bonds purchased are not (yet?) included in the re-direction. With more EU sovereigns, and the EU itself, issuing green bonds, this may be an element to be included in further steps towards fostering the green transition. **8.114**

Biodiversity is not part of the climate action plan, yet it is an element in the ECB's Environmental Statement[275] and is clearly in sight of the ECB's Board members.[276] Broadening the scope of the transitional policies to reflect biodiversity loss's danger to the planet and, by implication, to the economy of the euro area and its monetary and financial stability is a commendable next objective for the ECB.[277] The less visible impact of biodiversity loss and the absence of a binding international agreement with prominence like that of the Paris Agreement may explain (but not justify) the absence, hitherto, of biodiversity loss from the ECB's plans. **8.115**

3. What the ECB Had Already Undertaken

Prior to the monetary policy strategy review announcements on climate change action, the ECB had already undertaken various measures in this area. Beyond a 'Green ECB' campaign in its premises, exhorting staff and visitors to act 'green', the environmental impact of the central bank's activities is being mapped and steadily improved.[278] This includes energy and material efficiency, **8.116**

---

most progress. If these firms want to become climate-neutral, they are dependent on favourable financial conditions.' On buying green bonds only, she stated: 'a purely green asset purchase programme would not be realistic at present in any case.'

275 See the 2021 Update, at: www .ecb .europa .eu/ ecb/ orga/ climate/ green/ pdf/ ecb .environm entalstate ment202107~e1430ebcae.en.pdf. The 2023 Update is here: https://www.ecb.europa.eu/ecb/climate/green/html/ecb.environmentalstatement2023307~59d31f2afe.en.html.

276 Frank Elderson, *Patchy data is a good start: from Kuznets and Clark to supervisors and climate*, keynote speech at the ECB-EBRD joint conference on 'Emerging climate-related risk supervision and implications for financial institutions', Frankfurt am Main, 16 June 2021; at: www.ecb.europa.eu/press/key/date/2021/html/ecb.sp210616~44c5a95300.en.html.

277 NGFS Occasional Paper, *Biodiversity and financial stability: exploring the case for action*, at: www.ngfs.net/sites/ default/ files/ medias/ documents/ biodiversity_and_financial_stability_exploring_the_case_for_action .pdf.

278 As elaborated in the *2021 update of the ECB's Environmental Statement*, at: www.ecb.europa.eu/ecb/orga/climate/green/html/ecb.environmentalstatement202107~e1430ebcae.en.html.

also in producing banknotes, green procurement, biodiversity at the premises and reductions in travel.

8.117 Also, the ECB has established a Climate Centre[279] to centralize all research and policy-making in the field. A former employee of the Dutch central bank, which has been at the vanguard of climate change-related policies in the area of central banking, was appointed as its first head.[280]

8.118 The effects that climate change may have on monetary policy had been extensively mapped in 'Climate change and monetary policy in the euro area',[281] an issue in the Occasional Paper Series written in the context of the monetary policy review by the Eurosystem Work Stream on Climate Change and Monetary Policy'. The paper also maps the possible climate-related actions the Eurosystem may take, notably including climate change in modelling and in four specific areas (disclosure, risk assessment, collateral framework and the CSPP). The study goes in-depth into the relationship between climate and monetary policies but does not explore the potential expansion of climate-consciousness in other monetary policy instruments than these four areas.

8.119 In an op-ed[282] published *after* the adoption of the ECB's Climate Action Plan, Isabel Schnabel reiterated the three channels of influence between climate change and monetary policy. First, the transmission of monetary policy measures to financing conditions of households and firms may be impaired through physical risks or stranded assets on banks' balance sheets, and through 'a sharp and abrupt rise in credit risk premiums'. Also, central banks themselves may suffer losses through securities bought or collateral received. Second, climate change may lower or raise the equilibrium rate of interest (balancing savings and investments): lowering may through economic factors such as labour productivity, morbidity and mortality affected by climate change, through re-allocation of resources or through precautionary savings and reduced investments. Third, climate change and transition policies may influence inflation

279 *ECB sets up climate change centre*, press release, 25 January 2021, at: www.ecb.europa.eu/press/pr/date/2021/html/ecb.pr210125_1~3fc4ebb4c6.en.html.

280 *ECB appoints Irene Heemskerk as head of its climate change centre*, press release, 30 April 2021, at: www.ecb.europa.eu/press/pr/date/2021/html/ecb.pr210430~2042cc7f07.en.html.

281 F. Drudi, C. Holthausen, E. Moench, P. Weber (2021), Climate change and monetary policy in the euro area, *ECB Occasional Paper Series, at* www.ecb.europa.eu/pub/pdf/scpops/ecb.op271%7E36775d43c8.en.pdf?8068c39c5c19cd647e471b4ef8f60e5a.

282 ECB OP-ED, Climate change and monetary policy, contribution by Isabel Schnabel to the International Monetary Fund's magazine Finance and Development, Frankfurt am Main, 31 August 2021, at: www.ecb.europa.eu/press/blog/date/2021/html/ecb.blog210831~3a7cecbf52.en.html.

dynamics, such as climate shock or mitigation policies (for instance: carbon pricing).

An early action on climate change effected by the ECB was the innovative stress test for physical and transition risk announced[283] in spring 2021. Encompassing 'approximately four million companies worldwide and 2,000 banks – almost all monetary financial institutions in the euro area', the ECB, in cooperation with *Urgentem*[284] and *Four Twenty Seven*,[285] effected a climate change stress test based on scenario planning. In this first-of-its-kind exercise, the ECB mapped both physical and transition risks, finding that these are 'two sides of the same coin: greater policy action may increase the impact of transition risks, but at the same time reduce physical risks in later decades'.[286] The idea behind the effort was to 'help ensure that the financial system is resilient to the transition to a low-carbon economy, by providing more and better information to market participants on the risks from climate change'.[287] Just after the adoption of its climate road map, the ECB published the results of this stress test,[288] which assessed the impact of climate change on more than four million firms worldwide and 1,600 euro-area banks under three different climate policy scenarios.[289] Beyond this economy-wide stress test, the ECB submits the banks to a test of their climate-preparedness.[290] **8.120**

4. What the ECB Has Undertaken since Its Climate Action Plan

Beyond what was presented above, since the announcement of its climate agenda the ECB has clarified its stance and identified what can be done at short notice and what depends on further data or public sector rules. **8.121**

---

283 *Shining a light on climate risks: the ECB's economy-wide climate stress test*, THE ECB BLOG post by Luis de Guindos, ECB Vice-President, 18 March 2021, at: www.ecb.europa.eu/press/blog/date/2021/html/ecb.blog210318~3bbc68ffc5.en.html.

284 A data provider on emissions and climate risk: see www.urgentem.net/.

285 Currently Moody's ESG Solutions; see: https://427mt.com/.

286 *Shining a light on climate risks: the ECB's economy-wide climate stress test*, THE ECB BLOG post by Luis de Guindos, ECB Vice-President, 18 March 2021, at: www.ecb.europa.eu/press/blog/date/2021/html/ecb.blog210318~3bbc68ffc5.en.html: 'This relationship is one of the key elements captured and quantified in the ECB economy-wide climate stress test.'

287 Ibid.

288 Firms and banks to benefit from early adoption of green policies, ECB's economy-wide climate stress test shows, Press Release, 22 September 2021, at: www.ecb.europa.eu/press/pr/date/2021/html/ecb.pr210922~59ade4710b.en.html.

289 Spyros Alogoskoufis, Nepomuk Dunz, Tina Emambakhsh, Tristan Hennig, Michiel Kaijser, Charalampos Kouratzoglou, Manuel A. Muñoz, Laura Parisi and Carmelo Salleo, *ECB economy-wide climate stress test – Methodology and results*, ECB Occasional Paper Series, No 281, September 2021, at: www.ecb.europa.eu/pub/pdf/scpops/ecb.op281~05a7735b1c.en.pdf.

290 ECB Banking Supervision launches 2022 climate risk stress test, Press Release, 27 January 2022, at: www.bankingsupervision.europa.eu/press/pr/date/2022/html/ssm.pr220127~bd20df4d3a.en.html.

8.122 The role of monetary policy in the green transition has been set out in speeches, as well as the grinding progress towards C&E disclosure. Two speeches deserve special mention in this account of what the ECB has undertaken.

8.123 The prominent place of climate change in considerations at the ECB was highlighted by Frank Elderson's speech on climate litigation at the 2021 ECB Legal Conference.[291] Beyond the arguments for including climate change in the central bank's considerations and activities discussed here, Elderson emphasized 'climate-related human rights' in his reflections on climate litigation, referring to former United Nations High Commissioner for Human Rights Mary Robinson's definition of climate change as the 'greatest human rights issue of our time'.[292]

8.124 During the Glasgow meeting of the United Nations Climate Change Conference (COP 26),[293] the ECB issued a climate pledge.[294] Its statement starts: 'the ECB pledges to contribute, within its field of responsibility, to decisive action by policymakers to implement the Paris Agreement and mitigate the consequences of climate change'; recalls the Paris Agreement's aim of making financial flows compatible with the green transition; reiterates the financial sector's 'key role' 'by mobilising funds towards a more sustainable economy'; and makes undertakings relating to specific actions. The ECB pledged to

> [integrate] climate-related risks into financial stability monitoring and prudential supervision of banks, to [integrate] sustainability factors into own portfolio management, to [explore] the effects of climate-related risks on the Eurosystem monetary policy framework within our mandate, to [bridge] data gaps on climate-related data and to [work] towards higher awareness and intellectual capacity, also through technical assistance and knowledge sharing.[295]

291 *When you need change to preserve continuity: climate emergency and the role of law*, speech by Frank Elderson, ECB Legal Conference 2021, Frankfurt am Main, 25 November 2021, at: www.ecb.europa.eu/press/key/date/2021/html/ecb.sp211125~2da387f2ce.en.html.

292 Mary Robinson, Video Message to the Panel of Experts on Climate Leadership, on the eve of the Pacific Islands Forum, 2 September 2013, at: www.mrfcj.org/media/pdf/2013-09-04-MR-PIF-Video-Message.pdf.

293 See: https://ukcop26.org/.

294 The ECB pledge on climate change action, at: www.ecb.europa.eu/pub/pdf/other/ecb.pledge_climate_change_action211103~6af74636d8.pt.pdf.

295 Ibid.

8.125 In March 2022, Isabel Schnabel[296] expressed the need to address the three shocks resulting from transition to a CO_2-free economy:[297] 'climateflation' (inflation resulting from direct costs of climate change; (indirect) results of natural disasters and severe weather events); 'fossilflation' (price rises resulting from increased costs of oil and gas, due to the resurgence in use after the pandemic and the war in Ukraine but also 'the ability of energy producers to steer supply in an oligopolistic market'); and 'greenflation' (inflation induced by the increased use of metals and minerals for green technology which are scarce and more expensive than input in conventional production). These three types of inflation will not be addressed by increasing the inflation target or excluding energy from the price increase benchmark. What monetary policy *can* do is distinguish between the three in the ECB's policy response, and to 'green' the monetary policy framework. As Schnabel explained on the types of inflation she distinguishes:

> Climateflation and fossilflation share many of the characteristics of both an adverse supply shock and a terms of trade shock', whereas 'greenflation is much more likely to be the result of a strong and persistent positive demand shock, or investment boom, that re-establishes the 'divine coincidence' of monetary policy – that is, the ability of central banks to stabilise inflation and output simultaneously.[298]

8.126 Around the same time, Frank Elderson deplored the lack of progress in banks disclosing their C&E risk profiles in stark wording,[299] noting only marginal improvement in disclosure, and mostly at smaller banks: 'none of the 115 banks directly supervised by the ECB fully meets our supervisory expectations for disclosures.'[300] These words are telling:

---

296 *A new age of energy inflation: climateflation, fossilflation and greenflation*, speech by Isabel Schnabel, at a panel on 'Monetary Policy and Climate Change' at The ECB and its Watchers XXII Conference, 17 March 2022, at: www.ecb.europa.eu/press/key/date/2022/html/ecb.sp220317_2~dbb3582f0a.en.html.

297 While also eloquently putting into words the value of price rises in view of the green transition and the need to dissociate from Russian energy supply after the invasion into Ukraine: 'Today, our dependence on fossil energy sources is not only considered a peril to our planet, it is also increasingly seen as a threat to national security and our values of liberty, freedom and democracy.' And: 'There is a price to be paid for going green at a pace that reflects the dual objective of safeguarding both our planet and our right to self-determination. But that price, including the fiscal support required to protect the most vulnerable members of society, is worth paying.'

298 *A new age of energy inflation: climateflation, fossilflation and greenflation*, n 295.

299 *Full disclosure: coming to grips with an inconvenient truth*, keynote speech by Frank Elderson, 14th European Bank Institute Policy Webinar on the ECB's supervisory approach on climate-related and environmental risks, 14 March 2022, at: www.bankingsupervision.europa.eu/press/speeches/date/2022/html/ssm.sp220314~0422f4b854.en.html.

300 Saying: 'many of the banks raising the bar in C&E disclosures are small and medium-sized – showing that remarkable progress is achievable by all.' Ibid.

> Banks are trying to compensate for the poor quality of their disclosures by issuing a great volume of information around green topics. We end up with a lot of white noise and no real substance on what both markets and supervisors really want to know: how exposed is a bank to C&E risks and what is it doing to manage that exposure? It is of course relevant for banks to publicise their efforts to, for example, reduce the electricity consumption of their branches. However, it would be much more significant if they were to announce how they are steering their activities towards risk management practices that are aligned with a carbon-neutral economy. Looking at the world through green-coloured glasses' is not quite the same as a sound management of all material C&E risks.

8.127 What C&E risk disclosure, a permanent focus of the ECB's supervisory activities, means for commercial banks was spelled out in a subsequent speech:[301]

> banks should not misconstrue the ECB's actions as an outright call for divesting from carbon-intensive activities or from geographical regions vulnerable to physical risk. Rather, we are asking banks to fully grasp the physical and transition risks and to actively start managing them, with the aim of making their portfolios more resilient to C&E risks.

8.128 The lack of progress in C&E risk disclosure is also relevant for the greening of monetary policy, as Isabel Schnabel remarked in her speech three days later, with a reference to calls for green TLTROs:[302] 'Many banks, for example, do not yet effectively differentiate between green loans and other loans, making a green TLTRO difficult on a practical level.'

8.129 On 4 July 2022 the ECB issued its Climate Agenda 2022,[303] which begins with an excellent summary of its current (legal) thinking about its mandate. First, speaking as a monetary authority: 'Climate change and the transition to a greener economy affect our primary objective of maintaining price stability due to their impact on our economy and on the risk profile and value of the assets on the Eurosystem balance sheet.' Then, considering its prudential tasks: 'As a supervisory authority, it is our duty to contribute to the safety and soundness of the banking sector by ensuring the industry has made adequate preparations to manage climate-related risk.' Third comes secondary objectives-related considerations: 'Furthermore, as a European institution,

---

301 *Towards an immersive supervisory approach to the management of climate-related and environmental risks in the banking sector*, keynote speech by Frank Elderson, Industry outreach on the thematic review on climate-related and environmental risks, 18 February 2022, at: www.ecb.europa.eu/press/key/date/2022/html/ecb.sp220218~c55e646426.en.html.

302 Jens van 't Klooster and Rens van Tilburg, *Targeting a sustainable recovery*, September 2020, at: https://www.positivemoney.eu/wp-content/uploads/2020/09/Green-TLTROs.pdf.

303 ECB climate agenda 2022, at: www .ecb .europa .eu/ press/ pr/ date/ 2022/ html/ ecb .pr220704 _annex ~cb39c2dcbb.en.pdf.

acting within our mandate and without prejudicing our primary objective, it is our duty to play our part in supporting general economic policies which contribute towards the achievement of the EU's Treaty-based objectives. Such objectives include protecting the environment.'

These reflections precede an enumeration of the core objectives the ECB sees for itself in this context: (1) 'managing and mitigating the financial risks associated with climate change and assessing its economic impact'; (2) 'promoting sustainable finance to support an orderly transition to a low-carbon economy'; and (3) sharing of expertise 'to foster wider changes in behaviour'. The latter of the three goals pursued signals a messenger role. Improving its models and gathering more data will influence its climate strategy and actions, so the ECB states. The document then specifies, with deadlines, what actions it intends to undertake in six priority areas[304] with a focus on data gathering, analysis, risk assessment, considering climate-friendly monetary policy options and transparency. The accompanying press release is more explicit regarding several of the policy undertakings envisaged.[305] **8.130**

A striking feature is the absence of any reference to topics beyond the collateral framework and the CSPP: there's no indication of specific lending for transition purposes beyond '[r]esearch the potential role of central banks in financial markets and green innovation', an activity that seemed to have ended before the 2022 climate agenda was issued. The detailed specification of activities is to be lauded for the opportunity it provides to hold the independent central bank to account. **8.131**

The same holds for the letter to the European Parliament's Committee on Economic and Monetary Affairs of the same date,[306] in which President **8.132**

304 These are: (1) Assess the macroeconomic impact of climate change and mitigation policies on inflation and the real economy; (2) Improve the availability and quality of climate data to better identify and manage climate-related risks and opportunities; (3) Enhance climate change-related financial risk assessment; (4) Consider options for monetary policy operations and assess the impact of climate change on monetary policy (5) Analyse and contribute to policy discussions to scale up green finance; (6) Increase transparency and promote best practices to reduce the environmental impact.

305 The accompanying press release of 4 July 2020 (*ECB takes further steps to incorporate climate change into its monetary policy operations*) emphasizes (1) decarbonizing corporate bond holdings; (2) a 'new limits regime [that] aims to reduce climate-related financial risks in Eurosystem credit operations' for the collateral framework; (3) compliance with the Corporate Sustainability Reporting Directive (CSRD) as eligibility requirement for collateral in Eurosystem credit operations; and (4) 'urg[ing] rating agencies to be more transparent about how they incorporate climate risks into their ratings and to be more ambitious in their disclosure requirements on climate risks': www.ecb.europa.eu/press/pr/date/2022/html/ecb.pr220704~4f48a72462.en.html.

306 Letter from the ECB President to Irene Tinagli, ECON Chair, on progress on climate-related action plan, at: www.ecb.europa.eu/pub/pdf/other/ecb.mepletter220704_Tinagli~466b72513d.en.pdf?ef8c7e0645c2cbc204187b325879e8c9.

Lagarde informed Parliament on the progress since the climate action plan had been adopted. She wrote that 'the ECB has decided to adjust corporate bond holdings in the Eurosystem's monetary policy portfolios and its collateral framework, to introduce climate-related disclosure requirements and to enhance its risk management practices', specifying these along the lines of other ECB communications in early July 2022. Two further elements of this letter merit emphasis. First is the intention to review and, possibly, adapt the measures, with a view

> (1) to confirm that they continue to fulfil their monetary policy objectives; (2) to ensure – within its mandate – that the relevant measures continue to support the decarbonisation path to reach the goals of the Paris Agreement and the EU climate neutrality objectives; (3) to respond to future improvements in climate data and climate risk modelling or changes in regulation; and (4) to address additional environmental challenges, within its price stability mandate.[307]

8.133 Second, as in all its communications, the ECB squarely puts the onus on policy makers as the primary actors mandated to adopt the measures needed to address climate change[308] and, here, also holds politicians responsible for delays: 'the ECB is not acting in a vacuum, but rather in conjunction with the policies decided by other policymakers'; the actions announced 'are on track to meet the deadlines indicated in the climate roadmap' except for those 'that rely on the application of the forthcoming Corporate Sustainability Reporting Directive (CSRD)', whose implementation date is delayed, while possible 'further delay in the national transposition of the CSRD or the adoption of the harmonised reporting standards would have knock-on effects on the implementation of the ECB's actions'.[309] On this theme, the ECB President issues a clear call for legislative action:

> I am also counting on the co-legislators' ambition and willingness to further strengthen the regulatory framework underpinning climate-related disclosures and risk assessments, as well as to develop sound standards for sustainable financial products. For instance, improving climate disclosures and harmonised reporting of climate-related data for structured finance assets would help incorporate climate considerations into the treatment of those asset classes. In a similar vein, more ambitious regulatory requirements for CRAs' disclosure of climate risks are crucial to improving the Eurosystem's

307 Ibid.

308 'Although elected governments bear the primary responsibility of addressing climate change – and have more powerful tools to do so than central banks – the ECB is convinced that all policymakers need to take appropriate measures within their own mandates and respective areas of competence.' Ibid.

309 Ibid.

risk assessment capabilities. Swift agreement on the European green bond standard remains key to enhancing the credibility and effectiveness of green bonds.[310]

In a blogpost of 8 July 2022, two members of the Executive Board declared: 'the ECB can, within its mandate, act as a catalyst for greening the financial system.'[311] Isabel Schnabel and Frank Elderson bring to mind that the EU's trajectory towards climate neutrality by 2050 has 'implications for inflation during the transition phase', 'makes parts of the capital stock redundant and creates financial risks'. Turning away from 'market neutrality' in its corporate bond portfolio, which made this '[reflect] the existing bond universe', the ECB will diminish the 'carbon bias' in its portfolio and 'start tilting the reinvestments from maturing corporate bonds – around €30 billion every year – towards assets issued by companies with a better climate performance'. **8.134**

M. PRUDENTIAL SUPERVISION: A DIFFERENT ENVIRONMENT

1. The Legislative Framework for Prudential Supervision

In this separate[312] element of its mandate, the ECB is operating in a different environment. Although vested with the same level of independence as for monetary policy and all its tasks,[313] the fact of the matter is that prudential supervision concerns the application to supervised entities of standards set by the legislator. Thus, norms established elsewhere, both at Union level and beyond (global standard-setting bodies such as the BCBS[314] and the Financial Stability Board (FSB)), and at national level,[315] prescribe what the ECB can **8.135**

310 Ibid.

311 *A catalyst for greening the financial system*, ECB Blogpost, 8 July 2022, by Frank Elderson and Isabel Schnabel; at: www.ecb.europa.eu/press/blog/date/2022/html/ecb.blog220708~1c7076c7b1.en.html.

312 Article 25 SSM Regulation requires a separation between the prudential supervisory and monetary functions; an internal 'Chinese wall' maintaining different decision-making lines on distinct issues; monetary policy versus prudential policy and even versus systemic financial stability; the ECB's tasks in relation to the European Systemic Risk Board (ESRB) are also to be separated from the SSM-related tasks.

313 The basic provision on independence is Article 130 TFEU, which basically outlaws any interference from political bodies with the ECB's exercise of its powers and the carrying out of its tasks and duties. This is echoed in Article 7 ESCB Statute. The preamble to the SSM Regulation states the following: 'the ECB should exercise the supervisory tasks conferred on it in full independence, in particular free from undue political influence and from industry interference which would affect its operational independence' and follows up with Article 19 on independence of the ECB and the National Competent Authorities (NCAs), which carries the same language as Article 130 prohibiting the giving, or seeking, of instructions from bodies politic by members of the ECB's Supervisory Board.

314 See the BCBS' *Principles for the effective management and supervision of climate-related financial risks*, 15 June 2022, at: www .bis .org/ bcbs/ publ/ d532 .htm. These 18 principles set out how banks can manage climate-related financial risks and how supervisors should supervise these risks.

315 The ECB is to apply 'all relevant Union law, and where this Union law is composed of Directives, the national legislation transposing those Directives': Article 4(3) SSM Regulation.

do when it seeks to incorporate climate change in its supervision. It is for this reason that the ECB has to rely on the element of 'risk' as a basis for any furtherance of climate-related supervision. After all, risk is the pervasive factor in prudential regulation: avoiding and containing risk, or provisioning for its realisation, is what banks need to do and what supervisors look into.

8.136 The Union's prudential framework has hitherto been very modest when it comes to addressing climate change.[316] Even the most recent amendments to the Single Rulebook[317] only introduced a minimal greening. Apart from a requirement for the European Banking Authority to undertake a study and for the Commission, on the basis thereof, to *potentially* propose legislation for a dedicated treatment of ESG-relevant exposures,[318] and an additional requirement for the EBA to study[319] the inclusion of ESG factors in the annual Supervisory Review and Evaluation Process (SREP),[320] there are only modest disclosure requirements for credit institutions. Under CRR2, banks need to disclose 'information on ESG risks, including physical risks and transition risks, as defined in the [EBA] report referred to in Article 98(8) of [CRD5]'.[321] This disclosure is to take place annually for the first year, and biannually thereafter.[322]

8.137 The ECB has called for mandatory provisions in prudential regulation for banks to have net-zero transition plans, compliance with which the ECB can super-

316 See Box 8.3, prudential provisions relating to climate change and ESG.

317 See the interactive Single Rulebook at: www.eba.europa.eu/regulation-and-policy/single-rulebook/interactive-single-rulebook.

318 The EBA is to report by 28 June 2025 'whether a dedicated prudential treatment of exposures related to assets or activities associated substantially with environmental and/or social objectives would be justified', 'if appropriate' followed by a legislative proposal from the Commission: Article 501 c Capital Requirements Regulation (CRR)).

319 This study was issued on 23 June 2021: *EBA report on management and supervision of ESG risks for credit institutions and investment firms* (EBA/REP/2021/18); at: www.eba.europa.eu/sites/default/documents/files/document_library/Publications/Reports/2021/1015656/EBA%20Report%20on%20ESG%20risks%20management%20and%20supervision.pdf.

320 This is (in Basel parlance) 'Pillar 2' of supervision: the supervisor's annual exercise whether solvency, liquidity, risk management and governance of a supervised entity are sufficient, potentially leading to extra requirements for an individual bank beyond what is generally required: Articles 97 and 104 CRD5. Pillar 1 concerns the general solvency and liquidity requirements; Pillar 3 refers to the disclosure requirements that seek to infuse a market-induced correction to the assumption of excessive risks.

321 Article 449a CRR 2.

322 On 24 January 2022, the EBA has submitted to the Commission draft *Implementing Technical Standards (ITS) on prudential disclosures on ESG risks in accordance with Article 449a CRR*, EBA/ITS/2022/01, at: www.eba.europa.eu/implementing-technical-standards-its-prudential-disclosures-esg-risks-accordance-article-449a-crr#pane-new-7bdd87fb-e02f-492a-99d6-129449e3cf9d.

vise.[323] Support for the Banking Package 2021 was reiterated recently.[324] This Banking Package[325] proposed by the Commission would strengthen somewhat the green prudential standards, yet disappoints expectations of strong regulatory support for the green transition.[326] The requirement, in Article 501c CRR, to explore the imposition of ESG-related factors in risk weighing was brought forward in time (to end-2023) but weakened as the mention of a legislative proposal by the Commission was scrapped(!). A requirement to report ESG exposures to the competent authorities is added to Article 430 CRR. In the CRD, ESG risks are added to the issues the robust governance arrangements are required to address (Article 74), while Article 76 on a biannual risk review is strengthened, first by adding 'the current, short, medium and long-term impacts of environmental, social and governance factors' and second by requiring that the bank 'develops specific plans and quantifiable targets to monitor and address the risks arising in the short, medium and long-term from the misalignment of the business model and strategy of the institutions, with the relevant Union policy objectives or broader transition trends towards a sustainable economy in relation to environmental, social and governance factors'. Misalignment of business plans with government policy is thus a risk to be monitored, quantified and addressed, which *is* a remarkable yet wholly justifiable constraint on free enterprise: without adequately addressing climate change, there will be no room for any business. A credit institution needs to be more robust in addressing ESG risks as required by a new Article 87a CRR. This is taken further by adding to Article 401 on the SREP the possibility for the supervisors to require banks to alter their business models, governance

323 Bloomberg TV, interview with Frank Elderson, conducted by Francine Lacqua, on 2 November 2021, at: www.ecb.europa.eu/press/inter/date/2021/html/ecb.in211103~e8bcb85b25.en.html: 'My point would be that I would very much welcome in the new package of the European Commission that, at least in the European Union, there be a clear mandatory legal requirement for banks to have Paris-compatible transition plans so that we can easily supervise their alignment with the Paris Accord.'

324 *Good, bad and hopeful news: the latest on the supervision of climate risks*, keynote speech by Frank Elderson, 10th Annual Conference on Bank Steering & Bank Management at the Frankfurt School of Finance & Management, Frankfurt am Main, 22 June 2022, at: www.ecb.europa.eu/press/key/date/2022/html/ecb.sp220622~860a2aef6b.en.html: 'revisions to the Capital Requirements Directive currently under discussion by the EU co-legislators further reaffirm the ECB's mandate in this area by broadening the supervisory toolkit to address environmental, social and governance risks, and by explicitly requiring banks to have concrete plans to address C&E risks arising from misalignment with EU climate targets.'

325 See https://finance.ec.europa.eu/publications/banking-package_en.

326 See the Proposal for a Regulation of the European Parliament and of the Council amending Regulation (EU) No 575/2013 as regards requirements for credit risk, credit valuation adjustment risk, operational risk, market risk and the output floor, COM/2021/664 final, at: https://eur-lex.europa.eu/legal-content/EN/TXT/?uri=CELEX:52021PC0664; and the Proposal for a Directive of the European Parliament and of the Council amending Directive 2013/36/EU as regards supervisory powers, sanctions, third-country branches, and environmental, social and governance risks, and amending Directive 2014/59/EU, COM/2021/663 final, at: https://eur-lex.europa.eu/legal-content/EN/TXT/?uri=CELEX:52021PC0663.

strategies and risk management for this reason. Excerpts of the proposed changes are shown in Box 8.3.

8.138 The proposals are subject to amendments from the European Parliament.[327] One such amendment is most promising: the Greens propose to include a new Article 126b in the CRD under which a bank's fossil fuel exposures vis-à-vis corporate clients would be assigned heavy weightings; notably, *new* such exposures would be weighed at 1,250 per cent or, in other words, require 100 per cent capital.

2. Risk as a Central Element of Prudential Supervision

8.139 Being bound by the – thus far – minimalist approach of the legislator in this field of activity, the ECB has to rely on the element of risk, pervasive in supervisory standards, to include climate concerns in its supervision.[328] It has done so. The ECB published a *Guide on Climate-related and Environmental Risks* whose subtitle makes clear what it entails: *Supervisory Expectations relating to Risk Management and Disclosure.*[329] The Guide presents supervisory expectations for 'significant credit institutions' (that is, banks under direct supervision of the ECB)[330] which are said not to be binding but are to be taken on board in the supervisory dialogue with banks. Thus, even though formally non-binding, the Guide's 'expectations' will form the basis for SSM's engagement with the banks and may result in SREP decisions requiring changes to solvency requirements, governance and risk management. The Guide is rife with supervisory expectancies on understanding environmental risks, taking them into account in a bank's business strategy and risk management systems and own stress-testing, while arguing for disclosure according to the European Commission's *Guidelines on Non-financial Reporting: Supplement on Reporting Climate-related Information.*[331] In the October 2018 progress report, NGFS

327 Available at: www.europarl.europa.eu/doceo/document/ECON-AM-735427_EN.pdf. A political compromise has been achieved which could not be reflected here; see *Commission welcomes political agreement on EU banking package*, 27 June 2023, at https://finance.ec.europa.eu/news/commission-welcomes-political-agreement-eu-banking-package-2023-06-27.en.

328 Presaged by Andrea Enria in his speech in November 2019 when he said: 'so far, [banks] have addressed climate change from the angle of corporate social responsibility. Now they should expand their focus and approach it also from the angle of risk management and disclosure.'

329 *ECB publishes final guide on climate-related and environmental risks for banks*, press release, 27 November 2020, at: www.bankingsupervision.europa.eu/press/pr/date/2020/html/ssm.pr201127~5642b6e68d.en.html.

330 And with an exhortation to National Competent Authorities (NCAs) 'to apply the expectations set out in this guide in their supervision of less significant institutions in a manner that is proportionate to the nature, scale and complexity of the activities', in the interest of a 'consistent application of high supervisory standards across the euro area'.

331 [2019] OJ C209/1.

members acknowledged that 'climate-related risks are a source of financial risk. It is therefore within the mandates of central banks and supervisors to ensure the financial system is resilient to these risks.'[332]

3. Climate Change Considerations in Supervision

The question this chapter seeks to answer is whether such a climate-related approach by the ECB is within its mandate. Due to the instruction of the Treaty[333] and the legislator[334] to serve financial stability and the widely recognized negative potential effects of climate change on financial stability, there is no doubt in my mind that the ECB's mandate in this area also includes climate change-related approaches and measures – naturally, as indicated, within the framework of the hitherto modest legislative supervisory framework. **8.140**

Strong arguments can be made to include environmental–financial risks in supervision: a risk category combining biodiversity-related financial risks (BRFR) and climate-related financial risks (CRFR).[335] Additional reasons may be adduced here, based on the ECB's secondary mandate and on provisions discussed above (Articles 11 and 216(2) TFEU). After all, the secondary mandate to support economic policies in the Union also fully supports taking full account of the clear direction of EU policies to engage in a continent-wide conversion to a CO_2-free, circular economy by 2050. **8.141**

4. Recent Developments in Prudential Supervision

The early summer of 2022 was a busy time for the ECB in relation to climate change. Beside the announcements on the monetary policy front, the ECB gave away the preliminary findings resulting from its ongoing thematic review of climate-related and environmental risks (C&E risk). Most banks are still far from aligning their practices with the ECB's expectations in the *Guide on Climate-related Risks*.[336] **8.142**

---

332 Network for Greening the Financial System (2019), First Comprehensive Report: A call for action – Climate Change as a source of financial risk: www.ngfs.net/sites/default/files/medias/documents/ngfs_first_comprehensive_report_-_17042019_0.pdf.

333 Article 127(5) TFEU and Article 25.1 ESCB Statute.

334 The SSM Regulation mentions 'financial stability' 11 times, notably in recital 55 of the preamble: 'The conferral of supervisory tasks implies a significant responsibility for the ECB to safeguard financial stability in the Union, and to use its supervisory powers in the most effective and proportionate way.'

335 See, for instance, Katie Kedward, Josh Ryan-Collins and Hugues Chenet, Biodiversity loss and climate change interactions: financial stability implications for central banks and financial supervisors (2022) *Climate Policy*, DOI: 10.1080/14693062.2022.2107475, at: https://doi.org/10.1080/14693062.2022.2107475.

336 *Guide on climate-related and environmental risks Supervisory expectations relating to risk management and disclosure*, November 2020, at: www.bankingsupervision.europa.eu/ecb/pub/pdf/ssm.202011finalguideonclimate-relatedandenvironmentalrisks~58213f6564.en.pdf.

8.143 In a speech,[337] Frank Elderson did not hide the ECB's disappointment. He also called on banks to seize the opportunity that the green transition provides, saying: 'As the supervisor, our focus is on the safety and soundness of banks. Above all, we want to promote the stability of individual institutions and preserve financial stability. But banks should also want to effectively manage C&E risks and position themselves to benefit from the green transition.' He considered it 'reasonable that banks can be fully compliant with all our expectations by the end of 2024 at the latest'.

8.144 C&E risk inclusion in commercial banks' business had been advanced by the adoption by the BCBS of the *Principles for the Effective Management and Supervision of Climate-related Financial Risks*.[338] This 'principles-based approach to improving risk management and supervisory practices related to climate-related financial risks' contains 18 'high-level principles': 12 addressed to banks and 6 to prudential supervisors. The Principles reference other BCBS standards.[339] The BCBS argues that, because of longer than usual horizons for realization of climate risks, 'banks should take a prudent and dynamic approach to developing their risk management capacities'.

5. Climate-risk Litigation

8.145 Finally, as explained by Frank Elderson, the risk of climate litigation is to be taken into consideration. Supervisory authorities and central banks may become the subject of such litigation and, indeed, already are: 'While central banks and supervisors should of course not overstep their mandate, there is also a legal risk of being sued for failing to act and comply with legal obligations.'[340] Climate litigation[341] is a novel phenomenon leading to notable judicial decisions.[342] Although governments and corporations have been the

337 *Good, bad and hopeful news: the latest on the supervision of climate risks*, keynote speech by Frank Elderson, 10th Annual Conference on Bank Steering & Bank Management at the Frankfurt School of Finance & Management, Frankfurt am Main, 22 June 2022, at: www.ecb.europa.eu/press/key/date/2022/html/ecb.sp220622~860a2aef6b.en.html.

338 See n 314

339 They refer to the *Core principles for effective banking supervision* (BCPs; at: www.bis.org/basel_framework/standard/BCP.htm) and *Supervisory Review Process* (SRP; at: www.bis.org/basel_framework/standard/SRP.htm) as well as to the *Corporate governance principles for banks* (at: https://www.bis.org/bcbs/publ/d328.htm).

340 *The embrace of the horizon: Forcefully moving with the changing tide for climate action in financial sector policies*, speech by Frank Elderson, Chair of the Central Banks and Supervisors Network for Greening the Financial System, Member of the Executive Board and Vice-Chair of the Supervisory Board of the ECB, at The Green Swan Conference – Coordinating finance on climate, Frankfurt am Main, 3 June 2021, at: www.bankingsupervision.europa.eu/press/speeches/date/2021/html/ssm.sp210603~e0388eab0d.en.html.

341 Ivano Alogna, Christine Bakker and Jean- Pierre Gauci's edited volume *Climate Change Litigation: Global Perspectives* ([2021] Brill Nijhoff) provides an excellent overview of climate litigation across the globe.

342 See Chapter 11 of this book, by de Wit and Mills, on climate litigation.

main targets, central bank have come into the picture as well. A striking example concerns the proceedings started by environmental charity Client Earth[343] against the Belgian central bank[344] for 'failing to meet environmental, climate, and human rights requirements when purchasing bonds from fossil fuel and other greenhouse-gas intensive companies' in the context of the ECB's CSPP.[345] Their argument is based on violation of Article 11 TFEU (the environmental integration provision)[346] and Article 37 of the Charter of Fundamental Rights of the European Union[347] through the purchase of purchasing bonds from fossil fuel and other greenhouse gas-intensive companies. The plaintiff seeks a preliminary ruling from the CJEU on the issue. This could mean that a similar case to *Weiss* ensues: an NCB implied in litigation on its execution of Eurosystem-wide operations.[348] Although this litigation concerns monetary policy, not prudential supervision, it is a clear example of the risk of climate-related litigation facing central banks which may encompass all of their activities and policies.

An overview of climate litigations can be found at a website[349] co-hosted by the Sabin Center for Climate Change Law at Columbia Law School.[350] It contains two databases of climate change litigation, one for US climate change litigation and one for non-US cases. **8.146**

BOX 8.3 PRUDENTIAL PROVISIONS RELATING TO CLIMATE CHANGE AND ESG

Article 501c Capital Requirements Regulation (CRR2)[351]

Prudential treatment of exposures related to environmental and/or social objectives

EBA, after consulting the ESRB, shall assess, on the basis of available data and the findings

343 See www.clientearth.org/.

344 *Banque Nationale de Belgique/Nationale Bank van België/Belgische Nationalbank*; www.nbb.be/en.

345 *ClientEarth v Belgian National Bank*, reported at: http://climatecasechart.com/climate-change-litigation/non-us-case/clientearth-v-belgian-national-bank/.

346 See section G above.

347 This reads as follows: 'Article 37 Environmental protection: A high level of environmental protection and the improvement of the quality of the environment must be integrated into the policies of the Union and ensured in accordance with the principle of sustainable development.'

348 The difference being that in *Weiss* the plaintiffs relied on exceeding of the ECB's mandate and violation of the national constitution, whereas in *ClientEarth v BNB* the claims rest on violation of EU environmental law.

349 See: http://climatecasechart.com/.

350 See: https://climate.law.columbia.edu/.

351 From: Regulation (EU) No 575/2013 of the European Parliament and of the Council of 26 June 2013 on prudential requirements for credit institutions and amending Regulation (EU) No 648/2012, [2013] OJ L 176/1, as amended.

of the Commission High-Level Expert Group on Sustainable Finance, whether a dedicated prudential treatment of exposures related to assets or activities associated substantially with environmental and/or social objectives would be justified. In particular, EBA shall assess:

(a) methodologies for the assessment of the effective riskiness of exposures related to assets and activities associated substantially with environmental and/or social objectives compared to the riskiness of other exposure;
(b) the development of appropriate criteria for the assessment of physical risks and transition risks, including the risks related to the depreciation of assets due to regulatory changes;
(c) the potential effects of a dedicated prudential treatment of exposures related to assets and activities which are associated substantially with environmental and/or social objectives on financial stability and bank lending in the Union.

EBA shall submit a report on its findings to the European Parliament, to the Council and to the Commission by 28 June 2025.

On the basis of that report, the Commission shall, if appropriate, submit to the European Parliament and to the Council a legislative proposal.

Article 98(8) Capital Requirements Directive (CRD5)[352]

Technical criteria for the supervisory review and evaluation

8. EBA shall assess the potential inclusion in the review and evaluation performed by competent authorities of environmental, social and governance risks (ESG risks).

For the purposes of the first subparagraph, EBA's assessment shall comprise at least the following:

(a) the development of a uniform definition of ESG risks, including physical risks and transition risks; the latter shall comprise the risks related to the depreciation of assets due to regulatory changes;
(b) the development of appropriate qualitative and quantitative criteria for the assessment of the impact of ESG risks on the financial stability of institutions in the short, medium and long term; such criteria shall include stress testing processes and scenario analyses to assess the impact of ESG risks under scenarios with different severities;
(c) the arrangements, processes, mechanisms and strategies to be implemented by the institutions to identify, assess and manage ESG risks;
(d) the analysis methods and tools to assess the impact of ESG risks on lending and financial intermediation activities of institutions.

EBA shall submit a report on its findings to the Commission, the European Parliament and to the Council by 28 June 2021.

On the basis of the outcome of its report, EBA may, if appropriate, issue guidelines, in accordance with Article 16 of Regulation (EU) No 1093/2010, regarding the uniform inclusion

352 From: Directive 2013/36/EU of the European Parliament and of the Council of 26 June 2013 on access to the activity of credit institutions and the prudential supervision of credit institutions and investment firms, amending Directive 2002/87/EC and repealing Directives 2006/48/EC and 2006/49/EC, [2013] OJ L 176/338, as amended.

of ESG risks in the Supervisory Review and Evaluation Process performed by competent authorities.

Article 449a CRR2[353]

Disclosure of environmental, social and governance risks (ESG risks)

From 28 June 2022, large institutions which have issued securities that are admitted to trading on a regulated market of any Member State, as defined in point (21) of Article 4(1) of Directive 2014/65/EU, shall disclose information on ESG risks, including physical risks and transition risks, as defined in the report referred to in Article 98(8) of Directive 2013/36/EU.

The information referred to in the first paragraph shall be disclosed on an annual basis for the first year and biannually thereafter.

N. OTHER TASKS: PAYMENTS

A brief word on other tasks to end this exploration of the ECB's mandate in the context of climate change. Among the ECB's other tasks, most[354] are not relevant in this perspective; however the issue of euro banknotes[355] and the oversight function over the payment systems are. (The ECB's wider financial stability remit,[356] beyond prudential supervision,[357] is not discussed here, as the concerns and mandate issues relevant for the 'specific tasks' in the context of the Single Supervisory Mechanism (SSM) are applicable there as well.) **8.147**

Banknotes made of cotton are an area in which environmental and climate concerns are primary. In the *2020 Update of the ECB's Environmental Statement*,[358] the ECB makes clear how it assesses and addresses these issues. Manufacturers need to provide ISO certificates on the quality management, environmental management and health and safety aspects of the banknote production. Certified organic cotton is said to be used for more than half of **8.148**

353 From: Regulation (EU) No 575/2013 of the European Parliament and of the Council of 26 June 2013 on prudential requirements for credit institutions and amending Regulation (EU) No 648/2012, [2013] OJ L 176/1, as amended.

354 Its advisory function: consultation on national and Union legislation in its fields of competence (Article 127(4) TFEU; Article 4 ESCB Statute); and its external reserves and forex functions: to conduct foreign-exchange operations consistent with the provisions of Article 219 of that Treaty; and to hold and manage the official foreign reserves of the Member States (Article 127(2), second and third indent, TFEU, Article 3.1, second and third indent, ESCB Statute).

355 Article 128(1) TFEU, Article 16 ESCB Statute.

356 Set out in Article 127(5) TFEU and Article 25.1 ESCB Statute and relevant in the context of the ESRB.

357 Pursuant to Article 127(6) TFEU and Article 25.2 ESCB Statute.

358 At: www.ecb.europa.eu/ecb/climate/green/html/ecb.environmentalstatement202010~d0c3d15950.en.html. See also section 6.7 (bank notes) of the *ECB Environmental statement 2022* at: www.ecb.europa.eu/ecb/climate/green/html/ecb.environmentalstatement202207~dedabd566b.en.html#toc37.

the banknotes produced, with a 100 per cent target. There is no legal argument against taking environmental and climate considerations fully into account under the responsibility of the ECB to issue banknotes.[359]

8.149 With respect to the oversight of payment systems,[360] the instruction 'to promote the smooth operation of payment systems' has been taken to consist in the oversight by the Eurosystem of national payment systems and the provision of the TARGET[361] infrastructure payment services for settling financial transactions.[362] This is not the place to discuss the validity of this somewhat limited approach to the widely drawn mandate.[363] However, the impact of climate change and the transition to a CO_2-free economy do lend themselves to the following considerations.

8.150 Any further development of payment systems infrastructure and oversight may wish to take into account elements of the climate change challenge. The efficacy and efficiency of payment systems oversight may contribute to their environmental soundness.[364] The potential introduction of a Central Bank Digital Currency (CBDC)[365] raises issues of energy consumption of blockchain technology. Whatever the choices made in these areas,[366] from a legal perspective there is clarity on the inclusion of climate and environmental considerations in this part of the mandate as well. Here, as well as in respect of monetary policy and prudential supervision, the secondary mandate and the additional supporting elements adduced provide valid legal grounds for the inclusion of climate change considerations in the implementation of the ECB's tasks. Again, the conclusion is not that the ECB is *permitted* to include climate change but that it is *mandated* to do so.

---

359 The authorization of bank notes' issuance is an exclusive ECB competence; the issue of the notes themselves is reserved for the ECB and NCBs. Euro coins are issued by the Member States, with the ECB authorizing their volume (Article 128(2) TFEU).

360 Article 127(2), fourth indent, TFEU and Article 3.1, fourth indent, ESCB Statute.

361 TARGET stands for Trans-European Automated Real-time Gross settlement Express Transfer system.

362 These are: a real-time gross settlement (RTGS) system (TARGET2), a securities settlement platform (T2S) and a TARGET Instant Payment Settlement (TIPS) for instant payments in euro. See: www.ecb.europa.eu/paym/target/html/index.en.html.

363 One may question the approach of continuing with national payments systems instead of building an EU-wide system. This has legal and political ramifications and may be attributed to the choice of a decentralised model for the central banking system of the monetary union. This decentralized approach does nothing to instil a sense of coherence and irreversibility of the adoption of the single currency; it has been a source of divisive debate based on perceived credit channelled in a book-keeping system for cross-border transactions.

364 An environmentally inspired study may research whether less partitioning of the payments systems and more interaction across borders in the internal market would result in a lower environmental impact.

365 Christine Lagarde and Fabio Panetta, *Key objectives of the digital euro*, THE ECB BLOG, 13 July 2022, at: www.ecb.europa.eu/press/blog/date/2022/html/ecb.blog220713~34e21c3240.en.html.

366 See the Commission's proposal for a regulation on the establishment of the digital euro (COM/2023/369 final), at: https://eur-lex.europa.eu/legal-content/EN/TXT/?uri=CELEX%3A52023PC0369.

O. CONCLUDING REMARKS

Having reflected on the history of the interpretation of the European Central Bank's mandate, and discussed the international developments concerning climate change in the area of central banking and financial sector supervision (NGFS, TCFD, BIS), this chapter concludes as follows. The ECB's primary mandate of maintaining price stability is predominant, in the core provisions (Article 127(2) and 119(3) TFEU) and in the rules on exchange-rate policy (Article 219(1) and (2) TFEU). The ECB's secondary mandate (to support the general economic policies in the Union with a view to contributing to the achievement of the objectives of Article 127(2) TFEU) clearly supports an interpretation of its remit which takes climate change, and biodiversity loss, fully into account, since the economic policies in the EU and the EU's Climate Law make the direction of the Union's policy makers crystal clear. Similarly, the Union's objectives (Article 3 TEU) explicitly include climate change-related objectives: sustainable development; balanced economic growth; a high level of protection and improvement of the quality of the environment; solidarity between generations; protection of human rights, in particular the rights of the child; protection of the Union's citizens and sustainable development of the Earth. **8.151**

Beyond these strong arguments to read the mandate as not only *permitting* but *requiring* the ECB to take full account of climate change and biodiversity loss, additional arguments can be derived from the integration provisions (Articles 11 and 7 TFEU) and from the binding nature of the Paris Agreement (Article 216(2) TFEU). The EU's Charter of Fundamental Rights provides an additional legal argument (Article 37) for my preferred reading of the ECB's mandate. Whereas these legal arguments suffice, recourse to the primary mandate alone would be sufficient since the ever clearer consequences of climate change for price stability, and for financial stability, lead me – together with others – to conclude that there is a legal *requirement* to fully integrate climate change and biodiversity loss in the monetary policy operations of the ECB, not a mere *authorization* to do so. **8.152**

The open market principle (Articles 127(1) and 119(2) TFEU) does not form an obstacle to this reading. On the contrary, it requires the ECB to support well-functioning markets – from which the current price setting of financial and other products is currently far. There is no 'market neutrality principle' under EU law (even though central banks may have acted in accordance with this rule). An emergency situation reading of the mandate, and a focus on **8.153** the relationship between climate stability and primate stability, may further buttress this interpretation.

8.154 This reading may have consequences for a variety of operations of the ECB, from investing its own funds in green assets to reassessing and redirecting asset purchasing programmes for climate impact and requiring proof of 'green-ness' for collateral. All this presupposes the existence of a robust green taxonomy, which the EU has adopted and is fast developing, hiccups in the realization and diverse policy stances – notably on nuclear and gas – notwithstanding. Other elements of change may include taking a longer-term perspective in the price stability objective and incorporating climate and biodiversity variables in research, analysis[367] and policy-making. The results of the ECB's monetary policy strategy review and an overview of the actions already undertaken before and since show that the euro area's central banking system has firmly integrated work towards climate resilience and incorporation of climate change response into its activities. There is scope for widening the climate considerations into other elements of monetary policy.

8.155 The ECB's activities include prudential supervision, where the same legal grounds apply as in monetary policy. However, in this area, the legislative norms play a dominant role. Due to their – thus far – very limited integration of climate change and biodiversity loss into banking laws, the ECB will have to rely on the risk element inherent in any prudential standards in including climate change in its supervisory activities. It has done so already, *inter alia* with the adoption of its *Guide on Climate-related and Environmental Risks* and the implementation of a wide-ranging climate change stress test.

8.156 As to other ECB tasks, the promotion of the smooth operation of payment systems and the issue of banknotes seem most relevant from the perspective of climate change. The oversight of payments systems and the possible introduction of a CBDC both provide opportunities to include environmental soundness. It is concluded, on the basis of the same arguments as prevail in the context of monetary policy, that the ECB is legally bound to do so.

8.157 It is too early to provide an assessment of what has been undertaken thus far. As indicated, there is uncertainty about the exact scope of the taxonomy,

367 On central banks' analysis and climate mitigation scenarios, see the contribution assessing the NGFS's scenarios: Irene Monasterolo, Maria J. Nieto and Edo Schets, *The good, the bad and the hot house world: conceptual underpinnings of the NGFS scenarios and suggestions for improvement,* 6 September 2022, at: https://papers.ssrn.com/sol3/papers.cfm?abstract_id=4211384.

also since the full-scale Russian invasion of Ukraine.[368] And there are clear blank spots still in the ECB's climate action: unconventional monetary policy instruments[369] are only partially covered and 'green TLTROs' are hardly mentioned, while greening the foreign reserve portfolio of the Eurosystem seems not yet to have been contemplated either. Yet, recently realized movements on climate change, as well as the conclusions of the monetary policy strategy review, the climate action plan and the matters undertaken during the first year of its implementation, show a deep commitment and indicate a willingness to embrace the full rigour of the ECB's legal obligation in respect of climate change and biodiversity loss.

P. RECENT DEVELOPMENTS

1. Practice and Critique of ECB Decarbonizing

The ECB published details on decarbonizing its corporate bond holdings:[370] it **8.158** will rely on scores for companies' greenhouse gas (GHG) emissions to 'tilt its purchases towards issuers with a better climate performance'. In view of the changes in monetary policy in the face of the steep rise in inflation, there have been no new purchases under the CSPP since June 2022 and, since March 2023, the Eurosystem only partially reinvests the principal payments from maturing CSPP securities.[371] An in-depth explanation of the tilting approach and of possible greening of monetary policy instruments was given by ECB executive director Isabel Schnabel.[372] The ECB's greening record has been assessed very critically in a Greenpeace-supported report.[373] Disclosure of the

368 The full war unleashed by Russia in February 2022 has made investors re-appreciate the 'ESG' requirements, sometimes considering investment in defence equipment to fall within the 'S'. This does not affect the 'E'.

369 Acknowledging that these are on the retreat: quantitative easing is no longer part of the policy tools in view of high inflation figures – as of July 2022, no net purchases, only reinvestments of redemptions, are undertaken. Source: www.ecb.europa.eu/mopo/implement/app/html/index.en.html. See the ECB's Press Release, Monetary policy decisions, 21 July 2022, at: www.ecb.europa.eu/press/pr/date/2022/html/ecb.mp220721~53e5bdd317.en.html.

370 *ECB provides details on how it aims to decarbonise its corporate bond holdings*, press release, 19 September 2022, at: www.ecb.europa.eu/press/pr/date/2022/html/ecb.pr220919~fae53c59bd.en.html. See, also, the FAQs, at: www.ecb.europa.eu/mopo/implement/app/html/ecb.faq_cspp_climate_change.en.html, and the explainer at: www.ecb.europa.eu/ecb/educational/explainers/html/decarbonising_corporate_bond_holdings.en.html.

371 See: www.ecb.europa.eu/mopo/implement/app/html/index.en.html#cspp.

372 *Monetary policy tightening and the green transition*, speech by Isabel Schnabel at the International Symposium on Central Bank Independence, Sveriges Riksbank, Stockholm, 10 January 2023, at: www.ecb.europa.eu/press/key/date/2023/html/ecb.sp230110~21c89bef1b.en.html.

373 Yannis Dafermos, Daniela Gabor, Maria Nikolaidi, Jakub Gogolewski and Mauricio Vargas (2023), *Broken promises: the ECB's widening Paris gap*, SOAS University of London; University of Greenwich; University of the West of England; Greenpeace; at: www.greenpeace.de/publikationen/EZB_Report%20_Broken_promises.pdf.

ECB's own CSPP and PEPP portfolios and non-monetary policy portfolio (own funds and staff pension fund)[374] showed 'a decarbonization path' for Eurosystem bond holdings. In further application of norms with which the banks are expected to conform, the ECB stress-tested its own balance sheet for climate-related risks.[375] Eurosystem in-house credit rating assessment systems now also include climate-risk evaluations.[376]

2. Beyond Climate: Biodiversity

8.159 In a series of speeches, ECB Executive Director Frank Elderson explained that, beyond climate change, 'nature-related risks, including those associated with biodiversity loss' have macroeconomic implications and need to be addressed as 'a source of risk for individual financial institutions and for financial stability'.[377] Emphasising the 'E' in the ECB's *Guide on Climate-related and Environmental Risks: Supervisory Expectations relating to Risk Management and Disclosure*,[378] Elderson emphasized the need to look beyond climate-related metrics, such as GHG emissions, and include other metrics.[379] In a clear indication of where the ECB wishes banks to head, in terms of taking biodiversity-related risks into account, Elderson gave an interview to the *Financial Times*[380] in which he set out the economic and, hence, financial-sector risks of biodiversity loss.[381]

---

374 *Climate-related financial disclosures of the Eurosystem's corporate sector holdings for monetary policy purposes* and *Climate-related financial disclosures of the ECB's non-monetary policy portfolios*, 23 March 2023 at: www.ecb.europa.eu/pub/pdf/other/ecb.climate_related_financial_disclosures_eurosystem_corporate_sector_holdings_monetary_policy_purposes2023~9eae8df8d9.en.pdf and www.ecb.europa.eu/pub/pdf/other/ecb.climate_related_financial_disclosures_ECB_non_monetary_policy_portfolios2023~9199143410.en.pdf.

375 Maximilian Germann, Piotr Kusmierczyk and Christelle Puyo, *Results of the 2022 climate risk stress test of the Eurosystem balance sheet*, ECB Economic Bulletin, Issue 2/2023, at: https://www.ecb.europa.eu/pub/economic-bulletin/focus/2023/html/ecb.ebbox202302_06~0e721fa2e8.en.html.

376 Julia Körding and Florian Resch, *Common minimum standards for incorporating climate change risks into in-house credit assessment systems in the Eurosystem*, Economic Bulletin Issue 6, 2022, at: www.ecb.europa.eu/pub/economic-bulletin/focus/2022/html/ecb.ebbox202206_06~d7f88f706f.en.html.

377 *Natura finis magistra – acknowledging nature-related risks to make finance thrive*, speech by Frank Elderson at De Nederlandsche Bank/Official Monetary and Financial Institutions Forum conference on 'Moving beyond climate: integrating biodiversity into financial markets' at Artis Zoo in Amsterdam, 29 September 2022, at: www.ecb.europa.eu/press/key/date/2022/html/ecb.sp220929_2~d6497c36da.en.html.

378 See n 328.

379 'Even if the current focus of the ongoing work is still on climate-related risks, our ever-evolving understanding of the materiality of environmental risks and their transmission channels implies that these risks ultimately need to be taken into consideration in everything we do.'

380 Interview with the *Financial Times* conducted by Martin Arnold on 1 June 2023, published 8 June 2023, at: www.ecb.europa.eu/press/inter/date/2023/html/ecb.in230608~7247c0aaca.en.html. See also *The economy and banks need nature to survive*, THE ECB BLOG, Frank Elderson, 8 June 2023, at: www.ecb.europa.eu/press/blog/date/2023/html/ecb.blog230608~5cffb7c349.en.html.

381 'What I'm saying is that biodiversity and nature-related services generally are relevant for the economy. This is not some kind of a flower power, tree-hugging exercise. This is core economics. This is core financial stability, core macroprudential, core price stability.' Ibid.

Elderson announced the publication of an inventory of biodiversity-related losses in September 2023, revealing that '75% of bank loans are to firms that depend on ecosystem services'.[382] This interview is also revealing about the manner in which the prudential supervisory authority elaborates norms: based on statutory requirements to take risk into account,[383] it formulates supervisory expectations, requires banks to self-report on these and then conducts thematic reviews among the credit institutions, which may ultimately face specific measures.[384]

In this chapter, climate change is understood to encompass climate change and loss of biodiversity, as both developments produce risks for central banks and for the financial system, beyond threatening our economies and the survival of mankind on our planet. For more on this issue, see the Intergovernmental Science-Policy Platform on Biodiversity and Ecosystem Services.[385] **8.160**

3. Further Developments of Green Parameters

In January 2023 the ECB published statistical indicators on climate change.[386] The significance of climate-related disclosure requirements was underscored in a joint statement with the ESAs.[387] **8.161**

382 'Ecosystem services' are defined as 'outputs, conditions, or processes of natural systems that directly or indirectly benefit humans or enhance social welfare'; see www.britannica.com/science/ecosystem-services. In his ECB blog, Elderson gave the following example of services provided by nature: 'food, drinking water, timber and minerals; protection against natural hazards; or carbon uptake and storage by vegetation.'

383 Notably, Article 76 (bank's 'management body [needs to] approve [] and periodically review [] the strategies and policies for taking up, managing, monitoring and mitigating the risks the institution is or might be exposed to, including those posed by the macroeconomic environment in which it operates in relation to the status of the business cycle') and Article 74 (internal governance, including 'effective processes to identify, manage, monitor and report the risks they are or might be exposed to') CRD.

384 Such as SREP decisions or even sanctions (fines, periodic penalty payments): Article 1 of Council Regulation (EC) No 2532/98 of 23 November 1998 concerning the powers of the European Central Bank to impose sanctions, [1998] OJ L 318/4, as amended by Council Regulation (EU) 2015/159 of 27 January 2015, [2015] OJ L 27/1.

385 www.ipbes.net/.

386 *Towards climate-related statistical indicators*, at: www .ecb .europa .eu/ pub/ pdf/ other/ ecb .climate _change _indicators202301~47c4bbbc92.en.pdf.

387 *Joint ESAs–ECB Statement on disclosure on climate change for structured finance products*, 13 March 2023, at: www.ecb.europa.eu/pub/pdf/other/ecb.ESA_ECB_joint_statement~c1f96d353b.en.pdf?02fb3e782ccd745be3f3505071bf6d97.

8.162 The EU's green taxonomy developed further, with a new batch of delegated acts[388] under the Taxonomy Regulation[389] which fill in technical criteria for the economic activities substantially contributing to one or more of the objectives of the Taxonomy Regulation and a proposal for an ESG rating providers regulation.[390] Earlier, the CSFRD[391] entered into force. A consultation was held on a first batch of European sustainability reporting standards (ESRS).[392] A delegated act setting out these ESRS[393] was adopted by the Commission on 31 July 2023, watering down some of the mandatory requirements from earlier proposed texts with a 'materiality test'; this permits companies to exclude from disclosure items not deemed material, that is, not relevant in their particular circumstances, while identifying these non-material data points.[394] Such standards, and the requirement for corporates to disclose their climate and environmental risk exposure, assist the ECB in decarbonizing its assets and serve the C&E risk supervision of credit institutions by the SSM.

4. ECB Subject to the EU Climate Law?

8.163 The ECB's relationship with the EU Climate Law[395] was set out in another speech by Frank Elderson.[396] Elderson's inclination to the view that the ECB is not a 'relevant Union institution' in the sense of Article 2(2) of Regulation 2021/1119 as the central bank is a policy taker (not maker), and that Commission oversight of the central bank's climate actions would undermine its independence and circumvent Treaty provisions on amending the central

388 EU Taxonomy Delegated Acts: the Environmental Delegated Act, at: https:// finance .ec .europa .eu/ system/files/2023-06/taxonomy-regulation-delegated-act-2022-environmental_en_0.pdf, and amendments to the Climate Delegated Act, at: https://finance.ec.europa.eu/system/files/2023-06/taxonomy-regulation -delegated-act-2022-climate_en_1.pdf.

389 See Christos V. Gortsos and Dimitrios Kyriazis, *The Taxonomy Regulation and Its Implementation*, EBI Working Paper Series 2023 – no. 136, 08/03/2023, at: https://papers.ssrn.com/sol3/papers.cfm?abstract_id= 4381950.

390 Proposal for a Regulation of the European Parliament and of the Council on the transparency and integrity of Environmental, Social and Governance (ESG) rating activities, COM(2023) 314 final, 13 June 2023, at: https://eur-lex.europa.eu/legal-content/EN/TXT/?uri=CELEX:52023PC0314.

391 See text accompanying n 309. Under the CSRD (see n 238), companies need to disclose for the first time in annual reports published in 2025.

392 https:// ec .europa .eu/ info/ law/ better -regulation/ have -your -say/ initiatives/ 13765 -European -sustainability -reporting-standards-first-set_en.

393 Commission Delegated Regulation (EU) .../... of 31.7.2023 supplementing Directive 2013/34/EU of the European Parliament and of the Council as regards sustainability reporting standards, Brussels, 31.7.2023 C(2023) 5303 final, at: https://ec.europa.eu/finance/docs/level-2-measures/csrd-delegated-act-2023-5303_en.pdf.

394 European Commission, Questions and Answers on the Adoption of European Sustainability Reporting Standards, 31 July 2023, at: https://ec.europa.eu/commission/presscorner/detail/en/qanda_23_4043.

395 See David Brinkman's Chapter 7 in this book.

396 *The European Climate Law and the European Central Bank*, speech by Frank Elderson, Lustrum Symposium organised by Dutch Financial Law Association, Amsterdam, 1 December 2022, at: www.ecb.europa.eu/ press/key/date/2022/html/ecb.sp221201_1~435e6ea81a.en.html.

bank's objectives, is not shared by this author. I would consider the Commission competent to take stock of what the institutions do in terms of compliance with the Climate Law, and to assess whether they have fulfilled the requirement to 'take the necessary measures [...] to enable the collective achievement of the climate-neutrality objective set'.[397] The Commission's review of 'the consistency of Union measures with the climate-neutrality objective'[398] or with 'ensuring progress on adaptation [to climate change]'[399] should, in my perspective, also cover the ECB. Of course, the Commission cannot prescribe what the ECB is to do, just as it cannot impose on the Council and Parliament specific legislation in line with what it considers needed, or on the equally independent Court, as each have their own competences under the Treaty. Thus, when the Commission takes 'the necessary measures in accordance with the Treaties',[400] the ECB's independence guarantees that it sets monetary policy itself, yet the ECB would be required to explain any inconsistency that the Commission may have identified in climate-relevant aspects of ECB policy. I gladly note Elderson's view, expressed in the aforementioned speech,[401] that ECB policies and activities, while perhaps not covered by the Climate Law, still need to be consistent with it.[402]

5. Further Perspectives

The global work on climate-risk assessment has been inventoried in a speech at **8.164**
the IMF.[403] On the legal front, an academic proposal that the specification of the ECB's secondary objectives should take place via high-level coordination with the EU's political institutions should be mentioned,[404] as well as more publications on the ECB's green mandate[405] and on central banks and the

397 Article 2(2) European Climate Law.

398 Article 6(2)(a) European Climate Law.

399 Article 6(2)(b) European Climate Law.

400 Article 6(3) European Climate Law.

401 *The European Climate Law and the European Central Bank*, n 26.

402 Based on the consistency provisions: Articles 11 and 7 TFEU, discussed under G. INTEGRATION PROVISIONS.

403 *Policymakers as policy takers – accounting for climate-related and environmental factors in banking supervision and monetary policy*, speech by Frank Elderson at the Peterson Institute for International Economics, Washington DC, 21 April 2023, at: www.ecb.europa.eu/press/key/date/2023/html/ecb.sp230421~489cd977e0.en.html.

404 Jens van 't Klooster and Nik de Boer, 'What to do with the ECB's secondary mandate' (2023) JCMS, vol. 61, no. 3, 730–46, DOI: 10.1111/jcms.1340.

405 Pieterjan Heynen, 'The ECB going green: Impact on the interrelationship between monetary policy and banking supervision' (2022) *Maastricht Journal of European and Comparative Law*, vol. 29, no. 6, 667–84, and Pieterjan Heynen, *Greening the ECB: Issues and Developments*, Bank- en Financieel Recht/Droit Bancaire et Financier; Vol. 2022; issue 3; pp. 179–89. Earlier: Zsa Zsa Knödler, *Greening monetary policy measures: The Eurosystem's obligations with regards to the transition towards a low carbon economy*, European Banking Institute

greening of finance.[406] The inspiration to include climate change and biodiversity loss into central banking was, again, eloquently presented by Frank Elderson,[407] and the ECB's intention to enforce its supervisory expectations as regards banks' preparedness for climate change and biodiversity loss firmly underlined,[408] even with a reference to imposing periodic penalties.[409]

Working Paper Series 2021 – no. 100, posted: 11 August 2021, at: https://papers.ssrn.com/sol3/papers.cfm?abstract_id=3902039#.

406 David Ramos Muñoz, Antonio Cabrales and Ángel Sanchez, *Central banks and climate change. Fit, opportunity and suitability in the law and beyond*, EBI Working Paper Series 2022 – no. 119, 10/03/2022, at: https://papers.ssrn.com/sol3/papers.cfm?abstract_id=4054908; Omer Faruk Tekdogan, 'Green central banking: a new role for the central banks in the financial system', *Journal of Central Banking Law and Institutions* (2023), vol. 2, no. 2, 301–26.

407 *Beacons of hope to navigate the spring tide of urgency: from Terschelling to Frankfurt to Paris*, speech by Frank Elderson at the *Springtij* Forum, Terschelling, 20 September 2023, at: www.bankingsupervision.europa.eu/press/speeches/date/2023/html/ssm.sp230920_2~4036e4a9eb.en.html.

408 See Frank Elderson's *Interview with Market News International*, 27 September 2023, at: www.bankingsupervision.europa.eu/press/interviews/date/2023/html/ssm.in230927~af5bdc7426.en.html. See, also: ECB steps up climate work with focus on green transition, climate and nature-related risks, press release, 30 January 2024, at https://www.ecb.europa.eu/press/pr/date/2024/html/ecb.pr240130~afa3d90e07.en.html.

409 Which the ECB can impose thanks to the Council Regulation (EC) No 2532/98 of 23 November 1998 concerning the powers of the European Central Bank to impose sanctions, [1998] OJ L 318/4, as amended upon the activation of its prudential supervisory task by Council Regulation (EU) 2015/159 of 27 January 2015 amending Regulation (EC) No 2532/98 concerning the powers of the European Central Bank to impose sanctions, [2015] OJ L 27/1; this legal act added 'periodic penalty payments' to the ECB's arsenal of instruments.

9

SUSTAINABLE FINANCE AND REGULATION: A SOUTH AFRICAN PERSPECTIVE

Jonathan Maphosa

A. SOUTH AFRICA'S GREEN COMMITMENTS

9.001 South Africa is an energy-intensive economy that is highly dependent on coal as its main energy source. According to the National Treasury, as of 2020[1] electricity generation from fossil fuels contributed some 45 per cent of South Africa's greenhouse gas (GHG) emissions. This makes South Africa the 11th biggest contributor to GHG emissions in the world.[2] In this regard, South Africa made international commitments to the Paris Agreement on Climate Change to an emissions peak between 2020 and 2025, a plateau for the preceding decade and a decline from 2036 onwards.

9.002 In addition to this, during COP26, South Africa submitted a revised Nationally Determined Contribution (NDC) to reduce its domestic carbon emissions within an emissions range of between 420 CO_2-eq and 350 CO_2-eq by 2030.[3] The South African government has also made local commitments, which date back to 1965, in attempts to reduce and control air pollution; among these is the Atmospheric Pollution Prevent Act (Act No. 45 of 1965) ('APP Act'), the requirements of which were carried forward into the Bill of Rights codified in the Constitution of the Republic of South Africa in 1996.[4]

9.003 In essence, the APP Act is in tandem with the Bill of Rights in the Constitution of the Republic of South Africa[5] ('the South African Constitution'). Section 24 of the South African Constitution specifically relates to the environment. Section 24 states:

> Everyone has the right:
> a. To an environment that is not harmful to their health or well-being; and
> b. To have the environment protected, for the benefit of the present and future generations, through reasonable legislative and other measures that
> I. Prevent pollution and ecological degradation;
> II. Promote conservation; and

1 National Treasury. 2020. Financing a sustainable economy: Technical Paper 2020. Available online from www .treasury .gov .za/ publications/ other/ Sustainability %20technical %20paper %202020 .pdf accessed 13 January 2021.

2 Brand, J., Blumenthal, J., and Anstey, D. 2020. South Africa: Sustainable Finance and the South African Financial Services Sector. Available online from www.mondaq.com/southafrica/financial-services/975392/ sustainable-finance-and-the-south-african-financial-services-sector Accessed 13 January 2021.

3 Business Standard. 2021. South Africa Commits to Reducing Carbon Emissions after Foreign Financing. Available from www .business -standard .com/ article/ pti -stories/ south -africa -commits -to -reduce -carbon -emissions-after-usd-8-5b-foreign-financing-121110301812_1.html Accessed 12 November 2021.

4 Department of Environmental Affairs. 2018a. South Africa's Low-Emission Development Strategy 2050. Available online from www.environment.gov.za/sites/default/files/strategic_plans/southafricas_lowemission _developmentstrategy_dec2018draft.pdf Accessed 20 January 2021.

5 South African Constitution Act 108 of 1996.

III. Secure ecologically sustainable development and use of natural resources while promoting justifiable economic and social development.

Section 24 of the South African Constitution, among other local legislation, acts as a guide to air quality management in the country. South Africa has also ratified several multilateral air management agreements in an attempt to effectively manage air quality and is obligated to implement the given conditions for these agreements. These multilateral agreements require South Africa to address three major air quality issues, namely: persistent organic pollutants (POPs); greenhouse gases (GHGs) and associated climate change; and ozone layer depletion.[6] **9.004**

Recently, in an effort to reduce carbon emissions and meet the country's commitments to the Paris Agreement,[7] South Africa implemented a carbon tax law that requires organisations to report on their GHG emissions as part and parcel of the organisation's carbon footprint reports (Carbon Tax Act of 2019). To ensure that these requirements are met, the South African government also incorporated penalty fees for those who do not contribute to these efforts to reduce the country's GHG emissions. These are some of the local laws that have been implemented to support both international and local commitments to improve the environment, with climate change at the forefront. **9.005**

B. CLIMATE CHANGE IN SOUTH AFRICA

Climate change is recognised as a destabilising threat to economies and people's well-being, particularly the most vulnerable. There is an urgent global need to make a 'Just Transition' to a lower carbon economy as well as to achieve the Sustainable Development Goals (SDGs). According to the Climate Justice Alliance,[8] Just Transition refers to 'a vision-led, unifying and place-based set of principles, processes, and practices that build economic and political power to shift from an extractive economy to a regenerative economy'. This ensures that no communities are left behind from a socio-economic standpoint. **9.006**

6 Department of Environmental Affairs. 2018a. South Africa's Low-Emission Development Strategy 2050. Available Online from www.environment.gov.za/sites/default/files/strategic_plans/southafricas_lowemission_developmentstrategy_dec2018draft.pdf Accessed 20 January 2021.

7 The Paris Agreement is a legally binding international treaty on climate change. It was adopted by 196 Parties at the United Nation Conference of the Parties (COP) 21 in Paris, on 12 December 2015, and entered into force on 4 November 2016.

8 Climate Justice Alliance. 2021. Just Transition: A Framework for Change. Available online from https://climatejusticealliance.org/just-transition/ Accessed 12 November 2021.

9.007 Climate change has become a measurable global reality, which has vast negative impacts on developing countries due to their perceived lack of financial resilience. South Africa, among many other developing countries, is vulnerable to these negative impacts. The most prevalent negative impacts that have been witnessed in South Africa due to climate change are the increase in temperatures, water scarcity and food security issues, all of which negatively affect key sectors such as tourism and agricultural exports, among others.[9] This shows that climate change's impacts are interlinked with long-term economic and social risks.

9.008 According to the Department of Environmental Affairs,[10] local temperatures have increased at an average rate of 2°C per century, which is more than twice the global temperature rate increase. There is growing evidence of extreme weather events as a result of increasing global temperatures in South Africa. Climate zones across the country have been shown to have shifted, land degradation has become more prevalent, ecosystems have become degraded and veld fires have become more frequent.[11] This goes to show that climate change is a multifaceted challenge, which will have direct impacts on the environment and profound indirect negative effects on the rural communities, as well as on those who reside in the cities.

1. Climate-related Risks

9.009 The effects of climate change are widespread and affect everyone globally. The South African financial sector is no exception to this reality, and the following potential climate-related risks are identified:[12]

- Physical risks, which include but are not limited to extreme weather, which directly affects the financial institutions' operations or damages assets, and business finance and/ or default risks. There are also longer-term impacts such as increased water or heat stress, which may disrupt functionality across the supply chain.
- Transition risks, which result from disruptive technologies, change in policies and regulations and changes in market preferences. Such changes

9 UNDP. 2021. South Africa. Available online from www.adaptation-undp.org/explore/africa/south-africa Accessed 12 November 2021.

10 Department of Environmental Affairs (DEA). 2018b. South Africa's 3rd Climate Change Report. Available online from www.environment.gov.za/sites/default/files/reports/SouthAfricas-3rd-climate-change-report2017.pdf Accessed 13 January 2021.

11 Ibid.

12 Feridun, M., and Güngör, H. 2020. Climate-Related Prudential Risks in the Banking Sector: A Review of the Emerging Regulatory and Supervisory Practices. *Sustainability* 12, 5325. doi:10.3390/su12135325.

could prompt a reassessment of the value of assets. An example would be the increase in carbon taxes and the decline in the value of fossil fuel assets, which could lead to stranded assets as they would not be able to generate an economic return.

- Liability and disclosure risks, which result from rising insurance costs, loss and damages, disclosure failures and directors' liability.

To protect the South African economy and its citizens from major external shocks to the financial system, it is of utmost importance that financial institutions and the government build resilience through solvency and effective environmental and social risk management. Achieving long-term financial stability in South Africa requires financial institutions to develop a greater understanding of the environmental, social and governance risk exposures – particularly the risk posed by climate change – facing the financial sector. **9.010**

South Africa has made strides to work towards reducing its GHS emissions. **9.011** Recently, the President of the Republic of South Africa announced that private power producers could produce up to 100 megawatts each without a licence.[13] The drive for adopting renewables in South Africa has also been amplified due to the load-shedding crisis. The President announced a plan that not only seeks to end the Eskom power supply crisis but will aid in the country's efforts to fight climate change. The President brought forward the following solutions: the construction of solar and battery storage systems at targeted various power stations around the country; and the doubling of the generation capacity to be procured through Bid Window 6 from 2600 MW to 5200 MW.[14] Bid Window 6 forms part of the South African Renewable Energy Independent Power Producer Procurement Programme (REIPPPP). This is a competitive tender process that was designed to facilitate private sector investment into grid-connected renewable energy (RE) generation in South Africa.[15] Through these efforts, South Africa has shown its desire not only to combat its local energy crisis but also to reduce emissions and combat climate change.

13 Omarjee, L. 2021. A Breakthrough for Private Power Providers as Ramaphosa Makes a Big Move. News24. Available online from www.news24.com/fin24/economy/eskom/major-breakthrough-for-private-power-providers-as-ramaphosa-makes-big-move-20210610 Accessed 27 June 2021.

14 Bega, S. 2022. Ramaphosa Delivers a Plan to End Load-Shedding and Energy Insecurity. Available online from https://mg.co.za/news/2022-07-25-no-more-excuses-says-ramaphosa-as-he-delivers-energy-plan-to-end-loadshedding-and-energy-insecurity/ Accessed 14 August 2021.

15 Eberhard, A., Kolker, J. and Leigland, J. 2014. South Africa's Renewable Energy IPP Procurement Program: Success Factors and Lessons. World Bank Group, Washington, DC. Available online from https://openknowledge.worldbank.org/handle/10986/20039 License: CC BY 3.0 IGO.

9.012 Furthermore, following COP26, South Africa signed an international partnership which will facilitate the funding of USD 8.5 billion from Germany, France, the USA, the UK and the European Union over the next three to five years to aid in the country's transition towards a low-carbon economy.[16] This opens the opportunity for renewable energy Independent Power Producers (IPPs) to aid in the country's quest to reduce its GHG emissions and help resolve the ongoing electricity crisis in the country.

9.013 The changes in policy and formulation of new partnerships show South Africa's continuous efforts to tackle climate change. The South African government has also established a climate finance system, where funds are dedicated to tackling issues related to negative impacts caused by climate change. The following section shall highlight the current state of the South African climate finance system.

2. South African Climate Finance Systems

9.014 Some financial institutions in South Africa have received climate-dedicated funds from development agencies, namely the African Development Bank, the International Finance Corporation and the World Bank. The funding from the agencies has supported a vast range of projects which include (but are not limited to) the development of renewable energy sources, climate change resilience projects such as developing early warning systems for floods and droughts in communities and introducing climate change-resilient agriculture; for example, rainwater harvesting for crops and multi-cropping.[17]

9.015 However, in South Africa there is limited accountability and transparency as to how the climate finance funds have been spent, and that has become a major concern to the international community, especially concerning further funding of the country's climate change initiatives.[18] The DEA states that there are several contributing factors to these hurdles presented by the lack of funding. The lack of political will and the unwillingness to effectively implement strategies and policies that aim to reduce the impact of climate change has

---

16 Business Standard. 2021. South Africa Commits to Reducing Carbon Emissions after Foreign Financing. Available online from www.business-standard.com/article/pti-stories/south-africa-commits-to-reduce-carbon-emissions-after-usd-8-5b-foreign-financing-121110301812_1.html Accessed 12 November 2021.

17 Ngwenya, N. and Simatele, M.D. 2020. The Emergence of Green Bonds as an Integral Component of Climate Finance in South Africa. S Afr J Sci. 116(1/2), Art. #6522. Available online from https://doi.org/10.17159/sajs.2020/6522.

18 SANBI (South African National Biodiversity Institute). 2021. Money for Adaptation: The Adaptation Fund and Green Climate Fund in South Africa. Available from: www.sanbi.org/biodiversity/science-into-policy-action/nie-adaptation-fund/ Accessed 20 January 2021.

discouraged outside investment and left the country with no option but to use its resources, which are not sufficient. This, however, is rapidly changing for the better. South Africa recently signed a USD 8.5 billion international partnership with Germany, France, the USA, the UK and the European Union to aid in its transition towards a low-carbon economy.

According to Ngwenya and colleagues,[19] the climate finance mechanisms in South Africa are in the process of change and are adapting to the new emerging mechanisms. An example of the adoption of climate finance mechanisms is the implementation of the Principles for Managing Environmental and Social Risk by the Banking Association of South Africa. The Principles highlight the role that financial institutions could play in the implementation and promotion of environmental, economic and social rights in the country through sustainable banking practices.[20] These changes have begun to enable effective transformative changes towards becoming a low-carbon country. **9.016**

The issuance of green bonds has proven to be an effective climate finance mechanism globally, and their adoption within existing national financial structures seems promising, even for developing countries like South Africa. As well as climate change-related issues it is important to address other environmental and social issues, such as the protection of water resources, biodiversity and wetlands, and increasing access to infrastructure and sanitation.[21] **9.017**

This is where sustainable finance plays a pivotal role in enabling pro-environmental and social developments and creating new economic opportunities in a green economy. Sustainable finance is a broad concept that refers to the alignment of the financial system to the concept of sustainability. It is the combination of environmental, social and governance indicators in the financial decision-making process. **9.018**

19 Ngwenya, N. and Simatele, M.D. 2020. The Emergence of Green Bonds as an Integral Component of Climate Finance in South Africa. S Afr J Sci. 116(1/2), Art. #6522. Available online from https://doi.org/10.17159/ sajs.2020/6522.

20 Banking Association South Africa. 2015. Principles for Managing Environmental and Social Risk. Available online from http://sustainablefinanceinitiative.org.za/wp-content/uploads/2020/10/BASA-PRINCIPLES-FOR-MANAGING-ENVIRONMENTAL-AND-SOCIAL-RISK_Oct2015.pdf Accessed 20 January 2021.

21 National Treasury. 2020. Financing a Sustainable Economy: Technical Paper 2020. Available online from www.treasury.gov.za/publications/other/Sustainability%20technical%20paper%202020.pdf accessed 13 January 2021.

C. SUSTAINABLE FINANCE IN SOUTH AFRICA

9.019 Climate change-related problems are multifaceted and require financial resources and structural and socio-economic reforms. South Africa needs to mobilise towards sustainable finance products and resources to address this challenge, for the benefit of its citizens and to meet its global commitments. Sustainable finance is essential for balanced and inclusive economic growth,[22] as it is looking to identify and mitigate risks and also search for opportunities that are environmentally, economically and socially beneficial. The concept of sustainable finance encompasses the concepts of both green and socially focused financing. Sustainable finance is a relatively new concept, especially in the African context, and it requires large amounts of funding if it is to be implemented and reach its full potential.

9.020 The Intergovernmental Panel on Climate Change (IPCC), the OECD and other governing bodies have estimated that trillions of dollars will be needed every year, up to 2030, for investments in energy, transport, water and telecommunications infrastructure to sustain growth and mitigate climate effects. This will further require vast transitions within the global economy, which will present many risks. These risks cannot be prevented by any government but will require swift adaptation on the part of both private and public sector players.

9.021 To aid with the transitions, the Task Force on Climate-related Financial Disclosures (TCFD) published a set of recommendations to increase the understanding of financial risks related to climate change. The TCFD recommended financial disclosure to the G20, suggesting that global warming scenarios should be used to model the potential risks that companies and economic systems could face.[23] A systematic and credible method of disclosure is required to enable improved pricing and risk distribution and to also identify potential economic opportunities that are associated with climate change risk adaptation and mitigation.[24]

9.022 The South African government is making strides to tackle climate change-related risks, by enhancing its efforts to transition to a low-carbon economy. Several government agencies signed the Green Economy Accord (commonly known as the Accord) in 2011, alongside representatives of businesses, labour unions

---

22 Ibid.

23 TCFD (Task Force on Climate-Related Financial Disclosures). 2021. The Challenge We're Addressing. Available online from www.fsb-tcfd.org/about/ Accessed 27 June 2021.

24 Ibid.

and civil society.[25] The Accord aims to turn South Africa into a greener economy, which would include the development of green finance.

The South African financial industry itself has triggered sustainable/green finance. The adoption of the Code for Responsible Investing in South Africa (CRISA) in 2011 encourages the commitment and collaborative engagement of asset managers and institutional investors (mainly pension funds) to manage environmental, social and governance (ESG) issues in their asset ownership practices. Globally, South Africa was the second country, after the United Kingdom, to issue an ESG regulation for the pension fund sector.[26] **9.023**

The sustainable finance framework in South Africa does not have set requirements or standards regarding the development of green finance flows. However, the South African government has been committed to transitioning towards a greener economy. This framework also identifies economic opportunities that come with it and the potential job creation arising from the increase in green finance flow. The country made commitments to develop its green finance in 2011, through the Accord; Commitment 2 states that the country must undertake 'investment in the Green Economy'.[27] **9.024**

The commitment does not state any specific prescriptive measures for implementation; however, progress is currently under way to determine the barriers to the development of green finance within the country. The section above highlights that in South Africa sustainable finance initiatives have taken two distinct forms, namely those that are driven by the government through various regulations put in place and those that have been led by industry.[28] **9.025**

Thus, in the absence of overarching regulatory and policy frameworks, the primary force behind driving sustainable finance initiatives is the industry itself, largely through voluntary industry association-led initiatives or through international sector-specific initiatives. The following section briefly unpacks **9.026**

25 International Finance Corporation (IFC). 2020. Sustainable Finance Practices in South African Retirement Funds: Opportunities to Unlock Investment in Green and Climate Finance and Support a Resilient Economy. Available online from https://sustainablefinanceinitiative.org.za/assets_sfi/downloads/SustainableFinanceinSARetirementFunds_FINAL_08122020.pdf Accessed 20 January 2021.

26 Ibid.

27 Economic Development Department. 2011. New Growth Path: Accord 4 Green Economy Accord. Available online from www.economic.gov.za/communications/publications/green-economy-accord Accessed 15 January 2021.

28 ESRM Africa. 2022. Sustainability Initiatives in the South African Financial Sector. Available online from https://esrmafrica.org/south-africa-posts-5/ Accessed 14 August 2022.

the regulations and voluntary industry association-led initiatives that are being followed in South Africa.

1. Best Practices Adopted by South Africa Financial Institutions

9.027 The European Union has initiated a growing awareness of this area of law that has become part of a global response to climate issues. The concept of sustainable finance is relatively new in Africa. South Africa was one of the first countries on the continent, and among the emerging markets, to embrace the concept. The regulatory requirements for sustainable finance in South Africa have thus far focused mainly on the pension fund sector, through the amended Pension Funds Act[29] in 2012, which amendments consider ESG risks to be part of a fund's fiduciary responsibility. Thus, retirement funds take the leading role in sustainable finance in South Africa. The regulation of retirement funds is supported by the voluntary Code for Responsible Investing in South Africa (CRISA), which has been embedded in the King IV Code of Corporate Governance.[30]

9.028 The King IV report aims to encourage the leadership of organisations to address global realities such as climate change, inequality and radical transparency, among many issues.[31] The King IV report further states that business 'can no longer be seen as existing in its narrow universe [...] of stakeholders and the resources needed to create value – it also operates in and forms part of general society'.[32] The King IV report applies to all organisations in South Africa and is obligatory for the companies listed on the Johannesburg Stock Exchange (JSE).

9.029 In 2020 the International Finance Corporation (IFC) conducted a study to assess how well-positioned South Africa's retirement funds industry is to unlock investment opportunities towards green and climate finance' according to the IFC, an estimated $588 billion in investment is needed in South Africa alone up to 2030. The South African pension fund industry represents an

29 The Pension Funds Act 24 of 1956.

30 IFC (International Finance Corporation). 2018. Country Progress Report. Addendum to SBN Global Progress Report: South Africa. Sustainable Banking Network. Available online from www.ifc.org/wps/wcm/connect/bfede35f-5732-4c87-bfe2-fbcdd320b536/SBN+Country+Progress+Report+-+South+Africa.pdf?MOD=AJPERES&CVID=m746VJS Accessed 15 January 2021.

31 ECGI. 2021. King Report on Corporate Governance for South Africa-2016 (King IV Report). Available online from https://ecgi.global/code/king-report-corporate-governance-south-africa-2016-king-iv-report Accessed 27 June 2021.

32 IoDSA. 2016. King IV: Report on Corporate Governance for South Africa 2016. Johannesburg: Institute of Directors Southern Africa (IoS).

estimated R4 trillion (dollar equivalent) in assets under management (AUM); this industry is a major driver and influencer in the economy and plays an important role in many other emerging markets.[33] Accordingly, the retirement industry has an opportunity to contribute to the development of a sustainable economy that will secure benefits for current retirement fund members and for future generations to come.[34] Below is a summary of some of the principles that have played an integral role in the local retirement funds sector's leading role in sustainable finance in the country.

(a) Banking Association South Africa (BASA) – Sustainable Finance Principles

In 2014 BASA launched the Principles on Social and Environmental Risk Management, with the scope of the application specified to lending and investment.[35] These Principles outline the role that financial institutions can play in the promotion, protection and fulfilment of environmental, economic and social rights in South Africa. This can be achieved if financial institutions report on their business, lending and sustainability investment practices. It is expected that responsible corporate citizen members commit themselves to these Principles. To ensure that the Principles are promoted and understood nationally, BASA created a Sustainable Finance Committee to oversee their implementation. The objectives of the Principles are as follows:[36] **9.030**

- To promote sustainable banking by setting standards for environmental and social risk management by considering the relevant regulations.
- To increase consistency and transparency in the application of environmental and social risk management practices by the members.
- To promote confidence in the sustainability of the banking system.
- To support the cooperation between different stakeholders.

The objectives outline the intentions of the Principles and act as a composition for institutional investors. The Principles recognise the critical role that **9.031**

33 International Finance Corporation (IFC). 2020. Sustainable Finance Practices in South African Retirement Funds: Opportunities to Unlock Investment in Green and Climate Finance and Support a Resilient Economy. Available online from https://sustainablefinanceinitiative.org.za/assets_sfi/downloads/SustainableFinanceinSARetirementFunds_FINAL_08122020.pdf Accessed 20 January 2021.

34 Ibid.

35 IFC (International Finance Corporation). 2018. Country Progress Report. Addendum to SBN Global Progress Report: South Africa. Sustainable Banking Network. Available online from www.ifc.org/wps/wcm/connect/bfede35f-5732-4c87-bfe2-fbcdd320b536/SBN+Country+Progress+Report+-+South+Africa.pdf?MOD=AJPERES&CVID=m746VJS Accessed 15 January 2021.

36 Banking Association South Africa. 2015. Principles for Managing Environmental and Social Risk. Available online from http://sustainablefinanceinitiative.org.za/wp-content/uploads/2020/10/BASA-PRINCIPLES-FOR-MANAGING-ENVIRONMENTAL-AND-SOCIAL-RISK_Oct2015.pdf Accessed 20 January 2021.

financial institutions can play in the fulfilment of environmental, social and economic rights in South Africa. This can be achieved if financial institutions conduct and report on their investing practices and operations in a sustainable manner. There are no specifications on the measurement of adherence to the Principles for Managing Environmental and Social Risk. However, according to BASA,[37] all members of the Banking Association South Africa have agreed to adopt these Principles, which will be reviewed regularly by the BASA Sustainable Finance Committee.

(b) The Code for Responsible Investing in South Africa (CRISA)[38]

9.032 The CRISA was launched in July 2011 and later revised in 2020 to bring it up to date with changes in trends in the sustainable finance sector over the years. The CRISA consists of five principles that guide how institutional investors should execute their investment analysis and activities to promote governance. The five principles are summarised below:[39]

- Principle 1 requires institutional investors to develop policies that outline how they incorporate sustainability into their investment activities and analysis; this also includes the ESG aspects. Investors are required to ensure that this policy is implemented and that they establish sufficient processes to monitor their compliance with the policy. Through the implementation of the Code, South Africa became the second country in the world, after the UK, to formally encourage institutional investors to integrate sustainability issues such as ESG into their decision-making processes.
- Principle 2 requires institutional investors to demonstrate their acceptance of ownership responsibilities in investment arrangements and activities. Institutional investors should demonstrate a responsible approach by implementing a policy which outlines a detailed mechanism of intervention and engagement with companies when concerns have been identified, as well as when the concerns raised cannot be resolved by shareholders, among other things. The Code also requires a policy with a detailed approach to how voting at shareholder meetings is conducted, and this must include the

37 BASA (Banking Association South Africa). 2019. Global Principles for Responsible Banking. Available online from www.banking.org.za/news/global-principles-for-responsible-banking/ Accessed 15 August 2022.

38 CRISA. 2020. CRISA Code for Responsible Investment in South Africa. 2020 Revision Consultation Draft. Available online from https://cdn.ymaws.com/www.iodsa.co.za/resource/collection/1D7CF73B-B95B-453F-A8E3-D19829D18FBD/CRISA_2.0_Draft_for_public_comment.November2020__00000004_.pdf Accessed 27 June 2021.

39 IDSA (Institute of Directors South Africa). 2021. CRISA Summary of Principles. Available online from www.iodsa.co.za/page/crisasummary Accessed 21 January 2021.

criteria that are used in reaching voting decisions and the public disclosure of all voting records.

- Principle 3 requires institutional investors to consider collaborating to promote the acceptance and implementation of the principles of CRISA and other codes and standards. The principle encourages institutional investors to work with shareholders, investee companies, regulators, service providers and ultimate beneficiaries to promote CRISA and sound governance.
- Principle 4 requires institutional investors to identify the relationships that could lead to potential conflicts of interest and they should manage these when they arise. Institutional investors are further encouraged to develop a policy that outlines methods to prevent and manage conflicts of interest and to establish processes to monitor compliance with this policy.
- Principle 5 requires institutional investors to be transparent about the content of their policies, how they are implemented and how CRISA is applied to allow stakeholders to make detailed assessments. The Code further requires institutional investors to publicly disclose to stakeholders at least once a year the extent to which the Code has been applied.

Should institutional investors not apply any of the Principles of the Code, **9.033** they are required to disclose their reasons for not doing so. All disclosures and policies are required to be made accessible to the public. Institutional investors and their service providers are required to keep voting records confidential and carefully consider the reasons put forward to justify confidentiality. According to CRISA,[40] there are no provisions around either internal or external monitoring or enforcement of the principles and practice recommendations. The Principles of Code are standalone; thus, they should be capable of application in a self-regulated manner, without external oversight.

This has brought the effectiveness of the Code into question; therefore, the **9.034** Committee on Responsible Investing by Institutional Investors in South Africa are conducting an organisational review which includes the establishment of potential monitoring approaches that will enable the oversight of the implementation of the Code. These guidelines and frameworks for environmental and social (E&S) risk management provide a degree of commonality to the implementation of the industry's sustainable finance strategies, in a country

40 CRISA. 2020. CRISA Code for Responsible Investment in South Africa. 2020 Revision Consultation Draft. Available online from https:// cdn .ymaws .com/ www .iodsa .co .za/ resource/ collection/ 1D7CF73B -B95B -453F -A8E3 -D19829D18FBD/ CRISA_2 .0_Draft_for_public_comment .November2020__00000004_ .pdf Accessed 27 June 2021.

where there has been minimal consistency or coordination within industry sub-sectors.[41]

9.035 As highlighted in the preceding section, sustainable finance initiatives in South Africa rely predominantly on voluntary initiatives, the implementation of which is currently not supervised by any regulatory authorities.

(c) Green Finance Taxonomy

9.036 After a two-year consultation and development process, South Africa launched its first national Green Finance Taxonomy on 1 April 2022. It was launched by the Taxonomy Working Group as part of South Africa's Sustainable Finance Initiative. The Group was chaired by the National Treasury and hosted by the BASA, and included representatives from national government, financial sector regulators and the financial services sector.[42] The taxonomy not only supports national priorities but it is also aligned with international trends and the model which has been adopted by the European Union. The development of the taxonomy was supported by the IFC, through the IFC's Green Bond Market Development programme, in partnership with the Swedish International Development Cooperation Agency and the Swiss State Secretariat for Economic Affairs. Prior to the official launch, a draft was released in June for public comments and was tested in six financial institutions.[43]

9.037 The taxonomy has been designed to allow issuers, investors, lenders and other financial sector participants to track, monitor and demonstrate the credentials of their green activities.[44] The taxonomy further seeks to serve as an official classification of a minimum set of assets, projects and sectors eligible to be classified as environmentally friendly or green. According to Creamer,[45] the taxonomy will play a critical role in ensuring the promotion of transparency

41 ESRM Africa. 2022. Sustainability Initiatives in the South African Financial Sector. Available online from https://esrmafrica.org/south-africa-posts-5/ Accessed 14 August 2022.

42 Soofie, Z. 2022. New Green Finance Taxonomy Could Help South Africa Turn Green into Gold. Available online from www.dentons.com/en/insights/articles/2022/april/29/new-green-finance-taxonomy-could-help-south-africa-turn-green-into-gold Accessed 15 August 2022.

43 Creamer, M. 2022. Green Finance Taxonomy to Help Investors Make Green Project Decisions – Law Firm. Available online from www.miningweekly.com/article/green-finance-taxonomy-will-help-investors-make-green-project-decisions-says-law-firm-2022-04-05 Accessed 15 August 2022.

44 Soofie, Z. 2022. New Green Finance Taxonomy Could Help South Africa Turn Green into Gold. Available online from www.dentons.com/en/insights/articles/2022/april/29/new-green-finance-taxonomy-could-help-south-africa-turn-green-into-gold Accessed 15 August 2022.

45 Creamer, M. 2022. Green Finance Taxonomy to Help Investors Make Green Project Decisions – Law Firm. Available online from www.miningweekly.com/article/green-finance-taxonomy-will-help-investors-make-green-project-decisions-says-law-firm-2022-04-05 Accessed 15 August 2022.

within the financial sector and will serve as a bulwark against 'greenwashing', that is, deceptively showing something as environmentally friendly when it is not.

The taxonomy does not only focus on the environment, but it also incorporates criteria that aims at ensuring the implementation of South Africa's labour laws and policies. By considering both factors, the taxonomy shows that it supports South Africa's national policy and voluntary private sector initiatives that seek to promote sustainable finance by reducing the uncertainty and costs in classifying a core set of green activities.[46] According to Soofie,[47] the taxonomy aims to unlock several benefits, such as: **9.038**

- assisting with unlocking large-scale capital for climate-friendly and green investment in South Africa by increasing the credibility and transparency of green activities;
- reducing the costs associated with labelling and issuing green financial instruments;
- reducing financial risks through enhanced management of environmental and social performance;
- supporting regulatory and supervision oversight of the financial sector;
- providing clarity and certainty in selecting green investments in line with international best practices and national priorities and standards.

For each activity identified in the taxonomy, a technical screening criterion has been developed that includes both principles as well as metrics and thresholds. The principles inform the underlying rationale for how an activity will either result in substantial contribution or avoidance of harm to the environmental objective.[48] This is further developed by the methods with which the environmental performance of the economic activity will be measured. This in turn produces a guideline to determine whether a certain economic investment or activity is indeed green and in support of South Africa's sustainable policies and priorities.[49] **9.039**

---

46 National Treasury. 2020. Financing a Sustainable Economy: Technical Paper 2020. Available online from www.treasury.gov.za/publications/other/Sustainability%20technical%20paper%202020.pdf Accessed 13 January 2021.

47 Soofie, Z. 2022. New Green Finance Taxonomy Could Help South Africa Turn Green into Gold. Available online from www.dentons.com/en/insights/articles/2022/april/29/new-green-finance-taxonomy-could-help-south-africa-turn-green-into-gold Accessed 15 August 2022.

48 National Treasury. 2020. Financing a Sustainable Economy: Technical Paper 2020. Available online from www.treasury.gov.za/publications/other/Sustainability%20technical%20paper%202020.pdf Accessed 13 January 2021.

49 Soofie, Z. 2022. New Green Finance Taxonomy Could Help South Africa Turn Green into Gold. Available online from www.dentons.com/en/insights/articles/2022/april/29/new-green-finance-taxonomy-could-help-south-africa-turn-green-into-gold Accessed 15 August 2022.

9.040 This is another example of how South Africa has taken the initiative to ensure that the country is moving towards achieving its sustainability goals and obligations. Most financial institutions in the country look not only to the local guidelines but also to voluntary international guidelines and frameworks. According to ESRM Africa,[50] voluntary initiatives are a combination of adherence to locally and internationally developed standards. The application of these international guidelines by individual financial institutions varies and there is no standardised approach to environmental and social risk management in South Africa for most financial products. These guidelines include:

(d) The Equator Principles[51]

9.041 Several South African banks are signatories of the Equator Principles. The Equator Principles (EPs) are a risk management framework that has been adopted by financial institutions to determine, assess and manage environmental and social risks for project finance, project finance advisory, project-related corporate loans and bridge loans.[52]

9.042 There are currently 125 Equator Principles Financial Institutions (EPFIs) in 37 countries; they have all officially adopted the EPs, covering the majority of international project finance debt within developed and emerging markets. The EPFIs have committed to implementing the EPs in their internal environmental and social policies, procedures and standards for financing projects. The EPIS have all committed to not providing project finance or project-related corporate loans to projects where the client is not willing to or is unable to, comply with the EPs.[53]

9.043 While the EPs are not intended to be applied retroactively, EPFIs apply them to the upgrade of an existing project where changes in scale or scope may result in significant environmental and social risks and impacts on the existing project. The EPs have greatly increased the attention to corporate social responsibility within the project finance market, including robust standards

50 ESRM Africa. 2022. Sustainability Initiatives in the South African Financial Sector. Available online from https://esrmafrica.org/south-africa-posts-5/ Accessed 14 August 2022.

51 The Equator Principles Association. 2020. The Equator Principles. Available from https://equator-principles.com/about/ Accessed 20 January 2021.

52 ESRM Africa. 2022. Sustainability Initiatives in the South African Financial Sector. Available online from https://esrmafrica.org/south-africa-posts-5/ Accessed 14 August 2022.

53 Baloyi, G. 2019. The Benefits and Challenges of Implementing the Equator Principles: The Case of Four Large Banks in South Africa, through the Eyes of Project Finance Teams. A thesis submitted in partial fulfilment of the requirements for the degree of Master of Business Administration at the Rhodes Business School. Available online from http://vital.seals.ac.za:8080/vital/access/manager/PdfViewer/vital:35855/SOURCE1?viewPdfInternal=1 Accessed 15 August 2022.

for labour standards, indigenous peoples and consultation with locally affected communities. Furthermore, the EPs have also helped incite the development of responsible environmental and social management practices in the financial and banking sectors and have aided in the development of environmental and social risk management systems for member banks.[54]

Baloyi[55] used South African banks as a case study and identified that the EPs are applied during the Pre-Credit Committee, Credit Committee and onboarding processes. The Pre-Credit stage was the most popular among the local banks. The managers stated that they prefer to apply the EPs at the Pre-Credit stage because the risks can be highlighted to the borrower from the beginning. The study further highlighted that most banks have adopted these EPs to implement them and prevent reputational damage by overlooking environmental and social risks. The EPs have gained popularity in South Africa; however, they are not the only international guidelines that have been implemented. The Principles of Responsible Banking have also been widely adopted in South Africa. These are unpacked in the following section. **9.044**

(e) UNEP's Principles for Responsible Banking

In South Africa, five banks are signatories of UNEPs Principles for Responsible Banking.[56] According to BASA,[57] the Principles for Responsible Banking are a unique framework for ensuring that signatory banks' practices and strategies align with the vision society has set out for its future through the Paris Climate Agreement and Sustainable Development Goals. The framework consists of six Principles that are designed to bring ambition, purpose and vision to sustainable finance. They were created through a partnership between the United Nations and the founding banks. All the signatory banks commit to embedding these principles across all their business areas; that is, at the strategic, portfolio and transactional levels.[58] **9.045**

---

54 Equator Principles Association. 2017. Equator Principles. Available online from https://equator-principles.com./wp-content/uploads/2017/03/equator_principles_III.pdf Accessed 14 August 2022.

55 Baloyi, G. 2019. The Benefits and Challenges of Implementing the Equator Principles: The Case of Four Large Banks in South Africa, through the Eyes of Project Finance Teams. A thesis submitted in partial fulfilment of the requirements for the degree of Master of Business Administration at the Rhodes Business School. Available online from http://vital.seals.ac.za:8080/vital/access/manager/PdfViewer/vital:35855/SOURCE1?viewPdfInternal=1 Accessed 15 August 2022.

56 UNEPFI. 2022a. Signatories. Available online from www.unepfi.org/banking/bankingprinciples/prbsignatories/ Accessed 15 August 2022.

57 BASA (Banking Association South Africa). 2019. Global Principles for Responsible Banking. Available online from www.banking.org.za/news/global-principles-for-responsible-banking/ Accessed 15 August 2022.

58 Ibid.

9.046 The framework consists of six Principles designed to bring purpose, vision and ambition to sustainable finance. They were created in 2019 through a partnership between founding banks and the United Nations. Signatory banks commit to embedding these six principles across all business areas, at the strategic, portfolio and transactional levels. The six principles are as follows:[59]

1. *Alignment*: Signatories commit to aligning their business strategies to be consistent with, and contribute to the individual's needs and society's goals, as expressed in the Sustainable Development Goals, the Paris Agreement and all the other relevant national and regional frameworks.
2. *Impact and Target Setting*: The signatories commit to continuously increasing their positive impacts while reducing the negative impacts on and managing the risks to people and the environment resulting from their activities, products and services. Therefore, the signatories are required to set and publish their targets.
3. *Clients and Customers*: The signatories commit to working with their clients to encourage sustainable practices and enable economic activities that create shared prosperity for current and future generations.
4. *Stakeholders*: The signatories commit to engage, consult and partner with relevant stakeholders to achieve society's goals proactively and responsibly.
5. *Governance and Culture*: The signatories commit to implementing these Principles through effective governance and a culture of responsible banking.
6. *Transparency and Accountability*: The signatories commit to periodically review their individual and collective implementation of these Principles and be transparent and accountable about their positive and negative impacts and their contributions towards society's collective goals.

9.047 These are the six principles that guide the signatories to ensure that they are moving forward towards ensuring the Sustainable Development Goals and the other international global commitments. The signatories are guided by the following three-step process:

- *Impact Analysis*: Identifying the most significant impacts of products and services on the societies, economies and environments that the bank operates in.
- *Target Setting*: Setting and achieving measurable targets in a bank's areas of most significant impact.

59 UNEPFI. 2022b. Creating the Future of Banking. Available online from www .unepfi .org/ banking/ bankingprinciples/more-about-the-principles/ Accessed 15 August 2022.

- *Reporting*: Publicly report on progress on implementing the Principles, being transparent about impacts and contributions.

More than 270 banks, representing more than 45 per cent of banking assets worldwide, have become signatories of the principles. These banks are leading the way towards a future in which the banking community makes the kind of positive contribution to people and the planet from which society benefits. More South African banks should look to becoming signatories to ensure a faster transition toward the country becoming more sustainable and for it to reach its sustainability commitments. **9.048**

(f) The Task Force on Climate-related Financial Disclosures (Task Force)

As highlighted in section 3 of this chapter, the TCFDs are a systematic and credible method of disclosure required to enable improved pricing and risk distribution and to also identify potential economic opportunities that are associated with climate change risk adaptation and mitigation. The TCFDs were created to help identify the information needed by lenders, investors and insurance underwriters to assess and quantify and price climate-related opportunities and risks.[60] The Task Force's recommendations have gained much traction in the South African banking sector. They have been adopted by various financial sector organisations, including banks, asset managers, insurance companies and asset owners. According to Williams,[61] at the end of 2019 only two South African entities, namely SAICA and the FSCA, were official supporters of the TCFD recommendations. Despite the small number of supporters in the country, this goes to show that disclosure is slowly gaining prominence locally. **9.049**

According to Eccles and colleagues,[62] South Africa is one of the most advanced markets in terms of the implementation of integrated reporting of ESG factors in the world; however, climate-related financial disclosure is still considered to be in its infancy. The above principles act as guidelines and standards for sustainable finance and climate-related disclosures in South Africa. The principles have also resulted in increased sustainability awareness within banks and retirement funds and have also led asset managers to provide investment options that consider both ESG risks and take advantage of new green sustain- **9.050**

60 Williams, G. 2021. Climate-related Financial Disclosure in South Africa. Available online from www .dnaeconomics .com/ assets/ Usemosamo thoadnaeco nomicscom/ The _State _of _CFD _in _SA _Updated _UTW.pdf Accessed 16 August 2022.

61 Ibid.

62 Eccles, R.G., Krzus, M.P. and Solano, C. 2019. A Comparative Analysis of Integrated Reporting in Ten Countries. Available online from https://ssrn.com/abstract=3345590 Accessed 15 August 2022.

ability finance-orientated opportunities and products.[63] There are a variety of green financial products that can be used and have been adopted in the South African banking sector. The use of green finance in South Africa is highlighted in the following section.

D. GREEN FINANCE IN SOUTH AFRICA

9.051 South African financial institutions have adopted various voluntary guidelines and frameworks that have driven the development and growth of green finance in the country. As highlighted above, South Africa has developed the Green Finance Taxonomy to guide financial institutions and investors to make more informed decisions when it comes to 'green projects'. The taxonomy prevents things such as greenwashing in the financial industry. Green finance is defined as any structured financial activity that has been created to ensure a better environmental outcome.[64]

9.052 It constitutes various products, which include debt mechanisms and an array of loans and investments that are used to incentivise the development of green projects, or any projects that look to reduce the impact of climate change. Such projects include renewable energy, pollution control and prevention, biodiversity conservation, circular economy initiatives and the sustainable use of land and resources. Common green finance instruments that have had great traction globally and in South Africa are the green loans and the green bond.

1. Green Loans

9.053 The primary aim of the green loan market is mainly to support and assist environmentally sustainable economic activity in order to aid in the social transition to a more environmentally friendly way of life, such as the creation of environmentally friendly technologies. The IFC is the largest finance institution that supports the private sector in developing markets, and the leading provider of green loans.[65]

---

63 International Finance Corporation (IFC). 2020. Sustainable Finance Practices in South African Retirement Funds: Opportunities to Unlock Investment in Green and Climate Finance and Support a Resilient Economy. Available online from https:// sustaina blefinance initiative .org .za/ assets _sfi/ downloads/ Sustain ableFinanceinSARetirementFunds_FINAL_08122020.pdf Accessed 20 January 2021.

64 Fleming, S. 2020. What Is Green Finance and Why Is It Important? Available online from www.weforum .org/agenda/2020/11/what-is-green-finance/ Accessed 26 August 2022.

65 World Bank. 2021. What You Need to Know about Green Loans. Available online from www.worldbank .org/en/news/feature/2021/10/04/what-you-need-to-know-about-green-loans Accessed 15 January 2024.

Currently, developing countries account for $1.6 billion of the estimated $33 billion in outstanding green loans; however, with the rapid growth in the market, eventually green loans will outpace the growth of the green bond market in the near term.[66] Unlike the green bond, the green loan is typically smaller and undertaken in private operations. However, they are similar in that both raise capital for green-eligible projects and 100 per cent of their proceeds are meant for green-eligible activities only. Potential issuers in emerging markets with small green portfolios may feel more inclined to receive a green loan than to issue a green bond due to the higher transaction costs of bond issuance, the minimum bond size to be tradeable and the fact that only bonds above a certain size are tracked by various indices. **9.054**

Green loans are regulated by the Green Loan Principles (GLP). The GLP sets out a clear, understandable framework that outlines the characteristics of a green loan. The GLP is based on the following components:[67] **9.055**

1. Use of Proceeds: Designated green projects should provide clear environmental benefits, which will be assessed, measured, and reported by the borrower.
2. Process for Project Evaluation and Selection: The borrower of a green loan should clearly communicate how it is organised to assess and select projects that will receive loan proceeds. In addition, the borrower explains how it will manage environmental and social risks of eligible projects.
3. Management of Proceeds: The proceeds of a green loan should be credited to a dedicated account or tracked by the borrower to maintain transparency and promote the integrity of the product.
4. Reporting: The principles recommend the use of qualitative performance indicators and, where feasible, quantitative performance measures (for example, energy capacity, electricity generation, greenhouse gas emissions reduced/avoided, and so on).

Essentially, green loans should not be considered with loans that are not aligned with these mentioned components. The IFC adopted these principles to help clients receive additional financing to respond to environmental change. Through these green loans, the IFC partners with clients to develop a green finance regulatory framework, which articulates how the governance **9.056**

66 World Bank. 2021. What You Need to Know about Green Loans. Available online from www.worldbank.org/en/news/feature/2021/10/04/what-you-need-to-know-about-green-loans Accessed 15 January 2024.

67 ICMA (International Capital Market Association) 2018. Green Loan Principles: Supporting Environmentally Sustainable Economic Activity. Available online from www.lma.eu.com/application/files/9115/4452/5458/741_LM_Green_Loan_Principles_Booklet_V8.pdf Accessed 22 November 2022.

and systems of the client are used to manage and track the use of proceeds to ensure they are allocated only to eligible green projects.

9.057 In 2021, Africa received its first certified green loan that fully complied with the Green Loan Principles. The IFC provided ABSA Bank Ltd (South Africa's leading financial institution in financing renewable projects) with a loan of up to $150 million to support the bank's strategy to expand its climate finance business and assist South Africa in meeting its greenhouse gas reduction targets.[68] Notably, this was the IFC's fourth investment dedicated to green finance in South Africa. Furthermore, as an addition to the loan, the IFC further offered to provide technical advice and knowledge to assist ABSA in developing a green, social and sustainable bonds and loans framework. This was all done to assist South Africa to move towards becoming greener and more sustainable in the wake of the COVID-19 pandemic.

9.058 Lastly, the IFC estimates an approximately $588 billion investment opportunity between now and 2030 in climate mitigation across financial sectors in South Africa. ABSA Bank Ltd will be among the various financiers to assist financial markets in South Africa, Egypt, the Philippines and Mexico to mobilise funds for climate mitigation and align with Paris Climate Agreement Targets. As part of this initiative, the IFC disclosed a proposed investment of a green loan of up to US$200 million that will be issued in Africa, specifically in South Africa for a project that will help further develop Nedbank's climate finance platform to on-lend to renewable energy projects and contribute to expanding the bank's climate strategy through Equator Principles compliance projects.[69]

2. Green Bonds

9.059 Green bonds have emerged as one of the most promising and innovative climate finance mechanisms to date. Globally, the green bond market has grown by more than 90 per cent in the last decade.[70] Despite this exponen-

68 International Finance Corporation. 2021. IFC and Absa Bank Partner on Africa's First Certified Green Loan to Support Green Energy Projects. Available online from https://pressroom.ifc.org/all/pages/PressDetail.aspx?ID=26334 Accessed 22 November 2022.

69 International Finance Corporation (IFC). 2020. Sustainable Finance Practices in South African Retirement Funds: Opportunities to Unlock Investment in Green and Climate Finance and Support a Resilient Economy. Available online from https://sustainablefinanceinitiative.org.za/assets_sfi/downloads/SustainableFinanceinSARetirementFunds_FINAL_08122020.pdf Accessed 20 January 2021.

70 Ngwenya, N. 2019. South Africa's Green Bonds Show There Are Massive Opportunities for Growth. Business Live. Available online from www.businesslive.co.za/bd/opinion/2019-06-20-sas-green-bonds-show-there-are-massive-opportunities-for-growth/ Accessed 13 January 2021.

tial growth, the world still needs trillions of dollars to combat the negative impacts of global warming. Green bonds are a way for issuers to raise money for pro-environmentally friendly projects.[71] Investments from Green bond proceeds can go toward either new or existing projects that are meant to have positive environmental effects or mitigate climate change impacts. The spectrum of these projects is wide. It covers projects within the fields of (but not limited to) construction, energy, land rehabilitation, transport, waste management and water.

Green bonds are issued with the guidance of the Green Bond Principles (GBP), which serve as the market standard for green bonds globally.[72] The GBP are voluntary guidelines that have been designed to be flexible and can be used across the industry to support transparency, disclosure and integrity in the development of the Green Bond Market.[73] The GBP stipulates practices concerning project evaluation and selection, project eligibility, the use and management of bond proceeds, information disclosure and assurance.[74] Regarding market standardisation and guidelines, green bonds are supposed to serve the dual purpose of investment instrument and sustainable development instrument. **9.060**

In attempting to effectively implement green bonds and effectively transition South Africa to a resilient, low-carbon green economy, a Green Finance Taxonomy was created. According to the National Treasury,[75] a Green Finance Taxonomy is 'an official classification or catalogue that defines a minimum set of assets, projects, and sectors that are eligible to be defined as "green" in line with international best practices and national priorities'. This tool is essential as there has been no requirement for bond issuers or financial institutions to disclose taxonomic alignment to the investors. **9.061**

---

71 Pronina, L. 2019. What Are Green Bonds and How 'Green' Is Green? Available online from www.iol.co.za/personal-finance/what-are-green-bonds-and-how-green-is-green-20071020 Accessed 15 January 2021.

72 ICMA (International Capital Market Association). 2021. Green Bond Principles: Voluntary Process Guidelines for Issuing Green Bonds. Available online from www .icmagroup .org/ assets/ documents/ Sustainable-finance/2021-updates/Green-Bond-Principles-June-2021-140621.pdf Accessed 27 June 2021.

73 Duru, U., and Nyong, A. 2016. Why Africa Needs Green Bonds. Chief Economist Complex | AEB Volume 7 Issue 2.

74 ICMA (International Capital Market Association). 2021. Green Bond Principles: Voluntary Process Guidelines for Issuing Green Bonds. Available online from www .icmagroup .org/ assets/ documents/ Sustainable-finance/2021-updates/Green-Bond-Principles-June-2021-140621.pdf Accessed 27 June 2021.

75 National Treasury. 2021. Applying the Green Finance Taxonomy User Guidance to the Draft Green Finance Taxonomy: Draft. Available online from www .treasury .gov .za/ public %20comments/ GreenFinance2021/ Draft %20Green %20Finance %20Taxonomy %20User %20Guidance.pdf Accessed 11 November 2021.

9.062 Furthermore, it also allows all participants to track, monitor and demonstrate the credentials of their green activities confidently and efficiently. However, thus far there have been no reports or regulations passed that require financial intuitions or bond issuers to use the Green Bond Principles in their transactions. Despite the lack of stringent requirements in the application of the Green Bond Principles, South African banks and bond issuers have nevertheless taken it upon themselves to go ahead and issue green bonds.

9.063 In 2021, the IFC was an investor in a domestic medium-term note programme, where the first green bond was issued by a commercial bank in Africa that focused on green residential housing developments.[76] The IFC anchored Nedbank to issue green bonds as a way to assist in improving access to certified green homes in South Africa. This contributed to South Africa's reduced emissions targets and paved the way for Nedbank to expand its portfolio of green buildings certified under the IFC's EDGE programme. The first green bond was approximately R1.09 billion aligned with the ICMA GBP and was listed on the JSE in the sustainability segment. The availability of this green bond boosted South Africa's green building market. The trajectory of green bonds in South Africa is outlined in the following section.

3. The Green Bond Trajectory in South Africa

9.064 In South Africa, climate finance has taken a remarkable upturn and private investors have increasingly engaged in projects offering both environmental efficiency and financial return. The green bond market is demonstrating an upward trajectory. The World Bank has estimated that by 2030 there could be potentially $588 billion invested in climate-friendly projects in South Africa.[77] South Africa was the first country in the emerging markets to issue a green bond, in 2012. The first green bond issued in South Africa was issued by Nedbank and was worth $297.2 million.[78] The popularity of green bonds has increased since then, as both public and private entities issue green bonds. Notable government green bonds are the government-issued green bonds

---

76 International Finance Corporation 2021. IFC and Absa Bank Partner on Africa's First Certified Green Loan to Support Green Energy Projects. Available online from https://pressroom.ifc.org/all/pages/PressDetail.aspx?ID=26334 Accessed 22 November 2022.

77 Ngounou, B. 2020. South Africa: Standard Bank Raises $200 Million in Green Bonds; A Record. Available online from www.afrik21.africa/en/south-africa-standard-bank-raises-200-million-in-green-bonds-a-record/ Accessed 15 January 2021.

78 ALCB Fund. 2018. Understanding the African Green Bond Market. Available online from https://uploads-ssl.webflow.com/5f0f1ce96a1f6869277ccbbd/5f5b9224bcf30204da8a9e53_2018-03-05-African-Green-Bond-Market_Final.pdf Accessed 27 June 2021.

for the City of Cape Town, worth $84 million, in 2017, and for the City of Johannesburg, worth $136.9 million, in 2014.[79]

The City of Cape Town bond was the first to be listed on the JSE's new segment and is regarded as South Africa's first true green bond – it was also awarded a GB1 rating by Moody's and was further verified by KPMG against the CBS.[80] The municipal Green Bonds for South Africa's two cities are being primarily used to improve their water infrastructure and transport systems, and to finance projects that reduce greenhouse emissions in the cities. **9.065**

Substantial potential for growth has arisen in the green bond market since then. Green bonds have become integral to financing climate change and environmental projects and there are already vast success stories across the country. South Africa now has an active green bond sphere, where both its public and private sectors contribute to the issuance of green bonds. The proceeds have gone into projects such as renewable energy (wind and solar projects), energy-efficient buildings and low-carbon infrastructure such as low-emission transport.[81] **9.066**

These projects are all to reduce negative climate change impacts. South Africa is one of the hotspots for climate change.[82] Prolonged drought periods have resulted in water shortages, in turn having negative effects on the broader South African society and economy.[83] This is evident as the prolonged drought from 2014 to 2017 resulted in a decrease in GDP because of the negative impact on the agricultural sector.[84] **9.067**

The negative consequences of climate change have also accelerated the need to consider strategies to build social, environmental and economic resilience and **9.068**

79 Ibid.

80 Ibid.

81 Duru, U., and Nyong, A. 2016. Why Africa Needs Green Bonds. Chief Economist Complex | AEB Volume 7 Issue 2.

82 Ngwenya, N. and, Simatele, M.D. 2020. The emergence of green bonds as an integral component of climate finance in South Africa. S Afr J Sci. 116(1/2), Art. #6522. Available online from https://doi.org/10.17159/sajs.2020/6522; IPCC (Intergovernmental Panel on Climate Change). 2018. Summary for policymakers. In: Masson-Delmotte V, Zhai P, Pörtner HO, Roberts D, Skea J, Shukla PR, et al., editors. Global warming of 1.5°C. Geneva: World Meteorological Organization. Available online from https://report.ipcc.ch/sr15/pdf/sr15_spm_final.pdf.

83 Archer, E., Landman, W., Malherbe, J., Tadross, M., and Pretorius, S. 2019. South Africa's Winter Rainfall Region Drought: A Region in Transition? Clim Risk Manage 1–8. Available online from https://doi.org/10.1016/j.crm.2019.100188.

84 Le Page, D., Tyler-Davie, G., and Hamilton, G. 2019. Climate Change Must Be a Central Pillar of SA's Economic Growth. Business Live. Available online from www.businesslive.co.za/bd/opinion/2019-02-06-climate-change-must-be-a-central-pillar-of-sas-economic-growth/ Accessed 20 January 2021.

enforce national policies. Climate change adaptation and mitigation strategies have been reflected in numerous national policies and strategies, such as the Draft National Climate Change Adaptation Strategy (2019) and the National Climate Change Response White Paper (2011).[85]

9.069 The national policies and strategies are long-term plans to reduce South Africa's emissions as agreed during the Paris Agreement. Since 2011, South Africa has also established numerous climate finance systems, which are dedicated to climate adaptation and mitigation projects.[86] With the aid of local financial institutions and sustainable banking practices, green bonds and green loans are likely to become an integral component of climate finance in South Africa and further fund a range of environmental and climate-related projects.

4. South Africa's Green Finance Performance in Comparison to the Rest of Africa

9.070 Green finance has not only grown in relevance in South Africa but has also spread across the African continent. South Africa is the leading country when it comes to green bonds on the continent, with the rest of the continent lagging behind. Thus, one can argue that there is a gap in knowledge of the green bonds in Africa. This has in turn made Africa the slowest adopter of green bonds, and thus limited the potential for these innovative financial products to raise ancillary capital for sustainable development throughout the continent.[87] The African continent represents enormous potential for the growth of the green bond market.

9.071 However, specific steps need to be taken to guarantee that the market will be based on appropriate frameworks and mechanisms. There are three factors that could possibly have a significant influence on the growth of the green market in Africa. The first is the legal and regulatory frameworks; that is, to ensure that the green bond market operates in a system where there is openness and accountability from issuers, stringent legislative and regulatory frameworks must be in place. Second, there must be continuous monitoring and evaluation

85 Baudoin, M. A., Vogel, C., Nortje, K., and Naik, M. 2017. Living with Drought in South Africa: Lessons Learnt from the Recent El Niño Drought Period. Int J Disaster Risk Manage 23, 128–37. https://doi.org/10.1016/j.ijdrr.2017.05.005.

86 Ngwenya, N., and Simatele, M.D. 2020. The Emergence of Green Bonds as an Integral Component of Climate Finance in South Africa. S Afr J Sci. 116(1/2), Art. #6522. Available online from https://doi.org/10.17159/sajs.2020/6522.

87 Holtz, L., and Heitzig, C. 2021. Africa's Green Bond Market Trails Behind Other Regions. Available online from www.brookings.edu/blog/africa-in-focus/2021/03/26/africas-green-bond-market-trails-behind-other-regions/ Accessed 22 November 2022.

of the market to determine investor behaviour and impact evaluation as a means to enhance accountability and transparency and prevent greenwashing.[88] Last, there is a need for political will and institutional arrangements such as the African Development Bank green bond programme which was established to finance green projects. Should they not be implemented effectively, one would anticipate stagnant growth in green finance across the continent.

As shown in Figure 9.1, South Africa has nearly three-fourths of the total market share on the continent. It is followed by Morocco and Nigeria, and these three countries combined make up more than 97 per cent of total issuances of green bonds in Africa. **9.072**

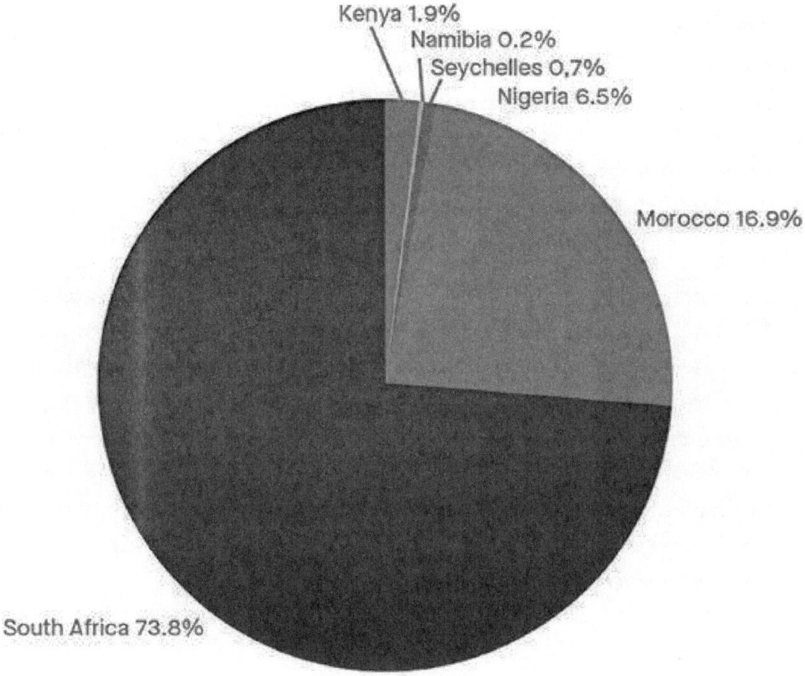

Source: George Marbuah, Stockholm Sustainable Finance Centre, 'Scoping the Sustainable Finance Landscape in Africa: The Case of Green Bonds' (2020), www.researchgate.net/publication/345842960_Scoping_the_sustainable_finance_landscape_in_Africa_The_case_of_green_bonds.

Figure 9.1 Share of total green bond issues by state

88 Ngwenya, N. 2019. South Africa's Green Bonds Show There Are Massive Opportunities for Growth. Business Live. Available online from www.businesslive.co.za/bd/opinion/2019-06-20-sas-green-bonds-show-there-are-massive-opportunities-for-growth/ Accessed 13 January 2021.

9.073 Africa is the recipient of 23 per cent of official climate finance, has less than 1 per cent of global green bond issuances and is paying more than double the interest rate of similarly rated peers to access markets.[89] Africa continues to face various challenges that include debt burden and historical high cost of borrowing, recovery post-COVID-19, climate change-related issues, energy and food shortages due to climate-related issues, civil war and political unrest, among various other factors. These challenges make it even more necessary for African states to benefit from new ways to raise money from private investors in a transparent and efficient framework and at reasonable rates.[90] Below are some case studies of a few green bonds that have been issued across the continent.

(a) Case Studies

9.074 This chapter shall look at case studies from the top three African countries, namely South Africa, Morocco and Nigeria, as shown in Figure 9.1. At the time of writing, these three countries reportedly held the following percentages of green bonds on the continent: Nigeria, 6.5 per cent; Morocco, 16.9 per cent; South Africa, 73.8 per cent.

(i) Nigeria

9.075 Nigeria, which is the biggest economy in Africa, issued its first green bond in 2017. The inaugural N10.69 (~US$26 million), 13.48 per cent five-year sovereign green bond was issued by the Federal Government of Nigeria (FGN). Various people contributed to and invested in the issuing of this bond: commercial banks, pension groups, asset management firms and the Nigerian investment community.[91] The proceeds were used to fund three significant green projects that aligned with the Sustainable Development Goals: the energising Education Project, the Afforestation Project and the Rural Electrification project.[92]

89 UNECA. 2022. Green Bonds to Serve Africa's Sustainable Investment Needs. Available online from www.un.org/africarenewal/magazine/june-2022/green-bonds-serve-africa%E2%80%99s-sustainable-investment-needs Accessed 12 December 2022.

90 UNECA. 2022. Green Bonds to Serve Africa's Sustainable Investment Needs. Available online from www.un.org/africarenewal/magazine/june-2022/green-bonds-serve-africa%E2%80%99s-sustainable-investment-needs Accessed 12 December 2022.

91 Ngwenya, N., and Simatele, M.D. 2020. The Emergence of Green Bonds as an Integral Component of Climate Finance in South Africa. S Afr J Sci. 116(1/2), Art. #6522. Available online from https://doi.org/10.17159/sajs.2020/6522.

92 Lexology. 2020. Climate Change Regulation for Financial Services Firms: A Global View. Available online from www.lexology.com/library/detail.aspx?g=5e01c104-0385-4c69-b117-9e2250caf4f2 Accessed 25 January 2021.

The success of the FGN green bond attracted local and international investors as investor confidence increased. This paved the way for the listing and issuance of corporate green bonds which include the N15 billion (~US$36 million) green bond issued by Access Bank of Nigeria Plc, the N8.5 billion (~US$21 million) Green Infrastructure Bond by North South Power Company (NSP) and the Series II N15 billion FGN seven-year sovereign green bond in 2019. This shows the upward trajectory of green bonds in Nigeria over a period of three years. Within a period of three years the Nigerian green bond market grew from zero to N49.19 billion (~$120 million) from issuances and listings.[93] This shows an upward trajectory of green bonds in the country and is likely to spread to the rest of West Africa. The development of the green bond market in Nigeria has paved the way for new projects to be established and undertaken, such as green building practices that will achieve the SGDs by providing affordable and sustainable energy for citizens of the country.[94] **9.076**

(ii) Morocco

The first green bond in Morocco was issued by the Moroccan Agency of Sustainable Energy SA (MASEN), which is a state-owned public limited company. It issued Morocco's first green bond in November 2016, which amounted to 1.15 billion Dirham (US$117 million). This green bond was helped by the development of three solar energy projects under the Noor I solar project. This opened the door for the many other green bonds in the country. Recently, with Morocco's future electricity generation capacity becoming firmly dependent on renewable energy sources, it has been attracting private financing for its new projects. Green bonds have become an increasingly viable option to help finance energy production in the kingdom. By 2019, the total amount of green bonds issued in Morocco had reached Dh3.65 billion (€328.3 million), showing the rapid growth and popularity of green bonds.[95] **9.077**

Initially, the funding was restricted to multilateral financial institutions; however, more private lenders and institutions are now partaking in the country's green bonds. Recently, a certified green bond was issued by the European Bank for Reconstruction and Development (EBRD), which has **9.078**

93 Chiemeka, J. 2021. Nigeria's Green Bonds Are a Key Step in Our Sustainable Finance Agenda. Available online from https://focus.world-exchanges.org/articles/nigeria-green-bonds.

94 Oguntuase, O.J., and Windapo, A. 2021. Green Bonds and Green Buildings: New Options for achieving Sustainable Development in Nigeria. Available online from https://link.springer.com/chapter/10.1007/978-981-33-4424-2_11.

95 Oxford Business Group. 2019. Morocco's green bonds supporting a switch to cleaner energy. Available online from https://oxfordbusinessgroup.com/reports/morocco/2019-report/economy/financing-change-green-bonds-are-starting-to-support-a-switch-to-cleaner-energy-but-attitudes-in-the-banking-sector-must-also-shift. Accessed 22 April 2022.

invested MAD 200 million (€19.2 million) to finance Morocco's national high-speed rail network. The EBRD has become the first foreign entity to contribute toward the needed MAD 1 billion (€95 million) green bond which was issued by Morocco's National Railways Office (ONCF) to refinance the debt used to boost the high-speed rail infrastructure across the country. This green infrastructure bond is set to support the implementation of the ONCF's rail strategy while consolidating the country's green financing market, which is currently valued at approximately $450 million.[96] This goes to show how popular green bonds and finance have become in the country over a short period of six years.

(iii) South Africa

9.079 In 2012, the first green bond was issued in South Africa by the Industrial Development Corporation (IDC) of South Africa Ltd. The IDC issued a R5 billion green bond that was set to be used to fund the growth of green and energy-efficient industries.[97] This paved way for the issuance of other green bonds. Between 2013 and 2014, the City of Johannesburg was the first South African municipality to list a green bond on the JSE. This bond was valued at R1.46 billion (~US$ 79 million). The proceeds were allocated to fund low-carbon transport and energy-saving measures such as solar water heating, all green projects.[98]

9.080 The success of the City of Johannesburg's green bond led to the City of Cape Town, another major metropolitan municipality, launching its green bond in July 2017. The City issued a R1 billion (~US$56 million) bond, and within two hours 29 investors made offers totalling R4.3 billion in response to the R1 billion that was being sold.[99] The City of Cape Town's green bond was certified by the Climate Bond Initiative and Moody's international rating agency as 'Excellent' by assigning a GB1 rating.[100]

96 Anouar, S. 2022. EBRD Invest €19.2 Million in Morocco's First Green Infrastructure Bond. Available online from www.moroccoworldnews.com/2022/07/350505/ebrd-invest-euro-19-2-million-in-moroccos-first-green-infrastructure-bond.

97 FANews. 2012. Nedbank Plays Pivotal Role in South Africa's First-ever Institutional Green Bond. Available online from www.fanews.co.za/article/company-news-results/1/nedgroup/1065/nedbank-plays-pivotal-role-in-south-africa-s-first-ever-institutional-green-bond/12837. Accessed 20 January 2021.

98 C40 Cities. 2016 C40 Good Practice Guides: Johannesburg – Green Bond. Available online from www.c40.org/case-studies/c40-good-practice-guides-johannesburg-green-bond/ Accessed 20 April 2022.

99 Blue Horizon. 2022. Financing Climate Change Adaptation: The Emergence of Municipal Green Bonds in South Africa. www.bluehorizon.energy/financing-climate-change-adaptation-the-emergence-of-municipal-green-bonds-in-south-africa/

100 Global Infrastructure Hub. 2021. Cape Town Green Bond. Available from: www.gihub.org/innovative-funding-and-financing/case-studies/cape-town-green-bond/#:~:text=In%202017%2C%20amid%20severe%20drought,to%20and%20mitigate%20climate%20change Accessed 22 November 2022.

Various financial institutions have also issued and listed their own green bonds. This includes Standard Bank, which has issued its first local Tier 2 capital-qualifying green bond, which looks to finance renewable energy projects in South Africa. The bank also increased its existing social bond, which was issued to finance mortgage loans in the affordable housing target market, focusing on women borrowers.[101] Nedbank listed an R1.09bn (~US$58 million) billion green bond on the JSE for green residential areas. This issuance boosted Nedbank's total green bond issuance on the JSE to R6.8 billion (~US$338 million).[102] **9.081**

The aforementioned are a few of the many green-financed projects in the country, as financial institutions have realised that the more they issue green loans and green bonds, the more positive the impact on their ESG performance. Thus, the South African banking system has played an integral role in ensuring the growth of green finance in the country. The following section unpacks the concept of sustainable banking in South Africa. **9.082**

E. SUSTAINABLE BANKING IN SOUTH AFRICA

There are 18 registered banks, 13 local branches of foreign banks, 5 cooperative banks, 4 mutual banks and 29 foreign banks with approved local representative offices in South Africa.[103] The banking sector is highly concentrated, with the top five banks – ABSA, Standard Bank, First National Bank, Capitec and Nedbank – representing an estimated 89.4 per cent of the total banking sector as of 31 March 2020.[104] **9.083**

The concept of sustainable banking in South Africa is still evolving as it is still in its infancy. Given the institutionalised inequality in South Africa's history, there has been pressure on the banking system to advocate for inclusivity, equity and a growing economy that provides employment and addresses poverty. The **9.084**

101 Burger, S. 2021. Standard Bank Issues Green, Social Bonds to Finance Renewable Housing Projects in South Africa. Available online from www.engineeringnews.co.za/article/standard-bank-issues-green-social-bonds-to-finance-renewable-housing-projects-in-south-africa-2021-12-13#:~:text=Financial%20services%20firm%20Standard%20Bank,a%20focus%20on%20women%20borrowers

102 Nedbank lists green residential bond on the JSE. Available online from www.jse.co.za/news/news/nedbank-lists-green-residential-bond-jse. Accessed 19 January 2022.

103 www .resbank .co .za/ en/ home/ publications/ publication -detail -pages/ prudential -authority/ pa -statistics -selected-trends---monthly/2021/Selected-SA-Banking-Sector-Trends---Monthly

104 Prudential Authority Annual Report. 2019/2020. Promoting and Enhancing The Safety, Soundness and Integrity of Regulated Financial Institutions. South African Reserve Bank. Available online from www.resbank.co.za/en/home/publications/publication-detail-pages/reports/pa-annual-reports/2020/10227. Accessed 19 January 2022.

early initiatives by banks during the post-apartheid transition mainly focused on addressing issues of financial inclusion and transformation of the demographic profile of bank ownership and management.[105] These initiatives have played a very important role in highlighting and addressing some of the key aspects required for social transitions concerning sustainable banking.

9.085 The initiatives in place, however, partially considered the environmental impact of banking and the impact that they have on South Africans. A search for 'transitions in the South Africa banking systems' would not throw up results specifically including terms such as environment or climate change but mostly focuses on the social transformation.[106] Environmental issues impact both the economy and society, mainly those marginalised and poor communities who are more vulnerable to the decline in environmental quality and economic inclusivity. Thus, it has been of great importance for South Africa to broaden its view of sustainable banking.

9.086 South African banks have engaged in the promotion of the green economy and have been at the forefront of introducing best practices in environmental and social risk management and helping to drive change on the continent.[107] This has been mainly due to the adoption of principles such as the Principles of Environmental and Social Risk Management and the Equator Principles. In 2014, the Banking Association of South Africa's (BASA) members (both local and international banks in South Africa) adopted the Principles of Environmental and Social Risk Management Principles.[108] The adopted principles apply to all financial activities, but their implementation is not mandatory.

9.087 The Principles on Environmental and Social Risk Management do not provide any technical guidelines that facilitate their implementation, nor do they require any disclosure of financial institutions' performance. Furthermore, because the banking sector in South Africa is run as a business, with all the large banks registered on several stock exchanges (and particular attention on the JSE), this means that the banks are obligated to apply the King IV Report

---

105 Ward, M., and Naude, R. 2019. Banking for a Sustainable Economy. Available online from www.bankseta .org .za/ wp -content/ uploads/ 2020/ 02/ BANKSETA -Sustainable -Banking -just -transition -FINAL .pdf Accessed 13 January 2021.

106 Ibid.

107 IFC (International Finance Corporation). 2018. Country Progress Report. Addendum to SBN Global Progress Report: South Africa. Sustainable Banking Network. Available online from www.ifc.org/wps/wcm/ connect/ bfede35f-5732 -4c87 -bfe2 -fbcdd320b536/ SBN+ Country+ Progress+ Report+ -+ South+ Africa .pdf ?MOD=AJPERES&CVID=m746VJS Accessed 15 January 2021.

108 Ibid.

on Corporate Governance.[109] To meet the requirements of the Principles and the King IV report, the top banks have had to adopt new tools and approaches that have allowed them to identify, plan, operationalise and report on how they have integrated sustainability aspects into their business.

The top four banks in South Africa were among the first emerging market signatories of the Equator Principles.[110] The Equator Principles are a risk management framework, and one which has been adopted by financial institutions all around the world.[111] These principles are used to determine, assess and manage environmental and social risk in projects and to support responsible risk-related decision-making. Over the years, it has become more apparent that banks must understand and manage the risks and negative impacts of banking activities for the environment and society. These regulations and principles have driven South African banks to look for opportunities to create value for the banking sector and broader society through sustainable banking. **9.088**

Through sustainable banking it has become more evident that banks could engage in various forms of value-driven business to increase their efforts towards being more sustainable. Some of the banks have started creating value through the development of innovative products and new forms of financing and business such as green bonds and green credit cards, among other products. For banks, these are long-term value products for both themselves and their clients. Sustainable banking is emerging as an important contributor to achieving sustainability at both global and local levels. **9.089**

The following two case studies provide insight into how South African banks are engaging, and have already engaged, with sustainable value creation both internally and externally, with regard to products and services that they provide to their clients and the different sectors of the economy, and how these banks compare to other banks that have adopted sustainable banking on the continent. **9.090**

---

109 Ward, M., and Naude, R. 2019. Banking for a Sustainable Economy. Available online from www.bankseta.org.za/wp-content/uploads/2020/02/BANKSETA-Sustainable-Banking-just-transition-FINAL.pdf Accessed 13 January 2021. See also IoDSA. 2016. King IV: Report on Corporate Governance for South Africa 2016. Johannesburg: Institute of Directors Southern Africa (IoS).

110 IFC (International Finance Corporation). 2018. Country Progress Report. Addendum to SBN Global Progress Report: South Africa. Sustainable Banking Network. Available [Online] from www.ifc.org/wps/wcm/connect/bfede35f-5732-4c87-bfe2-fbcdd320b536/SBN+Country+Progress+Report+-+South+Africa.pdf?MOD=AJPERES&CVID=m746VJS Accessed 15 January 2021.

111 Equator Principles. 2020. The Equator Principles: A Financial Industry Benchmark for Determining, Assessing and Managing Environmental and Social Risk in Projects. Available online from https://equator-principles.com/wp-content/uploads/2021/02/The-Equator-Principles-July-2020.pdf. Accessed 27 June 2021.

1. Case Study: Standard Bank

9.091 Standard Bank's approach to sustainability is guided by the United Nations Sustainable Development Goals, the African Union's Agenda 2063 and the South African government's National Development Plan.[112]

9.092 Sim Tshabalala, the CEO of Standard Bank, states that 'Standard Bank is committed to driving sustainable and inclusive economic growth across the continent we call home'.[113]

9.093 In the Standard Bank Group Report to Society 2019,[114] the bank outlined its approach to sustainability and further highlighted how this goes well beyond its internal operations to also extend to its external operations. The bank's initiatives and efforts to transition to more sustainable operations, which they have abbreviated as SEE (social, economic and environmental) will be summarised in the section below. Over the years Standard Bank's efforts towards sustainability have truly been noteworthy, where their financial products and services have taken to the market and have a strong core focus on sustainability.

(a) Internal sustainability operations

9.094 In alignment with its SEE goals, Standard Bank has taken various strides towards making its internal operations more sustainable. Among these efforts are working towards increasing employees' financial literacy, by hosting sessions which outline the importance of financial planning and investing with their end goals in mind. It is working towards empowering its employees and also giving back to society through financial inclusion. The bank has also taken strides to 'green' its offices and branches in South Africa as well as across the rest of the continent.

9.095 All new buildings and office construction is aligned with the Green Building Council of South Africa's sustainability rules and energy management systems are aligned with the ISO 50001 standard.[115] A prime example of this is the bank's office located at no.1 Simmonds Street in Johannesburg, which has a renewable energy parking facility that produces carbon-free electricity for the office building.[116] In 2017, R4.9 million was invested in energy efficiency

---

112 Standard Bank. 2017. Standard Bank's Report to Society 2017. Available online from http://annualreport2017.standardbank.com/downloads/Standard_bank_RTS2017_report_to_ society.pdf Accessed 27 January 2021.

113 Ibid.

114 Ibid.

115 Ibid.

116 Ibid.

improvements which contributed to the production of 1978 KW of renewable energy. These are some of the notable improvements and efforts made by Standard Bank to achieve sustainability in its internal operations.

(b) Sustainability in terms of financial services and corporate social investment: Affordable and clean energy

Standard Bank has committed to reducing its investments in fossil fuel energy and diverting this funding towards investments in renewable energy projects. To show its commitment to these efforts, Standard Bank engaged with the Centre for Environmental Rights (CER) and other environmental groups concerning the funding of coal-powered projects. Standard Bank stated: 'While minimising our direct environmental impacts is important, we must also consider the indirect impacts from businesses and projects we fund.'[117] **9.096**

It has demonstrably put its words into action, as from 2012 to 2017, 83 per cent of its power project finance was directed towards renewable energy while 17 per cent was directed towards lending to fossil fuel power projects in energy production in Africa.[118] Standard Bank further outlines that it is slowly transitioning towards only funding green energy because the socio-economic impacts related to the transition from carbon-intensive to low-carbon activities are not well understood for Africa, and that socio-political characteristics across the continent need to be developed to understand the transition risk.[119] **9.097**

Therefore, the bank has focused on two high carbon-emitting sectors, namely the mining and the energy sectors. The financing policies on coal power and mining ensure that the bank only supports developments that are essential to sustain the economic development in the countries in which the bank is investing.[120] For the projects that Standard Bank finances, it conducts detailed due diligence that is aligned with the Equator Principles and includes an assessment of the climate change-related risks.[121] Standard Bank has funded several green energy projects, such as the acquisition of five renewable energy generation plants in South Africa by the international power company Globeleq,[122] which created opportunities to boost social and economic development. **9.098**

117 Ibid p.68.

118 Ibid.

119 Standard Bank. 2019. Standard Bank's Group Report to Society 2019. Available online from https://sustainability.standardbank.com/documents/report-to-society-2019.pdf Accessed 27 January 2021.

120 Ibid.

121 Standard Bank. 2017. Standard Bank's Report to Society 2017. Available online from http://annualreport2017.standardbank.com/downloads/Standard_bank_RTS2017_report_to_ society.pdf Accessed 27 January 2021.

122 Standard Bank. 2019. Standard Bank's Group Report to Society 2019. Available online from https://sustainability.standardbank.com/documents/report-to-society-2019.pdf Accessed 27 January 2021.

9.099 In 2017, Standard Bank provided US$623 million of funding for Africa's biggest wind farm in Kenya's Lake Turkana, which is estimated to produce 310 MW, accounting for 15 per cent of Kenya's power capacity and providing power for up to a million homes.[123] In Uganda, Standard Bank partnered with M-hope to supply 22 primary schools with solar-powered electricity for their administration and classroom blocks, as part of their social investment programme. In South Africa, the bank also funded a solar energy farm at Nelson Mandela University, which subsides the university's energy use across its two main campuses.[124] These efforts show that Standard Bank is making strides towards achieving its SEE goals and becoming a sustainable bank.

(c) Climate change and sustainable finance

9.100 African states are extremely vulnerable to the negative effects of climate change, as they have major implications on the agricultural sector, food security, water accessibility, health and livelihoods of the various communities. Various parts of the continent are already experiencing water scarcity due to prolonged drought, which is also affecting the rain-fed yields across the continent. These changes in weather patterns across Africa have led to price shocks (driven by climate change), and this in turn has led to a demand for crop diversification to mitigate against climate-related risks. An example is the change in the rain patterns in Zambia, which has resulted in the country's agricultural practices shifting northwards.

9.101 Standard Bank Group invested US$200 million in Zambia's agricultural sector, in the hope of encouraging local farmers to diversify their business so that they remain sustainable.[125] Furthermore, in 2016, 38 clients in the agricultural sector in South Africa had their loans restructured to prevent them from defaulting as a result of the severe drought that was experienced at that time. This enabled the farmers to produce an estimated R176 million worth of field crops, horticulture and livestock. In an attempt to mitigate the impacts of the drought-stricken areas in South Africa, Standard Bank financed desalinisation plants in Monwabisi and Strandfontein in the Western Cape province of the country. These plants produce 7 million litres of potable water per day. These water purification plants are portable, as they are set up in containers and can

123 Standard Bank. 2017. Standard Bank's Report to Society 2017 (p.59). Available online from http:// annualreport2017 .standardbank .com/ downloads/ Standard _bank _RTS2017 _report _to _ society.pdf Accessed 27 January 2021.

124 Standard Bank. 2019. Standard Bank's Group Report to Society 2019. Available online from https:// sustainability.standardbank.com/documents/report-to-society-2019.pdf Accessed 27 January 2021.

125 Standard Bank. 2017. Standard Bank's Report to Society 2017. Available online from http://annualreport2017 .standardbank.com/downloads/Standard_bank_RTS2017_report_to_ society.pdf Accessed 27 January 2021.

be moved to new locations if need be. This project was initiated to address the long-term need for water infrastructure development.[126]

In its continued efforts to become a sustainable bank, Standard Bank developed the first sustainable finance business unit in Africa. This unit increases the bank's opportunities to deliver impactful investments and sustainable expertise to its stakeholders across an extensive range of growth themes.[127] The sustainable finance unit is responsible for merging with businesses to better serve clients, drive innovation and capture opportunities as the concept of sustainability grows and becomes increasingly important for investors, institutions and companies across the world. The unit has been involved in several projects, such as the provision of a sustainability-linked loan to Curro schools. This was the first sustainable finance deal in the African market. This loan will enable Curro to build additional schools and further develop its existing campuses. The loan is linked to the ESG targets and performance of the company; some of the target areas include reducing carbon emissions and the inclusion of diversity programmes. Furthermore, the unit also played a key role in the issuance of the first green bond in East Africa. An equivalent of R 611 million was raised to Nairobi property developer Acorn Group, in project finance over five years for environmentally friendly student accommodation in the city.[128] These efforts all indicate the upward trajectory of sustainable finance in South Africa, and how banks have contributed to sustainable development. **9.102**

2. Case Study: Nedbank

Nedbank states that it has an expanded, dynamic and multi-faceted view of sustainability that is directly influenced by the United Nations Sustainable Development Goals (SDGs). Using these universal sustainable development goals as a baseline, Nedbank created its Sustainable Development Framework.[129] The Nedbank Sustainability Framework incorporates all the 17 SDGs. Nedbank believes that its success is contingent on the extent to which it delivers value to society. **9.103**

126 Ibid (p.61).

127 Standard Bank. 2019. Standard Bank's Group Report to Society 2019. Available online from https://sustainability.standardbank.com/documents/report-to-society-2019.pdf Accessed 27 January 2021.

128 Ibid.

129 Nedbank. 2020. Nedbank Group: Integrated Report. Available online from www.nedbank.co.za/content/dam/nedbank/site-assets/AboutUs/Information%20Hub/Integrated%20Report/2021/2020%20Nedbank%20Group%20Integrated%20Report%20(High%20Res%20double-page).pdf Accessed 27 June 2021.

9.104 Nedbank acknowledges the role banks play in facilitating economic activities enabling sustainable growth and development.[130] Based on its annual sustainability review, which is additional to the Nedbank Group Integrated Report, the bank highlights that its sustainability efforts go well beyond driving its on-site operations in a more sustainable direction. The bank's initiatives to transition to more sustainable operations (mostly from an environmental sustainability standpoint) are briefly highlighted in the following section.

(a) Internal sustainability operations

9.105 Nedbank states that it has been carbon-neutral since 2010, following a 'reduce first, then offset' approach. The bank has managed to reduce its carbon footprint by prioritising raising internal awareness and steering behavioural change, then offsetting the remaining carbon through carbon credits from projects that demonstrate meaningful environmental and social impact.[131] The bank has invested R82.98m in its efforts to reduce its carbon output. It has invested in carbon-efficient systems and the purchasing of carbon credit offsets that allow it to meet their operational carbon-neutral obligations.

9.106 The bank has further reduced its paper consumption on a year-to-year basis. In 2017, it reduced its paper consumption by 23.2 per cent and also set a target of 35 per cent by 2025, based on its 2013 baseline.[132] The bank has also managed to maintain and somewhat reduce its water usage, despite occupying new buildings and an increase in the number of staff members.[133] Nedbank has also managed to reduce its waste output per individual and increase its recycled material. The bank states that it has managed to achieve these results through increased staff awareness, internal education campaigns and the establishment of on-site recycling at the different branches.[134]

130 Ibid.

131 Nedbank. 2019. Nedbank Group: Sustainable Development Review 2019. Available online from www.nedbank.co.za/content/dam/nedbank/site-assets/AboutUs/Information%20Hub/Integrated%20Report/2019/2019%20Sustainable%20Development%20Review(A).pdf Accessed 21 January 2021.

132 Nedbank. 2017. Sustainable Development Review for the Year ended 31 December 2017. Accessed online from https://nedbank.co.za/content/dam/nedbank/site-assets/AboutUs/Information%20Hub/Integrated%20Report/2017/2017%20Sustainability%20Review.pdf Accessed 21 January 2021.

133 Ibid.

134 Nedbank. 2019. Nedbank Group: Sustainable Development Review 2019. Available online from www.nedbank.co.za/content/dam/nedbank/site-assets/AboutUs/Information%20Hub/Integrated%20Report/2019/2019%20Sustainable%20Development%20Review(A).pdf Accessed 21 January 2021.

(b) Sustainability in terms of financial services and CSI

(i) Affordable and clean energy

Nedbank has taken several steps to realise its goal of providing affordable and clean energy. In 2012 the bank launched the Nedbank Green Savings Bond, which allowed its retail clients to make green investments. The funds invested in the bond by clients are designated for investment in renewable energy projects. Since its establishment, retail clients have invested more than R25.2 billion.[135] One of these projects includes Africa's first floating solar park. This R13.7 million solar park was established in the Western Cape, helping to mitigate the reoccurring challenges of load-shedding for the surrounding farms.[136] **9.107**

The bank has launched various initiatives not only to address the challenges and opportunities that come with affordable green energy but also to illustrate how digitalisation can be a significant driver to enable sustainability initiatives.[137] Nedbank has developed and piloted a mobile phone application that allows homeowners to control their geyser electricity usage digitally and remotely. The bank helped in the development of a device that is installed on geysers and has sensors that automatically shut off water and electricity supply once a leak or burst is detected.[138] This reduces the home's energy consumption and also its carbon footprint, which in turn contributes to efforts to minimise the impacts of climate change. **9.108**

Nedbank is also actively involved in working on the supply and demand side with both private and public stakeholders to develop funding solutions that assist in the alleviation of water shortages.[139] An example of a development project that clearly illustrates the intersection of environmental sustainability and social justice considerations is the funding of the 630 low-income housing units in Belhar Gardens, Cape Town. These housing units all have energy and water-saving features, which the City of Cape Town applauded, identifying the development as the new benchmark in social housing.[140] **9.109**

---

135 Nedbank. 2017. Sustainable Development Review for the Year ended 31 December 2017. Accessed online from https://nedbank.co.za/content/dam/nedbank/site-assets/AboutUs/Information%20Hub/Integrated%20Report/2017/2017%20Sustainability%20Review.pdf Accessed 21 January 2021.

136 Nedbank. 2019. Nedbank Group: Sustainable Development Review 2019. Available online from www.nedbank.co.za/content/dam/nedbank/site-assets/AboutUs/Information%20Hub/Integrated%20Report/2019/2019%20Sustainable%20Development%20Review(A).pdf Accessed 21 January 2021.

137 Nedbank. 2017. Sustainable Development Review for the Year ended 31 December 2017. Accessed online from https://nedbank.co.za/content/dam/nedbank/site-assets/AboutUs/Information%20Hub/Integrated%20Report/2017/2017%20Sustainability%20Review.pdf Accessed 21 January 2021.

138 Ibid.

139 Ibid.

140 Ibid.

9.110 In addition to the above, Nedbank invested R12 million in the WWF-SA Water Balance programme since its inception in 2011. It is dedicated to the removal of alien invasive species, which has led to more than 915,500 kilolitres of water being released into South Africa's water catchment annually.[141] In 2017, the bank focused on the active rehabilitation of cleared land; it initiated the planting of 20,000 indigenous plants and 6,000 days of work were created for the local communities.[142] The bank's partnership with the WWF also extended to support for a farming project to improve livestock grazing patterns and methods in the Matatiele district in Kwazulu-Natal. The project has helped farmers efficiently manage their cattle and grazing lands more sustainably, by educating them on the significance of rotational grazing. This initiative not only benefits the farmers and communities involved but also ensures the sustainable management of catchments in the local areas.

(ii) Green building finance

9.111 Nedbank prides itself in being the leader in terms of the financing of green buildings in South Africa. It states that R1.3 billion in funding was provided for the construction of buildings that conform to the green building standards in 2017.[143] That increased the bank's total investment in green buildings to R8.7 billion and more than 400,000 m^2.[144]

9.112 Both Standard Bank and Nedbank have shown themselves as leading in adopting and implementing sustainable banking in South Africa. According to Sustainalytics,[145] Standard Bank Group Ltd has a medium ESG risk rating. The ESG risk rating measures the company's unmanaged ESG risk. The ESG risk rating is composed of two main factors: exposure, which is the company's vulnerability to ESG risks; and management, which refers to the company's risk-mitigating actions. Standard Bank Group's rating for Exposure is medium and that for management is Average.[146] Standard Bank also has a moderate Controversy rating, this area including bribery and corruption, business ethics, the carbon impact of products, the negative environmental impact of products and customer incidents.[147]

141 Ibid.
142 Ibid.
143 Ibid.
144 Ibid.
145 Sustainalytics. 2021a. Company ESG Risk Ratings: Standard Bank Group Ltd. Available online from www.sustainalytics.com/esg-rating/standard-bank-group-ltd/1015959120 Accessed 27 June 2021.
146 Ibid.
147 Ibid.

On the other hand, Nedbank Group Ltd has a low ESG risk rating.[148] Like Standard Bank, Nedbank Group Ltd's Exposure rating is medium; its Management Risk rating is better, at Strong. Nedbank Group Ltd's Controversy rating is low, including business ethics and customer incidents.[149] This goes to show that despite their successes both banks can do more to improve their sustainability and ESG risk management. This also goes to show that sustainability in banking is not limited to being green or eco-friendly, but is also about being ethical, transparent and responsible towards all shareholders, customers, employees and society itself – which is heavily dependent on a stable financial services sector for responsible economic growth.[150] **9.113**

3. Banks' Progress to Sustainable Finance

The banking system in South Africa has been addressing sustainability issues in the context of risk management. While this practice remains incomplete and fragmented, it has increased in both sophistication and volume. The existing E&S risk focus and expertise in banks is at the transactional level, where these risks pose a threat to the potential source of credit or the reputation of the bank. Globally, all the leading banks also seek to obtain a better understanding of their exposure to their environmental risks and the potential social impacts these could provoke; for example, how exposure to climate change extreme events such as drought can lead to water scarcity, migration risk and reduction of the quality of life. **9.114**

Sustainable banking in South Africa mainly depends on voluntary initiatives; therefore implementation is currently not supervised by the financial regulatory authorities. The voluntary initiatives are a combination of internationally and locally developed standards and strategies. **9.115**

The South African government has recognised the need for a Just Transition. The government, alongside the Treasury and the National Planning Commission, are working to understand what is needed and stimulate the creation of new jobs. With the mobilisation of private sector funding for new and more sustainable projects, such as through the REIPP, the Treasury is facilitating the shift towards green infrastructure in both the national balance **9.116**

---

148 Sustainalytics. 2021b. Company ESG Risk Ratings: Nedbank Group Ltd. Available from: www.sustainalytics.com/esg-rating/nedbank-group-ltd/1008287966 Accessed 27 June 2021.

149 Ibid.

150 Eccles, R.G. and Serafeim, G. 2013. Sustainability in Financial Services Is Not about Being Green. Sustainability – *Harvard Business Review*. Available online from https://hbr.org/2013/05/sustainability-in-financial-services-is-not-about-being-green Accessed 27 June 2021.

sheet and private sectors. The National Treasury is working to establish a framework for financial institutions to better disclose their green initiatives and investments to improve stakeholders' understanding of the extent to which financial institutions are exposed to climate risk.[151]

9.117 A paper was published by the National Treasury that offers several recommendations as to how the different financial industries can move towards reducing their climate risk. However, the paper is not clear as to how climate change risk will be reduced or what role the South African Reserve Bank (SARB), as the macroprudential regulator, has in ensuring the protection and enhancement of the country's financial stability.[152]

9.118 It is of great importance that strategies are implemented as mandatory, for banks to focus on ensuring consistency in their approach and the outcomes of the standards. This would help banking sectors progress towards successful sustainable finance.

9.119 To ensure that South African banks implement the different suggested strategies to make the banking system more sustainable, the SARB, as the central bank, must restructure its monetary policy. In 2020 the SARB published a working paper titled 'Climate change and its implications for central banks in emerging and developing countries'.[153] In this paper, it proposes changes in certain macroprudential tools that will facilitate a low-carbon economy, increase climate-related risk disclosure and prescribe a portion of domestic assets for sustainable investment.[154]

9.120 On the other hand, banks in South Africa and the rest of the world have increasingly used bonds as a favoured means of raising sustainable finance, subject to criteria for categorisation and use of funds to ensure credibility. In South Africa, the BASA members have an estimated R18 billion (dollar equivalent) worth of green bonds for renewable energy. However, public disclosure of the terms of the lending and the impacts of disbursed funds are not entirely clear.[155] This goes to show that the progress towards sustainable

151 Goodspeed, I. 2020. Climate Risk Is Now on the Agenda of South African Financial Sector Regulators. Available online from https://financialregulationjournal.co.za/2020/06/30/climate-risk-now-on-the-agenda-of-south-african-financial-sector-regulators/#_ftn7 Accessed 27 June 2021.

152 Ibid.

153 Arndt, C., Loewald, C., and Makrelov. 2020. Climate Change and Its Implications for Central Banks in Emerging and Developing Economies. South African Reserve Bank Working Paper Series WP/20/04.

154 Ibid.

155 National Treasury. 2020. Financing a Sustainable Economy: Technical Paper 2020. Available online from www.treasury.gov.za/publications/other/Sustainability%20technical%20paper%202020.pdf Accessed 13 January 2021.

finance is very limited in South African banks. The lack of mandatory regulations and standards and an effective measurement methodology has slowed the progress of the growth of the concept of sustainable finance, as banks do not feel obligated to shift their practices and services towards becoming more sustainable as they know that their progress is not monitored or supervised by any financial boards.[156]

Therefore, the recommendations published by the National Treasury to try to push banks to move towards reducing climate risk are essential. However, these recommendations must be republished and provide more definitive steps and instructions as to how the local banks must reduce climate risk, and also outline the role of the SARB in this journey. Financial boards and regulatory authorities (Prudential and Financial Sector Conduct Authorities) must also be empowered to take on supervisory roles to ensure that the banks are truly and effectively implementing sustainable practices and adopting sustainable finance practices as per the regulations to which they commit. **9.121**

This is necessary to avoid confusion and ensure the effective implementation of the methods to reduce climate risk. The National Treasury must also create functional sustainability assessment methodologies to allow for measurement of the effectiveness of the implementation of sustainable practices throughout banks and their different practices. The implementation of compulsory regulations and the creation of a measurement methodology will prompt banks to implement these practices more effectively, which will in turn act as a catalyst to the adoption of sustainable finance in South Africa. **9.122**

4. Challenges

As in every other industry, the financial sector has its challenges. South African banks have and are still facing challenges which render the further development of sustainable finance in the country difficult, for various reasons that shall be highlighted in this section. The Basel III regulations require banks to reduce their exposure to long-term risk, especially liquidity risks in LCR and NSFT; this can pose a challenge for them.[157] This is because, under Basel III regulations, banks are required to hold at least 5 per cent of common equity of risk-weighted assets, and an additional capital conservation buffer of 2.5 per cent. Holding technologies such as renewable energy lead to an **9.123**

156 Ibid.

157 Van Dyk, F. n.d. Basel III: An Overview of the Safer 'Safety Net'. Available online from http://financialmarketsjournal.co.za/oldsite/13thedition/printedarticles/basel3.htm Accessed 27 January 2021.

increase in banks' capital charges. This is a considerable challenge for banks as they need to swap hard currency for local currency funding, which in turn creates additional inefficiencies and risks when it comes to considering these funding decisions.[158]

9.124 Furthermore, it is important to note that products, methodologies and practices are not uniform across the banking sector and that not all local banks subscribe to the voluntary principles. This illustrates that as yet no national benchmark or regulations are in place to ensure the uniform implementation of environmental and social risk assessment or management practices.[159] This makes it difficult for regulators to conclude the banks' exposure to climate change and other ESG risks from the disclosed information, as some banks only focus on publishing their operational facilities and selective information about their major transactions, such as those that fall within the Equator Principles.[160]

9.125 There is no system in place that assesses the performance maturity as there are no stringent requirements for South African banks to disclose the extent of the implementation of the BASA principles. On a global scale, there has been a growing demand for the financial sector as a whole (banks in particular) to recognise and acknowledge its role in sanctioning financial flows to address ongoing global challenges such as climate change.

9.126 Such growing pressure and demand can be a driver of regulatory adjustments, for both local and global financial institutions. It is of great importance for the financial sector to acknowledge the broader relationships between societal expectations and needs and the soundness of the financial system as to what has been previously accepted.[161] Furthermore, the growth in the mainstream focus of banks and banking regulators on topics that focus on financial inclusion sets an example for the involvement of financial institutions and their regulators in finding solutions to E&S risks.[162]

---

158 Ibid.

159 Ibid.

160 Lexology. 2020. Climate Change Regulation for Financial Services Firms: A Global View. Available online from www.lexology.com/library/detail.aspx?g=5e01c104-0385-4c69-b117-9e2250caf4f2 Accessed 25 January 2021.

161 National Treasury. 2020. Financing a Sustainable Economy: Technical Paper 2020. Available online from www.treasury.gov.za/publications/other/Sustainability%20technical%20paper%202020.pdf Accessed 13 January 2021.

162 Park, H., and Kim, J.D. 2020. The Transition towards Green Banking: The Role of Financial Regulators and Financial Institutions. Asian Journal of Sustainability and Social Responsibility 5(1). DOI: 10.1186/s41180-020-00034-3.

There are other challenges that the banking sector is facing, not just in South Africa but internationally, that need to be addressed to support further progress towards the effective implementation of E&S risk assessments and the transition towards sustainable finance. In the next section, I outline recommendations for the South African banks on how to transition towards sustainable finance and further improve the state of sustainability in the local finance sector. 9.127

5. Recommendations

1. To drive the local banking sector towards becoming more sustainable, the PA and FSCA need to do the following:[163]

- Engage with the local banks and set the minimum requirements for sustainable finance, which should include the banks' long-term climate strategy and also enforce portfolio-level risk management.
- Engage with the banks on the risks that come with international regulations, for example, the non-tariff barriers to trade, which are a consequence of South Africa's energy system not transitioning quickly enough to becoming less carbon-intensive.
- Undertake further analysis of practical regulatory instruments, which would focus on:
  - formal climate risk management strategies and policies, targets for disclosure, methodologies and performance data using international disclosure frameworks and methodologies; also incorporate climate risk management provisions and investment requirements into legal agreements, as well as disclose the bank's funding policies and exclusion lists.
  - alignment of requirements and standards for banks to publish their climate risk management policies and strategies with South Africa's international climate obligations, including supporting financial stability in the country. Also agreeing on minimum disclosure requirements, such as reporting on the portfolio exposure to the negative impacts of climate change.

2. The regulators and financial industry should:

- Partner and develop technical guidelines that will facilitate the implementation and disclosure of banks' performance concerning addressing climate impacts and other key E&S risks.

163 National Treasury. 2020. Financing a Sustainable Economy: Technical Paper 2020. Available online from www.treasury.gov.za/publications/other/Sustainability%20technical%20paper%202020.pdf Accessed 13 January 2021.

- Develop technical training programmes that will enable the banks' regulators and directors to exercise adequate oversight and for the bank management teams to effectively implement sustainable finance strategies.
- Collaborate and find solutions to the challenges that are linked to long-term risk and capital holding requirements as well as the tax implications that are involved when attracting and allocating international negotiating funding.

3. Banks should:

- Fast-track the implementation of strategies for international standards, which address both the SDGs and the impacts of climate change.
- Define internal roles, systems and methodologies and responsibilities and incorporate the BASA Principles into their oversight system.

9.128 These are some of the key recommendations that the financial sector in South Africa could consider in driving the state of sustainable finance forward in the country. The recommendations are not limited to the above; some other factors and strategies could be implemented to further drive the concept of sustainable finance in South Africa.

6. Conclusion

9.129 The notion of sustainable finance is in its infancy but is gaining ground rapidly in South Africa. Sustainable finance has been embraced as a concept but not much has been done to drive its implementation to its fullest potential. At present, there are no stringent or mandatory regulations to ensure that financial institutions mobilise and enforce practices and systems that encourage the growth of sustainable finance in the country. The regulations and principles that are in place, such as the BASA principles, are voluntary; therefore banks are not obligated to follow them. Had the banks been obligated to adopt and implement these principles, the South African sustainable finance system would likely be ahead of where it is today. Furthermore, the lack of measurement methodologies to assess the progress of the banks also takes away from the effectiveness of the principles.

9.130 Despite the lack of stable sustainable finance regulations, green bonds have gained popularity in the local market. The issuance of green bonds in South Africa is guided by the GBP. Banks such as Standard Bank and Nedbank have issued them and have also launched several sustainable finance products. Furthermore, banks in South Africa have mostly focused on implementing E&S risk assessments and management in their operations: a step in the right direction, but there are so many other issues to address, such as climate risk. Most banks use the Equator Principles as the go-to standard when it comes to assessing E&S risk. While there is notable progress, there remains a long way to go for banks and financial institutions in South Africa seeking to effectively implement sustainable finance. However, with the aforementioned recommendations, there is great potential for the sustainable finance market to grow in South Africa.

10

ARBITRATION IN CLIMATE CHANGE FINANCE

Georges Affaki[1]

10.01 'I ask all of you to use the great power of arbitration to help the world overcome conflict and hatred and build a future of dignity for all on a healthy planet.' These powerful words closed former United Nations Secretary-General Ban Ki-Moon's address at the 23rd Congress of the International Council for Commercial Arbitration.[2] Secretary-General Moon's words are undoubtedly the most inspiring message that the arbitration world could hope for, especially during this moment, in which the arbitration world must assume its responsibility to shape a better dispute resolution system for climate change disputes.

1 This chapter was originally published in the *Stockholm Arbitration Review*.

2 Arbitration Institute of the Stockholm Chamber of Commerce, *Ban Ki-Moon Commends International Arbitration* (24 May 2016).

Arbitration has a key role to play in the resolution of climate change disputes. This is even more critical given that disputes are expected to multiply with the exponential increase of green investments. For instance, in 2018, climate-related investments – or 'climate finance' – amounted to USD 546 billion worldwide.[3] In Europe alone in the first quarter of 2020, inflows to sustainable funds represented EUR 30 billion.[4] **10.02**

This chapter supports the case for arbitration as a preferred dispute resolution mechanism in climate change disputes, both as it now stands and as it should evolve. To that end, it will first address how the United Nations Framework Convention for Climate Change (UNFCCC) and the Paris Agreement's inducement for green investments will likely lead to a multiplication of disputes.[5] It will then discuss the role of international arbitration in the resolution of climate change disputes, showing that the investment arbitration framework is particularly apt for climate change-related disputes for both investors and host States. The chapter closes with a reflection on the procedural features of arbitration that particularly suit climate change disputes and the need for arbitral institutions to prepare to administer these disputes. **10.03**

A. CLIMATE FINANCE: A CATALYST FOR CLIMATE CHANGE DISPUTES

Since the adoption of the UNFCCC in 1992, the world has witnessed a substantial increase in public and private funding of green investments and projects. This increase in green finance and investments will inevitably lead to further climate change-related disputes. **10.04**

1. Financing a Green Transition

The current level of climate finance falls short of what is needed to comply with the commitments undertaken by the States Parties to the Paris Agreement,[6] as estimates of investment needed to reach the Paris Agreement's temperature reduction goals range between USD 1.6 trillion and USD 3.8 trillion annually from the time of writing to 2050.[7] To that end, Article 9(1) of the Paris **10.05**

3 Climate Policy Initiative, *Global Landscape of Climate Finance*, Report, p.2 (2019).
4 A. Mooney and P. Temple-West, *Climate Change: Asset Managers Join Forces with the Eco-Warriors*, Financial Times (26 July 2020).
5 United Nations Framework Convention for Climate Change (9 May 1992), T. S. No. 30822; Paris Agreement (12 Dec. 2015), T.S. No. 54113.
6 Climate Policy Initiative, *Global Landscape of Climate Finance*, n 3, p.3.
7 Ibid.

Agreement imposes concrete obligations on developed countries to increase their contributions to support developing countries' undertakings to mitigate climate change and to make a green energy transition.[8]

10.06 With massive investments needed, a number of climate change treaties have established dedicated public funds to stimulate climate finance.[9] The UNFCCC pioneered the use of financial mechanisms to combat climate change by creating two separate entities: the Global Environment Facility (GEF) and the Green Climate Fund (GCF). Since its creation in 1994, the GEF has financed more than 4,800 projects in 170 countries by providing USD 20.5 billion in grants and USD 112 billion in co-financing.[10] The GCF, for its part, seeks to finance developing countries in their commitment to combat climate change and to promote private financing in these countries.[11]

10.07 Other UN entities encourage climate finance by providing grants and support mechanisms. The United Nations Development Programme (UNDP), for instance, has dedicated USD 2.3 billion for climate change-related projects.[12] Likewise, in 2008, the World Bank established two additional funds through the Climate Investment Funds, namely the Clean Technology Fund and the Strategic Climate Fund.[13] Overall, the World Bank dedicated more than 30 per cent of its financing to climate change-related projects in 2018 and 2019, reaching USD 20.5 billion in 2018 and USD 17.8 billion in 2019.[14] To ensure sustainability of public climate finance through these funds, and to stimulate green investments on a long-term basis, the UN bodies in charge – and particularly the UNDP – should endeavour to ensure the good governance of climate funds. Allegations of fraud, such as those recently raised against the GEF, risk weakening this crucial system and slowing public climate finance. Should the UNDP fail to react with the appropriate level of seriousness, these risks will be further heightened.[15]

---

8 Wendy J. Miles and Nicolas Swan, 'Climate Change Financing and Dispute Resolution', *Finances in International Arbitration*, p.324 (Tung, Fortese et al., Kluwer Law International 2019): *Mitigation* investments aim at reducing or preventing greenhouse gases emissions, while investments for *adaptation* consist in the modification of existing infrastructures to minimise global warming and climate change.

9 *See* Article 9 Paragraphs 8 and 9 of the Paris Agreement.

10 Global Environment Facility, www.thegef.org/about-us (accessed 15 Oct. 2020).

11 Green Climate Fund, www.greenclimate.fund/about (accessed 15 Oct. 2020).

12 Wendy J. Miles and Nicolas Swan, 'Climate Change Financing and Dispute Resolution', n 8, p.326.

13 Alexander Thompson, 'The Global Regime for Climate Finance: Political and Legal Challenges', *Oxford Handbook of International Climate Change Law*, p.178 (Carlane et al., Oxford University Press 2016); Climate Investment Funds, *Timeline*, www.climateinvestmentfunds.org/timeline-cif (accessed 15 Oct. 2020).

14 World Bank, *World Bank Group Exceeds Its Climate Finance Target with Record Year*, 19 July 2018; World Bank, *Climate Finance*, www.worldbank.org/en/topic/climatefinance (updated 4 Oct. 2019).

15 E. White and L. Hook, *UN Body Accused of Climate Project Fraud*, Financial Times (1 Dec. 2020).

According to the European Commission, the European Union (EU), its Member States and the European Investment Bank are the largest contributors to public climate financing in developing countries.[16] In 2019 alone, they injected up to EUR 23.2 billion in climate finance.[17] EU institutions also continue to pursue green finance efforts. For instance, in July 2020 the President of the European Central Bank (ECB), Christine Lagarde, announced that the EUR 2.8 trillion ECB asset purchase scheme would be used to promote green objectives more efficiently and to fight climate change.[18] The President of the Deutsche Bundesbank, Jens Weidmann, suggested that the ECB should only purchase securities or accept them as collateral for monetary policy purposes if their issuers meet certain climate-related reporting obligations.[19] A further step that could be taken would be for financial institutions and their regulators to use ratings only from credit rating agencies that include climate-related financial risks in their credit assessments. **10.08**

However, the private sector remains the greatest contributor to climate finance. In 2017 and 2018, 56 per cent of climate finance contributions came from the private sector, representing USD 326 billion per year on average.[20] Private climate finance has also been boosted by the green bond market. Bond financing and refinancing projects, along with business activities promoting efforts against climate change, are available on this expanding market which, according to the Organisation for Economic Cooperation and Development (OECD), has already exceeded USD 80 billion labelled green bonds in 2020.[21] This significant growth in the green bond market led to the creation of 'Green Bond Principles' by the International Capital Market Association,[22] the purpose of which is to provide relevant information to bond issuers, allowing their bonds to be labelled as green bonds and to help investors assess the environmental impact of their investment.[23] **10.09**

---

16 European Commission, *International Climate Finance*, https:// ec .europa .eu/ clima/ policies/ international/finance_en (accessed 15 Oct. 2020).

17 European Council and Council of the European Union, *Climate Finance: EU and Member States' Contributions Continued to Increase in 2019*, Press Release (29 Oct. 2020).

18 R. Khalaf and M. Arnold, *Lagarde Puts Green Policy Top of Agenda in ECB Bond Buying*, Financial Times (7 July 2020).

19 J. Weidmann, *Central Banks Cannot Solve Climate Change on Their Own*, Financial Times (19 Nov. 2020).

20 Climate Policy Initiative, *Global Landscape of Climate Finance*, n 3, p.13.

21 Wendy J. Miles and Nicolas Swan, 'Climate Change Financing and Dispute Resolution', n 8, pp.328–9; OECD, *Growing Momentum for Sovereign Green Bonds* (29 Sept. 2020).

22 International Capital Market Association, *Green Bond Principles* (2018).

23 Ibid.

2. Expecting the Increase in Climate Finance Disputes

10.10 This staggering growth in green investments will undoubtedly lead to a proportional increase in disputes. In its November 2019 report 'Resolving Climate Change Related Disputes through Arbitration and ADR',[24] the International Chamber of Commerce (ICC) Arbitration Commission predicted that climate change disputes may arise in a broad variety of sectors, including energy, urban and infrastructure, land use systems, industry and new technologies, financing and insurance.[25]

10.11 Similarly, the Arbitration Institute of the Stockholm Chamber of Commerce (SCC) has identified three categories of potential climate change disputes (or 'green technology disputes'): those which arise directly or in connection with an international climate agreement or policy; disputes that are technical in nature; and non-technical disputes.[26]

10.12 According to the SCC, disputes directly related to international climate agreements and policies will increase as States Parties to the Paris Agreement have enacted more than 1,500 national regulations relating to climate change.[27] To date, most of the disputes in this category relate to carbon emission trading schemes established under Article 17 of the Kyoto Protocol and Article 6 of the Paris Agreement. However, as the regulations promulgated to enact these were lacking, disputes relating to these programmes unsurprisingly arose, involving issues ranging from unit registration and issuance to the revocation of trading-related decisions.[28]

10.13 Arbitration has been used frequently to resolve carbon trading disputes. The Permanent Court of Arbitration (PCA) has administered nine contract-based cases relating to carbon emission trading.[29] Similarly, the SCC has administered a dispute pertaining to a party's failure to transfer emission rights on time

24 International Chamber of Commerce, *Resolving Climate Change Related Disputes through Arbitration and ADR*, ICC Commission Report (2019).

25 Ibid, p.65, paras 25, 56, 63, 65, 67, 73.

26 S. Dwi Andrina, *Green Technology Disputes in Stockholm*, Arbitration Institute of the Stockholm Chamber of Commerce (2019).

27 S. Field and H. Laufer, *Climate Change, the Environment and Commercial Arbitration*, Kluwer Arbitration Blog (9 March 2020).

28 Wendy J. Miles and Nicolas Swan, 'Climate Change Financing and Dispute Resolution', n 8, p.339.

29 Ibid, pp.339–40; J. Levine and C. Pondel, *Updates on the Changing State of the Climate and International Arbitration*, 1 ACICA Review 35 (2019); ICC Commission Report, *Resolving Climate Change Related Disputes through Arbitration and ADR*, n 24, p.59, para. 44; Roda Verheyen and Cathrin Zengerling, 'International Dispute Settlement', *Oxford Handbook of International Climate Change Law*, p.423 (Carlane et al., Oxford University Press 2016).

within the EU emissions trading scheme, which resulted in the other party's payment of a penalty to the Environmental Protection Agency.[30] Recourse to arbitration in carbon trading disputes is not surprising, as carbon trading exchanges, such as the Intercontinental Exchange, sometimes impose dispute resolution through arbitration on their users.[31]

Regarding technical disputes, the SCC's docket includes cases involving software systems for the regulation of wind turbines, along with a case dealing with a partnership for the construction of a wind farm.[32] **10.14**

Finally, with respect to non-technical disputes, the SCC provides the example of cases arising from the unpaid delivery of wind energy converters and from a distribution agreement providing for the exclusive distribution of bioenergy products.[33] **10.15**

Alongside these green *technology* disputes, the number of green *investment* disputes is also on the rise, as revealed by institutions' own statistics. For instance, between 2012 and 2018, 28 per cent of cases registered by the SCC fell within the category of green investment disputes.[34] All of these disputes were filed under the Energy Charter Treaty (ECT), confirming that the ECT promotes the use of arbitration in climate-related investment disputes.[35] The International Centre for Settlement of Investment Disputes (ICSID) reported that in 2020 it administered 48 energy cases either directly or indirectly related to climate change: 16 per cent of that year's total cases.[36] The PCA's 2019 caseload included 20 cases involving issues of environmental impact or climate change-related projects, accounting for 12 per cent of disputes overall.[37] **10.16**

Investment treaty-based disputes relating to climate finance are likely to further expand, for two reasons. First, the European Commission decided that the subsidies and exemptions for renewable energies should be progressively phased out from 2020 through 2030.[38] The early termination of these incen- **10.17**

30 S. Dwi Andrina, *Green Technology Disputes in Stockholm*, n 26, p.12.
31 Wendy J. Miles and Nicolas Swan, 'Climate Change Financing and Dispute Resolution', n 8, p.339.
32 S. Dwi Andrina, *Green Technology Disputes in Stockholm*, n 26, p.12.
33 Ibid, p.13.
34 Ibid, p.18.
35 Ibid, p.19.
36 International Centre for Settlement of Investment Disputes, 2020 Annual Report, pp.20, 22 (2020).
37 J. Levine and C. Pondel, *Updates on the Changing State of the Climate and International Arbitration*, n 29, p.34.
38 European Commission, Communication, Guidelines on State Aid for Environment Protection and Energy 2014–2020, 2014/C 200/01, para. 108 (2014).

tives could cause a loss for investors, who may initiate treaty-based arbitration proceedings in cases in which jurisdictional conditions are met.

10.18 Second, investment disputes relating to climate finance may proliferate following the recent decision on jurisdiction in the *Portigon v Spain* ICSID arbitration, confirming that tribunals have jurisdiction over claims brought not only by equity investors but also by lenders to renewable energy projects under both the ICSID Convention and ECT.[39] In an earlier ICSID case, *Landesbank v Spain*,[40] concerning a similar set of facts (the claimant financial institution had provided more than 200 loans and financed dozens of renewable energy plants), the respondent did not even challenge that the financing of energy projects constitutes a protected investment under the ECT.[41] Cases such as *Portigon* and *Landesbank* may thus set the stage for the proliferation of ECT proceedings brought by lenders to renewable energy projects.

10.19 In addition to green technology and investment disputes, arbitration has been used in inter-State arbitrations involving environmental issues. In three of these cases, tribunals have held that States have a 'duty to prevent, or at least mitigate, significant harm to the environment when pursuing large scale construction activities',[42] and applied the 'polluter pays' principle. According to this principle, first articulated by the OECD in 1972, the polluter bears the cost of the pollution or the environmental damage it caused.[43] Although the 'polluter pays' principle lacks normative value by itself, it has been enshrined in various environmental treaties, such as the Convention for the Protection of the Marine Environment of the North-East Atlantic and the Convention on the Protection and Use of Transboundary Watercourses and International Lakes, as well as in both general regional treaties, such as the Treaty on the Functioning of the European Union, and specialised regional treaties, such as the Energy Charter Treaty.[44]

---

39 *Portigon AG v. Kingdom of Spain*, ICSID Case No. ARB/17/15, Decision on Jurisdiction, 20 August 2020 (decision not public).

40 *Landesbank Baden-Württemberg, HSH Nordbank AG, Landesbank Hessen-Thüringen Girozentrale and Norddeutsche Landesbank-Girozentrale v. Kingdom of Spain*, ICSID Case No. ARB/15/45.

41 D. Charlotin, *Greenwood-chaired Tribunal Offers Up Decision Dismissing intra-EU Objection in High-stakes 1.76 billion Dollar Energy Charter Treaty Claim*, IA Reporter (11 July 2019); L. Bohmer, *Majority Arbitrators Uphold Jurisdiction over Claims by Financial Institution which Funded Renewable Energy Projects in Spain*, IA Reporter (21 Aug. 2020).

42 *Iron Rhine Arbitration (Belgium v The Netherlands)*, PCA Case No. 2003-02, Award, 24 May 2005, para. 59; *Indus Waters Kishenganga Arbitration (Pakistan v India)*, PCA Case No. 2011-01, Partial Award, 18 February 2013, paras 451–452; *South China Sea Arbitration (The Republic of Philippines v The People's Republic of China)*, PCA Case No. 2013-19, Award, 12 July 2016, para. 945.

43 A. Boyle, *Polluter Pays*, Max Planck Encyclopaedia of Public International Law (2009), para. 1.

44 Ibid, paras 3, 6.

The first of these disputes articulating State responsibility to prevent or mitigate environmental harm is the 2005 *Iron Rhine Arbitration* between Belgium and the Netherlands, administered by the PCA.[45] The dispute concerned the Belgian reactivation of a railroad through Dutch territory, including a national park, under Belgium's transit rights over Dutch territory based on the 1839 Treaty of Separation. This reactivation gave rise to a disagreement on the allocation of costs and risks between the States related to the project's environmental impact.[46] Applying the 'polluter pays' principle, the tribunal concluded that Belgium was to bear the costs and financial risks of the reactivation of the railway for the segments that it used exclusively,[47] and costs and risks were allocated equally between the States for the segments of the railway used by both.[48] **10.20**

Similar environmental issues arose in the *Indus Waters Kishenganga* arbitration between Pakistan and India in 2013, initiated under the 1960 Indus Waters Treaty.[49] In response to India's plan to build a hydroelectric plant on the Kishenganga River, Pakistan contended that the project violated India's obligation not to obstruct the flow of the natural channels of the river in a manner likely to cause material and environmental damage.[50] The tribunal ruled that the treaty authorised India's planned project,[51] but that, in application to the State's duty to mitigate environmental damages, India was required to guarantee that the project ensured a minimum flow of water downriver.[52] **10.21**

The third of these cases was initiated by the Philippines against China in the *South China Sea* arbitration under the UN Convention on the Law of the Sea (UNCLOS).[53] These proceedings concerned, *inter alia*, whether Chinese construction of artificial islands in the South China Sea caused severe harm to the coral reef environment.[54] After an extensive review of the expert reports, the tribunal found that the Chinese artificial islands had caused devastating and long-lasting damage to the marine environment, amounting to a breach of its obligations under UNCLOS not to harm the marine environment.[55] **10.22**

45 *Iron Rhine Arbitration*, Award, 24 May 2005, n 42.
46 Ibid, paras 121, 206.
47 Ibid, paras 226, 236.
48 Ibid.
49 *Indus Waters Kishenganga Arbitration*, Partial Award, 18 February 2013, n 42.
50 Ibid, para. 256.
51 Ibid, para. 510.
52 Ibid, paras 451, p.201.
53 *South China Sea Arbitration*, Award, 12 July 2016, n 42.
54 *South China Sea Arbitration*, Award, 12 July 2016, n 42, para. 22.
55 Ibid, para. 983.

B. THE ROLE OF ARBITRATION IN THE RESOLUTION OF CLIMATE CHANGE DISPUTES

10.23 States have consented to the jurisdiction of arbitral tribunals for the settlement of climate change-related disputes in numerous treaties. While arbitration is often included as an available dispute resolution mechanism for inter-State disputes, the implementation process has never been fully completed by States parties. On the other hand, the use of investor-State arbitration for climate change-related disputes has expanded considerably.

1. Inter-State Arbitration in Climate Change Disputes: A Missed Opportunity

10.24 Recourse to arbitration for inter-State disputes arising out of international environmental and climate change agreements once appeared promising. This began with the adoption of the Vienna Convention for the Protection of the Ozone Layer (VCPOL) in 1985,[56] Article 11(3) of which invites parties to make declarations on whether they consent to the jurisdiction of arbitral tribunals and/or of the International Court of Justice (ICJ) for disputes arising out of the Convention. The parties adopted an Annex to the Convention tailoring the arbitral procedure to the specificities of these disputes, demonstrating their awareness of the particularities of environmental disputes and their willingness to consider recourse to arbitration.[57] This Annex establishes an arbitral procedure under the supervision of the Secretariat of the VCPOL.[58] Notably, this arbitral procedure is tailored for environmental disputes, as it provides that Contracting Parties with an interest in the arbitral proceedings have the right to participate therein, explicitly grants the respondent State the right to file counterclaims and requires the tribunal to render its decision within a five-month period, renewable only once.[59]

10.25 In 1992 the Parties to the UNFCCC followed the same path, as Article 14 of the Convention provides that disputes arising thereunder may be settled through arbitration. As with Article 11 of the VCPOL, Article 14 of the

---

56 Vienna Convention for the Protection of the Ozone Layer (22 March 1985), T.S. No. 26164.

57 W. Miles and M. Lawry-White, *Arbitral Institutions and the Enforcement of Climate Change Obligations for the Benefit of all Stakeholders: The Role of ICSID*, 24 ICSID Review 1, 11 (2019).

58 United Nations Environment Programme, *Handbook for the Vienna Convention for the Protection of the Ozone Layer*, 12th ed., pp.60–1 (2019).

59 Ibid.

UNFCCC invites the parties to declare their acceptance of the compulsory jurisdiction of the ICJ and/or arbitral tribunals.[60]

The Kyoto Protocol and the Paris Agreement followed a similar route: Article 18 of the Kyoto Protocol and Article 24 of the Paris Agreement incorporate Article 14 of the UNFCCC by reference.[61] Although an annex on arbitration was supposed to complement these arbitration mechanisms, the Parties to the UNFCCC, the Kyoto Protocol and the Paris Agreement never adopted these additional instruments.[62] **10.26**

This failure (or refusal) primarily reflects the Contracting Parties' unwillingness to consent to recourse to arbitration in environmental and climate change-related disputes. In 2020, only two (out of 197) Contracting Parties to the UNFCCC had made a declaration consenting to dispute settlement mechanisms (including arbitration) under Article 14.[63] With respect to the Kyoto Protocol, none of the 192 parties had made such declaration,[64] and the Netherlands is the sole State Party to have issued a declaration under Article 24 of the Paris Agreement consenting to the jurisdiction of the ICJ and arbitral tribunals.[65] **10.27**

2. The Suitability of Investment Treaty Arbitration to Deal with Climate Change Disputes

Recent investment treaty cases evince a trend of investors relying on the substantive protections provided under bilateral investment treaties (BITS), free trade agreements, and other multilateral investment treaties to seek recovery for climate change-related losses. In parallel, recent investment treaty cases also indicate a new trend in which host States can avail themselves of climate change-based defences against investors who are noncompliant with environmental regulations. **10.28**

60 Article 14 of the UNFCCC.

61 Article 18 of the Kyoto Protocol to the UNFCCC and Article 24 of the Paris Agreement both read: 'The provisions of Article 14 of the [United Nations Framework Convention on Climate Change] on settlement of disputes shall apply mutatis mutandis to this Agreement.'

62 W. Miles and M. Lawry-White, *Arbitral Institutions and the Enforcement of Climate Change Obligations for the Benefit of all Stakeholders*, n 57, p.10.

63 The Netherlands and the Solomon Islands made a declaration under Article 14 of the UNFCCC, consenting to the jurisdiction of arbitral tribunals: United Nations Framework Convention on Climate Change, *Declarations by Parties* (accessed 13 Oct. 2020).

64 United Nations Treaty Collection, Kyoto Protocol, *Declarations and Reservations* (accessed 13 Oct. 2020).

65 United Nations Treaty Collection, Paris Agreement, *Declarations and Reservations* (accessed 13 Oct. 2020).

(a) Investors' climate change-related arguments falling under the umbrella of the substantive protection of the investment treaty

10.29 The substantive protections offered to foreign investors under international investment agreements, including the Fair and Equitable Treatment (FET) and Full Protection and Security (FPS) standards, can provide a basis for investors to advance claims against States based on environmental and climate change-related losses.

10.30 An example of the application of the FET standard in this context is the *Novenergia v Spain* SCC case brought under the ECT.[66] The claimant had indirectly invested in photovoltaic plants in Spain following the adoption of Royal Decrees in 2000 and 2007 encouraging renewable energy production, resulting in the claimant's legitimate expectation that Spain would maintain this favourable regime.[67] However, following the economic crisis that occurred late in the first decade of this century, Spain issued a 2010 Royal Decree retroactively deleting feed-in tariff values for photovoltaic plants registered in 2007,[68] and subsequent regulations further altered the remuneration mechanism.[69] The tribunal agreed with the claimant and found that the investor had legitimate expectations arising out of Spain's initial Royal Decrees, which could not be radically or fundamentally altered,[70] and that this retroactive change of regulation required it to compensate the investor.[71]

10.31 The *Novenergia* award suggests that an investor may rely on its legitimate expectation, under an investment treaty's FET provision, that a State would continue to promote green energy investment and endeavour to ensure compliance with international environmental obligations.[72] Tribunals may indeed interpret the FET standard in light of the State's legitimate policy objective of

66 *Novenergia II – Energy & Environment (SCA), SICAR v Kingdom of Spain*, SCC Case No. 063/2015, Final Award, 15 February 2018.

67 *Novenergia II v Spain*, Final Award, 15 February 2018, n 66, para. 551.

68 *Novenergia II v Spain*, Final Award, 15 February 2018, n 66, para. 121; Royal Decree 1565/2010, 'Regulating and Modifying Specific Aspects Related to Energy Production in the Special Regime', 19 Nov. 2010.

69 *Novenergia II v Spain*, Final Award, 15 February 2018, *op. cit.* footnote 65, paras 132, 136, 139 and 145; G. Issac, *Luxembourg Fund Awarded EUR 53.3 Million for FET Breach Arising out of Spain's Curtailment of Renewable Energy Incentive Schemes*, International Institute for Sustainable Development (30 July 2018); Royal Decree-Law 2/2013 'Concerning Urgent Measures in the Electric System and Financial Sector', 1 Feb. 2013 and Royal Decree-Law 9/2013 'Adopting Urgent Measures to Ensure the Financial Stability of the Electric System', 13 July 2013.

70 Ibid, paras 666, 681.

71 Ibid, para. 697.

72 Royal Decree 661/2007 'Regulating Electricity Production Under the Special Regime', 25 March 2007: The second paragraph of the Royal Decree Preamble provides that the energy policy should encourage renewable energies and decrease gas emissions, as committed in the Kyoto Protocol.

complying with applicable international environmental law.[73] It will therefore come as no surprise that investors may rely on the FET standard moving forward as a basis for claims arising from a State's environmental and climate change action or inaction.

The 2018 *Zelena v Serbia* ICSID case appears to confirm this trend.[74] In *Zelena*, the claimant, an operator of a plant using animal by-products to produce energy, asserted that Serbia's failure to enforce its environmental and veterinary laws amounted to a FET violation, as it favoured the claimant's non-compliant competitors.[75] The tribunal agreed, ordering Serbia to compensate the claimant for the FET violation.[76] **10.32**

In addition to a host State's domestic law, the State's international obligations can also serve as a basis for an investor's claim. Broadly worded arbitration clauses (referring, for example, to 'all disputes relating to an investment'), together with Article 31(3)(c) of the Vienna Convention on the Law of Treaties (VCLT), which provides for the applicability of 'any relevant rules of international law applicable in the relations between the parties', allow tribunals to apply other international conventions when faced with an investment claim.[77] **10.33**

The ad hoc tribunal organised under the UNCITRAL Rules in the *S.D. Myers v Canada* case relied on treaties ratified by Canada to determine whether that the State had breached its obligations to the US investor under the North American Free Trade Agreement (NAFTA). In that case, the claimant, a waste treatment company, brought a claim against Canada when the State issued an interim order prohibiting export of the waste of a certain chemical compound.[78] In considering whether the order violated Canada's national treatment and minimum standard of treatment obligations under NAFTA, **10.34**

73 Annette Magnusson, 'New Arbitration Frontiers: Climate Change', *Evolution and Adaptation: The Future of International Arbitration*, p.1020 (Kalicki, Abdel Raouf, Kluwer Law International 2019).

74 *Zelena N.V. and Energo-Zelena d.o.o Inđija v. Republic of Serbia*, ICSID Case No. ARB/14/27, Award, 9 November 2018 (unpublished).

75 J. Hepburn, *Serbia Held Liable at ICSID in Case Alleging Failure to Enforce Environmental Regulations*, IA Reporter (10 Nov. 2018).

76 Ibid.

77 R. de Paor, *Climate Change and Arbitration: Annex Time Before There Won't Be a Next Time*, 8 J. Int. Disput. Settl. 179, 209 (2017); Zachary Douglas, 'The Enforcement of Environmental Norms in Investment Treaty Arbitration', *Harnessing Foreign Investment to Promote Environmental Protection*, pp.424–5 (Dupuy, Viñuales, Cambridge University Press, 2013). In addition, Article 42(1) of the ICSID Convention allows tribunals to apply 'rules of international law as may be applicable' in the absence of an agreement on the applicable by the Parties.

78 Ibid, para 8.

along with whether the order amounted to an expropriation, the tribunal considered the Canada–USA Transboundary Agreement on Hazardous Waste and the Basel Convention on the Control of Transboundary Movements of Hazardous Waste and Their Disposal.[79] In light of these treaty provisions the tribunal held that, although a State may achieve its chosen level of environmental protection 'through a variety of equally effective and reasonable means', Canada was obliged to adopt the alternative 'that is most consistent with open trade'.[80]

10.35 The FPS standard, which protects the physical integrity and the legal security of the investment and imposes a due diligence obligation on the host State,[81] can also protect investors in situations in which the action or inaction of the State has degraded the environment and, consequently, the value of the investment.[82]

10.36 For example, the claimant in the PCA case *Allard v Barbados* relied on the FPS standard after the Barbados Water Authority conducted an emergency discharge of raw sewage in a nearby swamp,[83] degrading the claimant's eco-tourism site.[84] The claimant contended that the FPS standard in the Barbados–Canada BIT included an obligation of due diligence, and that the State's failure to exercise such diligence resulted in an FPS violation.[85] Although the tribunal rejected the claimant's position, it nonetheless observed in *obiter dictum* that 'consideration of a host State's international obligations may well be relevant in the application of FPS standard to particular circumstances' and noted that Barbados had ratified the Convention on Biological Diversity and the Ramsar Convention on Wetlands of International Importance.[86]

10.37 Although the claimants were ultimately unsuccessful, the *obiter* in *Allard* opens the door to claims against States for violations of the FPS standard for their inappropriate actions or inactions on climate change.[87]

---

79 Ibid, paras 220–1.

80 Ibid.

81 August Reinisch, Christopher Schreuer, *International Protection of Investments: The Substantive Standards*, pp.558, 569, 580, paras 79, 129, 171 (Cambridge University Press, 2020).

82 Annette Magnusson, 'New Arbitration Frontiers: Climate Change', n 73, p.1021.

83 Ibid, paras 50, 43.

84 Flavia Marisi, *Environmental Interests in Investment Arbitration*, p.23 (Kluwer Law International 2020).

85 *Peter A. Allard v The Government of Barbados*, PCA Case No. 2012-06, Award, 27 June 2016, para. 249.

86 Ibid, para. 244.

87 Annette Magnusson, 'New Arbitration Frontiers: Climate Change', n 73, p.1021.

(b) Climate change-related defences for respondent states in investment arbitration

Not only does the investment arbitration framework allow investors to bring climate change-related arguments before arbitral tribunals; this same framework also provides a defence to respondent States. **10.38**

Investment treaties, for example, do not restrict States from adopting environmental regulations.[88] As recalled by the *Invesmart v Czech Republic* UNCITRAL tribunal, international investment agreements are not expected to prevent Contracting States from exercising their customary international law right to regulate.[89] Also known as the 'police powers' doctrine,[90] the right to regulate operates as a balance between the investor's private interests and the public purpose that the State pursues through action or abstention.[91] To that end, tribunals generally examine whether the State measure challenged by the claimant fulfils four criteria: whether the measure (i) was adopted in good faith, (ii) for a public purpose, (iii) is proportional to this purpose and (iv) is not discriminatory.[92] Environment protection has been routinely held by tribunals to be a public purpose on which police powers may be based.[93] As such, the State's right to regulate may constitute a successful defence against a claim regarding a polluting investment. **10.39**

Likewise, just as a claimant may invoke its legitimate expectations under the FET standard to challenge a State environmental measure, the respondent State can equally invoke FET principles as a defence. Tribunals generally **10.40**

---

88 *Methanex Corporation v United States of America*, UNCITRAL, Final Award, 3 August 2005, Part IV Ch. D paras 7, 9, 15; S. Schill, *Do Investment Treaties Chill Unilateral State Regulation to Mitigate Climate Change?* 24 J. Int. Arbitr. 469, 470 (2007).

89 *Invesmart B.V. v. Czech Republic*, UNCITRAL, Award, 26 June 2009, para. 498. See also *SAUR International v Argentine Republic*, ICSID Case No. ARB/04/4, Decision on Jurisdiction and Liability, 6 June 2012, para. 398.

90 Alain Pellet, 'Police Powers or the State's Right to Regulate', *Building International Investment Law: The First 50 Years of ICSID* (Fischer et al., Kluwer Law International, 2015); Yulia Levashova, *The Right of States to Regulate in International Investment Law: The Search for Balance Between Public Interest and Fair and Equitable Treatment* (Kluwer Law International, 2019); Catharine Titi, 'Police Powers Doctrine and International Investment Law', *General Principles of Law and International Investment Arbitration* (Gattini, Tanzi, Fontanelli, Brill Nijhoff, 2018).

91 S. Schill, *Do Investment Treaties Chill Unilateral State Regulation to Mitigate Climate Change?* n 88, p.471.

92 *See Saluka Investment BV v Czech Republic*, UNCITRAL, Partial Award, 17 March 2006, para. 255; SAUR *International v Argentine Republic*, ICSID Case No. ARB/04/4, Decision on Jurisdiction and Liability, 6 June 2012, para. 401; *Les Laboratoires Servier, S.A.S., Biofarma, S.A.S. and Arts et Techniques du Progrès S.A.S. v Republic of Poland*, UNCITRAL, Award, 14 February 2012, para. 569.

93 *Magyar Farming Company Ltd, Kintyre Kft and Inicia Zrt v Hungary*, ICSID Case No. ARB/17/27, Award, 13 November 2019, para. 366; *Crompton (Chemtura) Corporation v Government of Canada*, UNCITRAL, Award, 2 August 2010, para. 266; *Marvin Roy Feldman Karpa v United Mexican States*, ICSID Case No. ARB(AF)/99/1, Award, 16 December 2002, para. 103.

consider that investors' expectations are legitimate only when the investors exercised due diligence and carried out a risk assessment before investing.[94] This principle was articulated by the ad hoc tribunal established under the SCC Rules in the *Charanne v Spain* case, stating 'the Claimants should have made a diligent analysis of the legal framework for the investment' in order to attract investment treaty protection.[95]

10.41 As climate change agreements are now part of the public debate, it would thus be difficult for any investor to successfully argue that it was, for example, unaware of the Paris Agreement and a host State's obligation to reduce greenhouse gas emissions thereunder. The enactment of a regulation by a State Party to the Paris Agreement implementing its commitments under this treaty is therefore likely to be held as reasonable on the State's part and foreseeable to any prudent investor.[96] An investor making an investment in a polluting industry after the adoption of the Paris Agreement would correspondingly have difficulty arguing that it could not have legitimately expected the State to take measures against climate change. As a result, the increase in the number of climate change treaties and increasing public knowledge thereof may well constitute a defence for States faced with investment claims.

10.42 States may also assert climate change-related arguments against claimants through counterclaims. Although whether States can bring counterclaims is still the subject of debate,[97] and some commentators assert that States cannot file counterclaims when the obligation allegedly breached by the investor is not enshrined in the investment treaty,[98] 11 counterclaims have been filed by respondent States to date.[99] Out of these 11 counterclaims, tribunals have retained jurisdiction over only 5, and only 2 of those were ultimately successful.[100]

94 Yulia Levashova, *The Right of States to Regulate in International Investment Law*, n 88, pp.163–4; *See Biwater v Tanzania*, ICSID Case No. ARB/05/22 Final Award, 24 July 2008, para. 601; *Parkerings v Lithuania*, ICSID Case No. ARB/05/8 Award, 11 September 2007, para. 335; *Mamidoil Jetoil Greek Petroleum Products Société S.A. v Republic of Albania*, ICSID Case No. ARB/11/24, Award, 30 March 2015, para. 634; *Isolux Netherlands, BV v Kingdom of Spain*, SCC Case V2013/153, Award, 17 July 2016, para. 781.

95 *Charanne Construction v Spain*, SCC Case No. 062/2012, Award, 21 January 2016, para. 505 (unofficial translation).

96 M. Feria-Tinta, *The Role of International Law and Arbitration in Enforcing the Paris Agreement*, Kluwer Arbitration Blog (31 Dec. 2016).

97 Anne Hoffmann, 'Counterclaims', *Building International Investment Law: The First 50 Years of ICSID*, p.510 (Fischer et al., Kluwer Law International, 2015).

98 Ibid.

99 Flavia Marisi, *Environmental Interests in Investment Arbitration*, n 84, p.238.

100 Ibid; *Urbaser S.A. and Consorcio de Aguas Bilbao Bizkaia, Bilbao Biskaia Ur Partzuergoa v Argentine Republic*, ICSID Case No. ARB/07/26, Award, 8 December 2016, para. 1155; *Hesham T. M. Al Warraq v Republic of Indonesia*, UNCITRAL, Final Award, 15 December 2014, para. 664; *Perenco Ecuador Ltd. v Republic of*

Notwithstanding the limited use of counterclaims in the past, no fewer than four separate legal bases exist for an investment tribunal's jurisdiction over a respondent State counterclaim, depending on the circumstances.[101] First, the investment treaty may expressly grant the contracting State the right to bring a claim or counterclaim, though only four do so and most are silent on this issue.[102] Second, the applicable arbitration rules may expressly authorise counterclaims, as is the case with most arbitration rules.[103] Third, the parties may agree to confer jurisdiction to the tribunal over counterclaims, as in the *Burlington v Ecuador* ICSID case, discussed below.[104] Finally, a tribunal may base its jurisdiction over counterclaims on the applicable dispute resolution provision, in cases in which the provision is broadly worded, allowing the submission of 'all' or 'any' disputes related to investments.[105] **10.43**

Interestingly, the two State counterclaims that, to date, were successful were both based on environmental arguments. Both were filed by Ecuador, in the related *Burlington v Ecuador* and *Perenco v Ecuador* cases.[106] The claimants, Perenco and Burlington, formed a consortium and invested in two hydrocarbon blocks through ownership interests in Production Sharing Contracts (PSC) to operate in the Ecuadorian forest.[107] The disputes arose out of a significant increase in windfall taxes imposed by Ecuador on the claimants, although the PSCs provided that the State-owned oil company would cover **10.44**

Ecuador, ICSID Case No. ARB/08/6, Award, 27 September 2019, para. 1023(b); *Burlington Resources, Inc. v Republic of Ecuador*, ICSID Case No. ARB/08/5, Decision on Counterclaims, 7 February 2017, para. 1099.

101 Flavia Marisi, *Environmental Interests in Investment Arbitration*, n 84, p.239.

102 *See* Article 17 of the Slovak Republic–Iran BIT; Article 22 of the Slovak Republic–United Arab Emirates BIT; Article 28 of the Argentina–United Arab Emirates BIT; Article 9.19 of the Comprehensive and Progressive Agreement for Trans-Pacific Partnership.

103 *See* Article 46 of the ICSID Convention; Article 40(1) of the ICSID Arbitration Rules; Article 9 of the SCC Rules, Article 5 of the ICC Rules, Article 2(1)(iii) of the LCIA Rules, Articles 4(1)(b) and 25 of the SIAC Investment Rules; Article 21 of the 2010 UNCITRAL Arbitration Rules: Article 19(3) of the UNCITRAL Arbitration Rules originally authorised 'counter-claim[s] arising out of the same contract', but the reference to 'the same contract' was removed during the revision of the Rules in 2006 to leave no doubt on the permissibility of counterclaims in investment arbitration proceedings.

104 *Burlington Resources, Inc. v Republic of Ecuador*, ICSID Case No. ARB/08/5, Decision on Counterclaims, 7 February 2017, para. 60.

105 Flavia Marisi, *Environmental Interests in Investment Arbitration*, n 84, p.240; *See Urbaser S.A. and Consorcio de Aguas Bilbao Bizkaia, Bilbao Biskaia Ur Partzuergoa v. Argentine Republic*, ICSID Case No. ARB/07/26, Award, 8 December 2016, para. 1144.

106 *Burlington Resources Inc. v Republic of Ecuador*, ICSID Case No. ARB/08/5; *Perenco Ecuador Ltd. v Republic of Ecuador and Empresa Estatal Petróleos del Ecuador*, ICSID Case No. ARB/08/6.

107 M. Levine, *ICSID Tribunal Renders Interim Decision on Ecuador's Environmental Counterclaim in Long-running Dispute*, International Institute for Sustainable Development (26 Nov. 2015); J. Robalino Orellana, *Burlington Resources Inc v Republic of Ecuador (Decision on Ecuador's Counterclaims), ICSID Case No. ARB/08/5, 07 February 2017* (Contribution by ITA Board of Reporters, Kluwer Law International 2017).

future tax increases.[108] Perenco and Burlington filed separate ICSID arbitration claims in April 2008.[109] In both cases, Ecuador filed a counterclaim alleging that the claimants were liable for environmental damage caused by soil and groundwater pollution in the two hydrocarbon blocks they operated.[110] Although differently constituted, both tribunals retained jurisdiction over the counterclaim, and both unanimously found that the claimants were liable for environmental damage and ordered compensation to Ecuador based on its counterclaims.[111]

10.45 The respondent State's climate change-related defence may also directly derive from the letter of the applicable investment treaty. Out of the 2,342 BITS currently in force,[112] approximately 10 per cent include provisions addressing environmental issues.[113] More than 66 investment treaties refer to environmental matters in their preamble, including the recently ratified Agreement between the United States of America, the United Mexican States and Canada (USMCA), along with the ECT.[114] Some international investment agreements specify that non-discriminatory environmental measures do not amount to indirect expropriation,[115] and others encourage the Contracting Parties not to lower their environmental standards to attract investments.[116] Finally, some treaties deal with environmental issues directly in relation to investor-State dispute settlement. For instance, the Belgium/Luxembourg–Colombia BIT excludes State environmental measures from the scope of the dispute settlement clause entirely.[117]

108 *Perenco Ecuador Ltd. v Republic of Ecuador and Empresa Estatal Petroleos del Ecuador (Petroecuador)*, ICSID Case No. ARB/08/6, Decision on Jurisdiction, 30 June 2011, paras 15-21; International Institute for Sustainable Development, *Burlington v Ecuador*, Investment Treaty News (18 Oct. 2018).

109 *Perenco v Ecuador*, Decision on Jurisdiction, 30 June 2011, n 198, para. 21.

110 *Burlington v Ecuador*, Decision on Counterclaims, 7 February 2017, n 104, para. 52(i); *Perenco Ecuador Ltd. v Republic of Ecuador*, ICSID Case No. ARB/08/6, Interim Decision on the Environment Counterclaim, 11 August 2015, para. 36.

111 *Perenco Ecuador Ltd. v Republic of Ecuador*, ICSID Case No. ARB/08/6, Award, 27 September 2019, para. 1023(b); *Burlington v Ecuador*, Decision on Counterclaims, 7 February 2017, n 104, para. 1099.

112 Investment Policy Hub, *International Investment Agreements Navigator*, https://investmentpolicy.unctad.org/international-investment-agreements (accessed 7 Dec. 2020).

113 K. Gordon, J. Pohl, *Environmental Concerns in International Investment Agreements: A Survey*, OECD Working Papers on International Investment 2011/01, p.3 (2011).

114 Ibid, pp.11–13; The USMCA entered into force on 1 July 2020 and replaces NAFTA.

115 K. Gordon and J. Pohl, *Environmental Concerns in International Investment Agreements: A Survey*, OECD Working Papers on International Investment 2011/01, p.11 (2011).

116 Ibid.

117 Article VII(5) of the Belgium/Luxembourg-Colombia BIT deals with environment protection and policies, and provides that '[t]he dispute settlement mechanisms under Articles XII and XIII of this Agreement shall not apply to any obligation undertaken in accordance with this Article'.

These treaties encourage arbitral tribunals to consider environmental issues when dealing with an investment dispute. On this basis, arbitral tribunals' interpretation of investment treaties in light of climate change matters could undoubtedly support a respondent State's defence based on its environmental regulations. 10.46

C. THE SUITABILITY OF ARBITRATION PROCEEDINGS FOR THE RESOLUTION OF CLIMATE CHANGE DISPUTES

Arbitral institutions have increasingly acknowledged the role of arbitration in the resolution of climate change-related disputes. The PCA, for one, has been a pioneer, adopting in 2001 a special set of arbitration rules for environment-related disputes.[118] Adapted to disputes involving 'a natural resources, conservation, or environmental protection component',[119] the PCA Environmental Rules are accompanied by the establishment of a list of arbitrators specialised in environmental matters and a list of scientific and technical experts.[120] In addition, the PCA Environmental Rules allow the arbitral tribunal to appoint experts and order interim measures to preserve the environment from serious harm within the subject-matter of the dispute. These Rules have been applied in six contract-based disputes relating to carbon trading under the UNFCCC and the Kyoto Protocol.[121] 10.47

The ICC and the SCC have followed suit and taken initiatives to adapt arbitration proceedings administered under their rules to the specificities of disputes relating to climate change. These institutions have highlighted, and sometimes improved, the advantages that arbitration offers to resolve these disputes, including tribunal expertise, transparency and public participation and the expeditiousness of arbitral proceedings.[122] 10.48

1. Expertise on Climate Change Issues

Climate change disputes involve complex fields of law and require specific environmental and scientific knowledge.[123] As recalled by the ICC Arbitration 10.49

118 PCA Optional Rules for Arbitration of Disputes Relating to Natural Resources and/or the Environment.

119 Ibid, p.183.

120 The Panel of arbitrators for environmental disputes was established under Article 8(3) of the PCA Environmental Rules and the Panel of experts was established under Article 27(5) of the Rules.

121 J. Levine and C. Pondel, *Updates on the Changing State of the Climate and International Arbitration*, n 29, p.35.

122 ICC Commission Report, *Resolving Climate Change Related Disputes through Arbitration and ADR*, n 24.

123 D. Magraw, C. Giorgetti et al., *Model Green Investment Treaty: International Investment and Climate Change*, 36 J. Int. Arbitr. 95, 125 (2019); Wendy J. Miles and Nicolas Swan, 'Climate Change Financing and Dispute Resolution', n 8, p.342.

Commission Report on Climate Change, it is essential to ensure that 'appropriate expertise is available to the parties and the tribunal' to facilitate the 'understanding of disputes and their resolution techniques'.[124] Since international lawyers are not usually equipped with the necessary skills to deal with these issues,[125] arbitration may respond to the demands of climate change-related disputes in terms of expertise in two ways: through the appointment of arbitrators specialised in environmental issues and/or the specific sector at hand, and through the designation of competent experts.

10.50 To select arbitrators capable of understanding the issues in dispute, the parties may, for example, request that arbitral institutions provide publicly available information on the arbitrators' expertise or present a list of arbitrators qualified to deal with these matters.[126] As noted above, the PCA Environmental Rules do just that by establishing a panel of arbitrators specialised in environmental issues. The SCC, for its part, has observed that arbitrators specialised in the energy or in the construction sector are appointed in most disputes involving climate change elements.[127]

10.51 Arbitrator expertise is of such importance that an arbitrator's lack of the necessary skills to understand and rule on the dispute could give rise to a challenge.[128] In support of this view, the ICC Arbitration Commission Report on Climate Change relies on Article 14(1) of the ICC Arbitration Rules, under which an arbitrator may be challenged 'whether for an alleged lack of impartiality or independence, *or otherwise*' (emphasis added), and considers that '[t]he language "or otherwise" is a catch-all phrase that could include lack of requisite qualifications'.[129] To avoid such a situation, the appointment of an arbitrator with the appropriate expertise may be included in the arbitration agreement as a condition for the valid constitution of the Tribunal.[130]

---

124 ICC Commission Report, *Resolving Climate Change Related Disputes through Arbitration and ADR*, n 24, p.19.

125 Joint dissenting opinion of Judges Al-Khasawneh and Simma, *Pulp Mills on the River Uruguay* (Argentina v Uruguay), International Court of Justice, Judgement, 20 April 2010, p.109, para. 2: 'the Court has evaluated the scientific evidence brought before it by the Parties in ways that we consider flawed methodologically.'

126 ICC Commission Report, *Resolving Climate Change Related Disputes through Arbitration and ADR*, n 24, p.21.

127 S. Dwi Andrina, *Green Technology Disputes in Stockholm*, n 26, pp.15, 23.

128 ICC Commission Report, *Resolving Climate Change Related Disputes through Arbitration and ADR*, n 24, p.23, para. 5.19.

129 Ibid.

130 *See, e.g.*, *Indus Waters Kishenganga Arbitration (Pakistan v India)*, PCA Case No. 2011-01; Article IX(5)(4) of the 1960 Indus Waters Treaty requires that at least one highly qualified engineer compose the tribunal; Judith Levine, 'Adopting and Adapting Arbitration for Climate Change-Related Disputes: The Experience of the Permanent Court of Arbitration', *Dispute Resolution and Climate Change: The Paris Agreement and Beyond*, p.26 (Miles, ICC 2017), p.29.

The arbitral tribunal may alternatively seek assistance on technical issues by designating experts.[131] For example, in the *Perenco v Ecuador* case, the tribunal appointed its own independent expert, after it concluded that it was unable to determine which of the party- appointed experts was more reliable.[132] Similarly, in the *South China Sea* case, the tribunal appointed its own experts on coral reef environment to report and shed light on the potential consequences of the disputed construction activities.[133] **10.52**

As climate change-related disputes encompass a wide range of issues that do not necessarily pertain to environmental science alone, the SCC correctly observes that other areas of expertise may also bring meaningful contributions to the resolution of these types of disputes. This is, for instance, the case for finance and taxation experts who can guide the tribunal in understanding the consequences of States' incentive and support schemes in renewable energies, which are issues that appear increasingly in investment arbitration cases.[134] **10.53**

2. Transparency of the Arbitral Proceedings and Public Participation

Demand for transparency and public participation is growing in investment arbitration. This demand is particularly acute in climate change-related disputes, in light of actions initiated by citizens' groups and NGOs against States and corporations for environmental inaction.[135] **10.54**

In this context, the recent decision of the *Hoge Raad*, the Netherlands' Supreme Court, in *Urgenda Foundation v Netherlands* is particularly pertinent.[136] The Urgenda Foundation, together with a group of 900 Dutch citizens, initiated legal proceedings against the Dutch government to compel it to reduce greenhouse gas emissions.[137] On 20 December 2019 the *Hoge Raad*, in consideration of the UNFCCC, ordered the State to reduce greenhouse gases by at least 25 per cent compared to 1990 levels by the end of 2020.[138] This judgment inspired climate change cases in Europe, the Americas, Asia and Oceania, **10.55**

---

131 ICC Commission Report, *Resolving Climate Change Related Disputes through Arbitration and ADR*, n 24, p.24, paras 5.26–5.27.

132 *Perenco v Ecuador*, Interim Decision on the Environment Counterclaim, 11 August 2015, n 109, paras 585, 587.

133 *South China Sea Arbitration (Philippines v China)*, PCA Case No. 2013-19, Independent Expert Report on Coral Reef Environment, 26 April 2016.

134 S. Dwi Andrina, *Green Technology Disputes in Stockholm*, n 26, p.23.

135 J. Setzer and R. Byrnes, *Global Trends in Climate Change Litigation: 2020 Snapshot*, Policy Report (2020).

136 *Urgenda Foundation v The State of the Netherlands*, ECLI:NL:HR:2019:2007, 20 December 2019.

137 Ibid.

138 Ibid.

demonstrating that civil society is willing and, in some cases, able to compel governments to comply with international climate obligations.[139] Enhanced transparency would therefore reconcile the arbitral process with civil society, allow arbitration to gain legitimacy and ultimately facilitate public understanding of tribunal decisions.[140]

10.56 However, transparency may be subject to the consent of the parties to the dispute. Further, while transparency seems to be increasing in investment arbitration, it remains a rare feature in commercial arbitration, as confidentiality remains one of the reasons why parties to commercial contracts choose arbitration over litigation.

10.57 Most rules used in investment arbitration proceedings nevertheless provide for some amount of transparency. For instance, the adoption of the UNCITRAL Rules on Transparency in Treaty-Based Investor-State Arbitration (UNCITRAL Transparency Rules) in 2013 was a step forward for transparency in investment arbitration. The Transparency Rules provide for the publication of certain documents from the arbitration proceedings, such as the parties' submissions, exhibit lists, expert reports, witness statements and the tribunal's decisions.[141]

10.58 The use of the UNCITRAL Transparency Rules is expected to increase, along with an increase in the number of ratifications of the United Nations Convention on Transparency in Treaty-based Investor-State Arbitration (Mauritius Convention). Importantly, Article 2(1) of the Mauritius Convention provides that '[t]he UNCITRAL Rules on Transparency shall apply to any investor-State arbitration, whether or not initiated under the UNCITRAL Arbitration Rules, in which the respondent is a Party that has not made a relevant reservation under article 3(1)(a)'.[142] In 2020, seven States had ratified the

---

139 Urgenda, *Global Climate Litigation*, www .urgenda .nl/ en/ themas/ climate -case/ global -climate -litigation/ (accessed 30 Nov. 2020); *See* also the case 'Commune de Grande-Synthe' brought before the *Conseil d'Etat* (French Supreme Administrative Court): the city of Grande-Synthe, later joined by other French cities and foundations, initiated judicial proceedings against the French government for refusing to take measures to comply with its obligation to reduce greenhouse gases under the UNFCCC and the Paris Agreement. In a decision dated 19 November 2020, the *Conseil d'Etat* ordered the French government to justify within three months the reasons why the government refuses to take additional steps to reduce emissions and to explain whether this refusal is compatible with the objectives set in the Paris Agreement.

140 ICC Commission Report, *Resolving Climate Change Related Disputes through Arbitration and ADR*, n 24, p.41, para. 5.69; W. Miles and M. Lawry-White, *Arbitral Institutions and the Enforcement of Climate Change Obligations for the Benefit of all Stakeholders*, n 57, p.28.

141 ICC Commission Report, *Resolving Climate Change Related Disputes through Arbitration and ADR*, n 24, p.41, para. 5.68.

142 United Nations Convention on Transparency in Treaty-based Investor-State Arbitration (18 Oct. 2017), T.S. No 54749.

Mauritius Convention and none had made a reservation under Article 3(1)(a), meaning that the UNCITRAL Transparency Rules will apply in investment arbitration proceedings in which these States will appear as respondent.[143]

Similarly, the ICSID Arbitration Rules provide for transparency under certain conditions. Rule 48(4) of the ICSID Arbitration Rules provides that, should the parties refuse to consent to the award being made public, ICSID may nevertheless publish excerpts of the tribunal's legal reasoning, and Rule 32(2) permits the tribunal, with the parties' consent, to hold the hearings in public. These efforts towards transparency in ICSID proceedings are confirmed by the review of the ICSID Arbitration Rules currently under way. To date, the latest proposals provide that the ICSID 'shall' publish any order or decision taken by the tribunal, with necessary redactions, within 60 days the issuance of an order or decision, and that the tribunal 'shall' authorise any third person to observe hearings, unless the parties otherwise agree.[144] **10.59**

The recent increase in arbitral hearings conducted remotely allows tribunals to manage the attendance of non-party observers more easily, when the rules allow it. The opportunity for non-parties to observe arbitral hearings will further legitimise arbitration as an effective means of resolving disputes in which the public has an interest, which is particularly the case for environmental disputes. Remote hearings offer the particular advantage of allowing tribunals to deactivate observers' video and audio connections for *in camera* sessions, thereby reducing the inefficiency of requiring the tribunal to ensure that only counsel and party representatives are physically present in a hearing room. The hearing of the ICSID *Vattenfall v Germany* case,[145] for example, was recorded and made publicly available, which is particularly notable given the public interest in a case with environmental implications, as the *Vattenfall* claim was brought in response to Germany's decision to phase out nuclear power by 2022.[146] **10.60**

---

143 To date, the Mauritius Convention has been ratified by Australia, Bolivia, Cameroon, Canada, Gambia, Mauritius and Switzerland.

144 International Centre for Settlement of Investment Disputes, Proposals for Amendment of the ICSID Rules, Working Paper 4, Vol. 1, pp.65–6 (Feb. 2020).

145 *Vattenfall AB and others v Federal Republic of Germany*, ICSID Case No. ARB/12/12.

146 ICSID, *Vattenfall AB and others v Federal Republic of Germany (ICSID Case No. ARB/12/12) – Public Hearing*, Press Release (29 Sept. 2016); IA Reporter, *Germany Is Sued at ICSID by Swedish Energy Company in Bid for Compensation for Losses Arising out of Nuclear Phase-out* (1 June 2012).

10.61 The participation of non-parties to a dispute as *amici curiae* will also enhance transparency in the arbitral process.[147] Third party participation is possible under most arbitration rules. Article 25 of the ICC Rules provides that the tribunal may hear 'any other person', and Article 4 of the UNCITRAL Transparency Rules and Article 4 of the Appendix III to the 2017 SCC Rules authorise the tribunal to allow a non-disputing party to file written submissions. Similarly, ICSID Rule 37(2) states that the tribunal may authorise a non-disputing party to file a written submission to the tribunal, after considering whether the non-disputing party would assist the tribunal in determining a factual or legal issue related to the proceedings by bringing in a different perspective from that of the parties, whether the submission would address a matter within the scope of the dispute and whether the non-disputing party has a significant interest in the proceedings. The proposals for amendments of the ICSID Rules reaffirm this possibility in proposed amended Rule 67.[148]

10.62 In the context of climate change-related disputes, *amicus* briefs from non-parties may offer the tribunal another perspective and additional expertise, as demonstrated in *Foresti v South Africa*.[149] In that case, the claimant filed a claim for unlawful expropriation and the respondent State argued that the expropriation was lawful as it pursued the public purpose of protecting the environment and communities in the area.[150] The arbitral tribunal allowed four NGOs to file submissions on the issues of substantive equality, human rights, sustainable development and environmental protection in South Africa;[151] ordered the parties to give these non-disputing parties access to documents submitted to the tribunal; and invited the parties to comment on the *amicus* briefs.[152]

3. Expeditiousness of Arbitral Proceedings

10.63 Climate change-related disputes often involve an element of urgency and require prompt resolution.[153] If not dealt with expeditiously, the environmental

147 ICC Commission Report, *Resolving Climate Change Related Disputes through Arbitration and ADR*, n 24, p.42, para. 5.70; W. Miles and M. Lawry-White, *Arbitral Institutions and the Enforcement of Climate Change Obligations for the Benefit of all Stakeholders*, n 57, pp.28–9.

148 Proposals for Amendments of the ICSID Rules, n 144, p.67.

149 ICC Commission Report, *Resolving Climate Change Related Disputes through Arbitration and ADR*, n 24, pp.44–5, para. 5.90; *Piero Foresti, Laura de Carli & Others v Republic of South Africa*, ICSID Case No. ARB(AF)/07/01, Award, 4 August 2010.

150 Ibid; W. Miles and M. Lawry-White, *Arbitral Institutions and the Enforcement of Climate Change Obligations for the Benefit of all Stakeholders*, n 57, p.30.

151 *Foresti v South Africa*, Award, 4 August 2010, n 150, para. 27; *Foresti v South Africa*, Petition for Limited Participation as Non-Disputing Parties, 17 July 2009, para. 4.18.

152 Ibid, paras 28–29.

153 Ibid.

impact and the effect on populations in climate change-related disputes may be irreversible.[154] Parties may use various procedural options to expedite the resolution of the dispute. The ICC, for instance, recommends a host of measures to resolve a dispute efficiently, including the bifurcation of proceedings, deciding that some issues may be decided on a 'documents only' basis and the limitation of submissions to key climate change-related issues.[155]

Arbitration presents the immense advantage of procedural rules that are adaptable to fit the needs of parties. To resolve a dispute quickly, parties may agree on the application of an expedited procedure when arbitral institutions, such as the ICC and the SCC, offer this possibility.[156] In 2019, out of 586 cases administered by the ICC, 146 cases had been or were being conducted under the ICC Expedited Procedure.[157] Similarly, the SCC states that 19 per cent of the green technology disputes it administered between 2012 and 2018 were registered under the SCC Rules for Expedited Arbitrations and were terminated within a year, against an average of 16 months for rendering an award in other proceedings.[158] **10.64**

Should the circumstances of a climate change-related dispute require a decision prior to the constitution of the tribunal, the ICC Emergency Arbitrator Rules provide for the rendering of such a decision, but such a mechanism does not exist for treaty-based arbitration.[159] In such a situation, the President of the ICC Court will appoint an emergency arbitrator within no more than two days after the receipt of the application, and the emergency arbitrator will issue an order within 15 days after the receipt of the file.[160] In 2019, 23 Emergency Arbitrator applications were filed; half of them concerned disputes in the construction and energy sectors, two sectors particularly related to climate change.[161] **10.65**

154 ICC Commission Report, *Resolving Climate Change Related Disputes through Arbitration and ADR*, n 24, p. 26, para. 5.34.

155 Ibid, pp.26–7, para. 5.35.

156 Ibid, p.27, para. 5.36; *See* Article 30 of the ICC Arbitration Rules and the SCC Rules for Expedited Arbitrations.

157 International Chamber of Commerce, ICC Dispute Resolution 2019 Statistics, p.16 (2020).

158 S. Dwi Andrina, *Green Technology Disputes in Stockholm*, n 26, pp.8, 10.

159 ICC Commission Report, *Resolving Climate Change Related Disputes through Arbitration and ADR*, n 24, pp.35–6, paras 5.54–5.55.

160 Appendix V, Articles 2(1) and 6(4) of the ICC Arbitration Rules.

161 ICC Dispute Resolution 2019 Statistics, n 157, p.17.

D. CONCLUSION

10.66 As Wendy Miles KC correctly observes, arbitration may well become 'a tool of global climate governance',[162] as it offers the necessary mechanisms for the resolution of climate change disputes. With the number of climate change-related disputes being sure to increase thanks to increases in green investments made each year; recourse to climate change-related arbitration should be further promoted. Arbitral institutions, for their part, are engaged and determined to welcome climate change-related disputes.

10.67 The potential for the increased use of arbitration in these matters now lies in the hands of the parties. Private and public entities, when concluding a contract related to energy, construction or any other field in which climate or environmental issues may arise, should seriously consider including an arbitration clause. Likewise, States should complete the arbitration protocols in climate change treaties and incorporate climate change-related provisions in their investment promotion agreements.

10.68 The 'Model Green Investment Treaty' drafting competition launched by the SCC is an encouraging step towards incentivising States to ratify suitable investment agreements.[163] This Model Green Investment Treaty comprises express provisions promoting environmental actions and combating climate change. The first of these provisions pertains to States' rights to regulate generally, as well as to do so more specifically in relation to climate change.[164] The treaty also requires investors to comply with local law and with the World Bank Environmental and Social Standards and the International Finance Corporation Performance Standards.[165] To that end, the Model Green Treaty explicitly grants the respondent State the right to bring a counterclaim for a breach of international law and standards.[166] The Model Green Treaty also seeks to adapt arbitration proceedings to climate change-related disputes by requiring that arbitrators be familiar with the issues of climate change and sustainable development as well as with relevant laws and policies. Finally, the Model Green Treaty strengthens transparency by providing for public

162 Wendy J. Miles and Nicolas Swan, 'Climate Change Financing and Dispute Resolution', n 8, p.342.

163 A. Havedal Ipp, *Stockholm Treaty Lab: Combating Climate Change through Legal Crowdsourcing*, Kluwer Arbitration Blog (17 July 2020).

164 D. Magraw, C. Giorgetti et al., *Model Green Investment Treaty: International Investment and Climate Change*, 36 J. Int. Arbitr. 95, 99 (2019).

165 Ibid, p.118.

166 Ibid.

participation in the dispute resolution process and requiring reporting on the implementation of awards.[167]

In the same vein, the European Commission has proposed amendments to the ECT to introduce considerations of sustainable development and climate change.[168] In particular, the European Commission proposal seeks to reaffirm the Contracting Parties' right to regulate in environmental matters to fight climate change.[169] **10.69**

Similarly, out of the 26 international investment agreements concluded since the beginning of 2019, at least 17 include provisions addressing climate change issues. These agreements reaffirm the contracting State's right to regulate with respect to climate, include protection of the environment in the exception clause, provide that States should not lower environmental standards to promote investment and address corporate social responsibility. These treaties thus require investors to comply with the host State's environmental regulations.[170] As recent developments show, despite the calls for the establishment of an international court of environment,[171] States are determined to ensure the viability of arbitration in climate change-related disputes – and the arbitration system is up to the challenge. **10.70**

167 Ibid, p.96.

168 C. Sanderson, *EU Publishes Proposals for ECT Revamp*, Global Arbitration Review (28 May 2020).

169 Ibid.

170 *See* Belarus–Hungary BIT, Australia–Indonesia CEPA, Brazil–UAE BIT, CARIFORUM–UK FTA, Australia– Hong Kong BIT, Hungary–Cabo Verde BIT, Australia–Uruguay BIT, Burkina Faso–Turkey BIT, Uzbekistan– South Korea BIT, Morocco–Brazil BIT, Kyrgyz Republic–India BIT, Vietnam–EU FTA, Singapore–Myanmar BIT, Brazil–Ecuador BIT, Armenia–Singapore BIT, Morocco–Japan BIT, Brazil–India BIT.

171 International Bar Association, *Achieving Justice and Human Rights in an Era of Climate Disruption*, Report of the Climate Change Justice and Human Rights Task Force, p.28 (2014).

11

CLIMATE CHANGE LITIGATION

Elisa de Wit and Tamlyn Mills[1]

---

1 Written in collaboration with Ashleigh McCoach, Alyssa Glass and Sanjna Pramod, former Associates at Norton Rose Fulbright Australia. The authors are grateful to Caterina Presutti and Shaun Buckton for their contributions.

A. INTRODUCTION

Climate change litigation is becoming increasingly common across a broad spectrum of actors and industries. As of February 2022, more than 2400 climate change cases have been filed worldwide.[2] Cases have now been filed in at least 43 countries, in addition to cases brought in regional or international courts or commissions.[3] The vast majority of these cases have been commenced in the United States (US), Australia, the United Kingdom (UK), the European Union (EU), Canada and New Zealand.[4] Alongside this growth, actions are becoming more sophisticated, drawing on a wider array of legal rights and obligations as a basis for liability. **11.001**

Given the rapidly evolving legal landscape of climate change litigation, it is imperative for both prospective plaintiffs and defendants to be familiar with the growing body of cases in order to track trends and outcomes and **11.002**

2 Columbia University, Columbia Law School, Sabin Center for Climate Change Law, in collaboration with Arnold & Porter Kaye Scholer LLP, *Climate Change Litigation Databases* (accessed 10 February 2022) http://climatecasechart.com/.

3 Ibid.

4 Ibid.

to identify, assess and mitigate risk. Following climate change litigation can also help businesses develop appropriate policy settings around their emission reduction goals and proactively mitigate their exposure to climate-related risks. This chapter provides a consolidated and concise summary of selected leading climate change cases, focussing largely on cases from the past five years. Drawing on these summaries, this chapter also seeks to identify common themes, emerging trends and points of difference between jurisdictions.

11.003 Broadly defined, climate change litigation refers to legal proceedings brought before judicial, administrative or investigative bodies that raise issues of fact or law regarding climate change.[5] It includes strategic climate change litigation which is considered precedent-setting, in the sense that the claimants' motives for commencing proceedings go beyond individual concerns (or claims for monetary compensation for individual loss).[6] Strategic climate change litigation cases continue to gain in both volume and prominence.

11.004 The chapter is divided into five main sections, reflecting different legal bases for claims.[7] First, we address climate change litigation in which claimants rely on human rights and/or constitutional rights. Second, we consider climate change litigation based on tort law or duty of care. Third, we focus on cases concerning consumer protection. Fourth, we address claims against companies that fail to disclose climate-related risks to shareholders and investors. Finally, the fifth section focuses on cases concerning administrative, planning and permitting law.

11.005 The case summaries included in this chapter are current up to September 2022.

B. HUMAN RIGHTS AND CONSTITUTIONAL LAW ACTIONS

1. Introduction

11.006 Human rights and constitutional claims have been employed in climate change litigation against government bodies and more recently these rights have also been deployed in cases against corporations. The cases summarised in this section illustrate the range of possibilities and barriers which may arise when

5 Joana Setzer and Catherine Higham, *Global Trends in Climate Change Litigation: 2021 Snapshot* (Grantham Research Institute on Climate Change and the Environment, London School of Economics, 2021) 8.

6 Ibid 4, 12–13.

7 The boundaries between these categories are fluid and in some instances cases do not fit neatly into one category. Cases that do not fit neatly into one category have been categorised based on at least one of the grounds upon which the case was brought.

framing climate change as a human rights or constitutional issue. The *Urgenda*[8] judgment in the Netherlands has been heralded as the precedent-setting judgment of the Supreme Court of the Netherlands. It established that government inaction on climate change could violate the European Convention on Human Rights (ECHR) and ordered the Netherlands to reduce its greenhouse gas (GHG) emissions. According to the United Nations (UN) High Commissioner for Human Rights, the *Urgenda* decision 'provides a clear path forward for concerned individuals in Europe – and around the world – to undertake climate litigation in order to protect human rights'.[9] Since this decision, claimants worldwide have been increasingly relying on human rights law in climate change litigation. However, as demonstrated by *Juliana v United States*, *Union of Swiss Senior Women for Climate Protection v Switzerland* and *La Rose v Her Majesty the Queen in Right of Canada*, issues of standing, justiciability and separation of powers are prominent in these types of cases and often prevent a barrier for claimants. In some jurisdictions, national courts may be cautious about the judicial branch intervening in what could be considered matters of public policy. The *Juliana*[10] proceedings in the US demonstrate the potential limitations of court actions in the face of 'the complexity and long-lasting nature of global climate change'.[11]

That said, the role of the Courts in this space is still evolving. For example, in **11.007** the *Juliana* proceedings, the minority on appeal agreed with the Court below, and lamented that the majority had adopted an unnecessarily deferential approach to the political branches and appeared 'ready to yield even if those branches walk the Nation over a cliff'.[12] The *Urgenda* judgments showed a similar scepticism regarding deference to political decision making and a judicial willingness to carve out a meaningful role for the courts in addressing climate change issues, including the need for urgent mitigation of GHG emissions.

8 *The State of the Netherlands v Urgenda Foundation*, Case No 19/00135, Supreme Court of the Netherlands, Judgment of 20 December 2019 (English translation).

9 Office of the United Nations High Commissioner for Human Rights, *Bachelet Welcomes Top Court's Landmark Decision to Protect Human Rights from Climate Change* 20 December 2019) www.ohchr.org/en/press-releases/2019/12/bachelet-welcomes-top-courts-landmark-decision-protect-human-rights-climate.

10 *Juliana v United States*, 217 F Supp 3d 1224, 1234 (D. Or. 2016); *Juliana v United States*, 947 F 3d 1159 (9th Cir. 2020); *Juliana v United States*, 968 F 3d 1295 (9th Cir. 2021).

11 *Juliana v United States*, 947 F 3d 1159 1165, 1172 (9th Cir. 2020).

12 Ibid 1183–4.

2. Case Summaries

(a) *Urgenda Foundation v Netherlands*[13]

11.008 The Urgenda Foundation (Urgenda), a Dutch environmental group, filed a summons on behalf of itself and 886 Dutch citizens (Urgenda Plaintiffs) in the District Court of The Hague, requesting that the Court provide injunctive relief by ordering the State of the Netherlands to reduce its annual GHG emissions by 40 per cent, or at least by 25 per cent, relative to 1990 levels by the end of 2020.[14]

11.009 Urgenda advanced multiple legal bases for its claim, arguing that existing GHG emissions levels violated: (i) the State's obligation to keep the country habitable and to protect and improve the environment, pursuant to Article 21 of the Dutch Constitution; (ii) the State's obligation to exercise 'due care' in society, pursuant to the 'unwritten standard of care' codified in the Dutch Civil Code; and (iii) the State's human rights obligations under the ECHR, specifically the right to life (Article 2) and the right to respect for a person's private and family life (Article 8).[15]

11.010 On 24 June 2015, the District Court of The Hague upheld Urgenda's claim based on the standard of care under the Dutch Civil Code.[16] The District Court ordered a reduction of the Netherlands' annual GHG emissions by at least 25 per cent relative to 1990 levels by the end of 2020.[17] The District Court rejected Urgenda's human rights claims and its claims in relation to Article 21 of the Constitution, and dismissed the claims of the 886 individual claimants.[18]

11.011 The Netherlands appealed, and Urgenda cross-appealed the dismissal of its human rights claims. On 9 October 2018, the Hague Court of Appeal upheld

---

13 *Urgenda Foundation v The State of the Netherlands*, Case No C/09/456689/HA ZA 13-1396, District Court of The Hague, Judgment of 24 June 2015 (English translation) ECLI:NL:RBDHA:2015:7196 https://cer.org.za/wp-content/uploads/2015/10/Urgenda-v-State-of-the-Netherlands.pdf; *The State of the Netherlands v Urgenda Foundation*, Case No 200.178.245/01, The Hague Court of Appeal, Judgment of 9 October 2018 (English translation) ECLI:NL:GHDHA:2018:2610 http:// climatecasechart .com/ wp -content/ uploads/ sites/16/non-us-case-documents/2018/20181009_2015-HAZA-C0900456689_decision-4.pdf; *The State of the Netherlands v Urgenda Foundation*, Case No 19/00135, Supreme Court of the Netherlands, Judgment of 20 December 2019 (English translation) ECLI:NL:HR:2019:2007 http://climatecasechart.com/wp-content/uploads/sites/16/non-us-case-documents/2020/20200113_2015-HAZA-C0900456689_judgment.pdf.

14 *Urgenda Foundation v The State of the Netherlands*, Case No C/09/456689 / HA ZA 13-1396, District Court of The Hague, Judgment of 24 June 2015 (English translation) [2.4]; [4.104] ECLI:NL:RBDHA:2015:7196 https://cer.org.za/wp-content/uploads/2015/10/Urgenda-v-State-of-the-Netherlands.pdf.

15 Ibid [3.2], [4.35].

16 Ibid [4.53], [4.63].

17 Ibid [4.83], [5.1].

18 Ibid [4.45], [4.108]–[4.109].

the District Court's emissions reduction order and found in Urgenda's favour on the cross-appeal, concluding that the State's obligations under Articles 2 and 8 of the ECHR required it to protect current generations of Dutch citizens from the 'real threat of dangerous climate change'.[19]

The Netherlands instituted an appeal in cassation to the Supreme Court of the Netherlands. On 20 December 2019 the Supreme Court rejected the appeal, which meant that the order requiring the State to reduce GHG by the end of 2020 by at least 25 per cent compared to 1990 stood as the final order.[20] The Supreme Court held that Articles 2 and 8 of the ECHR should be interpreted 'in such a way that these provisions oblige the contracting states to do "their part" to counter that danger'.[21] It followed that the ECHR obliged the Netherlands to take appropriate measures against the threat of dangerous climate change, in accordance with its fair share of responsibility.[22] **11.012**

(b) *Juliana v United States*[23]

On 12 August 2015, 21 individual youth plaintiffs, the non-profit organisation Earth Guardians and a plaintiff identified as 'Future Generations' (Juliana Plaintiffs) commenced proceedings in the US District Court for the District of Oregon, alleging *inter alia* violations of their fundamental constitutional rights to life, liberty and property; irreversible discrimination against them in the exercise of those rights relative to prior and present adult generations; and violation of the public trust doctrine.[24] They sought to compel the US government to implement a national remedial plan to reduce GHG emissions and asked the Court to retain jurisdiction over the action to monitor and enforce the US government's compliance with that plan.[25] **11.013**

---

19 *The State of the Netherlands v Urgenda Foundation*, Case No 200.178.245/01, The Hague Court of Appeal, Judgment of 9 October 2018 (English translation) [40]–[43], [45] ECLI:NL:GHDHA:2018:2610 http://climatecasechart.com/wp-content/uploads/sites/16/non-us-case-documents/2018/20181009_2015-HAZA-C0900456689_decision-4.pdf.

20 *The State of the Netherlands v Urgenda Foundation*, Case No 19/00135, Supreme Court of the Netherlands, Judgment of 20 December 2019 (English translation) ECLI:NL:HR:2019:2007 http:// climatecasechart.com/wp-content/uploads/sites/16/non-us-case-documents/2020/20200113_2015-HAZA-C0900456689_judgment.pdf.

21 Ibid [5.7.9], [5.8]. See also [5.4.1], [5.6.3], [5.7.1].

22 Ibid [5.9.1].

23 *Juliana v United States*, 217 F Supp 3d 1224, 1234 (D. Or. 2016); *Juliana v United States*, 947 F 3d 1159 (9th Cir. 2020); *Juliana v United States*, 968 F 3d 1295 (9th Cir. 2021).

24 *Juliana v United States*, No. 6:15-cv-01517-TC, 2015 WL 4747094 (D. Or. Aug. 12, 2015) (complaint for declaratory and injunctive relief), [277]–[289] (substantive rights to life, liberty and property), [290]–[301] (equal protection of the law), [307]–[310] (public trust claim). The Juliana Plaintiffs are identified and described at [16]–[97].

25 Ibid, Prayer for Relief (see especially Orders 7 and 8).

11.014 The US government brought a motion to dismiss the proceeding and the questions before the Court on the hearing of the motion to dismiss included whether (i) the US government was responsible for some of the harm caused by climate change and (ii) the Juliana Plaintiffs could challenge the US government's climate change policy in court.[26]

11.015 On 10 November 2016, the District Court held that the Juliana Plaintiffs had standing, raised justiciable questions and stated a claim for infringement of a constitutional right to a 'climate system capable of sustaining human life'.[27]

11.016 The US government appealed,[28] and on 17 January 2020, a divided bench of the US Court of Appeals, Ninth Circuit allowed the appeal.[29] The Court 'reluctantly' held by majority that it was beyond its power to order, design, supervise or implement a national remedial plan.[30] The Court doubted its capacity to 'stop catastrophic climate change' or to ameliorate the Juliana Plaintiffs' injuries, given that reducing the global consequences of climate change 'calls for no less than a fundamental transformation' of the industrialised world.[31] These considerations went to the efficacy of the relief sought and to the Court's power to grant it, and precluded the Juliana Plaintiffs' standing to sue.

11.017 In dissent, Judge Staton acknowledged the majority's concern that any relief the Court could offer would be 'just a drop in the bucket'.[32] However, her Honour emphasised that 'we are perilously close to an overflowing bucket' and these 'final drops matter'.[33] Judge Staton considered that the Court *could* offer effective relief.[34]

---

26 *Juliana v United States*, 217 F Supp 3d 1224, 1234 (D. Or. 2016).

27 Ibid, 1250 (D. Or. 2016).

28 In the intervening period, the US Supreme Court denied the US government's motion for a stay of proceedings: *United States v U.S. District Court for District of Oregon*, 139 S.Ct. 1 (2018). The US government then moved for summary judgment. The District Court granted summary dismissal of certain confined aspects of the claim, but otherwise denied the US government's motions, again holding that the Juliana Plaintiffs had standing to sue: *Juliana v United States*, 339 F.Supp.3d 1062 (D. Or. 2018). The US government appealed both the District Court's 2016 interlocutory decision and this later 2018 decision of the District Court.

29 *Juliana v United States*, 947 F 3d 1159 (9th Cir. 2020). The appeal was allowed by a 2:1 majority, with Staton J dissenting.

30 Ibid 1165, 1171 (9th Cir. 2020), 5.

31 Ibid 1170–1 (9th Cir. 2020), 23.

32 Ibid 1182.

33 Ibid 1182.

34 Ibid 1184.

On 10 February 2021, the Ninth Circuit denied the Juliana Plaintiffs' petition for a rehearing.[35] On 17 February 2022, the Juliana Plaintiffs filed a notice of supplemental authority of a new opinion from the Ninth Circuit Court of Appeals issued on 7 February 2022 in *Barke v Banks*, which supported the Juliana Plaintiffs' motion for leave to file an amended complaint.[36] On 4 March 2022, a response was filed by the defendants to the Juliana Plaintiffs' notice of supplemental authority.[37] The Juliana Plaintiffs' motion for leave to file an amended complaint remains to be determined at the time of writing. **11.018**

(c) *Greenpeace Nordic v Norway*[38]

On 18 October 2016, Greenpeace Nordic Association (Greenpeace Nordic) and the environmental group 'Nature & Youth' commenced proceedings in the Oslo District Court to challenge the validity of a decision made by the Norwegian government to award 13 companies new production licences for petroleum in the Arctic Barents Sea (Licensing Decision). The Licensing Decision, in effect, opened new acreage to the oil and gas industry in the Barents Sea for the first time in 24 years.[39] **11.019**

At first instance, the plaintiffs alleged that the Licensing Decision was invalid on two grounds: (i) its climate impacts infringed the fundamental constitutional right of every person, including future generations, to a healthy environment (including a liveable climate); and (ii) the Licensing Decision was vitiated by procedural errors, including the failure to conduct an adequate assessment of impacts on the right to a healthy environment.[40] On 4 January 2018, the Oslo District Court ruled in favour of the Norwegian government.[41] **11.020**

On appeal, the plaintiffs added new grounds of invalidity, relying on the protection of the right to life and the right to private and family life in both **11.021**

---

35 *Juliana v United States*, 968 F 3d 1295 (9th Cir. 2021).

36 *Juliana v United States*, No. 6:15 cv 01517-AA, Document 524 (Filed 17 February 2022) (Notice of supplemental authority filed by plaintiffs).

37 *Juliana v United States*, No. 6:15 cv 01517-AA, Document 525 (Filed 4 March 2022) (Response filed by defendants to plaintiff's notice of supplemental authority).

38 *Greenpeace Nordic Association v Government of Norway*, Case No 16-166674TVI-OTIR/06, Oslo District Court, Judgment of 4 January 2018 (English translation); *Greenpeace Nordic Association v Government of Norway*, Case No 18-060499ASD-BORG/03, Borgarting Court of Appeal, Judgment of 23 January 2020 (English translation); *Greenpeace Nordic Association v Government of Norway*, HR-2020-2472-P, Case No 20-051052SIV-HRET, Supreme Court of Norway, Judgment of 22 December 2020 (English translation).

39 *Greenpeace Nordic Association v Government of Norway*, Case No 16-166674TVI-OTIR/06, Oslo District Court, Judgment of 4 January 2018 (English translation).

40 *Greenpeace Nordic Association v Government of Norway*, Oslo District Court, Writ of Summons, filed 18 October 2016 (English translation) Part 1 (Introduction).

41 *Greenpeace Nordic Association v Government of Norway*, Case No 16-166674TVI-OTIR/06, Oslo District Court, Judgment of 4 January 2018 (English translation).

the Norwegian Constitution and the ECHR.[42] On 23 January 2020, the Borgarting Court of Appeal dismissed the appeal.[43] A further appeal to the Supreme Court of Norway was also dismissed, on 22 December 2020.[44] In June 2021, Greenpeace Nordic and Nature & Youth, as well as six individuals, applied to the European Court of Human Rights (ECtHR), where the case is pending at the time of writing.[45]

11.022 The applicants sought relief in the form of: (1) non-pecuniary damages for 'mental harm due to the impending climate catastrophe'; (2) pecuniary damages of EUR 652,928.75 (being legal costs incurred in litigating the proceedings); (3) a declaration that Norway had breached Article 2, 8, 13 and 14 of the ECHR; (4) an order requiring Norway to conduct an assessment of the cumulative climate impacts caused by the Licensing Decision; (5) an order requiring Norway to withdraw the production licences for petroleum if the impact of the Licensing Decision is incompatible with the Paris Agreement; and (6) an order requiring that Norway cease issuance of further oil and gas exploration licences, or, alternatively, an order requiring Norway to conduct an environmental assessment prior to issuing new licences.[46]

11.023 The decisions of the Norwegian courts differ in their details, but have two noteworthy common aspects. First, all three courts applied a 'very high' threshold for finding a violation of the right to a healthy environment,[47] protected by

42 See *Constitution of the Kingdom of Norway*, Articles 93 and 102; *European Convention on Human Rights*, Articles 2 and 8.

43 *Greenpeace Nordic Association v Government of Norway*, Case No 18-060499ASD-BORG/03, Borgarting Court of Appeal, Judgment of 23 January 2020 (English translation).

44 *Greenpeace Nordic Association v Government of Norway*, HR-2020-2472-P, Case No 20-051052SIV-HRET, Supreme Court of Norway, Judgment of 22 December 2020 (English translation).

45 *Greenpeace Nordic Association v Norway*, Application No 34068/21, European Court of Human Rights, 15 June 2021 http://climatecasechart.com/wp-content/uploads/sites/16/non-us-case-documents/2022/20220504_Application-no.-3406821_na.pdf; European Network of National Human Rights Institutions, Written observations in application no. 34068/21 ENNHRI-third-party-intervention-in-Greenpeace-Nordic-et-al.-v.-Norway.pdf.

46 *Greenpeace Nordic Association v Norway*, Written observations on behalf of Applicants in app. no. 34068/21, Observations in reply to the Respondent's submissions, 29 June 2022 http://climatecasechart.com/wp-content/uploads/sites/16/non-us-case-documents/2022/20220629_Application-no.-3406821_reply.pdf, [173]–[188].

47 The Supreme Court described the threshold as 'very high' when the decision has been made legislatively, requiring a gross neglect of duties: *Greenpeace Nordic Association v Government of Norway*, HR-2020-2472-P, Case No 20-051052SIV-HRET, Supreme Court of Norway, Judgment of 22 December 2020 (English translation) [142]. The Borgarting Court of Appeal described the threshold as 'high' and 'relatively high': *Greenpeace Nordic Association v Government of Norway*, Case No 18-060499ASD-BORG/0, Borgarting Court of Appeal, Judgment of 23 January 2020 (English translation) Sections III(1), III(2.3). The Oslo District Court applied a 'certain threshold' without specification, but its reasons illustrate that the threshold it applied was in fact a high one: *Greenpeace Nordic Association v Government of Norway*, Case No

Article 112 of the Norwegian Constitution.[48] Second, the two appellate courts held that the Licensing Decision did not pose a 'real and immediate' risk of loss of life, nor was it in a 'direct and immediate' relationship with serious encroachments on the right to a private life, family life or home.[49] They held that it was too uncertain whether or to what extent the Licensing Decision would actually lead to GHG emissions, and that the possible impact on the climate would only be discernible 'in the more distant future'.[50] It was therefore held that there was no violation of Article 2 or Article 8 of the ECHR, nor of the corresponding articles of the Norwegian Constitution.[51]

(d) *Union of Swiss Senior Women for Climate Protection v Switzerland*[52]

On 25 November 2016, the Union of Swiss Senior Women for Climate Protection, together with four individual women (Swiss Applicants), filed a petition with multiple Swiss government bodies, including the Swiss Federal Council and the Swiss Federal Department of the Environment, Transport, Energy and Communications (DETEC).[53] **11.024**

The Swiss Applicants claimed that the Swiss government's inaction on climate change violated their right to life under the Swiss Constitution and the constitutional principles of sustainability and precaution, as well as their rights to **11.025**

16-166674TVI-OTIR/06, Oslo District Court, Judgment of 4 January 2018 (English translation) Section 5.2.2.

48 Article 112 of the Constitution of the Kingdom of Norway provides as follows: 'Every person has the right to an environment that is conducive to health and to a natural environment whose productivity and diversity are maintained. Natural resources shall be managed on the basis of comprehensive long-term considerations which will safeguard this right for future generations as well. In order to safeguard their right in accordance with the foregoing paragraph, citizens are entitled to information on the state of the natural environment and on the effects of any encroachment on nature that is planned or carried out. The authorities of the state shall take measures for the implementation of these principles.'

49 *Greenpeace Nordic Association v Government of Norway*, Case No 18-060499ASD-BORG/03, Borgarting Court of Appeal, Judgment of 23 January 2020 (English translation) Section III(4.2); *Greenpeace Nordic Association v Government of Norway*, HR-2020-2472-P, Case No 20-051052SIV-HRET, Supreme Court of Norway, Judgment of 22 December 2020 (English translation) [168], [171].

50 *Greenpeace Nordic Association v Government of Norway*, HR-2020-2472-P, Case No 20-051052SIV-HRET, Supreme Court of Norway, Judgment of 22 December 2020 (English translation) [168].

51 *Greenpeace Nordic Association v Government of Norway*, Case No 18-060499ASD-BORG/03, Borgarting Court of Appeal, Judgment of 23 January 2020 (English translation) Section III(4.2); Ibid [168], [171].

52 *Union of Swiss Senior Women for Climate Protection v Federal Department of the Environment, Transport, Energy and Communications*, Case No A-2992/2017, Federal Administrative Court of Switzerland, Judgment of 27 November 2018 (English translation); *Union of Swiss Senior Women for Climate Protection v Federal Department of the Environment, Transport, Energy and Communications*, Case No 1C_37/2019, Federal Supreme Court of Switzerland (Public Law Division I), Judgment of 5 May 2020 (English translation). No judgment has been issued in the ECtHR proceedings as of February 2022. *Union of Swiss Senior Women for Climate Protection v Switzerland*, Application No 53600/20, European Court of Human Rights, 26 November 2020.

53 *Union of Swiss Senior Women for Climate Protection v Swiss Federal Council*, Petition for Decision, filed 25 November 2016 (English translation).

life, to health and to physical integrity under the ECHR.[54] They sought relief under Swiss administrative law and pursuant to the rights to a fair trial and an effective remedy under the ECHR.[55] They petitioned the Swiss government to develop a regulatory solution to reduce GHG emissions by at least 25 per cent by 2020 and by at least 50 per cent by 2030, relative to 1990 levels.[56]

11.026 On 25 April 2017 DETEC dismissed the petition on the basis that the impugned public acts did not 'affect rights or obligations' of the Swiss Applicants, as required by Swiss administrative law.[57] Similar considerations meant that the Swiss Applicants lacked standing, in DETEC's view, for an individual application under the ECHR.[58]

11.027 The Swiss Applicants appealed DETEC's ruling to the Swiss Federal Administrative Court,[59] which dismissed the appeal on 27 November 2018.[60] The Court agreed with DETEC that the Swiss Applicants were not 'particularly affected' and therefore had no 'sufficient interest worthy of protection'.[61] On 5 May 2020 the Swiss Federal Supreme Court dismissed a further appeal for the same reasons, and emphasised the democratic, political avenues available to the Swiss Applicants to shape climate policy.[62]

11.028 In November 2020 the Swiss Applicants applied to the ECtHR, where the case is pending as of December 2022.[63] It is expected that a hearing will be held in April or May 2023, with a decision to follow in late 2023 or early 2024.[64] In

---

54 *Union of Swiss Senior Women for Climate Protection v Swiss Federal Council*, Petition for Decision, filed 25 November 2016 (English translation) [7].

55 Ibid 7.

56 Ibid 4–5.

57 *Union of Swiss Senior Women for Climate Protection v Swiss Federal Council*, Order of Swiss Federal Department of the Environment, Transport, Energy and Communications, 25 April 2017 (English translation) Section C.

58 Ibid.

59 *Union of Swiss Senior Women for Climate Protection v Federal Department of the Environment, Transport, Energy and Communications*, Appeal to Swiss Federal Administrative Court, filed 26 May 2017 (English translation).

60 *Union of Swiss Senior Women for Climate Protection v Federal Department of the Environment, Transport, Energy and Communications*, Case No A-2992/2017, Federal Administrative Court of Switzerland, Judgment of 27 November 2018 (English translation).

61 Ibid, [7.4.3].

62 *Union of Swiss Senior Women for Climate Protection v Federal Department of the Environment, Transport, Energy and Communications*, Case No 1C_37/2019, Federal Supreme Court of Switzerland (Public Law Division I), Judgment of 5 May 2020 (English translation) [4.3], [5.4]–[5.5].

63 *Union of Swiss Senior Women for Climate Protection v Switzerland*, Application No 53600/20, European Court of Human Rights, 26 November 2020.

64 Columbia Law School, Maria Tigre, 'Sabin Center files third-party intervention in the Klimaseniorinnen case at the European Court of Human Rights' (Blog Post, 7 December 2022) https://blogs.law.columbia.edu/climatechange/2022/12/07/sabin-center-files-third-party-intervention-in-the-klimaseniorinnen-case-at-the-european-court-of-human-rights/.

the ECtHR, the Applicants allege violations of their rights to effective access to a court and to an effective remedy (Articles 6(1) and 13 of the ECHR) as well as violations of their rights to life and to family and private life (Articles 2 and 8 of the ECHR).[65] The Swiss Applicants requested the Court to declare that: (1) the Applicants were victims under Article 34 of the ECHR and their claims were admissible; (2) Switzerland failed to protect the Applicants' right to life and private life under Articles 2 and 8 of the ECHR; and (3) the Applicants have a right of access to court under Article 6 and a right to an effective remedy under Article 13.[66] The Applicants also sought an award for their costs and expenses under Article 41 of the ECHR, and orders for general measures under Article 46, which required Switzerland to institute a legislative and administrative regime to prevent the increase of global temperatures beyond 1.5°C above pre-industrial levels.[67] In response, Switzerland invoked the separation of powers and the principle of subsidiarity, claiming that the application runs the risk of 'circumventing the democratic debate and complicating the search for politically acceptable solutions'.[68]

(e) *La Rose v Her Majesty the Queen in Right of Canada*[69]

On 25 October 2019, 15 youth plaintiffs (La Rose Plaintiffs) commenced proceedings in the Federal Court of Canada against the Canadian government in respect of its climate policy.[70] The La Rose Plaintiffs sought declarations that the Canadian government had unjustifiably infringed their human rights (specifically, rights to life, liberty and security of person, and rights to equality before the law) and the rights of all present and future generations of children and youth in Canada, as guaranteed under the Canadian Charter of Rights and Freedoms (Charter).[71] The La Rose Plaintiffs also sought a declaration **11.029**

65 Ibid; European Court of Human Rights, 'Grand Chamber to examine case concerning complaint by association that climate change is having an impact on their living conditions and health' (Press Release, 29 April 2022) http://climatecasechart.com/wp-content/uploads/sites/16/non-us-case-documents/2022/20220426_Application-no.-5360020_na-1.pdf.

66 *Union of Swiss Senior Women for Climate Protection v Switzerland*, Application No 53600/20, European Court of Human Rights, Observations on the facts, admissibility and the merits, 12 December 2022, 69–70 http://climatecasechart.com/wp-content/uploads/sites/16/non-us-case-documents/2022/20221202_Application-no.-5360020_petition.pdf.

67 Ibid.

68 *Union of Swiss Senior Women for Climate Protection v Switzerland*, Application No 53600/20, European Court of Human Rights, Comments of the Swiss Government on Admissibility and the Merits, 16 July 2021, [4]–[5].

69 *La Rose v Her Majesty the Queen in Right of Canada* [2020] FC 1008.

70 *La Rose v Her Majesty the Queen in Right of Canada*, Case No T-1750-19, Federal Court of Canada, Statement of Claim to the Defendants, filed 25 October 2019.

71 Ibid [6]; Justice Laws Website, *Constitution Act 1982* (Webpage, 15 September 2022) https://laws-lois.justice.gc.ca/eng/const/page-12.html#:~:text=Guarantee%20of%20Rights%20and%20Freedoms&text=1%20The%20Canadian%20Charter%20of,a%20free%20and%20democratic%20society .

that the Canadian government had failed to discharge its common law and constitutional obligations to protect the integrity of common natural resources that are fundamental to sustaining human life and liberties, relying on the public trust doctrine.[72]

11.030 The impugned conduct of the Canadian government included: (i) causing, contributing to and allowing GHG emissions incompatible with a stable climate system; (ii) adopting GHG emissions targets inconsistent with the best available science about what is necessary to avoid dangerous climate change and restore a stable climate system; (iii) failing to meet its own GHG emissions targets; and (iv) actively participating in and supporting the development, expansion and operation of fossil fuel industries and activities.[73]

11.031 In addition to declaratory relief, the La Rose Plaintiffs sought court orders compelling the Canadian government to develop and implement an enforceable plan to achieve GHG emissions reductions in accordance with the protection of public trust resources, and the La Rose Plaintiffs' constitutional rights.[74]

11.032 On 27 October 2020, the Canadian government succeeded in having the Statement of Claim struck out.[75] The Federal Court held that the La Rose Plaintiffs' claims under the Charter were non-justiciable and did not disclose a reasonable cause of action, because they were unduly broad and diffuse, and sought inappropriate remedies.[76] The claims 'effectively put the entirety of Canada's policy response to climate change in issue' and thus exceeded the bounds of the judicial function under the Charter.[77] The Court considered that the claims based on the public trust doctrine were justiciable,[78] but found that they did not disclose a reasonable cause of action.[79]

11.033 The La Rose Plaintiffs appealed the decision to the Federal Court of Appeal, and as at September 2022, the appeal is pending.

---

72 *La Rose v Her Majesty the Queen in Right of Canada*, Case No T-1750-19, Federal Court of Canada, Statement of Claim to the Defendants, filed 25 October 2019, [7].

73 Ibid [5].

74 Ibid [9].

75 See footnote 69.

76 Ibid [26], [40]–[48], [50]–[56], [62]–[63], [79].

77 Ibid [43].

78 Ibid [57]–[58].

79 Ibid [59], [87]–[93].

(f) *Neubauer v Germany*[80]

On 6 February 2020, nine plaintiffs (Neubauer Plaintiffs) filed a constitutional complaint with the Federal Constitutional Court of Germany.[81] The complaint alleged that by implementing a GHG emissions reduction target of 55 per cent by 2030 relative to 1990 levels (pursuant to the German Federal Climate Protection Act), the German legislature had violated the fundamental rights of the Neubauer Plaintiffs, including their rights to human dignity, life and physical integrity.[82] Those rights are protected under Germany's '*Grundgesetz*' (translation: 'Basic Law').[83] The Neubauer Plaintiffs sought orders compelling the legislature to implement a new GHG reduction quota.[84] **11.034**

In a judgment delivered on 24 March 2021, which addressed four related constitutional complaints (including the *Neubauer* complaint), the Court found that aspects of the Federal Climate Protection Act were incompatible with fundamental rights, but only insofar as the legislation lacked provisions for updating reduction targets for periods *after* 2030 in a way that would satisfy the constitutional requirements as the Court interpreted them.[85] The Court ordered that the legislature must enact provisions by the end of 2022 for updating reduction targets for periods from 2031.[86] The Court rejected the constitutional complaints in all other respects.[87] **11.035**

The Federal Constitutional Court held that: **11.036**

(i) The protection of life and physical integrity under the Basic Law extends to protection against risks to human life and health caused by climate change.[88] The fact that climate change is a genuinely global phenomenon and cannot be stopped by Germany on its own 'does not render it impos-

80 *Neubauer v Germany*, Case No 1 BvR 2656/18, 1 BvR 78/20, 1 BvR 96/20, 1 BvR 288/20, Federal Constitutional Court, Judgment of 24 March 2021 (English translation).

81 *Neubauer v Germany*, Constitutional Complaint regarding Federal Climate Protection Act, filed 6 February 2020 (English translation).

82 Ibid [1].

83 See Articles 1 and 2 of the Basic Law, in each case read in conjunction with Article 20a of the Basic Law, which provides that Germany must protect the natural foundations of life while being mindful of its responsibility towards future generations.

84 See footnote 81 [3].

85 *Neubauer v Germany*, Case No 1 BvR 2656/18, 1 BvR 78/20, 1 BvR 96/20, 1 BvR 288/20, Federal Constitutional Court, Judgment of 24 March 2021 (English translation) Order 2.

86 Ibid Order 4.

87 Ibid Order 3.

88 *Neubauer v Germany*, Case No 1 BvR 2656/18, 1 BvR 78/20, 1 BvR 96/20, 1 BvR 288/20, Federal Constitutional Court, Judgment of 24 March 2021 (English translation) Section B(II)(1)(aa).

sible or superfluous for Germany to make its own contribution towards protecting the climate'.[89]

(ii) It was not 'presently ascertainable' that the duty of protection had been violated; the German legislature had taken precautionary measures that were not 'manifestly unsuitable', and it retained 'a margin of appreciation and evaluation as well as leeway in terms of design' in this regard.[90] The protective framework adopted by Germany was not 'completely inadequate', nor did the challenged provisions fall 'significantly short' of the protection of life and health required.[91]

11.037 However, the Court did find that Germany had violated fundamental rights in one respect, because the emission amounts allowed by the Federal Climate Protection Act in the current period (that is, until 2030) were capable of giving rise to substantial burdens to reduce emissions in *later* periods.[92] The 2030 targets created 'disproportionate risks' that fundamental rights would be impaired in the future.[93] Protection of fundamental rights required precautionary measures to guarantee freedom over time and across generations, and the legislature would need to adopt measures aimed at mitigating the substantial emission reduction burdens which it had 'offloaded' onto the post-2030 period and which it would, after 2030, have to impose on the Complainants and others.[94]

(g) *ClientEarth v National Bank of Belgium*[95]

11.038 On 12 April 2021, ClientEarth filed a landmark legal action in the Court of First Instance of Brussels against the National Bank of Belgium (NBB), challenging the implementation of the European Corporate Sector Purchase Programme (CSPP).[96] Under the CSPP, six euro-area national central banks,

89 *Neubauer v Germany*, Case No 1 BvR 2656/18, 1 BvR 78/20, 1 Bvr 96/20, 1 BvR 288/20, Federal Constitutional Court, Judgment of 24 March 2021 (English translation), Section B(II)(1)(aa).

90 Ibid Section C(I).

91 Ibid Section C(I).

92 Ibid Sections C, C(III).

93 Ibid Sections C, C(III).

94 Ibid Sections C, C(III).

95 The court documents for this proceeding are not publicly available. However, it has been well documented in publications by ClientEarth and analysed in a working paper published by the European Central Bank, and the recent developments in the proceedings have been reported in the Belgian media. We rely on these sources for this summary.

96 ClientEarth, *The ECB's Monetary Policy Strategy Review: Corporate Sector Asset Purchases, Climate Change and the ECB's Legal Obligations* (Letter from ClientEarth to Christine Lagarde, President of the ECB, 12 April 2021) www.clientearth.org/media/jtxnhiba/2021-04-12-letter-from-clientearth-to-christine-lagarde.pdf.

including the NBB, are able to purchase bonds from eligible companies in an attempt to improve financing conditions by lowering debt costs.[97]

ClientEarth alleged that the CSPP was invalid due to the ECB not taking into account environmental protection requirements, specifically in relation to climate change, when deciding to establish the CSPP. ClientEarth also alleged that NBB's implementation of the CSPP was illegal due to breaches of the NBB's legal obligations to take into account environmental and human rights protection requirements, specifically in relation to climate change.[98] ClientEarth relied on the constitutional documents of the EU, namely the Treaty on the Functioning of the European Union (TFEU) and the Charter of Fundamental Rights of the European Union (EU Charter). In particular, ClientEarth argued that Articles 7 and 127(1) of the TFEU require the ECB and NBB to act consistently with the EU's climate objectives and policies, and that pursuant to Article 11 of the TFEU and Article 37 of the EU Charter, the ECB and NBB must take into account environmental protection requirements in the design and implementation of monetary policy.[99] **11.039**

ClientEarth sought a preliminary reference to the European Court of Justice to determine whether the decision to establish the CSPP was lawful, and thus the validity of the CSPP.[100] It requested relief including orders that the NBB stop purchasing bonds under the CSPP and that the ECB take all measures appropriate to remedy the illegality of the CSPP.[101] **11.040**

97 Joana Setzer et al, *Legal Working Paper Series: Climate Change Litigation and Central Banks* (European Central Bank Working Paper No 21, December 2021) 51–2.

98 ClientEarth, *Why ClientEarth Is Suing the Central Bank of Belgium for Climate Failings* (13 April 2021) www.clientearth.org/latest/latest-updates/news/why-clientearth-is-suing-the-central-bank-of-belgium-for-climate-failings; Joana Setzer et al, *Legal Working Paper Series: Climate Change Litigation and Central Banks* (European Central Bank Working Paper No 21, December 2021) 51–2; ClientEarth, *The ECB's Monetary Policy Strategy Review: Corporate Sector Asset Purchases, Climate Change and the ECB's Legal Obligations* (Letter from ClientEarth to Christine Lagarde, President of the ECB, 12 April 2021) www.clientearth.org/media/jtxnhiba/2021-04-12-letter-from-clientearth-to-christine-lagarde.pdf.

99 Joana Setzer et al, *Legal Working Paper Series: Climate Change Litigation and Central Banks* (European Central Bank Working Paper No 21, December 2021) 52–3; ClientEarth, *The ECB's Monetary Policy Strategy Review: Corporate Sector Asset Purchases, Climate Change and the ECB's Legal Obligations* (Letter from ClientEarth to Christine Lagarde, President of the ECB, 12 April 2021) www.clientearth.org/media/jtxnhiba/2021-04-12-letter-from-clientearth-to-christine-lagarde.pdf.

100 ClientEarth, *Why ClientEarth Is Suing the Central Bank of Belgium for Climate Failings* (13 April 2021) www.clientearth.org/latest/latest-updates/news/why-clientearth-is-suing-the-central-bank-of-belgium-for-climate-failings; Joana Setzer et al, *Legal Working Paper Series: Climate Change Litigation and Central Banks* (European Central Bank Working Paper No 21, December 2021) 52.

101 ClientEarth, *Why ClientEarth Is Suing the Central Bank of Belgium for Climate Failings* (13 April 2021) www.clientearth.org/latest/latest-updates/news/why-clientearth-is-suing-the-central-bank-of-belgium-for-climate-failings.

11.041 In December 2021, the Brussels Court of First Instance found in favour of the NBB, dismissing ClientEarth's claim and declining to refer the question of the validity of the CSPP to the European Court of Justice.[102] The Court of First Instance held that ClientEarth had failed to meet applicable procedural hurdles, basing its claim on rules of EU law that were too general to be invoked in court, and had not proved that the CSPP is harming the climate.[103] ClientEarth has reportedly appealed the decision.[104]

(h) *Silva v Minister for the Environment*[105]

11.042 On 13 April 2021, six Brazilian climate activists (Silva Plaintiffs) commenced proceedings against the Brazilian Government in the 14th Federal Civil Court of São Paulo, seeking the annulment of Brazil's revised Nationally Determined Contribution (NDC), submitted in December 2020 under the Paris Agreement.[106]

11.043 The Silva Plaintiffs argued that Brazil's revised NDC attempted a carbon-accounting manoeuvre, with the result that under the revised NDC Brazil's emissions would *increase* by 400 million tonnes of carbon dioxide (CO_2) equivalent.[107] It was alleged that this was contrary to the Paris Agreement's requirements of progressive and increased ambition in updated NDCs.[108]

11.044 Specifically, the Silva Plaintiffs alleged violations of: (i) the protection in Article 225 of the Brazilian Constitution of the right to an ecologically balanced environment for present and future generations; (ii) Brazil's domestic climate change laws and policies; and (iii) the Paris Agreement, as incorporated into Brazilian law through Decree No 9073/2017.[109] They sought interim relief in

102 ClientEarth, *Questions on Legality of ECB Lending Remain after Climate Case Ruling* (3 December 2021) www.clientearth.org/latest/press-office/press/questions-on-legality-of-ecb-lending-remain-after-climate-case-ruling.

103 The judgment does not appear to be publicly available as at September 2022: ibid; Bart Haeck, *La Banque Nationale Gagne Son Bras de Fer Juridique contre une ONG* (2 February 2022) www.lecho.be/economie-politique/europe/general/la-banque-nationale-gagne-son-bras-de-fer-juridique-contre-une-ong/10363954.html.

104 See e.g. *ClientEarth Perd Son Procès contre la Banque Nationale de Belgique* (RTBF, 3 February 2022) www.rtbf.be/article/clientearth-perd-son-proces-contre-la-banque-nationale-de-belgique-10927097; ClientEarth, *Why We're Going Back to Court against the Belgian National Bank* (Webpage, 31 January 2022) www.clientearth.org/latest/news/why-we-re-going-back-to-court-against-the-belgian-national-bank/.

105 *Silva v Minister for the Environment (Brazil)*, Case No 5008035-37.2021.4.03.6100, 14th Federal Civil Court of São Paulo, Judgment of 28 May 2021.

106 *Silva v Minister for the Environment (Brazil)*, Case No 5008035-37.2021.4.03.6100, 14th Federal Civil Court of São Paulo, Initial Petition, filed 13 April 2021, Section IV(1).

107 *Silva v Minister for the Environment (Brazil)*, Case No 5008035-37.2021.4.03.6100, 14th Federal Civil Court of São Paulo, Initial Petition, filed 13 April 2021, Section I.

108 Ibid, Sections I, IV(1).

109 Ibid, Sections I(1), III, IV(1).

the form of an injunction suspending the effects of Brazil's revised NDC and requiring the Brazilian government to present a new updated NDC compliant with the Paris Agreement and based on a participatory decision-making process with civil society involvement.[110] As final relief, the Silva Plaintiffs requested, *inter alia*, that the revised NDC be declared null and void.[111]

On 28 May 2021, the 14th Federal Civil Court of São Paulo dismissed the application for urgent interim relief.[112] The Court rejected Brazil's objection that there was no jurisdiction in respect of the Silva Plaintiffs' action, but found that the necessary elements for urgent interim relief were not established.[113] The Court held that Brazil's revised NDC had confirmed the previously set emissions reduction targets, and had expressly stated an objective to achieve climate neutrality by 2060.[114] Further, the Paris Agreement itself establishes mechanisms for technical review of parties' emissions inventories, and a change of calculation methodology was normal and expected.[115] As at September 2022 it appeared that an appeal of the Court's decision was still pending.[116] **11.045**

(i) *Plan B Earth v Prime Minister*[117]

On 1 May 2021, non-governmental organisation Plan B Earth and four individual claimants (Plan B Claimants) commenced judicial review proceedings against the UK government in the High Court of England and Wales.[118] **11.046**

The Plan B Claimants sought a declaration that the UK government had failed to take practical and effective measures to meet the central commitments of the Paris Agreement and the Climate Change Act 2008, in violation of the Plan B Claimants' rights to life and to family life, free from discrimination, protected by Articles 2, 8 and 14 of the ECHR as implemented into UK law by the Human Rights Act 1998.[119] They also sought orders compelling **11.047**

110 *Silva v Minister for the Environment (Brazil)*, Case No 5008035-37.2021.4.03.6100, 14th Federal Civil Court of Sao Paulo, Initial Petition, filed 13 April 2021, Section IV(1).

111 Ibid, Section IV(2).

112 *Silva v Minister for the Environment (Brazil)*, Case No 5008035-37.2021.4.03.6100, 14th Federal Civil Court of São Paulo, Judgment of 28 May 2021.

113 Ibid, 6.

114 Ibid, 8.

115 Ibid 9.

116 See Maria Antonia Tigre, *COP26: Perspectives from Latin America* (14 December 2021) www.gnhre.org/climate-change-2/cop26-perspectives-from-latin-america/, reporting on 14 December 2021 that the decision had been appealed.

117 *R (Plan B Earth) v Prime Minister* [2021] EWHC 3469 (Admin).

118 *R (Plan B Earth) v Prime Minister*, Case No CO/1587/2021, High Court of England and Wales, Statement of Facts and Grounds, filed 1 May 2021.

119 Ibid, [1], [4], [17], [34], [37].

the UK government to urgently implement a legal and regulatory framework sufficient to meet those commitments.[120] Without such a framework, the Plan B Claimants alleged, there would be 'nothing to prevent public and private institutions in the UK from actively investing and profiteering from projects that will lock-in gross violations of the rights of the Claimants, and all current and future generations'.[121]

11.048 On 21 December 2021, the High Court handed down judgment refusing to permit the Plan B Claimants to apply for judicial review.[122] The High Court held that unincorporated treaties such as the Paris Agreement do not form part of UK domestic law, in line with its dualistic approach to international law, and domestic courts cannot determine whether the UK has violated its obligations under an international treaty.[123] The claims under the Climate Change Act were, in the High Court's view, also untenable, because the statutory duties thereunder are not duties to achieve specific outcomes, only to prepare proposals and policies and to lay programmes before Parliament.[124] Further, the claims under the Human Rights Act faced the 'insuperable problem' that the UK does have in place a 'constantly evolving' administrative framework to address climate change under which the UK has met its first and second carbon budgets.

11.049 Ultimately, the High Court refused permission on all grounds, for reasons including (in addition to those canvassed above) the insufficiency of the evidence to meet the minimum evidential thresholds for claims under Articles 8 and 14 of the ECHR, and the Plan B Claimants' inability to establish an arguable status as 'victims' of a breach of rights under the ECHR.[125] The Plan B Claimants have applied for leave to appeal.[126]

120 *R (Plan B Earth) v Prime Minister*, Case No CO/1587/2021, High Court of England and Wales, Statement of Facts and Grounds, filed 1 May 2021, [37]–[38].

121 Ibid, [39].

122 *R (Plan B Earth) v Prime Minister* [2021] EWHC 3469 (Admin). Following that refusal, the Plan B Claimants renewed their application for permission, a renewal hearing was held in November 2021.

123 Ibid [25], citing *R (SC) v SSWP* [2021] UKSC 26, [2021] 3 WLR 428, [77], [84], [91] (Lord Reed).

124 Ibid [31]–[38].

125 Ibid [76]–[79].

126 *R (Plan B Earth) v Prime Minister*, Appellants' Skeleton Argument in Support of an Application for Permission to Appeal against the Refusal of Permission to Apply for Judicial Review, filed 29 December 2021.

(j) *African Climate Alliance v Minister of Mineral Resources and Energy*[127]

In November 2021, three civil society organisations, including the African Climate Alliance (ACA Applicants), instituted legal proceedings in the High Court of South Africa against the South African Government, specifically the Minister of Mineral Resources and Energy, the National Energy Regulator of South Africa (NERSA), the Minister of Forestry, Fisheries and the Environment and the President of South Africa.[128] **11.050**

This case concerns a constitutional challenge to the Minister's determination that 1500 MW of new energy capacity will be generated from coal-fired power stations in the next decade (Ministerial Determination),[129] which followed the publication of the revised Integrated Resource Plan (IRP) setting out similar plans.[130] NERSA concurred with the Minister's determination.[131] The ACA Applicants have applied to the Court seeking orders that the Ministerial Determination, NERSA's concurrence with the Ministerial Determination and the IRP are constitutionally invalid and should be set aside, to the extent that they provide for the procurement of 1500 MW of energy from new coal-fired power stations. **11.051**

The application is made on two legal bases. First, the ACA Applicants argue that the Ministerial Determination, NERSA's concurrence therewith and the IRP unjustifiably limit basic constitutional rights,[132] including the rights of present and future generations of South Africans, such as the right to a healthy environment under s 24 of the South African Constitution and related constitutional rights, including the rights of children, the rights to life, dignity and equality, and other implicated rights.[133] Second, the ACA Applicants seek review of the impugned decisions based on South Africa's Promotion of Administrative Justice Act (No 3 of 2000) or, in the alternative, the constitutional principle of legality.[134] **11.052**

127 No judgment has been issued in these proceedings as of February 2022. For the originating process, see *African Climate Alliance v The Minister of Mineral Resources and Energy*, Case No 56907/21, High Court of South Africa (Gauteng Division, Pretoria), Founding Affidavit, filed 3 November 2021.

128 *African Climate Alliance v The Minister of Mineral Resources and Energy*, Case No 56907/21, High Court of South Africa (Gauteng Division, Pretoria), Founding Affidavit, filed 3 November 2021.

129 Ibid [4]–[5].

130 Ibid [5]–[6].

131 Ibid [5]–[6].

132 Ibid [24.1], [324].

133 Ibid [15], [329]–[360].

134 Ibid [24.2], [325]–[326].

11.053 In December 2021, the Minister gave notice of his intention to oppose the application, and the President of South Africa gave notice that he will not oppose the application and will abide by the decision of the Court.[135] The proceedings were pending as of September 2022.

3. Conclusion

11.054 The intersection between human rights and climate change continues to evolve through litigation in domestic courts and regional human rights courts. The scope for, and approach to, human rights and constitutional claims depends very much on national law, but common themes emerge in the cases worldwide. Those themes include the role of the judiciary vis-à-vis the executive and legislative branches of government in taking action on climate change, the nature of appropriate relief in the face of the global problem of climate change, and the identification of persons with the legal entitlement (that is, standing) to bring claims in respect of inaction on climate change.

C. TORT LAW ACTIONS

1. Introduction

11.055 To date, torts cases make up only a small proportion of global climate change litigation.[136] This may be due to the significant hurdles faced by claimants, many of which are evident in the cases summarised in this section.

11.056 In common law jurisdictions, tort litigation has tended to centre on the torts of public nuisance and negligence. In civil law jurisdictions, tort litigation is typically based on statutory provisions codifying, for example, a standard of care requiring 'due care' to be exercised in society, civil liability for ecological damage or obligations to abate or remove unlawful interference with property. Across the differing legal landscapes in each jurisdiction, there are points of commonality and of contrast.

11.057 First, in any tort litigation, establishing causation of harm may be particularly difficult in the context of climate change, where, as the German Court

135 *African Climate Alliance v The Minister of Mineral Resources and Energy*, Case No 56907/21, High Court of South Africa (Gauteng Division, Pretoria) filed 8 December 2021 on behalf of the President of the Republic of South Africa.

136 See e.g. Douglas Kysar, 'What Climate Change Can Do About Tort Law' (2010) 41(1) *Environmental Law* 1.

indicated in *Lliuya v RWE AG*, the chain of causation is complex, multipolar, unclear and scientifically disputed – making it challenging 'to identify anything resembling a linear chain of causation from one particular source of emission to one particular damage'.[137] However, developments such as those in climate attribution have the potential to assist claimants seeking to link specific acts or omissions to an alleged loss.

Second, as in the human rights and constitutional cases discussed in the preceding section, concerns about the proper role of the judicial branch of government may give courts pause before, for example, imposing novel duties of care or granting injunctions enjoining defendants to adopt particular mitigation measures. The appellate decision of the Full Court of the Federal Court of Australia in *Minister for the Environment v Sharma*, overturning the lower court's imposition of a novel duty of care in negligence on a federal Minister, illustrates these concerns.[138] **11.058**

Broadly speaking, plaintiffs in civil law jurisdictions have had more success holding governments and corporate actors to account in tort, as cases such as *Milieudefensie v Royal Dutch Shell plc*[139] demonstrate. Perhaps this is because the codified obligations at play in such cases remove one of the biggest hurdles for plaintiffs at common law: establishing that a private law obligation or duty is owed in the first place. **11.059**

2. Case Summaries

(a) *Lliuya v RWE AG*[140]

On 23 November 2015, Mr Lliuya (Lliuya), a Peruvian farmer, commenced proceedings against RWE AG (RWE), Germany's largest electricity producer, in the District Court of Essen in Germany.[141] Lliuya's claims relied on §1004(1) of the German Civil Code, which provides for a cause of action in respect of interference with property ownership.[142] **11.060**

137 *Lliuya v RWE AG*, Case No 2 O 285/15, District Court of Essen (Second Civil Chamber), Judgment of 15 December 2016, 6–7.

138 *Minister for the Environment v Sharma* [2022] FCAFC 35.

139 *Milieudefensie v Royal Dutch Shell*, Case No C/09/571932 / HA ZA 19-379, District Court of The Hague, Judgment of 26 May 2021 (English translation).

140 *Lliuya v RWE AG*, Case No 2 O 285/15, District Court of Essen (Second Civil Chamber), Judgment of 15 December 2016; *Lliuya v RWE AG*, Case No 2 O 285/15, Higher Regional Court of Hamm (Fifth Civil Senate), Judgment of 30 November 2017.

141 *Lliuya v RWE AG*, Case No 2 O 285/15, District Court of Essen (Second Civil Chamber), Claim, filed 23 November 2015.

142 Ibid 2, 25.

11.061 Lliuya alleged that as the parent company of the RWE Group, RWE was responsible for large amounts of GHG emissions and therefore had been contributing to anthropogenic climate change for decades.[143] Lliuya claimed that his property in Huaraz, at the foot of the Andes, was acutely threatened by glacial melting, occurring at an accelerated pace and to an increasing extent due to climate change, and posing a heightened risk of glacial ice avalanches and flood waves.[144] Under §1004(1) of the German Civil Code, an owner is entitled to abatement of the disturbance or interference with their property.[145] Accordingly, Lliuya sought abatement or 'removal' of the impairment to his property, in the form of compensation for a proportion of the expenses for safety precautions to protect the property from a glacial flood.[146] The damages sought were said to be proportionate to RWE's contribution to the impairment of Lliuya's property, calculated by reference to RWE's share of global GHG emissions.[147]

11.062 One 15 December 2016 the District Court of Essen dismissed the claim.[148] One element of the cause of action under §1004(1) of the German Civil Code is the existence of a legally relevant causal link between the defendant's activity and the impairment to the plaintiff's property.[149] The District Court held that there was no legally relevant causation between RWE's GHG emissions and the impairment of Lliuya's property, especially because RWE's emissions were 'merely a fraction' of other pollutants and the hazards would not be eliminated in their absence.[150]

11.063 On 30 November 2017, the Higher Regional Court of Hamm reversed the first-instance decision, in essence finding that it had been premature to dismiss the claim for lack of causation in the absence of further evidence,[151] and held that the case should proceed to the evidentiary phase.[152] During 2018, the

143 Ibid 2.

144 *Lliuya v RWE AG*, Case No 2 O 285/15, District Court of Essen (Second Civil Chamber), Claim, filed 23 November 2015, 2.

145 Ibid 2, 25.

146 Ibid 1–2.

147 Ibid 2.

148 Ibid.

149 See Will Frank, Christoph Bals and Julia Grimm, 'The Case of Huaraz: First Climate Lawsuit on Loss and Damage Against an Energy Company Before German Courts', in Reinhard Mechler et al (eds), *Loss and Damage from Climate Change* (Springer, 2019) 475–82.

150 *Lliuya v RWE AG*, Case No 2 O 285/15, District Court of Essen (Second Civil Chamber), Judgment of 15 December 2016, 6.

151 *Lliuya v RWE AG*, Case No 2 O 285/15, Higher Regional Court of Hamm (Fifth Civil Senate), Judgment of 30 November 2017.

152 Ibid. In two further judgments in February 2018, the Higher Regional Court of Hamm rejected statements of objection filed by RWE against the Court's Order for the Hearing of Evidence, again confirming that climate damages can give rise to corporate liability.

Higher Regional Court of Hamm appointed experts to assess whether there is a serious threat of impairment to Lliuya's property.[153] In 2019, the experts recommended that the Court inspect the premises in Peru, and the COVID-19 crisis delayed the process of arranging for an inspection and the taking of evidence.[154] It appears the case is moving forward again with the Higher Regional Court of Hamm conducting a site visit in early June 2022 to examine whether the plaintiff's house is threatened by a flood wave from the glacial lake.[155]

(b) *City of Oakland v BP plc*[156]

On 19 September 2017, the City of Oakland and the City of San Francisco (Oakland Plaintiffs) commenced parallel proceedings in the California Superior Court against five major energy companies.[157] The Oakland Plaintiffs based their claims on public nuisance under the law of California.[158] **11.064**

The Oakland Plaintiffs alleged that: (i) global warming constituted an 'unlawful public nuisance'; (ii) the defendants had produced 'massive amounts of fossil fuels for many years [...] despite knowing – since at least the late 1970s and early 1980s if not earlier – that massive fossil fuel usage would cause dangerous global warming'; and (iii) that the defendants were therefore 'substantial contributors' to the public nuisance of global warming, causing injury to the inhabitants of Oakland and San Francisco for which they were jointly and severally liable.[159] The Oakland Plaintiffs sought orders requiring the **11.065**

153 See Germanwatch, *Saúl versus RWE – The Huaraz Case* (14 March 2022) www.germanwatch.org/en/rwe.

154 Ibid.

155 See Germanwatch, *Saúl versus RWE – The Huaraz Case* (6 October 2022) www.germanwatch.org/en/rwe.

156 *The People of the State of California v BP p.l.c.*, Case No C 17-06011 WHA, Case No C 17-06012 WHA, Order Denying Motions to Remand, 27 February 2018, 2018 WL 1064293 (N.D.Cal. 2018); *City of Oakland v BP p.l.c.*, Case No C 17-06011 WHA, Case No C 17-06012 WHA, 325 F.Supp.3d 1017 (N.D.Cal. 2018); *City of Oakland v BP p.l.c.*, Case No C 17-06011 WHA, Case No C 17-06012 WHA, Order Granting Motions to Dismiss for Lack of Personal Jurisdiction, 27 July 2018, 2018 WL 3609055 (N.D.Cal. 2018); *City of Oakland v BP p.l.c.*, Case No 18-16663, 969 F.3d 895 (9th Cir. 2020); *Chevron Corporation v City of Oakland*, 141 S.Ct. 2776 (2021); *The People of the State of California v BP p.l.c.*, Case No C 17-06011, Order Staying Case, 4 August 2021 (N.D.Cal. 2021).

157 The five defendants were BP plc, Chevron Corporation, ConocoPhillips Company, Exxon Mobil Corporation, and Royal Dutch Shell plc. See *The People of the State of California v BP p.l.c.*, Case No CGC-17-561370, Superior Court of California, County of San Francisco, 2017 WL 4161895, Complaint, filed 19 September 2017, [2]; *The People of the State of California v BP p.l.c.*, Case No RG17875889, Superior Court of California, County of Alameda, 2017 WL 4168934, Complaint for Public Nuisance, filed 19 September 2017, [2].

158 *The People of the State of California v BP p.l.c.*, Case No CGC-17-561370, Superior Court of California, County of San Francisco, 2017 WL 4161895, Complaint, filed 19 September 2017, [95]–[99]; *The People of the State of California v BP p.l.c.*, Case No RG17875889, Superior Court of California, County of Alameda, 2017 WL 4168934, Complaint for Public Nuisance, filed 19 September 2017, [94]–[98].

159 *The People of the State of California v BP p.l.c.*, Case No CGC-17-561370, Superior Court of California, County of San Francisco, 2017 WL 4161895, Complaint, filed 19 September 2017, [2], [10]; *The People of*

defendants to abate the alleged nuisance by funding an adaptation programme to build sea walls and other infrastructure to protect human safety and public and private property in Oakland and San Francisco, respectively.[160]

11.066 On 20 October 2017, the defendants removed the actions from the California Superior Court to the US District Court for the Northern District of California, claiming that the complaints arose under federal laws and treaties, presented substantial federal questions and made claims that were completely pre-empted by federal law.[161] The Oakland Plaintiffs filed motions to remand the proceedings to the state courts,[162] and on 27 February 2018, the District Court denied those motions.[163]

11.067 Subsequently, the Oakland Plaintiffs amended their complaints to assert nuisance claims under both federal and state law,[164] and the defendants filed motions to dismiss the complaints, *inter alia*, for failure to state a claim.[165] In

---

the State of California v BP p.l.c., Case No RG17875889, Superior Court of California, County of Alameda, 2017 WL 4168934, Complaint for Public Nuisance, filed 19 September 2017, [2], [10].

160 *The People of the State of California v BP p.l.c.*, Case No CGC-17-561370, Superior Court of California, County of San Francisco, 2017 WL 4161895, Complaint, filed 19 September 2017, [11]; *The People of the State of California v BP p.l.c.*, Case No RG17875889, Superior Court of California, County of Alameda, 2017 WL 4168934, Complaint for Public Nuisance, filed 19 September 2017, [11].

161 *The People of the State of California v BP p.l.c.*, Docket 3:17-cv-06012-EMC, Notice of Removal, filed 20 October 2017 (N.D.Cal. 2017), 1; *The People of the State of California v BP p.l.c.*, Docket 3:17-cv-06011-JCS, Notice of Removal, filed 20 October 2017 (N.D.Cal. 2017), 1.

162 *The People of the State of California v BP p.l.c.*, Docket 3:17-cv-06011-WHA, Plaintiff's Notice of Motion and Motion to Remand to State Court; Memorandum of Points and Authorities, filed 20 November 2017, 2017 WL 6993046 (N.D.Cal. 2017); *The People of the State of California v BP p.l.c.*, Docket 3:17-cv-06012-WHA, Plaintiff's Notice of Motion and Motion to Remand to State Court; Memorandum of Points and Authorities, filed 20 November 2017, 2017 WL 7716710 (N.D.Cal. 2017).

163 *The People of the State of California v BP p.l.c.*, Case No C 17- 06011 WHA, Case No C 17-06012 WHA, Order Denying Motions to Remand, 27 February 2018, 2018 WL 1064293 (N.D.Cal. 2018).

164 *The People of the State of California v BP p.l.c.*, Case No 3:17-cv-06011-WHA, Notice of Intent to Amend Complaint, filed 30 March 2018 (N.D.Cal. 2018); *City of Oakland v BP p.l.c.*, Case No 3:17-cv-06011-WHA, First Amended Complaint for Public Nuisance, filed 3 April 2018 (N.D.Cal. 2018).

165 *City of Oakland v BP p.l.c.*, Case No 3:17-cv-06011-WHA, Case No 3:17-cv-06012-WHA, Defendants' Motion to Dismiss First Amended Complaints; Memorandum of Points and Authorities, filed 19 April 2018, 2018 WL 11229200 (N.D.Cal. 2018); *City of Oakland v BP p.l.c.*, Case No 3:17-cv-06011-WHA, Case No 3:17-cv-06012-WHA, Defendant BP plc's Notice of Motion and Motion to Dismiss First Amended Complaints for Lack of Personal Jurisdiction; Memorandum of Points and Authorities in Support Thereof, filed 19 April 2018 (N.D.Cal. 2018); *City of Oakland v BP p.l.c.*, Case No 3:17-cv-06011-WHA, Case No 3:17-cv-06012-WHA, Notice of Motion to Dismiss First Amended Complaints for Lack of Personal Jurisdiction of Defendant Conocophillips; Memorandum of Points and Authorities in Support Thereof, filed 19 April 2018 (N.D.Cal. 2018); *City of Oakland v BP p.l.c.*, Case No 3:17-cv-06011-WHA, Case No 3:17-cv-06012-WHA, Defendant Exxon Mobil Corporation's Motion to Dismiss First Amended Complaint for Lack of Personal Jurisdiction and Memorandum of Points and Authorities, filed 19 April 2018 (N.D.Cal. 2018); *City of Oakland v BP p.l.c.*, Case No 3:17-cv-06011-WHA, Case No 3:17-cv-06012-WHA, Defendant Royal Dutch Shell PLC's Notice of Motion and Motion to Dismiss for Lack of Personal Jurisdiction, Insufficient Service of Process, and Failure to State a Claim; Memorandum of Points and Authorities in Support Thereof, filed 19 April 2018 (N.D.Cal. 2018).

judgments handed down on 25 June 2018 and 27 July 2018, the District Court granted the motions to dismiss.[166]

The Oakland Plaintiffs appealed the three adverse decisions of the District Court, namely, the orders: (i) denying the Oakland Plaintiffs' motions to remand; (ii) dismissing the cases for failure to state a claim; and (iii) dismissing the cases against four of the five defendants in any event for lack of personal jurisdiction.[167] On 26 May 2020, the US Court of Appeals, Ninth Circuit allowed the Oakland Plaintiffs' appeal and reversed the District Court's determination that the proceedings belonged in the federal rather than the state courts.[168] The defendants' attempts to pursue further appeals were unsuccessful.[169] **11.068**

The proceedings are again pending before the District Court. The Oakland Plaintiffs have filed renewed motions to remand to the state courts, as well as motions to amend their complaints (in effect, to return to their original form so that the sole claims are alleged violations of California's public nuisance law).[170] **11.069**

(c) *Notre Affaire à Tous v France*[171]

On 17 December 2018, four not-for-profit associations[172] (Associations) sent a letter of formal notice to the French Prime Minister and other members of the French government, taking the first step in legal proceedings against the **11.070**

166 *City of Oakland v BP p.l.c.*, Case No C 17-06011 WHA, Case No C 17-06012 WHA, 325 F Supp 3d 1017 (N.D.Cal. 2018); *City of Oakland v BP p.l.c.*, Case No C 17-06011 WHA, Case No C 17-06012 WHA, Order Granting Motions to Dismiss for Lack of Personal Jurisdiction, 27 July 2018, 2018 WL 3609055 (N.D.Cal. 2018).

167 *City of Oakland v BP p.l.c.*, Case No 3:17-cv-06011-WHA, Plaintiffs' Notice of Appeal, filed 24 August 2018 (N.D.Cal. 2018); *City of Oakland v BP p.l.c.*, Case No 3:17-cv-06012-WHA, Plaintiffs' Notice of Appeal, filed 24 August 2018 (N.D.Cal. 2018).

168 *City of Oakland v BP p.l.c.*, Case No 18-16663, 969 F 3d 895 (9th Cir. 2020).

169 On 12 August 2020, the Ninth Circuit denied the defendants' petition for a panel rehearing and/or a rehearing *en banc*, see: *City of Oakland v BP p.l.c.*, Case No 18-16663, 969 F 3d 895 (9th Cir. 2020), 901. On 14 June 2021, the US Supreme Court denied the defendants' petition for a writ of certiorari, see: *Chevron Corporation v City of Oakland*, 141 S.Ct. 2776 (2021).

170 *City of Oakland v BP p.l.c.*, Case No 3:17-cv-06011-WHA, Case No 3:17-cv-06012-WHA, The People's Notice of Renewed Motion and Motion to Remand; Memorandum of Points and Authorities in Support of Renewed Motion to Remand, filed 28 January 2021 (N.D.Cal. 2021); *City of Oakland v BP p.l.c.*, Case No 3:17-cv-06011-WHA, Case No 3:17-cv-06012-WHA, Plaintiffs' Notice of Motion and Motion for Leave to Amend, filed 28 January 2021 (N.D.Cal. 2021).

171 *Notre Affaire à Tous v France*, Petition No 1904967, 1904968, 1904972, 1904976/4-1 (Case No 44-008, 60-01-02-02 R), Paris Administrative Court (4th Section – 1st Chamber), Judgment of 3 February 2021 (English translation); *Notre Affaire à Tous v France*, Petition No 1904967, 1904968, 1904972, 1904976/4-1 (Case No 44-008, 60-01-02-02, 54-07-03 R), Paris Administrative Court (4th Section – 1st Chamber), Judgment of 14 October 2021.

172 Namely, Fondation pour la Nature et l'Homme, Greenpeace France, Notre Affaire à Tous, and Oxfam France.

French government.[173] They alleged that France has a duty to limit climate change, by virtue of constitutional and ECHR obligations to protect the environment, human health and security, and in light of international, European and domestic commitments related to emissions reduction.[174] The Associations requested the French government to remedy the moral and ecological damage resulting from the State's shortcomings in combating climate change and to end the ongoing violation of its duty.[175]

11.071 On 15 February 2019, the French government rejected these requests, leading the Associations to file petitions with the Paris Administrative Court.[176] The petitions, filed on 14 March 2019, sought court orders including:[177]

(i) that the State pay each Association the symbolic sum of €1 in compensation for moral damage suffered, and the symbolic sum of €1 in compensation for ecological damage suffered; and

(ii) enjoining the French government to cease breaching the State's legal obligations in relation to climate change, to alleviate the effects of climate change, and to remedy the ongoing ecological damage, by *inter alia* taking the necessary measures to reduce France's GHG emissions to a level compatible with containing the increase in global temperature to below 1.5°C compared to pre-industrial levels.

11.072 The Associations based their claims on a range of legal obligations, derived from private law, constitutional law, administrative law, international human rights law and international environmental law.[178]

11.073 In a judgment delivered on 3 February 2021, the Court relied on Article 1246 of the French Civil Code, which imposes civil liability for ecological damage.[179] The Court held that the ecological damage asserted by the Associations was

---

173 *Notre Affaire à Tous v France*, Letter of Formal Notice to French Government from Notre Affaire à Tous, Greenpeace France, Fondation pour la Nature et l'Homme, and Oxfam France, 17 December 2018 (English translation).

174 Ibid 1, 15, 19.

175 *Notre Affaire à Tous v France*, Letter of Formal Notice to French Government from Notre Affaire a Tous, Greenpeace France, Fondation pour la Nature et l'Homme, and Oxfam France, 17 December 2018 (English translation), 1.

176 See *Notre Affaire à Tous v France*, Petition No 1904967, 1904968, 1904972, 1904976/4-1 (Case No 44-008, 60-01-02-02 R), Paris Administrative Court (4th Section – 1st Chamber), Judgment of 3 February 2021 (English translation) 22–23.

177 Ibid 1–2, 11–12, 14–15, 17–18.

178 Ibid 2–5.

179 Ibid 24. Article 1246 of the French Civil Code provides: 'Any person responsible for ecological damage is obliged to remedy it.' By virtue of Article 1247 of the same Code, ecological damage consists of non-negligible harm to the elements or functions of ecosystems or to the collective benefits derived by man from the environment.

established, and that by failing to achieve substantial reductions in GHG emissions in the context of its first carbon budget, the State had aggravated that ecological damage.[180]

However, the Associations had not shown that the State would be unable to repair the ecological damage for which it was responsible, and the requests for payment of €1 were unrelated to the extent of that damage.[181] Those requests were therefore rejected. The Court ordered an additional investigation to ascertain what measures should be ordered to achieve compensation 'in kind' in relation to the State's liability for ecological damage,[182] deferring consideration of the request for injunctive relief. In view of the State's 'wrongful failure to implement public policies' to achieve the emission reductions targets it had set, the Court held that the Associations were entitled to compensation for moral damage, and ordered the State to pay the symbolic sum of €1 to each Association.[183] **11.074**

On 14 October 2021, the Court delivered a further judgment on the request for injunctive relief.[184] The Court held that the French government needed to remedy its emissions overshoots.[185] It enjoined the French government to take measures to repair the ecological damage and prevent the aggravation thereof by 31 December 2022.[186] **11.075**

(d) *Milieudefensie v Royal Dutch Shell plc*[187]

On 5 April 2019, a coalition of non-governmental organisations (NGOs) and 17,379 individual claimants (represented in the proceedings by one of the NGOs) commenced a public interest class action in the District Court of The Hague against Royal Dutch Shell (RDS).[188] The District Court of The **11.076**

180 Ibid 30–1.

181 Ibid 31.

182 See *Notre Affaire à Tous v France*, Petition No 1904967, 1904968, 1904972, 1904976/4-1 (Case No 44-008, 60-01-02-02 R), Paris Administrative Court (4th Section–1st Chamber), Judgment of 3 February 2021 (English translation), [31]–[32].

183 *Notre Affaire à Tous v France*, Petition No 1904967, 1904968, 1904972, 1904976/4-1 (Case No 44-008, 60-01-02-02 R), Paris Administrative Court (4th Section – 1st Chamber), Judgment of 3 February 2021 (English translation) 32–3.

184 *Notre Affaire à Tous v France*, Petition No 1904967, 1904968, 1904972, 1904976/4-1 (Case No 44-008, 60-01-02-02, 54-07-03 R), Paris Administrative Court (4th Section – 1st Chamber), Judgment of 14 October 2021.

185 Ibid 31.

186 Ibid.

187 *Milieudefensie v Royal Dutch Shell*, Case No C/09/571932/HA ZA 19-379, District Court of The Hague, Judgment of 26 May 2021 (English translation).

188 *Milieudefensie v Royal Dutch Shell*, Case No C/09/571932/HA ZA 19-379, District Court of The Hague, Summons, filed 5 April 2019 (English translation).

Hague accepted that six of the seven NGOs had standing under Dutch law to bring the proceedings, but declared the claims of the individual claimants inadmissible.[189]

11.077 The NGOs relied on the 'unwritten standard of care' under the Dutch Civil Code. Section 6:162 (2) of the Dutch Civil Code defines a 'tortious act' to be 'a violation of someone else's right (entitlement) and an act or omission in violation of a duty imposed by law or of what according to unwritten law has to be regarded as proper social conduct, always as far as there was no justification for this behaviour'.[190] Applying this standard of care, the NGOs argued that RDS was obliged to reduce the CO_2 emissions of the Shell energy portfolio through the corporate policy of the Shell group, in order to contribute to the prevention of dangerous climate change.[191]

11.078 On 26 May 2021, the District Court of The Hague declared that RDS must reduce the CO_2 emissions of the Shell group's activities globally by net 45 per cent by the end of 2030, relative to 2019 levels.[192] The Court reasoned that the standard of care required RDS, when determining the Shell group's corporate policy, to '*observe the due care exercised in society*'.[193] To deduce the content of this 'due care', the Court turned to what it identified as a 'widespread international consensus that human rights offer protection against the impacts of dangerous climate change and that companies must respect human rights'.[194] Referring *inter alia* to the UN Guiding Principles on Business and Human Rights (UNGP), the Court defined the content of RDS' duty of care by reference to the 'leverage' it could exercise over emissions, and held that the 'far-reaching control and influence of RDS over the Shell group' meant that RDS' reduction obligation was an 'obligation of result' for emissions connected to the activities of the Shell group itself.[195] In contrast, for the business relations of the Shell group (including end-users), RDS was held to have a 'significant best-efforts obligation', requiring it to 'take the necessary steps to remove or prevent the

189 See footnote 187, [4.2.1]–[4.2.7].

190 *Milieudefensie v Royal Dutch Shell*, Case No C/09/571932/HA ZA 19-379, District Court of The Hague, Summons, filed 5 April 2019 (English translation), [4.1.3], [4.4.1]–[4.1.2]. See also *Dutch Civil Code*, Book 6 the law of obligations, s 6:162(2).

191 Ibid [3.2].

192 Ibid [4.1.4].

193 Ibid [4.4.1]; de Rechtspraak, *Uitspraken* (Web page, 26 May 2021) https://uitspraken.rechtspraak.nl/details?id=ECLI:NL:RBDHA:2021:5339.

194 Ibid [4.4.11]–[4.4.21].

195 *Milieudefensie v Royal Dutch Shell*, Case No C/09/571932 / HA ZA 19-379, District Court of The Hague, Judgment of 26 May 2021 (English translation) [4.1.4], [4.4.11]–[4.4.21].

serious risks ensuing [...] and to use its influence to limit any lasting consequences as much as possible'.[196]

In July 2021, RDS confirmed that it would appeal the decision.[197] In April 2022, *Milieudefensie* addressed a letter to Shell's Board of Directors regarding an alleged lack of compliance with the Court's judgement. As of September 2022, RDS' appeal remains pending. **11.079**

(e) *Smith v Fonterra Co-operative Group Ltd*[198]

In August 2019, Mr Michael Smith, commenced a claim against seven companies[199] (Fonterra Defendants) in the High Court of New Zealand alleging public nuisance, negligence and breach of an inchoate duty to stop contributing to climate change.[200] With respect to the claim in public nuisance, he alleged that the Fonterra Defendants had interfered with 'public health, safety, comfort, convenience and peace' by causing GHG emissions.[201] He claimed that he would suffer special damage as a result, including the loss of physical land and 'sites of cultural and spiritual significance', damage to customary resources and an increased risk of adverse health impacts due to the special vulnerability of Māori communities.[202] With respect to the claim in negligence, he alleged that the Fonterra Defendants owed him a duty of care not to contribute to anthropogenic interference in the climate, and that they breached this duty of care by failing to reduce their GHG emissions.[203] Finally, he alleged that the Fonterra Defendants owed him an 'inchoate' duty, not previously recognised under the common law, to 'cease contributing to damage to the climate system, dangerous anthropogenic interference with the climate system and adverse effects of climate change through their emission of greenhouse gases'.[204] **11.080**

196 Ibid [4.1.4].

197 Royal Dutch Shell, *Shell Confirms Decision to Appeal Court Ruling in Netherlands Climate Case* (Press Release, 20 July 2021) www.shell.com/media/news-and-media-releases/2021/shell-confirms-decision-to-appeal-court-ruling-in-netherlands-climate-case.html.

198 *Smith v Fonterra Co-operative Group Limited* [2020] NZHC 419; *Smith v Fonterra Co-operative Group Limited* [2021] NZCA 552.

199 Namely, Fonterra Co-operative Group Ltd, Genesis Energy Ltd, Dairy Holdings Ltd, New Zealand Steel Ltd, Z Energy Ltd, The New Zealand Refining Company Ltd and BT Mining Ltd.

200 *Smith v Fonterra Co-operative Group Limited* [2020] NZHC 419, [2].

201 Ibid [11].

202 Ibid.

203 Ibid [13].

204 Ibid [15].

11.081 The plaintiff sought declarations that the Fonterra Defendants caused or contributed to a public nuisance and breached the alleged duties, and an injunction requiring the Fonterra Defendants each to reach net-zero emissions by 2030.[205]

11.082 The Fonterra Defendants brought an application to strike out the Statement of Claim. In March 2020, the High Court of New Zealand permitted the matter to proceed to trial in relation to the claim for breach of an inchoate duty only.[206] The Court was reluctant to conclude that 'the recognition of a new tortious duty which makes corporates responsible to the public for their emissions, is untenable'.[207]

11.083 The plaintiff appealed the High Court's decision to strike out the public nuisance and negligence claims, and the Fonterra Defendants cross-appealed with respect to the inchoate duty claim.[208] The Court of Appeal upheld the High Court's decision to strike out the public nuisance and negligence claims. Moreover, the Court of Appeal struck out the inchoate duty claim, finding that the refusal to strike out that claim was inconsistent with the High Court's strike out of the nuisance and negligence claims, and concluding that the 'bare assertion of a new tort' should not be sufficient to resist a strike-out application.[209]

(f) *Sharma v Minister for the Environment*[210]

11.084 On 8 September 2020, eight Australian children (Sharma Applicants) commenced proceedings in negligence against the Commonwealth Minister for the Environment in the Federal Court of Australia.[211] The Sharma Applicants alleged that the Minister owed them a duty of care in negligence when exercising her powers under Australia's Environment Protection and Biodiversity Conservation Act 1999 (EPBC Act) to approve an extension of an existing coal mine, the effect of which was to increase coal extraction from the mine.[212] The harms alleged to flow from the apprehended breach of the duty were personal injury, property damage and economic loss as a result of the effects of

---

205 Ibid [12], [14]–[15].

206 Ibid.

207 Ibid [103].

208 *Smith v Fonterra Co-operative Group Limited* [2021] NZCA 552.

209 Ibid [123]–[124], [126].

210 *Sharma v Minister for the Environment* [2021] FCA 560; (2021) 391 ALR 1; *Sharma v Minister for the Environment (No 2)* [2021] FCA 774; *Minister for the Environment v Sharma* [2022] FCAFC 35.

211 *Sharma v Minister for the Environment*, Case No VID 607/2020, Federal Court of Australia, Statement of Claim, filed 8 September 2020.

212 *Sharma v Minister for the Environment* [2021] FCA 560; (2021) 391 ALR 1, [1]–[2], [9]–[13].

climate change.[213] The Sharma Applicants sought an injunction to restrain an apprehended breach of the duty of care.[214]

On 27 May 2021, the Federal Court found in favour of the Sharma Applicants. The Federal Court imposed on the Minister a novel duty of care, being a duty to Australian children to exercise her power under ss 130 and 133 of the EPBC Act with reasonable care so as not to cause the children personal injury resulting from the extraction of coal and the emission of CO_2 into the Earth's atmosphere.[215] The Court considered that key 'salient features' of the relationship between the Minister and the Sharma Children supported the recognition of the duty, such as the reasonable foreseeability of harm.[216] The Federal Court declined to issue the injunctive relief sought by the Sharma Applicants, but awarded declaratory relief on 8 July 2021 to give effect to its earlier judgment.[217] **11.085**

The Minister appealed and, on 15 March 2022, the Full Court of the Federal Court unanimously allowed the appeal.[218] The Full Court did not disturb the factual findings made below, which were based on the unchallenged evidence led by the Sharma Applicants.[219] However, it concluded that a novel duty of care should not be imposed. Reasons given by one or more members of the Full Court against imposing the duty included: **11.086**

(1) The content and scope of the posited duty would, at the stage of the breach inquiry, necessitate judicial evaluation of high public policy in a manner unsuited to the role of the judicial branch.[220]
(2) The imposition of the duty would be incoherent and inconsistent with the statutory regime established by the EPBC Act.[221]
(3) The Minister lacked control over the harm (as distinct from control over a small contribution to the overall risk of damage from climate change).[222]
(4) Australian children lacked special vulnerability in the legal sense.[223]

---

213 Ibid [11]–[13].
214 Ibid [10].
215 Ibid [92].
216 Ibid [96]–[109], [143]–[148], [247]–[315].
217 *Sharma v Minister for the Environment (No 2)* [2021] FCA 774.
218 *Minister for the Environment v Sharma* [2022] FCAFC 35.
219 Ibid [2], [277]–[278], [280], [283], [285], [290] (Allsop CJ); [403]–[408], [412] (Beach J), [834] (Wheelahan J).
220 Ibid [260]–[264] (Allsop CJ).
221 Ibid [267] (Allsop CJ), [850]–[852] (Wheelahan J).
222 Ibid [334]–[337] (Allsop CJ).
223 *Minister for the Environment v Sharma* [2022] FCAFC 35, [338]–[340] (Allsop CJ).

(5) The liability flowing from imposition of the posited duty would be indeterminate.[224]

(6) There was disproportionality between the small increase in risk and lack of control, on the one hand, and ongoing liability into the future for all damage by heatwaves, bushfires and rising sea levels to all Australian children, on the other hand.[225]

(7) There was no sufficiently close and direct connection between the Minister's exercise of statutory power and the likely risk of harm to Australian children.[226]

(8) Sharma Applicants did not pursue a special leave to appeal to Australia's apex court, the High Court of Australia.

(g) *Ministério Público Federal v de Rezende*[227]

11.087 On 7 April 2021, the Government of Brazil's Amazon Task Force, established by Brazil's federal public prosecution office, the Ministério Público Federal (MPF), filed a tort action in the 7th Federal Environmental and Agrarian Court of the Judiciary Section of Amazonas against farmer Dauro Parreiras de Rezende, seeking to hold him accountable for the deforestation of 2,488.56 ha of Amazonian rainforest between 2011 and 2018.[228]

11.088 The MPF's claim relies on Brazilian law imposing civil liability for environmental damage and on Article 225 of the Constitution of the Federal Republic of Brazil, which enshrines the right to a healthy environment and provides in §3 that persons responsible for 'conduct and activities considered harmful to the environment' are subject to 'criminal and administrative sanctions'.[229] The MPF argues that Mr de Rezende failed in his duty to cooperate in the protection of the environment and maintain a climate equilibrium, and violated the rights of traditional communities. According to the MPF's claim, Mr de Rezende is liable for: (i) climate damage, by reference to the emissions that deforestation has caused; (ii) the collective pain and suffering resulting from violation of human rights (moral damage); (iii) environmental damage; and (iv) compensation for illegal profits derived from deforestation.[230]

---

224 Ibid [341]–[342] (Allsop CJ), [742]–[747] (Beach J).

225 Ibid [343] (Allsop CJ).

226 Ibid [695]–[701] (Beach J).

227 *Ministério Público Federal v de Rezende*, Case No 1005885-78.2021.4.01.3200, 7th Federal Environmental and Agrarian Court of the Judiciary Section of Amazonas, Judgment of 16 April 2021.

228 *Ministério Público Federal v de Rezende*, Case No 1.13.000.001719/2015-49, 7th Federal Environmental and Agrarian Court of the Judiciary Section of Amazonas, Petition, filed 7 April 2021.

229 Ibid 22–23.

230 *Ministério Público Federal v de Rezende*, Case No 1.13.000.001719/2015-49, 7th Federal Environmental and Agrarian Court of the Judiciary Section of Amazonas, Petition, filed 7 April 2021; Maria Antonia Tigre

In the interim, the MPF sought urgent provisional relief, in the form of orders obliging Mr de Rezende to remove all cattle from his properties and prohibiting the issuance of any transport permits or invoices for cattle from such areas, so as to prevent any legal transaction resulting in the movement of cattle to or from the rural properties the subject of the action.[231] In a preliminary decision delivered on 16 April 2021, the Brazilian Court found that the requirements for the grant of interlocutory relief were satisfied, and issued the injunction sought by the MPF.[232] The case remained pending before the Brazilian courts as of September 2022. **11.089**

(h) *Metz et al v Wintershall Dea AG*[233]

On 4 October 2021, three representatives of a German not-for-profit environmental association (Metz Plaintiffs) commenced proceedings against Wintershall Dea AG (Wintershall) in the Regional Court of Kassel, seeking injunctive relief to restrain Wintershall from violating their fundamental rights by consuming more than its 'fair share' of Germany's limited remaining total emissions budget.[234] **11.090**

The Metz Plaintiffs rely on the Federal Constitutional Court's decision in *Neubauer v Germany*,[235] claiming that the decision constitutionally enshrined the fact that Germany has a limited total CO_2 emissions budget at its disposal.[236] They claim that their fundamental rights, which the Federal Republic of Germany is constitutionally obliged to protect, have an 'indirect third-party effect', with the result that Wintershall owes obligations to the Metz Plaintiffs under private law in respect of those rights.[237] In essence, the Metz Plaintiffs argue that the interpretation and application of German tort law should be **11.091**

---

and Colombia University, *Guest Commentary: Brazilian's First Tort Climate Case for Illegal Deforestation in Amazonia* (Blog Post, 16 June 2021) http://blogs.law.columbia.edu/climatechange/2021/06/16/guest-commentary-brazilians-first-tort-climate-case-for-illegal-deforestation-in-amazonia/#more-7481.

231 *Ministério Público Federal v de Rezende*, Case No 1005885-78.2021.4.01.3200, 7th Federal Environmental and Agrarian Court of the Judiciary Section of Amazonas, Judgment of 16 April 2021, 3.

232 Ibid.

233 No judgment has been issued in these proceedings as of September 2022. For the statement of claim, see *Metz et al v Wintershall Dea AG*, Regional Court of Kassel, Statement of Claim, filed 4 October 2021.

234 *Metz et al v Wintershall Dea AG*, Regional Court of Kassel, Statement of Claim, filed 4 October 2021, 58–67.

235 *Neubauer v Germany*, Case No 1 BvR 2656/18, 1 BvR 78/20, 1 BvR 96/20, 1 BvR 288/20, Federal Constitutional Court, Judgment of 24 March 2021 (English translation).

236 See footnote 234, 58–67. See also, *Metz et al v Wintershall Dea AG*, Letter of Demand, 3 September 2021 (English translation).

237 Ibid 58–67. See also, *Metz et al v Wintershall Dea AG*, Letter of Demand, 3 September 2021 (English translation).

informed by their fundamental rights and freedoms under German constitutional law. The legal basis for their claims lies in tort. They rely on:[238]

(1) §823(1) of the German Civil Code, which provides that '[a] person who, intentionally or negligently, unlawfully injures the life, body, health, freedom, property or another right of another person is liable to make compensation to the other party for the damage arising from this'; and
(2) §1004(1), second sentence, of the German Civil Code, which applies in cases of unlawful interference with property and provides that '[i]f further interferences are to be feared, the owner may seek a prohibitory injunction'.

11.092 The Metz Plaintiffs are seeking orders that stop Wintershall from extracting natural gas and/or crude oil that emits more than 0.62 Gt CO_2 (natural gas) or more than 0.31 gigatonne CO_2 (crude oil) when burned (calculated as of 1 January 2021), unless Wintershall can establish GHG neutrality for any additional CO_2 emissions exceeding those amounts. The Metz Plaintiffs are also seeking orders that stop Wintershall from opening new oil or gas fields, either nationally or internationally, after 31 December 2025, and that stop Wintershall participating in such openings through company participation. The proceedings are ongoing as of September 2022.

(i) *Pabai Pabai v Commonwealth of Australia*[239]

11.093 In October 2021, First Nations leaders from the Gudamalulgal Nation of the Torres Strait Islands commenced class action proceedings in the Federal Court of Australia, against the Commonwealth of Australia. The proceedings are brought by the Applicants on their own behalf and on behalf of all persons of Torres Strait Islander descent who, from about 1985 and continuing, have suffered loss and damage due to Australia's alleged inaction on climate change.[240]

11.094 The Applicants allege that small and low-lying islands like the Torres Strait Islands are particularly vulnerable to the impacts of climate change,[241] including sea level rises, inundation and coastal erosion,[242] which will extinguish

238 Ibid 1–2, 58–62, 87–9.

239 No judgment has been issued in these proceedings as of September 2022. For the originating process, see *Pabai Pabai v Commonwealth of Australia*, Federal Court of Australia, Statement of Claim, filed 22 October 2021.

240 Ibid [1].

241 Ibid [28]–[29].

242 Ibid [57].

native title rights and interests over the Torres Strait Islands because the islands will disappear.[243]

The Applicants claim that Australia owes them a duty of care, relying on factors including special vulnerability,[244] an 'extremely significant' degree of harm,[245] control,[246] assumption of responsibility,[247] knowledge[248] and reasonable foreseeability.[249] It is alleged that, in breach of that duty, Australia has failed to take reasonable steps to avoid injury and harm to Torres Strait Islanders and implement necessary mitigation and adaptation measures.[250] That breach is said to have caused loss and damage, including environmental degradation, loss of customs and traditions and loss of native title rights.[251] It is pleaded that the ongoing breach of the duty of care will cause an increase in emissions,[252] a material contribution to the impacts of climate change[253] and physical and psychological injury to Torres Strait Islanders.[254] **11.095**

The proceedings were pending before the Federal Court as of September 2022. **11.096**

3. Conclusion

Tortious liability for inaction on climate change and the associated harms to individuals is one of the more untested, novel and challenging areas of climate change litigation. In many ways, the move to use private law obligations to hold governments and corporate actors to account remains a nascent trend, which has gathered momentum particularly in the preceding five years. As the physical consequences of climate change take an increasing toll, in terms of personal injury, property damage and economic loss, one would expect further claims based in tort. It will be interesting to see whether judicial and social perceptions about the imposition of duties of care, and attribution of liability shift. We expect efforts to push the boundaries of the established principles **11.097**

243 Ibid [58].
244 Ibid [78].
245 Ibid [62].
246 Ibid [76].
247 Ibid [73].
248 Ibid [77].
249 Ibid [80].
250 Ibid [82]–[83].
251 Ibid [86].
252 No judgment has been issued in these proceedings as of September 2022. For the originating process, see *Pabai Pabai v Commonwealth of Australia*, Federal Court of Australia, Statement of Claim, filed 22 October 2021, [87].
253 Ibid [87].
254 Ibid [88].

which govern issues such as duty of care, causation, and compensation will continue. Notably, several of the proceedings are still pending or under appeal.

D. CONSUMER LAW ACTIONS

1. Introduction

11.098 A common basis for climate-related litigation is alleged misleading conduct, typically directed at consumers or shareholders. To date, this type of action can be broadly separated into two categories. The first category is a series of actions commenced by US States against major carbon emitters based on claims of fraud, failure to warn and violations of State laws prohibiting consumer fraud, deceptive trade practices and false statements in advertising. The second category are more traditional actions based on prohibitions on misleading conduct, brought by regulators, consumers or investors in the form of regulatory enforcement proceedings, class actions or complaints to authorities such as an advertising standards body. These cases can provide a mechanism to test controversial issues, for example the effectiveness of certain carbon reduction technologies, such as carbon capture and storage and the underlying veracity of particular carbon offset programmes.

11.099 Significant growth in these types of cases is expected as businesses across a broad range of sectors make public commitments to carbon reduction initiatives and goals, consumers become increasingly focused on green and sustainability credentials and regulators increase scrutiny of potential 'greenwashing' claims. For businesses, it is not enough to commit to objectives such as 'net zero' or spruik green credentials; they must be able to demonstrate a credible plan for how these goals will be realised and be able to demonstrate a proper basis for any claims.

2. Case Summaries

(a) *ACCC v Volkswagen*[255]

11.100 On 1 September 2016, the ACCC instituted proceedings in the Federal Court of Australia against Volkswagen Akteingesellschaft and Volkswagen Group Australia Pty Ltd (Volkswagen Defendants).[256] The proceedings arose out of

255 *Australian Competition and Consumer Commission v Volkswagen Aktiengesellschaft* [2019] FCA 2166.

256 Australian Competition & Consumer Commission, 'ACCC takes action against Volkswagen over diesel emission claims' (September 2016) MR 157/16 www.accc.gov.au/media-release/accc-takes-action-against-volkswagen-over-diesel-emission-claims.

the use of 'two-mode' software installed on vehicles imported into Australia. During regulatory testing, the software switched to a mode which altered the vehicle's operation, such that it reduced the total level of oxides of nitrogen (NO_x) emissions.[257] This was performed in order to circumvent NO_x emissions limits set by regulators.[258] During normal function, vehicles produced higher overall levels of NO_x.[259]

The ACCC alleged that the Volkswagen Defendants deceived and misled Australian regulators using the two-mode software so that Volkswagen vehicles could be imported and sold in Australia.[260] The Volkswagen Defendants made various admissions of wrongdoing and negotiated a proposed civil penalty of $75 million with the ACCC.[261] The Court held that this proposed penalty was manifestly inadequate[262] and should be set at $125 million for the extensive breaches of the Australian consumer law.[263] The fact that the Volkswagen Defendants did admit to wrongdoing was taken into account, although it did not substantially reduce the company's overall liability.[264] **11.101**

The Volkswagen Defendants unsuccessfully appealed the decision to the Full Federal Court.[265] A special leave application to the High Court was also unsuccessful, such that the decision of the first instance Court stands.[266] **11.102**

(b) *The People of the State of New York v Exxon Mobil Corporation*[267]

On 10 October 2018, the New York Attorney General commenced an action in the Supreme Court of the State of New York alleging that Exxon Mobil Corporation (Exxon) had engaged in securities fraud under s 352 of the New York General Business Law, and persistent fraud or illegality under s 63(12) of the New York Executive Law, as well as common law fraud by perpetrating a longstanding scheme concerning the management of business risks relating **11.103**

257 *Australian Competition and Consumer Commission v Volkswagen Aktiengesellschaft* [2019] FCA 2166, [85].
258 Ibid [85].
259 Ibid [85].
260 Ibid [82].
261 Ibid [30].
262 Ibid [273].
263 *Australian Competition and Consumer Commission v Volkswagen Aktiengesellschaft* [2019] FCA 2166, [274].
264 Ibid [261](a).
265 *Volkswagen Aktiengesellschaft v Australian Competition and Consumer Commission* [2021] FCAFC 49, [214]–[215].
266 Australian Competition & Consumer Commission, 'High Court denied Volkswagen leave to appeal $125 million penalty' (12 November 2021) MR 179/21 www.accc.gov.au/media-release/high-court-denies-volkswagen-leave-to-appeal-125-million-penalty.
267 *People of the State of New York v Exxon Mobil Corporation* (Supreme Court of the State of New York County of New York, Index No. 452044/2018, 10 December 2019).

to climate change in order to deceive investors and the investment community.[268] It was alleged that over a number of years, Exxon made misleading and fraudulent representations to investors by applying more conservative risk calculations internally than were represented publicly.[269] It was also alleged that Exxon was inconsistent in its application of 'proxy costs' for carbon emissions and failed to apply appropriate costs to risk assessments of carbon-intensive assets such as oil sands.[270] As a result, it was alleged that climate-related risks to Exxon's business and assets were significantly under reported, particularly in relation to long-term assessments of asset value, demand and price projections and business risks posed by a two-degree scenario.[271]

11.104 The State sought relief to prevent Exxon from making false or misleading claims about climate change risk management, to compel curative disclosures to investors, and for all appropriate monetary relief for Exxon's fraudulent conduct, including disgorgement of amounts gained or retained as a result of the fraud, damages, restitution and costs.[272]

11.105 The Supreme Court of the State of New York found Exxon not guilty of the allegations stating that the Attorney General had failed to prove that Exxon made material misrepresentations that misled any reasonable investor.[273] The case largely turned on the finding that the alleged misrepresentations were not 'material'.[274] The Court noted that its decision did not absolve Exxon from responsibility for contributing to climate change.[275]

---

268 *People of the State of New York v Exxon Mobil Corporation* (Supreme Court of the State of New York County of New York, Index No. 452044/2018, 10 December 2019) complaint filed 24 October 2018, [21].

269 Ibid [131].

270 Ibid [72]–[78].

271 Ibid [78]–[85].

272 *People of the State of New York v Exxon Mobil Corporation* (Supreme Court of the State of New York County of New York, Index No. 452044/2018, 10 December 2019) complaint filed 24 October 2018, [21].

273 *People of the State of New York v Exxon Mobil Corporation* (Supreme Court of the State of New York County of New York, Index No. 452044/2018, 10 December 2019).

274 Ibid.

275 Ibid.

(c) *Commonwealth of Massachusetts v Exxon Mobil Corporation*[276]

On 24 October 2019, the Commonwealth of Massachusetts Attorney General filed a complaint in the Suffolk County Superior Court under the Massachusetts Consumer Protection Act, alleging that Exxon had:[277] **11.106**

(1) misrepresented and failed to disclose material facts regarding systemic climate change risks to its investors, in violation of Massachusetts General Laws;
(2) made materially false and misleading statements to Massachusetts investors regarding its use of a proxy cost of carbon, in violation of Massachusetts General Laws;
(3) deceived Massachusetts consumers by misrepresenting the purported environmental benefit of using its 'Synergy' and 'green Mobil 1' products and failed to disclose the risks of climate change caused by fossil fuel products, in violation of Massachusetts General Laws; and
(4) deceived Massachusetts consumers by promoting a false and misleading 'greenwashing' campaign, in violation of Massachusetts General Laws.

The Commonwealth of Massachusetts sought declaratory relief, injunctive relief and the statutory penalty of $5000 for each violation of the Massachusetts Consumer Protection Act.[278] Exxon sought to have the case moved to federal jurisdiction, which was denied by the District Court of Massachusetts on 17 March 2020.[279] **11.107**

On 22 June 2021, the Massachusetts Suffolk County Superior Court denied Exxon's motion to dismiss on personal jurisdiction grounds or for failure to state a claim.[280] The Court held that the Commonwealth had shown that its claims regarding investor deception arose from Exxon's contacts with Massachusetts, and the claims relating to consumer deception arose from **11.108**

---

276 *Commonwealth of Massachusetts v Exxon Mobil Corporation* (Suffolk County Superior Court, Massachusetts, Civil Action No. 1984CV03333-BLS1, 22 June 2021) Memorandum of Decision and Order on Defendant's motion to dismiss amended complaint, 22 June 2021; *Commonwealth of Massachusetts v Exxon Mobil Corporation* (Suffolk County Superior Court, Massachusetts, Civil Action No. 1984CV03333-BLS1, 22 June 2021) Memorandum of Decision and Order on Defendant's special motion to dismiss amended complaint, 22 June 2021.

277 *Commonwealth of Massachusetts v Exxon Mobil Corporation* (Suffolk County Superior Court, Massachusetts, Civil Action No. 1984CV03333-BLS1, 22 June 2021) complaint filed 24 October 2019.

278 Commonwealth of Massachusetts v Exxon Mobil Corporation (Suffolk County Superior Court, Massachusetts, Civil Action No. 1984CV03333-BLS1, 22 June 2021) complaint filed 24 October 2019.

279 *Commonwealth of Massachusetts v Exxon Mobil Corporation* (United State District Court, District of Massachusetts, Civil Action No. 19-12430-WGY, 18 March 2020).

280 *Commonwealth of Massachusetts v Exxon Mobil Corporation* (Suffolk County Superior Court, Massachusetts, Civil Action No. 1984CV03333-BLS1, 22 June 2021) Memorandum of Decision and Order on Defendant's motion to dismiss amended complaint, 22 June 2021, 15.

Exxon's advertisements through its Massachusetts franchisees. The Court further found that the Commonwealth had shown its claim against Exxon to be viable.

11.109 On the same date, in a second decision, the Court denied Exxon's special motion to dismiss under the Massachusetts anti-Strategic Litigation Against Public Participation statute (anti-SLAPP).[281] The Court found that Exxon had failed to establish that it had made statements 'solely, or even primarily, to influence, inform, or reach any government body, directly, or indirectly'.[282] Further, the Court found that Exxon had failed to discharge the burden of establishing that the Commonwealth of Massachusetts' claims were based on 'petitioning activity' protected by the anti-SLAPP statute.[283]

11.110 On 8 November 2021, Exxon appealed the decision denying Exxon's motion to dismiss to the Commonwealth of Massachusetts Appeals Court.[284] Exxon argued that by denying its motion the Court below had jeopardised foundational First Amendment protections. The Court affirmed the dismissal of Exxon's motion on 24 May 2022, holding that the anti-SLAPP statute did 'not apply to government enforcement actions brought by the Attorney General'.[285]

(d) Complaint to the UK Advertising Standards Authority regarding Ryanair advertisements[286]

11.111 In 2019, a complaint was made to the UK Advertising Standards Authority (ASA) regarding Ryanair advertisements. It was alleged that the advertisements were misleading in relation to the airline's GHG emissions.[287] There were three advertisements that were alleged to be misleading. The first featured the statement 'Europe's Lowest Fares, Lowest Emissions Airline'. The

281 Ibid; The EU Commission has proposed similar legislation to 'improve protection of journalists and human rights defenders from abusive court proceedings' or SLAPPs: European Commission, *Press Corner*, 'Commission tackles abusive lawsuits against journalists and human rights defenders "SLAPPs"' (27 April 2022) https://ec.europa.eu/commission/presscorner/detail/en/ip_22_2652.

282 Ibid 7, 8.

283 *Commonwealth of Massachusetts v Exxon Mobil Corporation* (Suffolk County Superior Court, Massachusetts, Civil Action No. 1984CV03333-BLS1, 22 June 2021) Memorandum of Decision and Order on Defendant's special motion to dismiss amended complaint, 22 June 2021, 4.

284 *Commonwealth of Massachusetts v Exxon Mobil Corporation* (Commonwealth of Massachusetts Appeals Court, No. 2021-P-0860) Appellant's Brief, 8 November 2021.

285 *Commonwealth of Massachusetts v Exxon Mobil Corporation* (Massachusetts High Court, No. SJC-13211, 24 May 2022).

286 Advertising Standards Authority decision regarding complaint no. G19-1035778, 5 February 2020 www.asa.org.uk/rulings/ryanair-ltd-cas-571089-p1w6b2.html.

287 Ibid.

second advertisement included the statement 'Fly Ryanair. Europe's low fare, low CO_2 emissions airline from just £14.99. Book Ryanair today'. The third advertisement was put on the radio, which stated 'Fly Ryanair. Europe's low fare, low CO_2 emissions airline from just £14.99 one way [...] Ryanair, low fares, low CO_2 emissions. Based on the top 27 European airlines.'[288]

In response to the complaint, Ryanair stated that its claims were substantiated, and that the metric it used to measure CO_2 emissions was grams of CO_2 per passenger kilometre (that is, every passenger flown one kilometre). It claimed that the advertisements clearly explained the basis of the comparison with other airlines and that 'low CO_2 emissions' meant less than average.[289] **11.112**

On 5 February 2020, ASA concluded that Ryanair's claims in the three advertisements breached the UK Code of Non-broadcast Advertising and Direct and Promotional Marketing,[290] including rules regarding misleading advertising, substantiation and environmental claims. ASA considered that the claims in Ryanair's advertisement regarding low emissions would be understood, and was satisfied that the metric they used to measure CO_2 emissions was satisfactory. However, ASA determined that the basis of the claims had not been made clear in the advertisements, and that there was not sufficient evidence to demonstrate that Ryanair was the lowest CO_2-emitting airline based on the metric of grams of CO_2 per passenger kilometre. ASA ultimately found that the advertisements must not appear again in the same form that they were in at the time of the decision.[291] **11.113**

(e) Specific instance complaint filed with the UK National Contact Point for the OECD Guidelines against BP regarding advertising[292]

On 3 December 2019, ClientEarth filed a 'Specific Instance' complaint with the UK National Contact Point for the Organisation for Economic Cooperation and Development Guidelines for Multinational Enterprises **11.114**

288 Ibid.

289 Ibid.

290 Committee of Advertising Practice, 'The UK Code of Non-broadcast Advertising and Direct & Promotional Marketing' (2014) (Edition 12) www.asa.org.uk/static/47eb51e7-028d-4509-ab3c0f4822c9a3c4/The-Cap-code.pdf.

291 Advertising Standards Authority decision regarding complaint no. G19-1035778, 5 February 2020 www.asa.org.uk/rulings/ryanair-ltd-cas-571089-p1w6b2.html.

292 No judgment has been issued in these proceedings as of September 2022. For the complaint, see Client Earth, 'Complaint against BP in respect of violations of the OECD Guidelines' (Complaint, 12 April 2019) http://climatecasechart.com/climate-change-litigation/wp-content/uploads/sites/16/non-us-case-documents/2019/20191204_NA_complaint-1.pdf.

(OECD Guidelines) against BP regarding allegedly misleading advertising.[293] A 'Specific Instance' is a complaint regarding non-observance of the OECD Guidelines.[294]

11.115 ClientEarth alleged that BP's 2019 advertising campaign launched under the titles 'Keep Advancing' and 'Possibilities Everywhere' is misleading, and in turn is in conflict with the OECD Guidelines, in that it creates false perceptions regarding BP's business and strategy, climate issues and sustainable consumption choices. Specifically, ClientEarth argues that the advertising campaign gives a false perception of the relative scale of BP's renewable and low-carbon energy activities in comparison to its fossil fuel use,[295] misleadingly omits full lifecycle emissions for gas,[296] provides an emissions saving against coal combustion that is allegedly inaccurate,[297] and asserts that an increase in global energy demand is inevitable and necessary for human progress and development.[298]

11.116 ClientEarth requested that BP take steps to correct the allegedly misleading information, including by withdrawing specific advertisements until they are revised to conform with the OECD Guidelines, and make a public statement explaining the withdrawal and/or correction of the advertisements. The complaint further asks that the UK National Contact Point for the OECD Guidelines conclude that BP's advertising breaches the OECD Guidelines if BP does not ensure its advertising complies with the OECD Guidelines.[299]

11.117 In February 2020, BP announced that it would cease, and not replace, the advertising campaign that was the subject of the complaint.[300] Subsequently, the UK Contact Point for the OECD Guidelines determined in June 2020

---

293 Client Earth, 'Complaint against BP in respect of violations of the OECD Guidelines' (Complaint, 12 April 2019) http:// climatecasechart .com/ climate -change -litigation/ wp -content/ uploads/ sites/ 16/ non -us -case -documents/2019/20191204_NA_complaint-1.pdf.

294 OECD, *Specific instance handling under the OECD Guidelines for Multinational Enterprises* (Web Page) https://mneguidelines.oecd.org/specificinstances.htm.

295 Client Earth, 'Complaint against BP in respect of violations of the OECD Guidelines' (Complaint, 12 April 2019) http:// climatecasechart .com/ climate -change -litigation/ wp -content/ uploads/ sites/ 16/ non -us -case -documents/2019/20191204_NA_complaint-1.pdf [6.1].

296 Ibid [121].

297 Ibid [6.2].

298 Ibid [168].

299 Client Earth, 'Complaint against BP in respect of violations of the OECD Guidelines' (Complaint, 12 April 2019) http:// climatecasechart .com/ climate -change -litigation/ wp -content/ uploads/ sites/ 16/ non -us -case -documents/2019/20191204NAcomplaint-1.pdf [216].

300 Client Earth, 'BP pulls advertising campaign just months after our legal complaint' (14 February 2020) www.clientearth.org/latest/latest-updates/news/bp-pulls-advertising-campaign-just-months-after-our-legal -complaint/.

that, notwithstanding the fact that BP had withdrawn the campaign, the complaint was 'material and substantiated'.[301]

(f) *State of Minnesota v American Petroleum Institute et al.*[302]

11.118 On 24 June 2020, the Attorney General for the State of Minnesota filed a complaint in the Ramsey County District Court against American Petroleum Institute, Exxon, Koch Industries and Flint Hills Resources on the basis of internal documents dating back to the 1970s and 1980s which allegedly confirm that the companies 'well understood the devastating effects that their products would cause to the climate'.[303]

11.119 The Attorney General alleges, inter alia, that notwithstanding this knowledge, the defendants have profited from 'avoiding the consequences and costs of dealing with global warming'[304] and have deliberately undermined 'the science of climate change, purposefully downplaying the role that the purchase and consumption of their products played in causing climate change'.[305]

11.120 The Attorney General's claims against the defendants include that they breached the Minnesota Statutes by making fraudulent, false and misleading statements in marketing materials connected with the sale of fossil fuel products,[306] failing to warn of the impacts of fossil fuel consumption on climate change,[307] creating uncertainty about current climate change science[308] and presenting themselves as experts on the impact of fossil fuel products, such that consumers, regulators, policy makers and the general public relied on the defendants.[309] The Attorney General has also alleged that the defendants breached the False Statement in Advertising Act by making a variety of deceptive and misleading statements with the intention of driving increased consumption of fossil fuels.[310]

---

301 Client Earth, 'BP greenwashing complaint sets precedent for action on misleading ad campaigns' (17 June 2020) www.clientearth.org/latest/latest-updates/news/bp-greenwashing-complaint-sets-precedent-for-action-on-misleading-ad-campaigns/.

302 No judgment has been issued in these proceedings as of September 2022. For the complaint, see *State of Minnesota v American Petroleum Institute, Exxon Mobil Corporation & Ors*, Complaint, 24 June 2020.

303 *State of Minnesota v American Petroleum Institute, Exxon Mobil Corporation & Ors*, Complaint, 24 June 2020, [3].

304 Ibid [7].

305 Ibid [8].

306 Ibid [184]–[188].

307 *State of Minnesota v American Petroleum Institute, Exxon Mobil Corporation & Ors*, Complaint, 24 June 2020, [203].

308 Ibid [204].

309 Ibid [217].

310 Ibid [238]–[239].

11.121 The Attorney General seeks relief in the form of, inter alia: (i) disgorgement of profits made by Exxon and Koch as a result of their alleged unlawful conduct;[311] (ii) injunctions against the defendants preventing them from engaging in conduct that breaches the Minnesota Statutes;[312] (iii) an order requiring the defendants to publicly disclose all internally conducted research related to climate change;[313] and (iv) an order requiring the defendants to fund a corrective public education campaign focused on climate change.[314]

11.122 The defendants filed a notice of removal on 27 July 2020 seeking to transfer the case from the District Court of the State of Minnesota to the US District Court for the District of Minnesota.[315] In response, the Attorney General filed a motion to remand the case to the State courts. The US District Court for the District of Minnesota upheld the motion, remanding the case to the State courts on 31 March 2021.

11.123 The motion to remand has been appealed to the US Court of Appeals on 4 April 2021. As of September 2022, the appeal is pending.

(g) *District of Columbia v Exxon Mobil Corporation et al.*[316]

11.124 On 25 June 2020, the Attorney General for the District of Columbia filed, in the Superior Court of the District of Columbia, a complaint against Exxon, BP, Chevron and Shell alleging that they 'systematically and intentionally misled consumers in Washington DC [...] about the central role their products play in causing climate change'.[317]

11.125 The Attorney General claimed that the defendants breached the DC Consumer Protection Procedures Act by participating in a marketing campaign that fostered 'climate change denialism' with the intention of driving consumption for fossil fuel products,[318] making various misrepresentations about the scientific consensus concerning human impacts on climate change,[319] holding them-

---

311 Ibid [249].

312 Ibid [244].

313 Ibid [245].

314 Ibid [246].

315 *State of Minnesota v American Petroleum Institute, Exxon Mobil Corporation & Ors*, Notice of Removal, 27 July 2020.

316 No judgment has been issued in these proceedings as of September 2022. For the complaint, see *District of Columbia v Exxon Mobil Corp. and others*, The Superior Court of the District of Columbia, Complaint, 25 June 2020, 1.

317 *District of Columbia v Exxon Mobil Corp. and others*, The Superior Court of the District of Columbia, Complaint, 25 June 2020, 1.

318 Ibid 67–77.

319 Ibid.

selves out as renewable energy leaders, making various misleading statements concerning their carbon footprint and the extent to which they were investing in sources of renewable energy[320] and failing to disclose the risks of combusting fossil fuels when marketing their fossil fuel products.[321]

The Attorney General is seeking an order that the defendants cease the alleged disinformation campaigns, provide financial relief for consumers and pay civil penalties.[322] **11.126**

On 17 July 2020, Exxon, on behalf of the defendants, filed a notice of removal to transfer the case from the District of Columbia Superior Court to the US District Court for the District of Columbia on the grounds inter alia that the case raised issues falling under federal statutes and regulations concerning the management of GHG emissions,[323] federal common law concerning 'transboundary pollution, foreign relations and the navigable waters of the United States',[324] and federal enclaves (exclusive territories of the federal government).[325] Further, the defendants argued that their activities were taken at federal direction and the Court had jurisdiction under the Federal Officer Removal Statute[326] and under the Outer Continental Shelf Lands Act,[327] and that the action commenced by the Attorney General is essentially a class action on behalf of consumers in the District of Columbia[328] such that jurisdiction is enlivened under the Class Action Fairness Act,[329] and the consumers had 'diversity of citizenship'.[330] **11.127**

The District of Columbia filed a motion to remand the case to the District of Columbia Superior Court on 17 August 2020. As of September 2022, the US District Court for the District of Columbia had not made a determination with respect to the motion to remand.[331] **11.128**

---

320 Ibid.

321 Ibid.

322 *District of Columbia v Exxon Mobil Corp. and others*, The Superior Court of the District of Columbia, Complaint, 25 June 2020.

323 *District of Columbia v Exxon Mobil Corp. and others*, United States District Court District of Columbia, Notice of removal, 17 July 2020, [20].

324 Ibid.

325 Ibid.

326 Ibid.

327 Ibid.

328 Ibid.

329 *District of Columbia v Exxon Mobil Corp. and others*, United States District Court, District of Columbia, Notice of removal, 17 July 2020, [20].

330 Ibid.

331 *District of Columbia v Exxon Mobil Corp. and others*, United States District Court District of Columbia, Plaintiff's Notice of Supplemental Authority, 25 May 2022; Defendants' Response to Plaintiff's Notice of Supplemental Authority, 17 June 2022.

(h) *State of Delaware v BP America Inc et al.*[332]

11.129 In September 2020, the Delaware Attorney General filed a lawsuit in the Superior Court of Delaware against 31 fossil fuel companies as well as the American Petroleum Institute.[333] The lawsuit alleged four causes of action.

11.130 In the first cause of action concerning negligence, the State alleged that the defendants had a duty to warn the State of Delaware, the general public and consumers of the risks associated with using their fossil fuel products,[334] and had breached this duty of care.[335] Further, it was alleged that the defendants 'knew or should have known' of the negative climate effects associated with fossil fuel consumption,[336] including sea-level rise, increased precipitation and their consequences.[337] Further, that the defendants took steps to conceal the risks of the negative climate effects,[338] and that the defendant's conduct 'was a direct and proximate cause' of the harm suffered by the State, including injuries to public resources that interfere with the rights of the State and its residents.[339] The State sought an award of punitive damages.[340]

11.131 Second, with respect to trespass, the State alleged that the defendants 'intentionally, recklessly, or negligently' caused, inter alia, flood water and other materials to enter the State's real property,[341] and that the State's real property was rendered unusable by flood waters, rising sea levels and precipitation.[342] It was also alleged that the State had further suffered damages due to funds spent on addressing 'sea level-rise related damages'.[343]

11.132 Third, with respect to nuisance, the State alleged that the defendants were involved in the 'fossil fuel product supply chain',[344] had concealed information concerning the risks of continued use of fossil fuel and had produced

332 No judgment has been issued in these proceedings as of September 2022. For the complaint, see *State of Delaware v BP America Inc., and others*, The Superior Court of the State of Delaware, Complaint, 10 September 2020.
333 *State of Delaware v BP America Inc., and others*, The Superior Court of the State of Delaware, Complaint, 10 September 2020.
334 Ibid [235].
335 Ibid [236].
336 Ibid [238].
337 Ibid [237].
338 Ibid [240].
339 Ibid [244].
340 Ibid [246].
341 *State of Delaware v BP America Inc., and others*, The Superior Court of the State of Delaware, Complaint, 10 September 2020, [249].
342 Ibid [251].
343 Ibid [252].
344 Ibid [257].

misleading material on climate change.[345] Therefore the State alleged that the defendants contributed to the creation of a public nuisance[346] and the State had suffered special injury caused by the alleged public nuisance.[347] The State sought injunctive relief and punitive damages.[348]

Fourth, regarding alleged breaches of the Consumer Fraud Act,[349] the State alleged that the defendants made various misleading statements about the risk of fossil fuel products causing climate change and the extent of their investment,[350] and deliberately concealed information about the contribution of fossil fuel products to climate change.[351] The State sought punitive damages and $10,000 penalties against the defendants for each wilful violation of the Consumer Fraud Act.[352] **11.133**

On 23 October 2020, the defendants issued a notice of removal, moving the case to the US District Court for the District of Delaware.[353] The plaintiff filed a motion to remand the case back to the Delaware Superior Court.[354] The Court granted the motion to remand and ordered that the case should be transferred to the Delaware Superior Court.[355] The defendants appealed this order to the United States Court of Appeal for the Third Circuit.[356] As of September 2022, the appeal is pending. **11.134**

(i) *Lawyers for Climate Action Complaint to the Advertising Standards Board*[357]

In July 2021, climate activist group, Lawyers for Climate Action NZ, lodged a complaint with the New Zealand Advertising Standards Complaints Board (ASCB) in relation to a television and YouTube advertisement for energy company, Firstgas Group (Firstgas).[358] The advertisement showed different images of people using gas for cooking and heating hot water. A voiceover said: 'New Zealand's heading towards zero carbon so we're ensuring our gas **11.135**

345 Ibid [257].
346 Ibid.
347 Ibid [259].
348 Ibid [263].
349 Ibid [267].
350 Ibid [268]–[270].
351 Ibid [268].
352 Ibid 217.
353 Ibid 1.
354 Ibid.
355 Ibid.
356 Ibid.
357 *Lawyers for Climate Action and others v Firstgas Group*, ASA Complaints Board, Complaint No. 21/194, 6 July 2021.
358 Ibid.

is going zero carbon too. You know what that means for you? Absolutely nothing. You can continue doing what you love. And help change the world, without changing too much of yours. Find out more at gasischanging.co.nz.'[359]

11.136 The complaint alleged that the advertisement stated, without qualification, that Firstgas was 'ensuring its gas is going zero carbon', and that consumers could be misled into believing that its gas was carbon neutral.[360] It also alleged that the advertisement contained statements which could not be backed by scientific evidence, presumed the industry would be able to produce zero emission gas, utilised an uncertain timeline and encouraged wasteful use of fossil fuels.[361]

11.137 The ASCB reviewed the advertisement by reference to the advertising standards code, which requires that an advertisement must be prepared with recognition of a social responsibility to consumers and society and that the content must not encourage environmental damage and must be truthful and not mislead or be likely to mislead consumers. Under the code, environmental claims must be accurate and able to be substantiated by evidence that reflects scientific and technological developments.

11.138 The ASCB upheld the complaint in part and ordered that the advertisement be removed.[362] It found Firstgas' claims were misleading as there was no evidence that they would produce zero-carbon gas soon.[363] However, by majority the ASCB rejected the claim that the advertisement encouraged environmental damage or was in breach of the principle that advertising should 'be prepared with a due sense of social responsibility'.[364]

(j) *Jochims v Oatly Group AB*[365]

11.139 On 26 July 2021, Kai Jochims instituted securities class actions in the District Court of the Southern District of New York, alleging that Oatly Group AB (Oatly) and its officials and directors had made false statements, failed to disclose adverse facts about Oatly, artificially inflated share prices and made false statements deceiving public investors, causing plaintiffs and other members of the Class to purchase shares at inflated prices.

---

359 Ibid 1.
360 Ibid.
361 Ibid 7.
362 *Lawyers for Climate Action and others v Firstgas Group*, ASA Complaints Board, Complaint No. 21/194, 6 July 2021, 5.
363 Ibid 4.
364 Ibid 4.
365 No judgment has been issued in these proceedings as of September 2022. For the complaint, see *Kai Jochims et al v Oatly Group AB et al*, Complaint for the violation of the Federal Securities Laws, filed on 26 July 2021.

The plaintiffs' claim alleges that share prices in Oatly's initial public offering were inflated because its registration statements filed with the US Securities and Exchange Commission (SEC) allegedly made misleading statements about Oatly's financial metrics, sustainability and growth in China. In particular, Oatly allegedly included misleading statements regarding GHG emissions and the energy consumption of its product. In June 2021 Oatly also published an investor presentation online, which allegedly made misleading statements regarding the same issues.[366] **11.140**

On 14 July 2021 a short seller's report alleged several improprieties on the part of Oatly, including improper accounting practices and greenwashing. After the report was released, the price of Oatly's shares dropped. The plaintiffs that had purchased the shares suffered economic loss from the inflated prices of shares that could no longer be sold at a similar price.[367] The decline in the price of the shares was alleged to be the direct result of Oatly's conduct being revealed to the market as the plaintiffs claimed that the fall in share prices occurred too quickly for it to have been caused by market conditions or industry factors.[368] The plaintiffs have sought a declaration that the action is a proper class action, and also seek damages, including interest, for the economic loss caused by purchasing Oatly shares at inflated prices.[369] **11.141**

On 4 March 2022 the plaintiff filed a consolidated amended complaint. The defendants subsequently filed a motion to dismiss the amended complaint on 8 April 2022. The plaintiff then filed a further amended complaint, which, as at September 2022, the Court was yet to consider.[370] **11.142**

(k) *Australasian Centre for Corporate Responsibility v Santos Limited*[371]

On 25 August 2021, the Australian Centre for Corporate Responsibility (ACCR), a shareholder advocacy group, commenced proceedings in the Federal Court of Australia against Santos Limited (Santos),[372] a natural gas supplier. **11.143**

---

366 Ibid [36], [41].

367 Ibid [58].

368 Ibid.

369 Ibid 19.

370 *Kai Jochims et al v Oatly Group AB et al*, District Court of the Southern District of New York, Case No. 1:21-cv-06360, Amended Complaint, 17 August 2022.

371 No judgment has been issued in these proceedings as of September 2022. For the Originating Application, see *Australasian Centre for Corporate Responsibility v Santos Limited*, Originating Application, filed on behalf of ACCR, dated 25 August 2021.

372 Ibid.

11.144 ACCR alleged that Santos had engaged in misleading and deceptive conduct in breach of sections 18 and 33 of the Australian Consumer Law and Section 1041H of the Corporations Act 2001 by making misleading representations in its 2020 Annual Report.[373] In particular, the ACCR relied on representations by Santos that natural gas is a 'clean energy' and 'clean fuel' and Santos' statement that it has a plan to achieve 'net zero' Scope 1 and Scope 2 GHG emissions by 2040 without disclosing a range of qualifications or assumptions made to reach this target, and without disclosing that Santos intends to increase its emissions in the short term.

11.145 ACCR seeks declarations that Santos has engaged in misleading or deceptive conduct, or conduct that is likely to mislead or deceive' an injunction prohibiting Santos from engaging in the same conduct in the future' and an injunction requiring Santos to issue a corrective statement regarding the environmental impacts of its operations.[374] As of September 2022, this proceeding was ongoing.

(l) Complaint to the Dutch Advertising Committee regarding Shell advertisements[375]

11.146 On 26 August 2021, a group of nine law students (Shell Complainants) made a complaint to the Dutch Advertising Committee (Committee) in relation to advertisements in the Shell campaign 'Make the difference. Drive CO_2 Neutral'. In the campaign, Shell promoted the offsetting, or 'compensation', of CO_2 emissions caused by its fossil fuel products, essentially claiming that environmental damage caused by the CO_2 emissions can be neutralised by offsetting the CO_2 emissions. The Complainants alleged that the advertisement effectively stated that if a customer paid one extra cent per litre of fuel purchased from Shell, the carbon emissions produced by their driving would be offset.[376]

11.147 The Committee monitors compliance with the Dutch Advertisement Code (Nederlandse Reclame Code) (NRC), which includes multiple special codes, such as the Environmental Advertisement Code (Milieu Reclame Code) (MRC). In their complaint, the Shell Complainants alleged that by promoting

---

373 *Australasian Centre for Corporate Responsibility v Santos Limited,* Concise Statement, filed on behalf of ACCR, dated 25 August 2021.

374 See footnote 381.

375 Advertising Code Committee, Recommendation, File 2021/00190, dated 26 August 2021 www.reclamecode.nl/uitspraken/resultaten/vervoer-2021-00190/304997/.

376 Advertising Code Committee, Recommendation, File 2021/00190, dated 26 August 2021 www.reclamecode.nl/uitspraken/ resultaten/vervoer-2021-00190/304997/.

the offsetting of CO_2 emissions caused by its fossil fuel products, Shell was making an environmental claim that did not meet the requirements in Article 3 of the MRC, as the advertisements were not demonstrably accurate.[377] The complaint was also based on, *inter alia*, Article 2 of the MRC, which provides that environmental claims must not contain statements, images or suggestions that would mislead the consumer about environmental aspects of the advertised products or about the advertiser's contribution to maintaining and promoting a clean environment in general.[378]

The Committee found that the statements regarding the offsetting, or 'compensation', of CO_2 did not comply with Article 3 of the MRC as Shell could not prove that it was fully offsetting CO_2 emissions caused by its fossil fuel products.[379] The Committee stated that Shell should have been able to demonstrate that the effect of the offsetting could be measured so precisely that the measurement could serve as a basis for the claim that, by paying one extra cent per litre purchased, the adverse effect on the environment with regard to the use of the fossil fuel was guaranteed to be eliminated.[380] Although the Committee considered it plausible that the offsetting programme being advertised involved some degree of offsetting, it was held that Shell's claim regarding offsetting went beyond this.[381] The Committee found that the fact that it could be assumed that there was some offsetting did not alter the fact that there is (and remains) uncertainty about the comparability of CO_2 emissions on the one hand and offsetting on the other, and therefore about the precision with which the effect of offsetting measures can be measured.[382] **11.148**

The Committee also found that as the statements regarding offsetting did not comply with Article 3 of the MRC, they also were in violation of Article 2 of the MRC. The Committee recommended that Shell no longer advertise in the manner that gave rise to the original complaint.[383] **11.149**

377 Shell Complainants, Complaint, Advertising Code Commission, File 2021/00190, https:// ve rbiedfossi elereclame.nl/wp-content/uploads/2021/04/def-Complaint-RCC-Shell-Rij-CO2-neutraal-campaign.pdf.

378 Dutch Advertisement Code, Environmental Advertisement Code (Milieu Reclame Code), Art 2.

379 Advertising Code Committee, Recommendation, File 2021/00190, dated 26 August 2021 www.reclamecode .nl/uitspraken/resultaten/vervoer-2021-00190/304997/.

380 Ibid.

381 Ibid.

382 Ibid.

383 Advertising Code Committee, Recommendation, File 2021/00190, dated 26 August 2021 www.reclamecode .nl/uitspraken/ resultaten/vervoer-2021-00190/304997/.

3. Conclusion

11.150 As the case summaries in this section demonstrate, climate change actions based on consumer protection laws, including laws that prohibit misleading conduct, can take a variety of forms. They can include actions commenced by governments, consumers, investors or regulators and encompass class actions, complaints to advertising standards bodies, international organisations and civil claims.

11.151 Sustainability, green credentials and climate change are now firmly on the agenda for consumers and investors.[384] As the demand for eco-friendly products and services grows, so too does the risk of companies overstating their sustainability credentials in order to attract and retain customers and investors. In the UK, the Competition and Markets Authority recently published a new Green Claims Code to provide guidance to businesses on their obligations under consumer protection law when it comes to making environmental claims about their goods and services and has announced its intention to crack down on misleading environmental claims.[385] In Australia, the ACCC has announced that issues concerning 'environmental claims and sustainability' will be a priority enforcement issue.[386] ASIC is also intending to enhance climate risk disclosures provided by corporations through targeted surveillance and external communications.[387]

11.152 Importantly, these kinds of actions are not limited to large emitters. Any business in any sector that makes environmental and sustainability claims is potentially exposed to court action if those claims are exaggerated or imprecise or cannot be properly substantiated with objective evidence, including that there is a credible plan to achieve any stated decarbonisation commitments.

---

384 Norton Rose Fulbright, *Climate change and sustainability disputes: Greenwashing* (February 2022) www .nortonrosefulbright.com/ en/ knowledge/ publications/ aaa46f8f/ climate-change-and-sustainability-disputes -greenwashing.

385 Competition & Markets Authority, 'Green Claims Code' (ND), *Green Claims Code: Get your green claims right* (webpage, undated) https:// greenclaims .campaign .gov .uk/ . See also The Netherlands Authority for Consumers and Markets, 'Guidelines: Sustainability claims' (ND) www .acm .nl/ sites/ default/ files/ documents/guidelines-suistainability-claims.pdf.

386 Australian Competition and Consumer Commission, *2022–2023 Compliance and Enforcement Priorities* (web page, 2022), 1 www.accc.gov.au/system/files/ce-priority.pdf.

387 Australian Securities and Investment Commission, *ASIC Corporate Plan 2021–2025* (August 2021), 23 https:// download .asic .gov .au/ media/ qzcaljce/ asic -corporate -plan -2021 -25 -focus -2021 -22 -published -26 -august-2021.pdf.

E. CORPORATION LAW ACTIONS

1. Introduction

Climate change can have a myriad of impacts on businesses across all sectors. These include the impact of extreme weather events, supply chain disruption, resilience and adaptation costs, insurance, access to finance, changes in consumer demand and geopolitical risks related to climate disruption. One form of climate change litigation has targeted companies for their failure to adequately identify, consider and disclose the impact of climate risk on their business. It is also possible in many countries for action to be taken against individual directors for failing to comply with their obligations to the company and its shareholders. **11.153**

As the energy transition gathers urgency and momentum, businesses also now need to grapple with the resulting opportunities and challenges on an unprecedented scale and at an unprecedented pace. This poses additional challenges for executives and boards in setting strategy and managing risk. Recent years have seen a growth in investor focus on climate change and sustainability issues with activist investors placing increasing pressure on companies to take meaningful action to tackle climate change and commit to ambitious carbon reduction targets, often now with support from institutional investors. This activism can take the form of shareholder resolutions, aggressive scrutiny at shareholder meetings and board spills. **11.154**

The case summaries below demonstrate how cases based on established principles of corporations law have evolved. While failure to disclose climate risk remains a common feature, shareholders are also accessing a broader range of legal remedies, such as statutory rights to access company records, with a view to testing whether companies are effectively implementing their climate change policies. **11.155**

2. Case Summaries

(a) *In re Peabody Energy Corp.*[388]

In June 2007, the New York Office of the Attorney General (NYAG) investigated disclosures made by Peabody Energy Corporation (Peabody) concerning **11.156**

---

388 No judgment will be issued in these proceedings as the investigation has been resolved. For the Assurance of Discontinuance, see Attorney General of the State of New York Environmental and Investor Protection Bureaus, In the Matter of Investigation by Eric T. Schneiderman, Attorney General of the State of New

climate change and the potential effects of climate change policy on Peabody's future business.[389]

11.157 The NYAG found that the disclosures were incomplete and omitted less favourable projections of future coal demand.[390] In response to the NYAG's finding, on 8 November 2015 Peabody issued an Assurance of Discontinuance, resolving the investigation by agreement.[391] Peabody neither admitted nor denied the NYAG's findings in the Assurance of Discontinuance, but agreed to make more extensive disclosures in future. [392]

(b) *Abrahams v Commonwealth Bank of Australia*[393]

11.158 On 8 August 2017, certain shareholders of the Commonwealth Bank of Australia (CBA) brought an action against CBA in the Federal Court of Australia, alleging that CBA had failed to properly disclose the risk climate change posed to the business in CBA's Financial Report for the 2016 financial year in breach of ss 292(1)(b), 295 and 297 of the Corporations Act 2001, and in CBA's Directors' Annual Report for the 2016 financial year in breach of ss 292(1)(b), 298(1), 298(1AA) and 299A(1) of the Corporations Act 2001. The action focused on an allegation that the CBA knew, or ought to have known, that any form of financial support to the controversial Adani Carmichael coal mine project in Queensland posed major risks to CBA's business.[394] The shareholders sought an injunction compelling CBA to make adequate disclosure in future annual reports.[395]

11.159 The proceeding was discontinued after CBA's 2017 annual report included an acknowledgement from its directors that climate change posed a significant risk to the bank's operations, with a commitment to undertake climate change

York, of Peabody Energy Corporation, Assurance No. 15-242 https:// ag .ny .gov/ pdfs/ Peabody -Energy -Assurance-signed.pdf February 2022.

389 Attorney General of the State of New York Environmental and Investor Protection Bureaus, In the Matter of Investigation by Eric T. Schneiderman, Attorney General of the State of New York, of Peabody Energy Corporation, Assurance No. 15-242 https://ag.ny.gov/pdfs/Peabody-Energy-Assurance-signed.pdf February 2022.

390 Ibid.

391 Ibid.

392 Ibid.

393 No judgment will be issued in these proceedings, as they have been discontinued. For the concise statement, see *Abrahams v Commonwealth of Australia* (Federal Court of Australia, VID879/2017, commenced 8 August 2017) concise statement filed by the applicant on 8 August 2017.

394 *Abrahams v Commonwealth of Australia* (Federal Court of Australia, VID879/2017, commenced 8 August 2017) concise statement filed by the applicant on 8 August 2017.

395 *Abrahams v Commonwealth of Australia* (Federal Court of Australia, VID879/2017, commenced 8 August 2017) concise statement filed by the applicant on 8 August 2017.

scenario analysis on its business in the upcoming year to assess the risk.[396] In addition, CBA published its first climate policy position statement,[397] stating it would target an average emissions intensity decrease of its business lending portfolio consistent with its commitment to a net-zero emissions economy by 2050. CBA also stated that it would not lend money to Adani's Carmichael coalmine.[398]

(c) *Mark McVeigh v Retail Employees Superannuation Pty Ltd*[399]

On 23 July 2018, 23-year-old Mark McVeigh commenced proceedings against Retail Employees Superannuation Pty Ltd (REST) in the Federal Court of Australia, alleging that REST had breached s 1017C of the Corporations Act 2001 by failing to provide adequate information to allow the claimant to make an informed judgment about the management and financial condition of REST.[400] **11.160**

The claimant filed an amended concise statement on 21 September 2018 further alleging that REST had breached its duties as a trustee under s 52 of the Superannuation Industry (Supervision) Act 1993 (SIS Act) by not having an adequate climate change policy, and by failing to require its investment managers to provide information on investment performance and capability pursuant to s 102(1) of the SIS Act.[401] **11.161**

The claimant contended that since the 2016 financial year, public information had been available showing that climate change posed and would continue to pose material or major risks to the financial position of many of REST's **11.162**

396 Commonwealth Bank of Australia, *Annual Report 2017* www.commbank.com.au/content/dam/commbank/about-us/shareholders/pdfs/annual-reports/annual_report_2017_14_aug_2017.pdf.

397 Commonwealth Bank of Australia, *Reaffirming Commitment to Addressing Climate Change* (August 2017) www.commbank.com.au/guidance/newsroom/our-climate-commitment-201708.html#:~:text=CBA%20Media%20%2D%200291186919-,Commonwealth%20Bank%20of%20Australia%20(CBA)%20has%20released%20its%20first%20Climate,Reduce%20our%20own%20emissions; Gareth Hutchens, 'Commonwealth Bank shareholders drop suit over nondisclosure of climate risks' (September 2017) www.theguardian.com/australia-news/2017/sep/21/commonwealth-bank-shareholders-drop-suit-over-non-disclosure-of-climate-risks.

398 Gareth Hutchens, 'Commonwealth Bank shareholders drop suit over nondisclosure of climate risks', *The Guardian* (21 September 2017) www.theguardian.com/australia-news/2017/sep/21/commonwealth-bank-shareholders-drop-suit-over-non-disclosure-of-climate-risks.

399 No judgment will be issued in these proceedings, as they have been settled. For the concise statement, see Mark McVeigh v Retail Employees Superannuation Pty Ltd (Federal Court of Australia, NSD1333/2018, commenced 24 July 2018) Concise Statement, dated 23 July 2018.

400 *Mark McVeigh v Retail Employees Superannuation Pty Ltd* (Federal Court of Australia, NSD1333/2018, commenced 24 July 2018) Concise Statement, dated 23 July 2018.

401 *Mark McVeigh v Retail Employees Superannuation Pty Ltd* (Federal Court of Australia, NSD1333/2018, commenced 24 July 2018) Amended Concise Statement, dated 21 September 2018.

investments and sought to understand how REST was responding to these risks.[402]

11.163 The claimant sought the following relief:

(1) declarations that REST had breached ss 52(2)(b), 52(2)(c) and 52(2)(j) of the SIS Act;
(2) a declaration that REST had breached its equitable duties to the complainant; and
(3) injunctions pursuant to s 315 of the SIS Act and in the equitable jurisdiction of the Court, restraining REST from continuing to breach its obligations outlined in (1) and (2) above.

Alternatively, the claimant sought:

(1) a declaration that REST had contravened s 1017C of the Corporations Act 2001 and/or s 52(2)(j) of the SIS Act;
(2) a declaration that REST was under an equitable obligation to give further climate change information to him; and
(3) an injunction under s 1324(1) of the Corporations Act 2001, s 315 of the SIS Act, and/or in the equitable jurisdiction of the Court requiring REST to give him further information on how REST was managing climate change risk.

11.164 The parties settled the proceedings prior to trial. Under the terms of the settlement, REST agreed to incorporate climate change financial risks in its investment strategy and implement a 'net zero by 2050' carbon footprint goal.[403]

(d) Kathleen O'Donnell v Commonwealth of Australia & Ors[404]

11.165 On 22 July 2020, Kathleen O'Donnell, a holder of and investor in exchange-traded Australian Government Bonds (eAGBs), commenced proceedings in the Federal Court of Australia against the Australian government, specifically the Secretary to the Department of Treasury and the Chief Executive of the Australian Office of Financial Management (AOFM).[405]

402 *Mark McVeigh v Retail Employees Superannuation Pty Ltd* (Federal Court of Australia, NSD1333/2018, commenced 24 July 2018) Concise Statement, dated 23 July 2018.

403 REST, 'Media Release: Rest reaches settlement with Mark McVeigh' (2 November 2020) https://rest.com.au/why-rest/about-rest/news/rest-reaches-settlement-with-mark-mcveigh.

404 No judgment has been issued in these proceedings as of September 2022. For the Concise Statement, see Kathleen O'Donnell v Commonwealth of Australia & Ors (Federal Court of Australia, VID482/2020, commenced 22 July 2020) Concise Statement, dated 22 July 2020.

405 *Kathleen O'Donnell v Commonwealth of Australia & Ors* (Federal Court of Australia, VID482/2020, commenced 22 July 2020) Concise Statement, dated 22 July 2020.

O'Donnell alleged that in promoting and arranging for the trading of eAGBs on the ASX, the Commonwealth engaged in misleading and deceptive conduct by failing to disclose information about climate change risks in Australian in disclosure documents. O'Donnell alleged that this breached s 12DA(1) of the Australian Securities and Investments Commission Act 2001. O'Donnell claimed that this failure to disclose also constituted a breach of the fiduciary duty of utmost candour and honesty that the Commonwealth owed to investors who acquired eAGBs.[406] Further, O'Donnell alleged that the AOFM, which is within the Treasury portfolio, has responsibility for the management and administration of Australian government debt and breached its duty to exercise its powers, perform its functions and discharge its duties with reasonable care and diligence under s 25(1) of the Public Governance, Performance and Accountability Act 2013 by failing to disclose climate change risks on behalf of the Commonwealth. Ms O'Donnell argues that climate change is a risk to the value of investments in government bonds, which must be disclosed to potential investors as it is material to an investor's decision to trade in such bonds. Ms O'Donnell sought a declaration that the duties outlined above were breached and an injunction preventing the government from promoting eAGBs until it complies with its duty of disclosure.

On 8 October 2021, the Federal Court handed down a decision concerning applications made by the Commonwealth to strike out Kathleen O'Donnell's Amended Statement of Claim and refuse leave to file a Second Further Amended Statement of Claim.[407] Murphy J held that, while the pleadings did not identify with specificity the material facts necessary to demonstrate how the risk of climate change would adversely impact the Commonwealth's financial position and the value of eAGBs,[408] this was due (in part) to the information asymmetry between the parties.[409] Accordingly, Murphy J declined to strike out the misleading and deceptive conduct claim made by Kathleen O'Donnell.[410] However, Murphy J held that Kathleen O'Donnell lacked standing to bring the fiduciary duty of disclosure and Public Governance, Performance and Accountability Act 2013 claims against the Commonwealth.[411] Therefore, the parts of the Statement of Claim dealing with these matters were struck **11.166**

406 *Kathleen O'Donnell v Commonwealth of Australia & Ors* (Federal Court of Australia, VID482/2020, commenced 22 July 2020) Concise Statement, dated 22 July 2020, [19]–[20].

407 *O'Donnell v Commonwealth of Australia* [2021] FCA 1223, [1] (Murphy J).

408 *O'Donnell v Commonwealth of Australia* [2021] FCA 1223, [102]–[103] (Murphy J).

409 Ibid [104]–[105] (Murphy J).

410 Ibid [117] (Murphy J).

411 Ibid [155] (Murphy J).

out. Kathleen O'Donnell was directed to prepare and file a further amended Statement of Claim after discovery.[412]

11.167 As of September 2022, the matter was ongoing before the Federal Court.

(e) *Abrahams v Commonwealth Bank of Australia*[413]

11.168 On 26 August 2021, Guy Abrahams and Kim Abrahams as trustees for the Guy & Kim Abrahams Family Trust (Abrahams Applicants), filed an application under Section 247A of the Corporations Act 2001 in the Federal Court of Australia seeking access to all documents created by the CBA in relation to the bank's reported involvement in seven specified gas and fossil fuel projects (Projects).[414] Section 247A of the Corporations Act 2001 allows shareholders of a company to apply to the Court for an order authorising the shareholders to inspect the books of the company.

11.169 The Abrahams Applicants sought all documents created by CBA for the purpose of:

(1) carrying out an assessment of the environmental, social and economic impacts of the Projects;
(2) carrying out an assessment of whether the Projects are in line with the goals of the Paris Agreement; and
(3) discharging any obligation or responsibility that any unit, division or employee of CBA has under its internal Environmental and Social Policy (E&S Policy).[415]

11.170 The Abrahams Applicants relied on CBA's Environmental & Social Framework (a public version of its E&S Policy), which states:[416]

> We ensure our business lending policies support the responsible transition to a net zero emissions economy by 2050, by [...] only providing Banking and Financing activity to New oil, gas or metallurgical coal projects if supported by an assessment of the environmental, social and economic impacts of such activity, and if in line with the goals of the Paris Agreement.

---

412 Ibid [9] (Murphy J).

413 No judgment has been issued in these proceedings as of September 2022. For the Concise Statement, see *Abrahams v Commonwealth Bank of Australia* (Federal Court of Australia, NSD864/2021, commenced 26 August 2021).

414 *Abrahams v Commonwealth Bank of Australia* (Federal Court of Australia, NSD864/2021, commenced 26 August 2021).

415 Ibid.

416 Commonwealth Bank of Australia, *Environmental & Social Framework* (2021) www.commbank.com.au/content/dam/commbank/about-us/download-printed-forms/environment-and-social-framework.pdf.

On 4 November 2021, the Court ordered by consent that CBA provide a more limited scope of documents for inspection in two tranches on 9 December 2021 and 10 February 2022. **11.171**

It is possible that the Applicants may bring a further claim against CBA if they consider that the documents produced demonstrate that the Projects did not satisfy CBA's E&S Policy or that the assessments undertaken by CBA were insufficient or inadequate. **11.172**

3. Conclusion

It is now widely accepted that businesses, including but not limited to financial institutions and large emitters, should consider climate change in the context of their strategic and operational risk management. Failure to adequately disclose these risks, or misleading investors regarding the impacts of climate change, can expose companies to climate change litigation. **11.173**

Scrutiny of companies' disclosures is likely to increase with a growing number of jurisdictions adopting or moving to adopt specific and expansive climate change disclosure obligations (see for example the two Exposure Drafts released by the International Sustainability Standards Board for public comment in 2022).[417] **11.174**

While these type of cases do not provide a ready vehicle for compelling companies to take specific steps to reduce emissions, they are most recently being used as a way for investors to scrutinise whether operational practices and decision making are consistent with public commitments to climate change action. Like many other kinds of climate change action, these cases often expose companies to public scrutiny, carry reputational risk and can result in companies that have been slow to recognise climate risk and to implement appropriate climate change policies, to take further action. **11.175**

417 International Financial Reporting Standards Foundation (IFRS), 'Exposure Draft and comment letters: General Sustainability-related Disclosures', *IFRS Website* (Webpage, undated) www .ifrs .org/ projects/ completed -projects/2023/ climate -related -disclosures/ exposure -draft -and -comment -letters/; International Financial Reporting Standards Foundation (IFRS), 'Exposure Draft and comment letters: Climate-related Disclosures', *IFRS Website* (Webpage, undated) www .ifrs .org/ projects/ work -plan/ climate -related -disclosures/exposure-draft-and-comment-letters/.

F. ADMINISTRATIVE AND ENVIRONMENTAL LAW ACTIONS

1. Introduction

11.176 Actions in administrative, planning and permitting law are increasingly being brought against projects that involve the production or use of fossil fuels, such as coal mines, coal-fired power generation or oil and gas projects. Many jurisdictions have long incorporated obligations relating to ecological sustainable development into their planning controls. Some jurisdictions have laws which require consideration of GHG emissions, or adaptation to and mitigation of climate change specifically in the development of policy or approval of projects. This provides scope for claimants to push for the widest possible interpretation of such obligations to address the impact of individual projects or policies may have on climate change.

11.177 For example, in Gloucester Resources Limited v Minister for Planning[418] the New South Wales Land and Environment Court (NSWLEC) was required to decide on the merits of the project as though it were standing in the shoes of the Minister as the consent authority, and the consent authority was required to consider an assessment of GHG emissions when determining whether or not to approve a planning application for a mine.

11.178 In some cases, legislation outside traditional planning and administrative law can be employed. For example, in the landmark decision of Waratah Coal Pty Ltd v Youth Verdict Ltd,[419] a group of young Indigenous and non-Indigenous Australians challenged the proposed Waratah Coal mine in Queensland's Galilee Basin. The case marks the first time that human rights-based arguments have been used in climate change litigation in Australia, and shows how Queensland's human rights legislation (and possibly those of other jurisdictions) can be applied to planning and administrative law decisions.

2. Case Summaries

(a) *Gloucester Resources Limited v Minister for Planning*[420]

11.179 On 19 December 2017, Gloucester Resources Limited (GRL) commenced judicial review proceedings in the NSWLEC against the Minister for Planning, concerning the Minister's decision to refuse GRL's application to

418 *Gloucester Resources Limited v Minister for Planning* [2019] NSWLEC 7.
419 *Waratah Coal Pty Ltd v Youth Verdict Ltd* [2020] QLC 33.
420 *Gloucester Resources Limited v Minister for Planning* [2019] NSWLEC 7.

construct an open-cut coal mine, commonly known as the Rocky Hill Coal Project.[421]

The Minister for Planning (by their delegate, the Planning and Assessment Commission) was required to consider the public interest in determining whether to grant development consent for the project. The Minister initially refused development consent for three reasons, including that the project was not in the public interest.[422] **11.180**

During the proceedings, the Court was required to make a new decision on the merits as though it were standing in the shoes of the Minister as the consent authority. On 8 February 2019, the Court found that the project should be refused development consent.[423] The Court ruled that the adverse social and environmental impacts of the project outweighed the public benefits of the project. There were multiple reasons given for refusing the application. One of those reasons was that the GHG emissions of the project would likely contribute to adverse impacts on the climate system, environment and people.[424] **11.181**

The requirement for a consent authority to consider an assessment of GHG emissions included an assessment of the project's downstream emissions.[425] An issue was how much weight should be given to those considerations. The Court found that approval of the mine would counter measures being undertaken to limit climate change.[426] This finding was framed around the concept of the 'carbon budget', a commonly used approach to determine the limit of emissions which must be met in order to reduce global temperature rises to a particular temperature, such as the 2 degree limit set by the Paris Agreement. The Court agreed that further fossil fuel extraction from new sources, whether or not in Australia, would almost certainly exceed the relevant carbon budget set by the Paris Agreement.[427] **11.182**

421 Ibid.
422 Ibid [22].
423 Ibid [699].
424 Ibid [556].
425 State Environmental Planning Policy (Mining, Petroleum Production and Extractive Industries 2007), clause 14(2).
426 *Gloucester Resources Limited v Minister for Planning* [2019] NSWLEC 7, [526]–[527].
427 *Gloucester Resources Limited v Minister for Planning* [2019] NSWLEC 7, [441], [527], [550]–[556].

(b) *R (on the application of Friends of the Earth Ltd) v Secretary of State for Transport; R (on the application of Friends of the Earth Ltd and others) v Heathrow Airport Ltd*[428]

11.183 In 2018, multiple proceedings concerning the Airports National Policy Statement (ANPS) were commenced in the High Court of England and Wales against the Secretary of State for Transport (Secretary). The ANPS, which was designated by the Secretary of State under the Planning Act 2008, supported the extension of Heathrow Airport. Four of the multiple proceedings, one of which was brought by Friends of the Earth, were heard together by the High Court. Heathrow Airport Limited and Arora Holdings Limited were interested parties in each proceeding. The claimants relied on 22 grounds of challenge to the ANPS. In relation to climate change, the grounds included, *inter alia*, that the Secretary, when deciding to designate the ANPS, limited his considerations of climate change issues more than was required. On 1 May 2019 the High Court dismissed each of the claims.[429] Multiple claimants, including Friends of the Earth, appealed the decision to the Court of Appeal of England and Wales.

11.184 On 27 February 2020, the Court of Appeal ruled that the ANPS was invalid and its designation as a National Policy Statement was unlawful on several grounds relating to climate change, including that it failed to take into account the UK government's commitment to the 2015 Paris Agreement.[430] At the time of designation of the ANPS, the UK had legislated a 2050 target of achieving at least an 80 per cent reduction in its GHG emissions from 1990 levels.[431] The Secretary took this target into account but, on legal advice, chose not to take the Paris Agreement into account.[432] The Court determined that the UK government's commitment to the Paris Agreement was part of 'Government policy' and was required to be taken into account.[433]

---

428 *R (on the application of Spurrier and others) v Secretary of State for Transport* [2019] EWHC 1070 (Admin); R (Friends of the Earth) v Secretary of State for Transport and Others [2020] EWCA Civ 214; *R (on the application of Friends of the Earth Ltd and others) v Heathrow Airport Ltd* [2020] UKSC 52.

429 *R (on the application of Spurrier and others) v Secretary of State for Transport* [2019] EWHC 1070 (Admin), [668].

430 Norton Rose Fulbright, *R (Friends of the Earth) v Secretary of State for Transport and Others [2020] EWCA Civ 214* (ND) www.nortonrosefulbright.com/en-au/knowledge/publications/74cb9a68/climate-change-commitments-lead-to-invalidity-of-heathrow-airport-extension-policy#autofootnote5.

431 On 27 June 2019, the 2050 emissions reduction target in the Climate Change Act 2008 (UK) was amended to require net-zero emissions by 2050, in line with the Paris Agreement.

432 *R (Friends of the Earth) v Secretary of State for Transport and Others* [2020] EWCA Civ 214, [233].

433 *R (Friends of the Earth) v Secretary of State for Transport and Others* [2020] EWCA Civ 214, [233].

In May 2020, the Supreme Court granted an appeal from the Court of Appeal's ruling. On 16 December 2020 the Supreme Court overturned the Court of Appeal's decision that the UK government had acted unlawfully by designating the ANPS without considering the country's commitment to meeting the Paris Agreement goals. The Court agreed with four grounds of Heathrow Airport's appeal, mainly that: (i) the Paris Agreement does not constitute government policy under the Planning Act 2008; (ii) the Secretary of State did not fail to act with the objective of sustainable development by failing to consider the Paris Agreement; (iii) the Secretary did not treat the Paris Agreement as legally irrelevant to the Strategic Environmental Assessment; and (iv) the Secretary did not act irrationally in excluding post-2050 and non-CO_2 emissions.[434] **11.185**

(c) *Friends of the Earth France et al v Total SA*[435]

On 29 October 2019, proceedings were commenced in the French Nanterre Judicial Court by six NGOs, including Friends of the Earth France, against Total SA (Total). The proceedings concern the Tilenga project and the East African Crude Oil Pipeline project (EACOP), which are oil projects that are yet to be developed. Both projects are being carried out by a joint venture involving Total E&P Uganda BV, a wholly owned subsidiary of Total. The Tilenga project involves the development of a crude oil treatment plant located at Lake Albert in Uganda. The EACOP involves the development of a pipeline that will transport oil extracted near Lake Albert to the Tanzanian coast.[436] **11.186**

The French Corporate Duty of Vigilance Law provides that certain companies, including Total in this case, have the obligation to develop, publish and implement a Vigilance Plan 'intended to prevent the risk of serious breaches of human rights and fundamental freedoms, the health and safety of individuals and the environment, which may result from its activities and those of the companies it controls and of its usual subcontractors or suppliers'.[437] **11.187**

434 *R (on the application of Friends of the Earth Ltd and others) v Heathrow Airport Ltd* [2020] UKSC 52.

435 Friends of the Earth France et al v Total SA, Nanterre Judicial Court (Nanterre) 19/02833, DB3R-W-B7D-VIPX, referral order dated 30 January 2020 (English translation); Friends of the Earth France et al v Total SA, Versailles Court of Appeal, 20/01692, DBV3-V-B7E-T2A7, judgement dated 10 December 2020 (English translation); Friends of the Earth France et al v Total SA, Court of Cassation, 21-11.883 and 21-11.959, judgement dated 15 December 2021 (English translation).

436 *Friends of the Earth France et al v Total SA*, Nanterre Judicial Court 19/02833, DB3R-W-B7D-VIPX, judgement dated 30 January 2020 (English translation).

437 Ibid. See also Respect, European Coalition of Corporate Justice, *French Corporate Duty of Vigilance Law (English Translation)* (2016) https://respect.international/french-corporate-duty-of-vigilance-law-english-translation/.

11.188 On 20 March 2019, Total published its Vigilance Plan addressing the Tilenga project and the EACOP. The plaintiffs allege that Total failed to adequately assess the human rights and environmental impacts of the projects in the Vigilance Plan, including by not properly accounting for the projects' potential lifecycle GHG emissions.[438] Accordingly, the plaintiffs summoned Total for interim measures, arguing that Total's alleged disregard of its due diligence obligations constituted manifestly unlawful disturbance, and that urgent action must be ordered to put an end to that disturbance. In the alternative, the plaintiffs alleged that Total's failure to comply with its due diligence obligations justifies an order that Total must comply with its obligations relating to the establishment, publication and effective implementation of vigilance measures in accordance with the relevant provisions of the French Commercial Code.

11.189 Total argued that the Nanterre Judicial Court was not competent to judge the proceedings. The Nanterre Judicial Court agreed and referred the case to the Commercial Court of Nanterre. The question of competency was considered by the Versailles Court of Appeal and then the Court of Cassation, which on 15 December 2021 recognised the competency of the Nanterre Judicial Court to judge the proceedings.[439] As at September 2022 the case remains pending before the Nanterre Judicial Court.

(d) *KEPCO Bylong Australia v Independent Planning Commission and Bylong Valley Protection Alliance*[440]

11.190 On 16 December 2019, KEPCO Bylong Australia Pty Ltd (KEPCO) commenced judicial review proceedings at the NSWLEC, challenging the refusal of a thermal coal mine by the Independent Planning Commission (IPC). Reasons for the IPC refusing the development application included the failure of the project to manage Scope 3 GHG emissions and that the project would impose inequitable costs on future generations.[441] KEPCO argued that the IPC had made eight legal errors in coming to its decision. One of the legal errors, KEPCO claimed, was that when considering the development's management of GHG emissions, the decision maker had erroneously taken into account the New South Wales (NSW) government's Climate Change

---

438 Friends of the Earth France and Survie, *Manquements Graves à La Loi Sur Le Devoir De Vigilance: le cas total en Ouganda* (Report, June 2019) http://climatecasechart.com/climate-change-litigation/wp-content/uploads/sites/16/non-us-case-documents/2019/20191023_NA_na.pdf.

439 *Friends of the Earth France et al v Total SA*, Court of Cassation, 21-11.883 and 21-11.959, judgment dated 15 December 2021 (English translation).

440 *KEPCO Bylong Australia Pty Ltd v Independent Planning Commission (No 2)* [2020] NSWLEC 179; *KEPCO Bylong Australia Pty Ltd v Bylong Valley Protection Alliance Inc* [2021] NSWCA 216.

441 *KEPCO Bylong Australia Pty Ltd v Independent Planning Commission (No 2)* [2020] NSWLEC 179.

Policy Framework and the Paris Agreement. KEPCO argued these were not policies regarding the assessment of GHGs contemplated by the legislation. On 18 December 2020, the Court rejected this construction and dismissed all grounds of appeal.[442]

In March 2021 KEPCO appealed the decision to the NSW Court of Appeal. The NSW Court of Appeal upheld the decision of the NSWLEC, including by confirming that the IPC was entitled to take into account the NSW government's Climate Change Policy Framework when assessing the development's management of GHG emissions.[443] **11.191**

In October 2021, KEPCO applied for special leave to have the case heard by the High Court of Australia. On 10 February 2022, the High Court declined to grant special leave.[444] **11.192**

(e) *R (on the application of ClientEarth) v Secretary of State for Business, Energy and Industrial Strategy & Anor*[445]

On 30 January 2020, judicial review proceedings were commenced in the High Court of England and Wales by ClientEarth, against the Secretary of State for Business, Energy and Industrial Strategy, challenging her decision to grant development consent to build and operate two new gas-fired generating units at the Drax Power Station. ClientEarth made its judicial review application on multiple grounds, including, *inter alia*, that the Secretary of State: **11.193**

- misinterpreted the Overarching National Policy Statement for Energy (EN-1) on the approach to assessing a nationally significant energy infrastructure project's contribution to satisfying the need for the type of infrastructure proposed;
- misinterpreted EN-1 on the approach to assessing GHG emissions; and
- misapplied Section 104(7) of the Planning Act 2008.[446]

On 22 May 2020, the High Court dismissed ClientEarth's judicial review application.[447] In July 2020, the Court of Appeal granted ClientEarth's appli- **11.194**

---

442 Ibid.

443 *KEPCO Bylong Australia Pty Ltd v Bylong Valley Protection Alliance Inc* [2021] NSWCA 216.

444 Environmental Defenders Office, *It's Over: Final Victory as Bylong Coal Project Appeal Rejected* (10 February 2022) www.edo.org.au/2022/02/10/its-over-final-victory-as-bylong-coal-project-appeal-rejected/.

445 *R (on the application of ClientEarth) v Secretary of State for Business, Energy and Industrial Strategy* [2020] EWHC 1303 (Admin); *R (on the application of ClientEarth) v Secretary of State for Business, Energy and Industrial Strategy & Anor* [2021] EWCA Civ 43.

446 *R (on the application of ClientEarth) v Secretary of State for Business, Energy and Industrial Strategy* [2020] EWHC 1303 (Admin).

447 Ibid.

cation to appeal the High Court's decision but ultimately dismissed the appeal by ClientEarth.[448]

11.195 ClientEarth pursued the appeal on the same three grounds that were relied on in the High Court hearing.[449] In relation to the first ground, ClientEarth argued that a quantitative assessment was required to calculate a project's particular contribution to satisfying the need for new energy infrastructure. The Court of Appeal disagreed, finding instead that the decision maker should give substantial weight to considerations of 'need' and that this should be proportionate to the project's anticipated contribution to meeting the need.[450]

11.196 In relation to the second ground, the Court of Appeal found against ClientEarth on the basis that the Secretary of State had acknowledged that 'the significant adverse impact of the proposed Development on the amount of greenhouse gases that will be emitted to atmosphere, but recognised that that should not "displace the presumption [set out in EN-1] in favour of granting consent"'.[451]

11.197 In relation to the third ground, ClientEarth argued that the Secretary of State had failed to discharge its obligation under Section 104(7) of the Planning Act 2008, which requires it to weigh the 'adverse impact' of the proposed development against its 'benefits'. They claimed that instead, the Secretary of State simply reiterated his or her assessment under Section 104(3) of the Planning Act 2008 which required her to consider the application in accordance with any relevant National Policy Statement.[452] The Court of Appeal held that the Secretary of State had acted lawfully by giving due weight to the need for gas supply infrastructure as recognised in the EN-1, and setting that against any harm the development may cause in accordance with the requirements of Section 104(7) of the Planning Act 2008.

11.198 ClientEarth has confirmed that it will not appeal the Court of Appeal's decision.

448 *R (on the application of ClientEarth) v Secretary of State for Business, Energy and Industrial Strategy & Anor* [2021] EWCA Civ 43.

449 Ibid.

450 Ibid.

451 Ibid.

452 Ibid.

(f) *Waratah Coal Pty Ltd v Youth Verdict Ltd*[453]

In April 2020, a coalition of individuals led by non-profit organisation Youth Verdict Ltd (Youth Verdict) filed objections to the mining lease and environmental authority applications of Waratah Coal Pty Ltd (Waratah Coal).[454] On 3 May 2020, Waratah Coal's applications and Youth Verdict's objections were referred to the Land Court of Queensland.[455] The Court's function is to recommend to the ultimate administrative decision-makers the grant or refusal of final approval for the mining project.[456] **11.199**

Australia does not have a constitutional 'bill of rights'. However, several Australian states and territories have enacted human rights legislation, including Queensland.[457] The Human Rights Act 2019 (HR Act) came into effect on 1 January 2020 in Queensland, and enshrines multiple human rights derived from international law.[458] Youth Verdict argued that granting Waratah Coal's applications would be unlawful under the HR Act, because it would cause GHG emissions which would contribute to climate change, and in turn would ultimately infringe young Australians' human rights (including the right to life and the right to culture).[459] Waratah Coal applied to the Court to strike out any objections that relied upon the HR Act, arguing (among other things) that the Court did not have jurisdiction to consider those objections.[460] **11.200**

On 4 September 2020, the Court dismissed Waratah Coal's application.[461] The Court held that it did have jurisdiction to hear the submissions regarding human rights issues, as Section 108(1) of the HR Act provides that the HR Act **11.201**

453 *Waratah Coal Pty Ltd v Youth Verdict Ltd* [2020] QLC 33; *Waratah Coal Pty Ltd v Youth Verdict Ltd & Ors (No 2)* [2021] QLC 4; *Waratah Coal Pty Ltd v Youth Verdict Ltd & Ors (No 3)* [2021] QLC 36.

454 Youth Verdict Ltd, *Objection Form for a Mining Lease Application* (3 April 2020) www.youthverdict.org.au/_files/ugd/b4b563_ce38fb382bc143eb94764f3e4c1ad7e0.pdf; Youth Verdict Ltd, *Objection to an Application or Amendment Application for Environmental Authority (Mining Lease or Mining Claim)* (3 April 2020) www.youthverdict.org.au/_files/ugd/b4b563_79470ad1e8e64cca95428299f8ed4d1a.pdf.

455 *Waratah Coal Pty Ltd v Youth Verdict Ltd* [2020] QLC 33, [1].

456 Ibid [1], [9]–[11]; *Mineral Resources Act 1989* (Qld), ss 268–269; *Environmental Protection Act 1994* (Qld), ss 222–223.

457 The other Australian jurisdictions which have enacted human rights legislation are Victoria (*Charter of Human Rights and Responsibilities Act 2006* (Vic)) and the Australian Capital Territory (*Human Rights Act 2004* (ACT)).

458 *Human Rights Act 2019* (Qld).

459 *Waratah Coal Pty Ltd v Youth Verdict Ltd* [2020] QLC 33, [3]; Youth Verdict Ltd, *Objection Form for a Mining Lease Application* (3 April 2020) www.youthverdict.org.au/_files/ugd/b4b563_ce38fb382bc1 43eb94764f 3e4c1ad7e0 .pdf, Attachment A, [1.3]; Youth Verdict Ltd, *Objection to an Application or Amendment Application for Environmental Authority (Mining Lease or Mining Claim),* (3 April 2020) www.youthverdict.org.au/_files/ugd/b4b563_79470ad1e8e64cca95428299f8ed4d1a.pdf, Attachment A, [2.3]. See Human Rights Act 2019 (Qld), ss 16, 28.

460 Ibid [4].

461 *Waratah Coal Pty Ltd v Youth Verdict Ltd* [2020] QLC 33.

applies to all legislation and instruments, and thus the Court has jurisdiction to consider human rights issues in making its recommendations. Specifically, the Court held that its recommendation on an application for a mining lease or environmental authority is an 'act' or 'decision' of a public entity under the HR Act.[462] Further, it held that it was required to give 'proper consideration' to human rights in deciding what recommendations to make on the applications, and to reach an outcome that is, in substance, compatible with those rights.[463]

11.202 Subsequently, Waratah Coal revised its proposed mine plan insofar as it affected a protected nature refuge.[464] The parties are in dispute over whether this revision has the effect that Waratah Coal is required to lodge a fresh application for a new project, such that the Court should no longer proceed to hear the original applications and objections.[465] As of September 2022, the case remains before the Court.

(g) *Thomas v EPA*[466]

11.203 On 21 May 2020, a Guyanese scientist filed judicial review proceedings in the High Court of the Supreme Court of Judicature of Guyana against the Environmental Protection Agency (EPA) of Guyana.[467] The applicant claimed that the EPA had acted beyond its power and without legal authority in granting permits to Esso Exploration and Production Guyana Ltd (Esso Exploration) for oil exploration for periods exceeding 23 years.[468] The regulations under the Environmental Protection Act CAP: 20:05 provided that a permit could be granted for no more than five years.[469]

11.204 The applicant sought court orders to quash the decision of the EPA to grant the permits to Esso Exploration, and to direct the EPA to issue corrected permits that were effective until a fixed date not beyond five years from the date on which the permit is granted.[470] In the applicant's affidavit, they made a number of statements relating to the impact of climate change, including that breaching the regulations under the Environmental Protection Act exposes

---

462 Ibid [17]–[64]; *Human Rights Act 2019* (Qld), ss 9(1)(f), 9(4)(b), 10(1)(a), 58(1).

463 Ibid [71]–[77], [86]; *Human Rights Act 2019* (Qld), ss 58(5), 108(1).

464 *Waratah Coal Pty Ltd v Youth Verdict Ltd (No 3)* [2021] QLC 36, [2]–[3], [5].

465 Ibid [13]–[14].

466 No judgment will be issued for these proceedings as the case settled. For the Application for Judicial Review, see *Thomas v EPA*, Application for Judicial Review, made on behalf of the applicant Troy Thomas, dated 21 May 2020.

467 *Thomas v EPA*, Application for Judicial Review, made on behalf of the applicant Troy Thomas, dated 21 May 2020.

468 Ibid.

469 *Environmental Protection Regulations 2000.*

470 See footnote 479.

'Guyana and the rest of the world to serious, if not irreparable, harm and adverse consequences from climate change'.[471]

In October 2020, the Supreme Court of Guyana issued a consent order regarding an agreement that was reached between the parties. The terms of the settlement required the EPA to reduce the terms of the permits to five years, and to file amended permits demonstrating compliance with that order.[472] **11.205**

(h) *R (on application of Friends of the Earth Ltd) v Secretary of State for International Trade, UK Export Finance and the HM Treasury*[473]

On 8 September 2020, Friends of the Earth brought an Aarhus Convention claim to the High Court of England and Wales, challenging the UK government's decision to provide approximately USD 1 billion in financial support for the development of a liquefied natural gas (LNG) project with Total in Mozambique.[474] Friends of the Earth challenged the legality of decisions made by the Secretary of State for International Trade, HM Treasury and UK Export Finance in respect of the project. Specifically, it was alleged that the UK government's decision to invest in the LNG project was unlawful because the UK government incorrectly decided that the investment was consistent with both the UK's and Mozambique's commitments under the Paris Agreement.[475] Friends of the Earth stated that the investment also breached 'a number of other international law standards on the environment and human rights', and criticised the decision of UK Export Finance to withhold disclosure of the assessment undertaken in respect of the environmental impact of the project.[476] **11.206**

On 22 April 2021, Friends of the Earth were granted permission to proceed to hearing on one ground, namely that the defendants 'proceeded on the legally and/or factually erroneous basis that the project was consistent with the United Kingdom's commitments under the Paris Agreement and/or assisted Mozambique to achieve its commitments under the Paris Agreement', or in the alternative, the defendants 'failed to ask themselves the right questions and/or failed to carry out essential analysis in order properly to determine **11.207**

471 *Thomas v EPA*, Plaintiff's affidavit, dated 21 May 2020, [20].

472 *Thomas v EPA*, Consent order, dated 5 October 2020.

473 R (on application of Friends of the Earth Ltd) v Secretary of State for International Trade, UK Export Finance and the HM Treasury [2021] EWHC 2369.

474 *R (on application of Friends of the Earth Ltd) v Secretary of State for International* Trade, UK Export Finance and the HM Treasury [2021] EWHC 2369.

475 Friends of the Earth, *Briefing: UK Export Finance – climate litigation* (June 2021) https://cdn.friendsoftheearth.uk/sites/default/files/downloads/UKEF_Briefing_updated_June_2021.pdf?_ga=2.113878725.332313814.1644299277-735258458.1629178577.

476 Ibid.

whether the decision aligned with the United Kingdom and Mozambique's commitments under the Paris Agreement'.[477] The hearing took place in London at the Royal Courts of Justice from 7 to 9 December 2021[478] and resulted in a split judgment from the High Court.[479] Friends of the Earth were granted permission to appeal and as at September 2022 the case was pending before the Court of Appeal.[480]

3. Conclusion

11.208 There is an increasing trend to use planning, environmental and administrative law to oppose developments, which are alleged to result in increased GHG emissions, particularly new coal, oil and gas projects. This represents an additional approval risk that companies need to be aware of and adequately address in the application and assessment process.

11.209 Increasingly, it can be expected that challenges will be lodged in relation to developments which are likely to generate significant GHG emissions and against government policies that support fossil fuel developments, particularly where these developments are alleged to be inconsistent with the goals of the Paris Agreement. As we have seen with the Heathrow Airport decision in the UK and Gloucester Resources Limited v Minister for Planning in Australia, courts will, in appropriate circumstances, use international or national policies, laws or regulation to refuse new development that are found to increase climate change risk. These actions often exhibit a tension between what is seen as necessary to support increased energy needs and the dangers posed by climate change.

G. CONCLUSION

11.210 Climate change litigation has increased in number and sophistication, reflecting changing attitudes and an increasing sense of urgency with respect to avoiding climate change impacts. Landmark decisions such as *Urgenda* set the scene for a continued increase in the type and number of claims being filed.

477 *R (on application of Friends of the Earth Ltd) v Secretary of State for International Trade*, UK Export Finance and the HM Treasury [2021] EWHC 2369, [2].

478 Friends of the Earth, *What's Happening in Mozambique* (9 April 2021) https://friendsoftheearth.uk/climate/whats-happening-mozambique.

479 Friends of the Earth, 'Judge rules UK government decision to support mega gas project in Mozambique unlawful' (originally published 18 March 2022; last updated 5 September 2022) https://friendsoftheearth.uk/climate/judge-rules-uk-government-decision-support-mega-gas-project-mozambique-unlawful.

480 Ibid.

Human rights is likely to remain an active basis for new litigation against both governments and corporations. Other trends are likely to encompass actions against companies for alleged greenwashing, damage claims for spending on adaptation measures and alleged failure to disclose and manage climate change risks.[481] We also expect the trend of cases which seek to restrict high emissions activities or developments to continue.

It can be expected that strategic claims may start to increase against the private **11.211**
sector actors, particularly given the decisions in *Milieudefensie v Royal Dutch Shell plc*. Further, increased disclosure requirements will lead to enhanced scrutiny of corporations and potential exposure to regulatory or private actions. In our view, litigation will continue to be used as a tool to achieve outcomes consistent with a net-zero emissions future.

However, while the risks associated with climate change and climate change **11.212**
litigation are significant and not to be taken lightly, risks can also provide opportunities. Those who monitor and keep abreast of climate change-related risks may also identify opportunities that result in improved reputation, increased competitiveness and new investment avenues in the energy transition.

481 Joana Setzer and Catherine Higham, *Global Trends in Climate Change Litigation: 2021 Snapshot* (Grantham Research Institute on Climate Change and the Environment, London School of Economics, 2021).

INDEX